## DATE DUE

| | | | |
|---|---|---|---|
| ~~Dec 2~~ '74 | | | |
| | | | |
| | | | |
| | | | |
| | | | |
| | | | |
| | | | |
| | | | |
| | | | |
| | | | |
| | | | |
| | | | |
| | | | |
| | | | |
| | | | |
| GAYLORD | | | PRINTED IN U.S A |

# MUNICH

# MUNICH

*by Keith Eubank*

UNIVERSITY OF OKLAHOMA PRESS : NORMAN

By Keith Eubank

*Paul Cambon: Master Diplomatist* (Norman, 1960)
*Munich* (Norman, 1963)

The publication of this volume has been aided
by a grant from the Ford Foundation.

This book has been printed on paper bearing
the watermark of the University of Oklahoma
Press and designed for an effective life
of at least three hundred years.

*940.5312*
*Eu / m*
*59287*
*Oct. 1967*

*LIBRARY OF CONGRESS CATALOG CARD NUMBER:* 63-8987

*To my parents*

Weaver K. Eubank and Grace Holden Eubank

# Preface

THE WORDS "appeasement" and "Munich" have a peculiar meaning to the generation that fought World War II. To some they mean a false peace and a mustached Englishman flapping a piece of paper in the September breezes of a London airport. Others remember the joy of victory without bloodshed bestowed on Germany by Adolf Hitler. Among Czechoslovaks there are memories of betrayal and defeat. In the mouths of politicians, these words have become powerful symbols. "Another Munich" can damn a policy as cowardly surrender. "Appeasement" is a nasty word.

The events of 1938–39 have become shrouded in myth. Those who favored the Munich Agreement believed the Sudeten German problem had originated with the Versailles Treaty and felt the "logical" solution was only a matter of frontier adjustment for the purpose of self-determination. Thus, proponents of the Agreement erroneously ignored history which showed that the problem was a legacy of the Hapsburg Empire, but the opponents had their myths also. They felt Great Britain and France needed only to call the aggressor's bluff, and victory would be theirs without bloodshed.

After Dunkirk and the fall of France, the men of Munich stood condemned, their opponents vindicated. Yet, the men of Munich were not alone in their guilt: the destruction of Czechoslovakia was the responsibility of many governments. Too long have Great Britain and France borne the entire burden of shame, and one can argue that without Munich, Germany could have won the Battle of Britain.

The story of the Munich Agreement has often stopped with the Munich Conference or with the seizure of Bohemia and Moravia. This was not the end. The Agreement contributed to the unleashing of war in September, 1939, and affected its conduct and the peace treaties. To the Sudeten Germans and the Czechoslovaks, it brought sorrow and heartache. Only the Union of Soviet Socialist Republics profited from it.

Surrounding Munich, there is a riddle. Was the Agreement only the result of a historical process to be faced realistically? Was it a sordid tale of cowardice, of freemen tamely submitting to a strutting dictator? Could the aggressor have been stopped by calling his bluff? In 1938 the answer to the riddle seemed easy to those without responsibility.

The history of the Munich Agreement is an example of a problem often faced by a head of state. How can he stop the totalitarian aggressor who threatens a small nation? Should the threat be ignored because the victim is far away? Should world war be risked over an unimportant land of funny people who cannot speak English? Where will the aggressor stop? Can the head of state, in good conscience, subject millions to the threat of war and destruction? Dare he hazard the future of millions yet unborn? Will the crippled, the blind, the dead curse his name throughout eternity? Is it cowardice if he seeks some peaceful means to avoid conflict? Is it better to give the aggressor a portion and satisfy him if millions live out their lives in peace?

In 1938, Western statesmen grappled with these problems and struggled to avoid another holocaust like World War I with its more than eight million dead. Since 1945 statesmen in the free world have wrestled with the same problem. Here is the significance of the story of Munich. It is not a tale of diplomats making conversations over cocktails. It is a tale of tragedy, of knaves, fools, and frightened men and women.

Research is always a co-operative venture. I am deeply grateful for the help given me by so many. The Faculty Research Committee of North Texas State University aided my task with research grants and a lightened teaching load. Otoker Odložilík of the University of Pennsylvania and Edward Táborsky of the University of Texas gave freely of their knowledge. Vinita B. Davis, Louise Evans, Elaine A. Ledlow, and others on the library staff of North Texas State University helped greatly to make this book possible. My colleagues, William T. Hagan and Richard N. Kottman, read and criticized portions of the manuscript. Lucy Griffiths and Carol Oakey bore the burden of typing the manuscript. Janice Boatman prepared the maps. My labors have been eased by the help and encouragement of my wife, Marilyn.

Keith Eubank

Denton, Texas
March 1, 1963

# Contents

xi

# Illustrations, Maps

MUNICH

# MUNICH

# I

## One September Evening

IN THE DARKNESS of the September evening, Czech sentries kept watch along the German frontier for the expected attack by the mighty German *Wehrmacht*. Using the shadows for concealment, bands of Sudeten German Free Corps attacked lonely Czech soldiers on patrol. Citizens of Prague hurried home through the blackout wondering if German bombers would destroy the beautiful city before dawn. In Paris that evening, posters called up men to their units, and requisitioned buses carried troops to the Maginot Line. In Britain the government prepared to issue the available gas masks. Already slit trenches had been dug in parks in preparation for the air raids. In London mothers hurried home from shopping forays seeking blankets and clothes for their children who were to be evacuated from the city. The antiaircraft units of the Territorial Army had set up their guns and searchlights in London and its suburbs. Throughout Germany that evening of September 26, 1938, soldiers of the *Wehrmacht* moved to their appointed posts for the invasion of Czechoslovakia.

In Berlin, radios and loudspeakers urged the good citizens to show their national spirit by listening to the speech of their leader, Adolf Hitler, that night in the *Sportpalast*. By nightfall over fifteen thousand men, women, and children awaited the words of their *Führer* with joy. In restaurants, in railroad stations, and wherever there was a loud speaker, Germans gathered under the eyes of the Storm Troopers to lend their ears to the *Führer's* words.

In the *Sportpalast,* bands blared forth party tunes in a vain effort to get the noisy throng to sing. Around the walls hung banners proclaiming, *"Ein Volk, Ein Reich, Ein Führer!"* Over the speaker's platform hung a banner with words from one of Hitler's latest pronouncements: "The Germans in Czechoslovakia Are Neither Defenseless nor Forsaken!" Outside the *Sportpalast,* Storm Troopers lined the street all the way to the Reichschancery where Hitler was preparing his speech. Slowly the Nazi hierarchy strolled in to take its place on the platform. Reichsmarshal Hermann Göring was cheered until he acknowledged the crowds. Someone yelled, "Turn the bombs loose!" Laughter swept the hall.

At last Hitler entered, accompanied by Propaganda Minister Joseph Paul Goebbels and followed by a detachment of Sudeten German refugees and the Sudeten Free Corps, still dressed in the shabby clothes they wore when they slipped across the frontier. Hitler sat down beside Göring to await the solemn parade of party standards. Goebbels introduced him, proclaiming, "In this historic hour every German is behind you!" The crowd roared its allegiance. Around the world, foreign ministries listened in by short wave radio for the expected declaration of war.

Hitler told the world that he spoke for the German people. "At this second the whole people in its millions agrees word for word with my words, confirms them, and makes them its own oath!" The crowd answered, *"Sieg Heil!"* Germany, Hitler declared, was not troubled so much by Czechoslovakia as by "Mr. Beneš." He told the world about Germany's peaceful foreign policy, her suffering under the Versailles Treaty, her rearmament, and finally of Czechoslovakia and the Sudeten German problem.

This problem, Hitler said, had begun when "certain crazy, so-called 'statesmen' " tore up Central Europe without regard for the origins and wishes of the people. From this process came Czechoslovakia. "This Czech state began with a single lie, and the father of this lie was named Beneš," Hitler screamed. The crowds shrieked, "Hang Beneš!"

Inside that state, Hitler continued, was a German minority, three and one-half million Sudeten Germans, who had lost their right of self-determination. Beneš had begun a reign of terror to exterminate them. Now they had the highest death rate, and experienced the greatest poverty of all the German peoples. This tyranny must be

4

ended by returning the Sudetens to Germany immediately. The crowd interrupted him again and again yelling, *"Heil, Sieg Heil!* We march tonight!"

England and France, he continued, had told Beneš to set the Czechs free. Hitler insisted that he did not want any Czechs, but the Sudetens must come home to Germany. The decision for peace or war was in the hands of Beneš. At last, after an hour of frenzy, screams, and hysteria, Hitler concluded, "We are determined! Now let Mr. Beneš make his choice."[1]

That September evening, Europe was on the brink of world war because of a quarrel over a minority, the Sudeten Germans, living in Czechoslovakia. Too many people, ignorant of the history of the problem, accepted Hitler's version.

The problem of the Sudetens and their Czech neighbors was not as recent as many Europeans thought on that September evening in 1938. Most people would have blamed the men who wrote the Versailles Treaty for tearing the Sudetens from the homeland to which they now longed to return, but the Sudetenland had never been a part of the German Empire founded in 1871. The Sudeten Germans in September, 1938, were descendants of migrants who entered Bohemia and Moravia (central and western Czechoslovakia) in the twelfth century. Gradually the Germans came to dominate the area in which they lived, and their power increased when the Hapsburgs began to rule Bohemia and Moravia in 1526. Czech attempts to rebel were always futile.

In the eighteenth century, the tide of German migration swelled again as Empress Maria Theresa and her son, Joseph II, welcomed emigrants from Bavaria, Thuringia, Saxony, and Hanover. Everywhere the Germans were the masters, and the Czech peasants were often landless and saddled with heavy taxes.

By the nineteenth century, the German flood had subsided, but the Czech birthrate grew so that the Sudetens opposed all changes in the government that might give the Czechs any home rule. The Romantic movement gave an impetus to the revival of Czech culture and language, helping to make the dream of political independence stronger. The Czechs fought for their own schools so that their children would not be forced to learn German. Czech nationalists de-

[1] *The Speeches of Adolph Hitler, April, 1922–August, 1939* (ed. by Norman H. Baynes), II, 1508–27.

manded equality of Czech and German languages in the administration of the land.

The Germans knew little of the Czech intellectual development. To the average Sudeten, the Czech language was for servants and unfit for an educated German. In Eger, a Sudeten town in Bohemia, signs hung in the hotels and cafes, "Czechs, Jews, dogs, not allowed here."

World War I added to the strife. The Sudetens eagerly volunteered in the Austro-Hungarian army. The Czechs loathed service under the Hapsburg flag; wholesale desertions to the Russians were the rule among Czech soldiers. The Czech nationalists solicited the help and approval of the Allied governments, and in the fall of 1918, the Allied powers recognized the independence of Czechoslovakia, formed by a union of Czechs, Slovaks, and Ruthenes, led by the Slovak scholar, Tomáš Masaryk.

When the Paris Peace Conference met in 1919, the Sudeten Germans were more interested in their loss of prestige and status than in belonging to the Weimar Republic. During the Conference, the Czechoslovak Commission considered the frontier question and advocated a line which followed the old Hapsburg frontier, one of the oldest in Europe. To apply the ethnological principle entirely, the committee argued, and to compose the nation according to the desire of every hamlet and crossroads would produce "a country as discontinuous as the spots on a panther's skin."[2] Although four small changes were made in the Hapsburg frontier, the old historic boundaries between Germany and Bohemia remained much as they had in the past.

The old way made economic sense. Bohemia could not exist without the peripheral areas in which German-owned industry was concentrated, and the agricultural hinterland was dependent upon this industry. The market for Sudeten industry had always been within the old Hapsburg Empire, not Hohenzollern Germany.

In the new republic, nationalist Czechs remembered German domination of the past centuries and felt their turn had come. That the Czechs were sometimes bad mannered could not be denied, but it was far from the truth to claim, as Hitler did in the *Sportpalast* speech, that the Sudetens were being exterminated by Beneš. Czech

---

[2] *Foreign Relations of the United States,* (hereafter cited as *FRUS*), *1919 Peace Conference,* III, 877–81.

treatment of the Sudetens was no worse than the treatment given minority groups in other nations and often much better. Minorities in Poland, Italy, Yugoslavia, and Russia received far worse treatment than the Sudetens.

The Sudetens blamed the Czechoslovak government for many of their troubles which were out of the government's control. Cheap Japanese textile exports competed with Sudeten mills and caused unemployment. The Czechs were blamed. World depression brought unemployment to the Sudeten Germans. Although many Czechs were also out of work, the Sudetens blamed them.

Hitler did not tell his audience that there had been no serious friction between the Weimar Republic and Czechoslovakia before his accession to power. The Berlin government deliberately rejected any policy of interference in Czechoslovak affairs. In 1923 the German Foreign Ministry advised the Sudetens to recognize the existence of Czechoslovakia and make the best of the new regime. Gustav Stresemann, foreign minister from 1923 to 1929, refused to join any Sudeten activities for the cause of autonomy. When the Czech foreign minister, Eduard Beneš, visited Berlin in 1928, no one mentioned the Sudeten problem.[3]

Until 1933 the Sudeten German problem was not one of international importance. Statesmen were more troubled by the depression and disarmament. The Nazi victory in Germany altered this situation, as Hitler's Pan-Germanism transformed the Sudeten problem into an international question.

Hitler did not create the Sudeten-Czech hostility. It was already there, a result of eight hundred years of history. Neither the Paris Peace Conference nor the Versailles Treaty had created this problem. Perhaps, given time, patience, and prosperity, the Czechs and the Sudeten Germans would have found the solution. Because they had not found it, Adolf Hitler had an issue that opened Central Europe to his armies.

[3] J. W. Bruegel, "German Diplomacy and the Sudeten Question before 1938," *International Affairs,* Vol. XXXVII (July, 1961), 323–31.

# 2
## 1933-37

ADOLF HITLER became German chancellor on January 30, 1933. This event changed the entire relationship between the Czechs and the Sudetens. As a son of the old Hapsburg Empire, he regarded the Czechs as subhuman. Infected with the disease of Pan-Germanism, he preached the union of all German peoples within the Reich. If necessary, he would expel non-Germans from their homeland to achieve his goal. To him Czechoslovakia was the embodiment of the Versailles Treaty, but it was also the key to military dominance of Central Europe. Hitler perceived that Czechoslovakia was a threat to German security because Bohemia extended into the heart of Germany and would make a perfect base for an air attack on central Germany.

Hitler was forced to move warily in foreign policy until rearmament could be accomplished. For the moment his aggressive policies towards the Czechs had to be furthered by the Sudeten German party, a Nazi organization, led by Konrad Henlein. In his rimless spectacles, Henlein seemed an earnest man seeking justice for his people. A veteran of the Austrian army, he fought on the Italian front until taken prisoner in 1918. After the war he became a bank clerk and later a gymnastics teacher, traveling over the Sudeten area as leader of the German Gymnastics Society. He accepted the leadership of the Sudeten Nazis after an invitation from the Reich party in 1933. Henlein moved his home to Asch, surrounded on three sides by Germany and within two miles of the frontier.

By 1935, Henlein was ready to broaden his party's work because he had a subsidy from Berlin. Using threats, violence, boycotts, and beatings Henlein's party made themselves the spokesmen for the Sudeten Germans. The antics of the Nazis soon were thought to express the wishes of three and one-half million Sudeten Germans. There were other political parties among the Sudetens who did not desire to become a part of the Third Reich, but their voices were either silent or ignored.

The average Sudeten German wanted less control from Prague and some degree of autonomy. He wanted German officials and German police, but not necessarily Nazis. He wanted a good market for Sudeten products and perhaps imagined that Germany would provide it. In contrast to his German cousins, he could freely criticize his government and read newspapers which complained about the Czech bureaucrats and President Beneš.

In 1935, Eduard Beneš became president of Czechoslovakia. A son of peasants, born in a village of two hundred inhabitants within two miles of the German frontier, Beneš early became a Socialist. In the University of Prague, he came under the influence of Tomáš Masaryk who infused him with a desire for Czech independence. In 1915, Beneš escaped from the Austro-Hungarian Empire to better serve the cause of Czech freedom. His wife and daughter were arrested and imprisoned with prostitutes—a deed which only deepened his hatred for the Hapsburgs. When a government was formed for the new nation, he was named Czechoslovak foreign minister, and he served in this capacity until his election to the presidency, upon the resignation of Masaryk in 1935.

Beneš' appearance was not distinctive. His physique was small and wiry. Subjecting himself to spartan discipline, even to abstention from tobacco and liquor, he devoted all his time and talents to the nation which he helped to create.

To protect Czechoslovakia, Beneš negotiated a treaty with France pledging both nations to concert their foreign policies when national security was threatened or the treaties of 1919 were endangered. As a corollary to the Locarno Treaty, France and Czechoslovakia joined in a Treaty of Mutual Assistance on October 16, 1926. If the Locarno Treaty broke down and the League of Nations failed to control the situation, France and Czechoslovakia would lend each other aid if there were an unprovoked attack.

Czechoslovakia made a peculiar arrangement with France and Russia in 1935. On May 2, 1935, France and Russia agreed to give each other "immediate" aid if attacked without provocation. If the matter were referred to the Council of the League of Nations and the machinery broke down, each would give the other aid. Czechoslovakia signed a treaty with Russia on May 16, 1935, similar to the Franco-Russian treaty except that the provisions for aid went into effect only if France first helped the victim of the aggression.

Seemingly both Czechoslovakia and Russia would benefit from the agreement. Russia would not fight Germany alone. France would keep Czechoslovakia out of the Communist orbit. The alliance would check German aggression. However, there were no provisions for staff consultations. There were no practical discussions over methods for France and Russia to aid Czechoslovakia. Between France and Czechoslovakia there was some liaison through the efforts of General Louis Faucher, the French military attaché in Prague. The entire system depended on France, whose diplomats had insisted on the Czech state in 1919. Should France repudiate its promises, Russia would be free and Czechoslovakia doomed.

On the surface this treaty seemed to place Russia under obligation to defend Czechoslovakia by fighting Germany. Stalin and his colleagues had no intentions of taking on such a formidable opponent amid the great purges and the ordeal of industrialization. When Maxim Litvinov, the shrewd commissar for foreign affairs, was questioned about the problem of fighting Germany for Czechoslovakia, he replied: "Don't tell me about our treaty with Czechoslovakia. I drafted that treaty. Read the text again more carefully and you will see that you are wrong. We are obliged to come to the aid of the Czechs under the League of Nations machinery and then only if France has assumed her obligations."[1] Through his unique sources of information, Litvinov was certain that France would not fight: thus Russia was relieved of an obligation which she had no intention of fulfilling.

Czechoslovakia was also a member of the Little Entente. The purpose of this alliance was to unite Czechoslovakia, Rumania, and Yugoslavia against Hungary. An attack upon one was not an attack upon all, unless Hungary were the attacker.

Hitler first attempted to penetrate the Czechoslovak defenses by

1 John Whitaker, *We Cannot Escape History*, 269.

negotiating a special agreement as he had already done in Austria through the Agreement of July 11, 1936.[2] By claiming special privileges for his followers, he could gradually extend his influence throughout Czechoslovakia. With luck the trick might be as successful in Czechoslovakia as it was proving to be in Austria.

In the fall of 1936, through his agents, Graf zu Trauttmansdorff and Albrecht Haushofer, Hitler offered Beneš a German-Czechoslovak agreement, including a non-aggression treaty in case of a Soviet attack. Beneš was interested in a non-aggression treaty based on the German-Czech treaty of arbitration signed at Locarno in 1925. He was willing to negotiate over German-Czech trade and Sudeten economy and culture but not Sudeten autonomy.

Negotiations continued into the new year when Haushofer presented Hitler a draft treaty. Haushofer proposed to expand the arbitration treaty and end mutual press attacks; the Czechs would curtail refugee activities directed at the Nazi government, and a cultural agreement and trade pact would be concluded.

Although the Czech government pressed for negotiations, nothing was done by Berlin except to keep Prague waiting. The exact reason for Hitler's lack of interest is unknown, but certainly he now thought a pact with Czechoslovakia was unnecessary. The need to neutralize Czechoslovakia was no longer so pressing because the purges in the higher military ranks of the Soviet Union had sapped the strength of the armed forces by 1937. Probably Hitler had begun to think along different lines regarding Czechoslovakia: he could utilize the Sudeten Germans.[3]

The proposed German-Czechoslovak agreement was similar in spirit to that of July 11, 1936, between Austria and Germany. Hitler would have used it to force greater concessions to German interests, but he was not seeking to help the Sudeten Germans: never did his

[2] Keith Eubank, "Conquest by Diplomacy," *The Southwestern Social Science Quarterly*, Vol. XXXIX (June, 1958), 18–27. The agreement of July 11, 1936, laid the foundations for the *Anschluss* in 1938. By continued complaints of infractions, real or imagined, the Germans gradually forced concessions from the Schuschnigg government. When Schuschnigg tried to break out of the web he saw Hitler spinning, German troops were ordered across the frontiers.

[3] Edvard Beneš, *Memoirs: From Munich to New War and New Victory*, 14–20; Boris Celovsky, *Das Münchener Abkommen von 1938*, 88–91; Gerhard L. Weinberg, "Secret Hitler-Beneš Negotiations in 1936–37," *Journal of Central European Affairs*, Vol. XIX (January, 1960), 366–74.

agents press this point during the negotiations. For Hitler the Sudetens were always a means to an end.

To counter the growing demands from the Sudetens, on February 18, 1937, the Czechoslovak government offered concessions. Government orders for manufactured goods would be placed in accordance with the degree of need of the areas. In German areas, local workmen would be employed first. Relief would be granted in accordance with the need of the area. The government promised modifications of language regulations. Henlein replied on February 28, demanding autonomy and the rectification of the wrongs committed in 1919. The issue was now plain: a group friendly to Nazi Germany demanded a measure endangering the security of the Czechoslovak state. Henlein's demands were refused.

On September 16, 1937, the Czech prime minister, Milan Hodža, met Henlein privately in the prime minister's home. Henlein demanded self-determination, defining it as autonomy; he charged the government with supporting his opposition and contributing nothing but talk toward settling the Czech-Sudeten problem. Hodža complained that the Sudeten German question disturbed relations between Berlin and Prague. Direct intervention from Berlin would not be permitted. Henlein retorted that he had no answer because this was not his business. The prime minister wanted full understanding with the Sudeten Germans. Although he favored an improvement in relations with Henlein's party, he asked Henlein to avoid making the Sudeten party appear to be a branch of Hitlerism. Henlein made no promises.[4]

Henlein's statements meant nothing. His goal was the destruction of the Czechoslovak state through demands for autonomy. He wanted his cries of martyrdom to arouse the sympathies of nations beset by guilt over the Versailles Treaty. Until ordered to the contrary, he pledged Berlin to hide the National Socialism of his party and to appear a sincere parliamentarian. His goal, the incorporation of the Sudeten German areas within the Reich, remained unchanged.[5] In Central Europe, Hitler now had a fifth column prepared to destroy Czechoslovak independence at his command.

German diplomatic pressure on the Czechoslovak government in-

[4] Eisenlohr to the German Foreign Ministry, October 8, 1937, *Documents on German Foreign Policy* (hereafter cited as *DG*), Series D, II, 1–9.

[5] Henlein to Neurath, November 10, 1937, *ibid.*, 49–62.

creased during the fall of 1937. On October 9, Ernst Eisenlohr, the German minister in Prague, complained to Kamil Krofta, Czechoslovak foreign minister, over the expulsion of Reich Germans in the frontier areas as a result of national defense needs. Eisenlohr demanded permission for the sale of *Mein Kampf* and a relaxation of the censorship.

Eisenlohr returned on November 4 to denounce the protection of refugee papers published within the Czechoslovak frontiers. On November 11, Eisenlohr repeated the same complaints to Beneš, adding a fresh complaint over the "arrest psychosis."[6]

Germany applied pressure also through the press. The Czechs were damned as "outposts of Bolshevism." Stories were spread across the front page of German papers that the Russian general staff was using Czechoslovakia to prepare an attack on Germany. Horror stories informed the excited reader that the Czechs starved Sudeten German children and tortured their fathers in loathsome prisons. That the land of Dachau and Oranienburg should print such stories infuriated the Czechs.

By November 1937, Germany's situation was so secure and the West was so unsuspecting that Hitler could consider future opportunities for expansion. To a meeting in the Reichschancery on November 5, he summoned his chief agents: Field Marshal Werner von Blomberg, war minister; Colonel General Baron Werner von Fritsch, commander in chief of the army; Admiral Erich Raeder, commander in chief of the navy; Colonel General Hermann Göring, commander in chief of the *Luftwaffe;* and Baron Konstantin von Neurath, the foreign minister.

Hitler announced that his remarks were his last will and testament and his basic ideas for Germany's future. For the future, Germany's chief problem was space, he declared. Germany could not maintain her present position and prepare for the future on the basis of economic self-sufficiency within her present frontiers. Additional resources must be found elsewhere, Hitler explained. Increased world trade would weaken Germany militarily because Britain dominated the world trade routes. The only remedy was living space in proximity to Germany and, therefore, German expansion in Europe. Britain

6 Eisenlohr to the German Foreign Ministry, October 11, 1937, *ibid.,* 11–15; Eisenlohr to the German Foreign Ministry, November 4, 1937, *ibid.,* 29–30; Eisenlohr to the German Foreign Ministry, November 11, 1937, *ibid.,* 36–44.

and France would be the opponents of German expansion. They were not very formidable because the British Empire was weakening, in Hitler's view, and French strength was severely sapped by internal national problems.

The *Führer* admitted that the problem of space could only be solved by force. The solution must come before 1943; after that date Germany would weaken as the opponents' counter measures increased. Germany would expand first into Austria and Czechoslovakia. From these nations Germany could obtain additional foodstuffs, a more easily defended frontier, the release of forces for other duties, and a new source of troops. Hitler was insistent that Czechoslovakia be overthrown because he feared a Czech attack should Germany weaken. He believed that Britain and France had already written off the Czechs and were reconciled to a German settlement. If the plans were successful, he doubted that Italy would object and believed that Poland would remain neutral. They must, however, be prepared for any counter action from Russia.

Hitler mistakenly prophesied an Anglo-French struggle with Italy over the Spanish Civil War by the summer of 1938. Germany could use the opportunity to acquire Austria and Czechoslovakia. Britain would not fight because of the Italian war; France would not move if Britain did nothing.

When the *Führer's* musings were finished, his listeners raised objections. Blomberg was fearful of the weakness of the western German fortifications and the strength of the Czechoslovak fortifications. Fritsch was worried about French troops available on the French-German frontier. Neurath could not see any war of France, Britain, and Italy by the summer of 1938. Within three months this trio was forced out of office. The meeting ended after a discussion of specific problems relating to armaments which would be needed if Hitler's thoughts became reality.[7] No one objected to the moral question: that Germany should seize two independent nations was accepted by the leaders of the Reich. Six years later, those who had been present at this conference and survived the Nazi defeat had to answer the question in the dock at Nuremberg.

[7] Hossbach memorandum, November 10, 1937, *DG*, I, 29–39. Although Hitler did not outline any plans at this meeting, I cannot agree with A. J. P. Taylor, *The Origins of the Second World War*, 133–34. Taylor argues that Hitler's statements were meaningless because subsequent events did not bear them out.

Contrary to past contentions, Hitler did not lay down any firm plans at this conference. Assuredly he revealed his growing interest in gaining access to Central Europe and its resources. The key to Central Europe was Czechoslovakia. It thrust far into the European "heartland." German occupation could enable Hitler's armies to threaten Poland, Hungary, Rumania, Bulgaria, and Yugoslavia. Hitler's forces would be brought nearer to the Russia he must ultimately defeat in order to dominate Central Europe. The destruction of Czechoslovakia would remove the Bohemian salient aimed against Germany.

The key to Czechoslovakia was the Sudetenland, inhabited by the Sudeten Germans, where the Czechoslovak government had built a line of fortifications to stop a German invasion. Once Hitler possessed this area, all Czechoslovakia would be at his mercy. The Sudeten Germans would be the key to the Sudetenland. Control of Austria was necessary because this country outflanked Czechoslovakia. Once Hitler controlled Austria, a German attack could be launched on Czechoslovakia from three sides if necessary. The Czechs would have no alternative but to withdraw from the Sudetenland. The same result could be achieved if the Czech government could be forced to give the Sudeten Germans self-determination. Applying this force was Hitler's new task.

# 3

## A New Policy

Of all the politicians prominent in the history of the Munich Agreement, none has had a more controversial role than Neville Chamberlain. On May 28, 1937, he kissed hands as the King's prime minister. Born in Birmingham in 1869, he was the son of Joseph Chamberlain, the dynamic British politician of the late Victorian era. In his early years, Neville was overshadowed by the political reputation of this elder half-brother, Austen, who served as foreign secretary in Stanley Baldwin's second cabinet.

Neville Chamberlain was trained for a business career. He became a prominent member of the business community in Birmingham, eventually becoming lord mayor. Lloyd George called him to Whitehall for the first time in 1916 to become minister of national service. Denied cabinet status, his powers curbed, Chamberlain was happy to resign in August 1917. Returning to national politics a year later, he was elected to Parliament in the "Coupon Election" at the age of 49. He served as minister of health; he was chancellor of the exchequer in Baldwin's cabinets and in Ramsay MacDonald's national government. As minister of health, he pushed through a solid program of social welfare involving housing, town planning, poor law revision, food and drugs regulation, and national health service. As a cabinet minister, he knew his subject well and administered his department with a firm hand, constantly paying attention to details.

Chamberlain was neither a coward nor a meek, obsequious politician. He was a hard-working businessman with an analytical mind who had entered politics. His nature was not gregarious; his likes and dislikes were pronounced. His shyness led to brusqueness, particularly with the Opposition. As prime minister he amazed many in Whitehall by his detailed comprehension of each department.

Chamberlain was not a pacifist, for he introduced the rearmament bills in the mid 1930's and fought for them against the Laborites. Unlike his former chief, Baldwin, who cared little about foreign affairs, Chamberlain was determined to improve the international situation. Believing that the ways of professional diplomats were too slow and that haste was imperative, he by-passed the Foreign Office and took control of foreign policy into his own hands. Because he opposed Chamberlain's policies, Robert Vansittart was elevated out of the way from the office of Permanent Undersecretary of State for Foreign Affairs to the exalted position of Chief Diplomatic Adviser to the Government in late 1937.

Although Chamberlain called his policy "appeasement," he did not mean peace at any price. Appeasement was the study and peaceful solution of problems that could cause war. By removing these causes, he hoped to avoid the war. Another world conflict with millions dead and wounded was, to him, an unspeakable horror, and he was willing to do everything in his power to prevent such a catastrophe. Extreme sacrifice was worthwhile if it would prevent a repetition of 1914–18.

The great weakness of Chamberlain was his failure to comprehend that a head of government would deliberately plan a world war. Such an idea was ridiculous to him. Because Hitler was the head of the German government, Chamberlain reasoned that the *Führer* must have common sense and would be happy to avoid war if the causes were removed. Through face-to-face meetings with the heads of governments, Chamberlain believed he could settle the problems that might lead to war. He would refuse any solution that was not orderly and peaceful.

Chamberlain's appeasement policy was useless because Hitler was determined to dominate Europe. Too much precious time was lost before Chamberlain grasped this fact. With his background in mind, his failure to understand Hitler's intentions can be explained if not defended. Chamberlain did not read *Mein Kampf* until after his return from Munich, and even then he probably discounted it as political propaganda.

As his chief adviser, Chamberlain had installed Sir Horace Wilson in an office in No. 10 Downing Street. Wilson was a competent civil servant who had labored long and faithfully in the Ministry of Labor, rising to be permanent secretary. In 1930 he was appointed Chief Industrial Adviser to the Government, and he was sent to the Treasury in 1937 for special duties with the prime minister. Chamberlain found him there and brought him to work with the cabinet as a liaison with the Foreign Office. Untrained in foreign affairs, Wilson left Chamberlain open for criticism.

Chamberlain set up an inner cabinet which advised him during the Czech crisis. This group included: Sir Samuel Hoare, a competent home secretary; Sir John Simon, chancellor of the exchequer; and Lord Halifax, who succeeded Anthony Eden as foreign secretary in 1938. The trio came from much the same social and religious background as Chamberlain; they shared his prejudices in foreign affairs.

Chamberlain's policies were eagerly furthered in Berlin by Sir Nevile Henderson. A career diplomat, Henderson had not read *Mein Kampf* until appointed to Berlin as ambassador in 1937. He was the classic English clubman, always immaculately dressed with a flower in his lapel. He was disdainful of his standing among the Berlin diplomatic corps who did not like him. He based his work on the belief that he was divinely ordained to stop another world war. Eagerly he joined in the search for an Anglo-German settlement. His excessive zeal occasionally brought reproof from his superiors in Whitehall. Accused of being pro-Nazi, he was more inclined to be a naïve gentleman. Because Chamberlain took so prominent a role in making foreign policy, the influence of Henderson has often been overlooked.

Chamberlain was still eager for closer contact with the Nazi leaders. Anthony Eden, the foreign secretary who had labored so arduously at Geneva for collective security, was not the man for such a contact. Lord Halifax, then lord president of the Council, was more inclined to Chamberlain's idea and happily lacked Eden's unfortunate connections with Geneva. When an invitation came to Halifax from Göring in the fall of 1937 to visit Germany for the International Exhibition of Hunting, Chamberlain eagerly pushed an acceptance. Here was an opportunity for a quiet, heart-to-heart talk without interference from the diplomats and their protocol. Such a meeting matched Chamberlain's experience of a private businessmen's meeting at a club to settle matters over drinks in the smoking room.

On November 19, Halifax saw Hitler in the presence of Neurath. Halifax "welcomed the opportunity to bring about a better understanding between England and Germany, by means of a personal conversation with the Chancellor." He had come "to discover in what way an opportunity could be made for a comprehensive and open discussion of all questions of interest to both countries." Hitler was agreed. Both men accepted the reality of Germany as an important force and acknowledged the injustices and mistakes of the Versailles Treaty. Britain, Halifax explained, wanted to make her influence felt to prevent adjustments to new conditions occurring through force. Whenever he attempted peaceful solutions, Hitler retorted, the democratic countries rejected them.

Halifax commented on Central Europe, observing that Austria, Czechoslovakia, and Danzig were possible changes in Europe which might come with time. Halifax declared that England was "interested to see that any alterations should come through the course of peaceful evolution and that methods should be avoided which might cause far-reaching disturbances, which neither the Chancellor nor other countries desired." Hitler retorted that Czechoslovakia would herself help to clear away the difficulties, for "she only needed to treat the Germans living within her borders well and they would be entirely happy."

The impression left by Halifax on Hitler can be gained by reading the following excerpt from the circular sent to some of the German embassies reporting on the conversation:

> The British did not believe that the *status quo* had to be maintained under all circumstances. Among the questions in which changes would probably be made sooner or later were Danzig, Austria, and Czechoslovakia. England was only interested in seeing that such changes were brought about by peaceful development.[1]

Unwittingly Chamberlain's representative had implied that if the

[1] Neurath to Henderson, November 20, 1937, *DG*, Series D, I, 54–68; German Foreign Ministry to German embassies in Italy, Great Britain, France, and the United States, November 22, 1937, *ibid.*, 68–71.

seizure of Austria and Czechoslovakia could be attained peacefully, Britain would not interfere. There was nothing objectionable in the changes provided all was peaceful. Overlooked was the danger to the security of Europe and the world.

Halifax judged the talk to be of little value although personal contact had at last been established without the diplomats. He received the "impression that apart from colonies there was little or nothing Hitler wanted from Britain, and that as regards European problems he felt time to be on his side."

Field Marshal Hermann Göring entertained Halifax at luncheon on November 20. The commander in chief of the *Luftwaffe* appeared "dressed in brown breeches and boots all in one, green leather jerkin surrounded with a green leather belt, on which hung a dagger in a red leather sheath." Although Halifax found the food "uneatable," he was delighted to meet "a modern Robin Hood." Throughout the luncheon, Halifax kept wondering "how many people he had been responsible for getting killed." Göring was blunt in his remarks. In Europe, Germany wanted special spheres of influence. Britain and France had best not "block any agreements Germany might reach with her neighbors."[2]

The talk between Halifax and Hitler made a significant impression on Chamberlain. He believed the trip a success. It created an "atmosphere in which it is possible to discuss with Germany the practical questions involved in a European settlement." For the present, he accepted the statements of Hitler and Göring that they did not want war. Chamberlain believed they wanted domination of Eastern Europe, close union with Austria without incorporation into the Reich, and "the same things for the *Sudetendeutsche* as we did for the *Uitlanders* in the Transvaal." The Prime Minister thought there was a fair basis for discussion if Germany gave assurances that force would not be used in Austria and Czechoslovakia. If Germany obtained her goals in Eastern Europe peacefully, Chamberlain was willing that Britain give assurances not to oppose Germany.[3]

Chamberlain lacked any grasp of the strategic importance of Central Europe. The peaceful changes he contemplated would give Hitler an empire from which to launch an attack on the West or the East. Like many of his generation, Chamberlain failed to see that the peace

2 Earl of Halifax, *Fulness of Days,* 188–91.
3 Keith Feiling, *The Life of Neville Chamberlain,* 332–33.

settlement of 1919 splintered Central Europe into a collection of many weak nations and one strong nation—Germany. None of Germany's small neighbors possessed the requisite industrial system to outbuild her; each tried to throttle the other in tariff wars; each lacked the population to create a large army. Any addition to German territory, no matter how peacefully it might be added, would only further upset the balance of power in Germany's favor.

Halifax's trip to Germany frightened France. Was another deal being prepared behind the back of the French government? Perhaps another Anglo-German Naval Agreement? To reassure the French government, and in order that Chamberlain could become better acquainted with his French counterpart, Halifax invited Camille Chautemps, the premier, and Yvon Delbos, the foreign minister, to London for a conference in late November.

Halifax pacified the French by recounting his trip to Germany. The moderation of Hitler over Czechoslovakia had impressed him. At the most, he thought, the Germans would push for the desired adjustments "in a comparatively orderly fashion, but not take any action in any manner that would give other governments cause to oppose or intervene."[4]

Delbos proposed, and the British accepted his plan for, a trip to Central Europe to reassure and tighten the Little Entente. With the full backing of the British government, Delbos would press Prague for better understanding with the Sudeten Germans and direct settlement between Berlin and Prague. Such action, the conference thought, would facilitate the orderly adjustment in Central Europe without dangerous consequences.

Neurath met Delbos for about thirty minutes in his railway coach as the French statesman passed through Berlin on December 2. Delbos assured his host that France had no intention of blocking German development in Central Europe. Undeterred by French courtesy, Neurath criticized the communiqué issued to the press after the November conference in London. It created the impression that France and Britain wanted to tell Germany how to pursue her own interests. Germany rejected this tutelage forever. Germany had given proof of good will and readiness for peace without any response from France and Britain. Delbos' explanations were cut off by Neurath's condem-

[4] British Embassy to the Department of State, December 15, 1937, *FRUS, 1937,* I, 196–202.

nation of the "lack of discipline" in the democratic press. Only the departure of the train for Warsaw ended Neurath's attack.

The reports of the rest of Delbos' trip were gratifying to the German foreign office, for his reception in Poland, Rumania, and Yugoslavia was correct but unenthusiastic.

In Prague there was more enthusiasm for the French foreign minister and more sincerity in the toasts. Delbos presented the Anglo-French desire for settlement of the Sudeten question by concessions. The Czechs resented the pressure; they would discuss the question in a friendly fashion but not negotiate with a foreign government over an internal question of Czech citizens. To emphasize his feelings, Delbos pointedly conferred with three Sudeten German deputies after the foreign ministers' dinner on December 16. Only thus could he impress on the Czech government the desire in London and Paris for a peaceful settlement of this pressing question.[5]

The New Year brought a warning from Henlein that until the Sudeten Germans were satisfied, any Czech agreement with Germany was impossible. Those Sudeten Germans who did not support him, Henlein threatened with the traitor's fate.

Hitler's speech to the *Reichstag* on February 20 did little to calm the situation. His audience knew full well his meaning when he lamented the "ten million Germans who live in two of the states adjoining our frontiers." They had been prevented in 1919 "against their will from forming a union with the Reich." These Germans should not be deprived "of their rights as members of a national community." It was intolerable to Hitler that Germans across the frontier "suffer severe persecution simply because of their sympathy, their feeling of union with Germany, because of their common fate, their common point of view." Hitler declared that a peaceful settlement could be obtained using good will. "If one tries to prevent the solution of the problem in this way," he warned, "and uses force in so doing, then one day this violence will be returned with violence." He swore to protect the freedoms of the Germans who lived beyond the frontiers of the Reich.[6]

Chamberlain made no direct reference to Hitler's words over

5 Memorandum of Neurath, December 3, 1937, *DG*, Series D, I, 94–95; Eisenlohr to the German Foreign Ministry, December 17, 1937, *ibid.*, II, 71–72; Eisenlohr to the German Foreign Ministry, December 21, 1937, *ibid.*, 79–89.

6 *The Speeches of Adolph Hitler, April, 1922–August, 1939*, II, 1404–1406.

Czechoslovakia and Austria. Speaking in the House of Commons on February 21, he hinted for the first time at a four-power settlement of problems in Europe as a means of saving the peace of Europe for "a generation."[7] In Paris before the Chamber of Deputies, Delbos pledged "the affection of France for the brave Czechoslovak people to whom, should the occasion arise, our engagements will be faithfully fulfilled."

Not until March 4 did Hodža make a formal statement in reply to Hitler before the Czechoslovak Parliament. Never would the Czech government allow foreign interference in internal affairs. Although they desired peace, the Czechs would fight rather than have a settlement with Germany at the expense of Czech independence.[8]

Hodža's words were a reflection of Beneš' ideas that Czechoslovakia must resist German aggression. If Czechoslovakia were conquered by Germany, he believed that Russia and Germany would then partition Central Europe, destroying the independence of the small nations. To prevent this catastrophe, he expected Britain and France to support Czechoslovakia if only for their best interests. Without their assistance Czechoslovakia "would at once become a vassal of Germany."

At the urging of Jan Masaryk, the son of Tomáš Masaryk and Czechoslovak minister in Great Britain, Beneš appealed for Anglo-French support through an interview printed in the March 6 issue of the *Sunday Times*. He would not let the Sudeten question become a matter for negotiation with foreigners, but he would place any information desired at the disposal of the British and French. He was willing to negotiate a settlement with Germany. Concessions to the Sudetens already under study, but he would not sacrifice Czechoslovak national unity. Czechoslovakia, he declared, was "bound to the evolution of Western Europe."[9]

Beneš' attitude was contrary to the policies already being pursued by Chamberlain. In December, 1937, he had approached Joachim von Ribbentrop, a former champagne salesman who now passed for the German ambassador. The prime minister explained that senti-

---

[7] *Parliamentary Debates, House of Commons,* Fifth series, Vol. 332, col. 64.

[8] *Survey of International Affairs,* II, 55–60.

[9] William V. Wallace, "The Foreign Policy of President Beneš in the Approach to Munich," *The Slavonic and East European Review,* Vol. XXXIX (December, 1960), 108–18.

ment in Parliament was favorable for a settlement with Germany. He assured Ribbentrop that it was "a well-known fact that I am not one of those who consider understanding with Germany to be impossible." Even a solution of the Sudeten question was possible, once negotiations were started.[10]

Late in January, 1938, Henderson was ordered to obtain an interview with Hitler to discuss the basis for Anglo-German settlement. On March 3, Henderson finally saw Hitler in the company of Ribbentrop. Henderson announced that Britain was interested in arms limitation, "appeasement in Czechoslovakia and Austria," and an examination of the colonial question. He did not seek a bargain but rather "to create a basis for friendship." Great difficulties must be surmounted, but the British government would accept peaceful changes based on the use of reason rather than force. At the end of the longest continuous statement that Henderson ever made to Hitler, the *Führer* scowled and launched forth into a tirade against the British press. He warned against interference when Germany tried to improve the lot of Germans in Austria. The Sudeten Germans must be granted their rightful autonomy. If Germans were fired on in Austria or Czechoslovakia, he was ready to intervene.

Throughout the conversation, Hitler was brusque, rude, and offensive. He was courteous and agreeable only when Ambassador Henderson asked him to autograph a drawing of the *Führer* for a lady from New Zealand.[11]

Ribbentrop came to London a week later to present his letter of recall. Germany, Ribbentrop announced, wanted self-determination for the ten million Germans in Austria and Czechoslovakia. "No power on earth can stop this inevitable development toward the German view," he warned. Once these problems were settled, Germany's nationality problems in the east would be solved and the negotiations could proceed to arms limitation and colonial questions. Bluntly Ribbentrop summarized Hitler's feelings on the nationality question: "For the oppression of a foreign people, not a single German soldier would be sacrificed, but for the preservation of the Ger-

10 Ribbentrop to the German Foreign Ministry, December 17, 1937, *DG*, Series D, I, 131–34.

11 Memorandum of Ribbentrop, March 3, 1938, *ibid.*, 236–38; Nevile Henderson, *Failure of a Mission: Berlin, 1937–1939*, 113–18.

man nationality in Europe, the entire German nation would be employed."

Somewhat taken back by this bellicose reply to British accommodation, Halifax, who had succeeded Eden as foreign secretary in February, assured Ribbentrop that Britain recognized the reality of the German point of view in Austria and Czechoslovakia and would use her influence in Prague for a peaceful solution. Hitler had "it in his power more than any other to go down in history as the great architect of peace and a great benefactor of countless men, women and children in Europe who were yet unborn," Halifax pleaded. "Conditions in this country today were favorable for the effort that so great a purpose deserved. The prime minister had set himself with energy to the task." Halifax begged Ribbentrop not to let this opportunity pass to achieve peace.[12]

Hitler replied to Halifax' plea on March 11. Chamberlain entertained the Ribbentrops at lunch; before the guests had departed from No. 10 Downing Street, two telegrams were handed to Halifax announcing that the German government had given Kurt von Schuschnigg an ultimatum to resign. Before the day was over, a Nazi agent, Artur von Seyss-Inquart, replaced Schuschnigg. By March 13, German troops had occupied Austria. Hitler made his triumphal entry into Vienna on March 14. Czechoslovakia had been outflanked; the Sudeten party would function as a Nazi front and as a cause to arouse the sympathies of France and Britain; the Czechs would play the role of persecutor, and Adolf Hitler would be the long-awaited savior of the Sudetenland.

[12] Conversation, Halifax-Ribbentrop, March 11, 1938, *DG*, Series D, I, 263-62. 264–69.

# 4

## The First Alarm

THE NEWS of the *Anschluss* interrupted a luncheon at No. 10 Downing Street honoring Ribbentrop. The German government had demanded the resignation of Schuschnigg by a definite deadline. Momentarily the hosts were excited. It was "an exceedingly serious situation," Chamberlain exclaimed. To Halifax the ultimatum was an "intolerable" method in foreign relations. Ribbentrop denounced Schuschnigg for arranging a plebiscite without consulting Germany. Finally Chamberlain confessed that he understood the situation; even Halifax calmed down.

Later in the day, Halifax called on Ribbentrop for tea and any additional information. Their chat was interrupted by the announcement of Schuschnigg's resignation. Halifax condemned the German method as an indication that the German leaders preferred force to negotiation. Ribbentrop compared German tactics in Austria with those of the British in Ireland. The tea party soon ended.

Halifax instructed Henderson to get an accurate warning quickly to Hitler. Henderson made no attempt to reach Hitler because he did not think that he could see him. Instead, about 5 P.M. on March 11, he protested the German actions to Neurath, who was no longer influential in the formation of German foreign policy.

That evening Henderson, with the other members of the diplomatic corps, attended a ballet and concert given by Göring. While the guests awaited the arrival of the host, the first secretary of the

British embassy, Ivone Kirkpatrick, entered and handed Henderson a message from Halifax instructing him to protest the ultimatum sent to Schuschnigg demanding his resignation. Nervous diplomats awaited the arrival of Göring, delayed by the crisis. At last the perspiring Reichsmarshal made his entrance and seated himself at the table of honor, surrounded by diplomats. Göring handed Henderson a note, across the wife of the American ambassador, asking the British ambassador to see him as soon as the music stopped.

After the ballerinas finished dancing to the strains of "The Beautiful Blue Danube," Göring and Henderson hurried out to a private room. There Henderson protested the ultimatum, but Göring denied that there was any ultimatum from Germany: it was merely one set of Austrians sending an ultimatum to another set. Henderson admitted that Göring had scored a point on a technicality. According to Göring, Schuschnigg broke the agreement with Hitler, echoing the line taken in London by Ribbentrop. Henderson confessed that Schuschnigg acted with "precipitate folly."

So distasteful was the situation to Henderson that he begged Halifax to relieve him of any more protests. Only force could save Austria from Schuschnigg's "ill-conceived and ill-prepared folly." Halifax was in agreement with this conclusion. The German government duly rejected Henderson's protest: Britain was not the protector of Austria. With the rejection, the British government considered the incident closed.[1]

On March 14, Chamberlain recounted the story of the crisis to the House of Commons and read Neurath's reply, rejecting the British protest. The Prime Minister replied that Britain would interest herself in the affairs of a member of the League of Nations. After condemning the methods used, he denied rumors that the government had either encouraged or consented to the *Anschluss*. There were no British commitments towards Austria, except to consult with the French and Italian governments. This had been done, he said. Although the event damaged confidence in Europe, German action

---

1 Memorandum of Ribbentrop, March 11, 1938, *DG*, Series D, I, 273–75; Halifax to Henderson, March 11, 12, 1938, *Documents on British Foreign Policy*, (hereafter cited as *DBFP*), Third Series, 8, 21–23, 29–33; Henderson to Halifax, March 12, 1938, *ibid.*, 23–26, 30–32; Henderson, *Failure of a Mission*, 124–26; Joachim von Ribbentrop, *The Ribbentrop Memoirs*, 85–86.

could not have been stopped unless Britain and France had been prepared to use force. He promised a review of the rearmament program.

In the House of Lords on March 16, Halifax confessed intimating to the Germans that there could be a change in the *status quo* in Europe, but not one by violence. In his opinion, there was no protection for Austria, short of force, either in international law or in the League of Nations. He noted that the events created a new position for Czechoslovakia; he was glad that the German government had promised to respect the Czechoslovak frontiers.[2]

Both men condemned the methods because they threatened appeasement. They were not aghast at Hitler's goals, but at his ungentlemanly methods. While the German troops invaded Austria, Halifax paced the foreign office muttering, "Horrible! Horrible! I never thought they would do it![3]

Upon learning of the *Anschluss,* the Czechoslovak government informed Eisenlohr that it did not intend to intervene in this crisis. On the night of March 11, at the *Haus der Flieger,* Göring gave Vojtech Mastny, the Czech minister, a hearty greeting and announced that on his word of honor the entry of German troops into Austria was just a family affair. There was no need for alarm. After informing his government, Mastny returned about 1:00 A.M. Göring repeated his declaration and gave "the word of the supreme head of the state." In the afternoon of March 12, Mastny called on Neurath, who assured him that the occupation was not directed against Czechoslovakia. The troops would remain at least fifteen to thirty kilometers from the frontier. Göring again assured Mastny, on March 13, that the operation was not aimed at Czechoslovakia and that German aircraft had been ordered to stay at least thirty kilometers from the frontier. Three days later, speaking for Ribbentrop, Secretary of State Georg von Mackensen assured Mastny that rumors of threatening German troops in Bavaria and Saxony were "sheer nonsense." Mastny declared that he was not worried now because he had Göring's word of honor. If someone woke him at midnight with alarming news, he would mention Göring's word of honor and fall asleep.[4]

2 *Parliamentary Debates, House of Commons,* Fifth series, Vol. 333, cols. 45–52; *House of Lords,* Fifth series, Vol. 108, cols. 176–83.

3 Alan Campbell Johnson, *Viscount Halifax: A Biography,* 456.

4 Mastny to Prague, March 12, 1938, *Europäische Politik, 1933–1938, im Spiegel*

The repeated assurances given to Mastny indicated the German fears that the Czechoslovak forces might upset the *Anschluss*. The performance of the German army had revealed serious weaknesses in training as scores of armored vehicles broke down on the roads to Austria. A sudden move by the armed forces of Czechoslovakia could have placed Hitler's armies in an embarrassing situation. Beneš, however, had no desire to use his small, well-trained army to save the seat of the Hapsburg might which had so long ruled Bohemia and Moravia. The Germans hoped to trick Beneš into believing that the *Anschluss* would work out well for Czechoslovakia in the future. Nowhere in the assurances was there any promise to respect the integrity of Czechoslovakia.

The *Anschluss* found France without a government because the Chautemps cabinet fell on March 10. As foreign minister in a caretaker government, Delbos could do little more than warn Johannes Welczeck, the German ambassador, that such incidents could lead to a general war. Welczeck retorted that the *Anschluss* was a family affair. Delbos informed Štefan Osusky, the Czechoslovak minister, that France would regard an attack on Czechoslovakia as an attack on France.

André François-Poncet, the French ambassador in Berlin, presented a protest on March 11 over the use of violence and coercion against an independent state. The protest was rejected.

On March 13, Léon Blum formed a government with Joseph Paul-Boncour as foreign minister. The latter declared to Osusky on March 14 that if Czechoslovakia were attacked, France would keep her agreement regardless of British action. Paul-Boncour inquired about British intentions in view of the changes in Central Europe. Despite his statement to Osusky, the foreign minister wanted a public announcement that Britain would support France if she went to the aid of Czechoslovakia in a war brought on by a German attack. Halifax rejected any prior commitments and proposed a high level meeting with the French ministers. Chamberlain refused until the French government was more firmly established.

With Charles Corbin, the French ambassador, Halifax raised

---

*der Prager Akten* (ed. by Fritz Berber), (hereafter cited as *Europäische Politik*), 94–95; reports of Eisenlohr, March 12, 13, 1938, *DG*, series D, II, 156, 158–60; memorandum of Neurath, March 14, 1938, *ibid.*, 161–62; memorandum of Mackensen March 16, 1938, *ibid.*, 168–69.

another question. How would France help Czechoslovakia in a practical way when the *Anschluss* made that more difficult? To find an answer, Paul-Boncour called a meeting of the Permanent Committee of National Defense on March 15. Édouard Daladier, the minister of national defense, declared that initially direct aid could not be given Czechoslovakia: France would mobilize her forces and hold the German troops along the frontiers. General Maurice Gamelin, the army chief of staff, was cool to a French attack along the German frontier because the area would be well fortified. He did not expect much help from Russia. General Joseph Vuillemin, chief of staff for air, doubted that much help could come from Russia by air because her planes had to fly over Poland and Rumania. The Czechoslovak airfields were few in number, and Germany could easily knock them out. Vuillemin confessed that he had done nothing to have the Czechs build larger airfields to accommodate the Russian planes. Blum concluded that, although some German troops might be held up by mobilization of French troops, France could do little to aid Czechoslovakia.[5]

When Paul-Boncour met the German ambassador, Johannes Welczeck, on April 14, he warned that if Germany attacked, France would help Czechoslovakia; but Welczeck reported that the French government hoped to prevent any war involving obligations to Czechoslovakia. Paul-Boncour's declarations contrasted strongly with press tirades against using the French nation as cannon fodder to defend Czechoslovakia. Even moderate French newspapers insinuated that Czechoslovakia was threatened with internal collapse.

On April 5, Paul-Boncour presided at a meeting of French diplomats accredited to Central and Eastern European capitals. He wanted their opinions on French policy regarding Czechoslovakia, which the government had promised to defend. Only the opinions of Léon Noël, ambassador to Poland, are known. He argued that under the prevailing conditions France could do little for Czechoslovakia. As he enlarged his ideas, someone hissed, "That's defeatism!" Ignoring his critic, Noël stressed that France was too weak in armaments and had relied too much on vague pacts and discussions in Geneva to maintain great power status. He reported that Poland would not help Czechoslovakia and would fight Russian troops seeking to aid the Prague

[5] Joseph Paul-Boncour, *Entre deux guerres*, III, 83–84, 88; Welczeck to the German Foreign Ministry, March 15, 1938, *DG*, Series D, I, 603; Maurice Gamelin, *Servir*, II, 322–28.

government. Robert Coulondre, the ambassador to Russia, gave a pessimistic report on the possibility of Russian aid. The conference failed to come up with any bold policy. This fact was soon known to the German government.[6]

The problem for France was complicated by ignorance of the intentions of the Soviet Union. On March 15, Maxim Litvinov, the people's commissar for foreign affairs, informed the Czechoslovak minister, Zdenek Fierlinger, that the Soviet Union was ready to carry out its obligations towards Czechoslovakia. In Paris, the Soviet ambassador announced that the Soviet Union would stand behind the Czechoslovak-Soviet Treaty of Mutual Assistance. Litvinov informed newsmen on the same day that Russia would intervene in defense of Czechoslovakia if France did. When asked how this could be accomplished without a common frontier with Germany, he replied that "the means would be found." His hearers pointed out that his statement meant the creation of a corridor; he seemed to agree with their conclusion.

To Paris, London, Washington, and Prague on March 17, Litvinov dispatched a written statement, less aggressive in tone. The *Anschluss* had created a menace to the independence of small nations in Central Europe: the threat to Czechoslovakia could develop into a world war. Russia would join in collective action to stop "the further development of aggression and the elimination of the increased danger of a new world slaughter." Litvinov avoided any mention of defending Czechoslovakia from German aggression.

The commissar for foreign affairs did not actually call for a four-power conference as some have claimed. He only said that the Soviet Union was "ready as before to participate in collective action. . . . It is prepared immediately to take up . . . deliberations . . . on practical measures when circumstances demand." This was not a stirring call to defend Czechoslovakia by force of arms.

The inclusion of the United States and Great Britain was strange. That the United States would reject the proposal must have been known to Moscow before the note was dispatched. Chamberlain made his statement to the House of Commons before the note was sent; thus, the attitude of the British government was public. On March 24, the London government rejected the proposal. By including two nations who would reject a four-power conference, the Soviet Union

[6] Léon Noël, *L'aggression Allemande contre la Pologne*, 196–97.

could proclaim for the record that an attempt had been made at collective security, but that the other nations had refused to co-operate. Actually, only France and Czechoslovakia needed to be consulted. Certainly Soviet agents had reported on the attitude of these governments. The note gave the Soviet Union a good basis for its contribution to the Munich myth.

In private conversation, Litvinov was less aggressive and very pessimistic. He told Viscount Chilston, the British ambassador, that Hitler's next step would be against Czechoslovakia; neither Britain, France, nor the League of Nations held any terrors for Hitler. To Joseph E. Davies, the United States ambassador, Litvinov declared his expectation of trouble over Czechoslovakia during the summer. He feared lest Czechoslovakia surrender to Germany because of her isolation and lack of confidence in France. Litvinov believed that France had no confidence in the Soviet Union, who, he confessed to Davies, had no confidence in France.[7]

In the Sudeten area, the effects of the *Anschluss* were decisive. A wave of feeling for a united front swept across the Sudetenland. Many rushed to apply for membership in the Sudeten party. The Sudeten press demanded incorporation into the Reich instead of mere autonomy. The Activist Front, made up of those German parties who co-operated with the government, was broken. Representatives of these parties hastened to resign from the cabinet. The German Agrarian party united with the Sudeten German parliamentary party, and the German Social Democrats joined the opposition.

The enlarged Sudeten party showed its strength in the Sudetenland on March 27 in thirty-six meetings of five hundred thousand members. The forbidden party flags waved over the town halls of Asch and Eger. In defiance of an order forbidding the Nazi salute, the speaker in Göckaulugun proclaimed: "On behalf of you all I salute our *Führer* and the entire German people with upraised hand." Following their orders, the police only watched; sometimes, under duress, they saluted the Sudeten German flag.

Within the Czech government, the *Anschluss* created some agreement on internal policy. The Henlein party would have to be ad-

7 Litvinov statement, March 17, 1938, *New Documents on the History of Munich* (hereafter cited as *NDM*), 22–24; Tippelskirch to the German Foreign Ministry, March 17, 21, 1938, *DG*, Series D, II, 176–77, 184; Chilston to Halifax, March 15, 17, 1938, *DBFP*, I, 54–56; Joseph E. Davies, *Mission to Moscow*, 290–92.

mitted to the government. Beneš was prepared to appoint inspectors who would eliminate practices irritating to the Sudeten Germans. For the Sudeten Germans, Hodža promised "self administration," which he defined as the appointment of local officials by the German party victorious in the elections: German officials would be transferred to German areas.

Beneš believed that Germany sought domination in Southeastern Europe, and now he would only negotiate with Germany if Britain and France supported him as the guarantors of any agreement. With Britain and France backing Czechoslovakia, Beneš was ready to reach an agreement with Germany which would be " 'manly, dignified, honest and clear.' " Without the knowledge and approval of France and Great Britain, he would consider nothing. Once this condition was met, Czechoslovakia would fight.[8]

By this decision, Beneš delivered his foreign policy into the hands of Great Britain and France. He saw the *Anschluss* as a warning of the fate threatening to overtake small nations who tried to negotiate with Germany in isolation. The tie which he now sought with the Western powers would prevent isolation, thereby avoiding a Czechoslovak *Anschluss*. Their victories would be the victories of Prague, so Beneš thought. He assumed that the foreign policies advocated by London and Paris would be advantageous to Czechoslovakia because it would be to the best interests of his Western friends to support him.

Beneš had made a fateful decision, for he had thrust the future of Czechoslovakia into the unwilling hands of the British and French governments. Czechoslovak foreign policy would now be made in Paris and London; the mistakes of French and English diplomats would affect Prague. Beneš had surrendered something of Czechoslovak independence to Britain and France, believing that such a policy was best. He did not turn to Russia because he was not of the East and feared Russian ambitions in Central Europe.

Czechoslovak military planning also followed Beneš' pro-Western slant. The general staff expected war with Germany within a year or two at the latest, but they were confident of victory because of French and Russian aid and possible help from Britain. Their planning was

---

[8] Newton to Halifax, March 20, 21, 22, 29, 1938, *DBFP*, Third series, I, 72–78, 103–108; Wallace, "The Foreign Policy of President Beneš in the Approach to Munich," *The Slavonic and East European Review*, Vol. XXXIX (December, 1960), 118–38.

based on the assumption of French mobilization to relieve German pressure on the Czechoslovak frontiers. The unanswered question was: could they continue the struggle alone? They might succeed if the *Anschluss* had awakened Paris and London sufficiently to the German threat. Paris seemed aware of the German threat to Czechoslovakia and had called for British support. The Chamberlain government had yet to declare its position.

# 5

## *Policies and Plans*

THE *Anschluss* forced a reassessment of British foreign policy in which Neville Chamberlain's opinions were decisive. The pressure to "give a clear, decided, bold, and unmistakable lead" he dismissed as "twaddle . . . calculated to vex the man who has to take the responsibility for the consequences." He found little solace in Winston Churchill's idea of a "Grand Alliance." The Germans could overrun Czechoslovakia if they desired, and Britain could not help "unless we had a reasonable prospect of being able to beat Germany to her knees in a reasonable time, and of that I see no sign." Seeing that luck could not be trusted to bring victory when the odds so favored defeat, Chamberlain made up his mind neither to guarantee Czechoslovak independence nor to support French obligations to Czechoslovakia.[1]

Chamberlain stated the government's policy on March 24. Britain was obligated to France under the terms of the Locarno Treaty. Membership in the League of Nations required intervention to restore peace or to maintain order if events made it appropriate. The Prime Minister rejected any firm commitment to Czechoslovakia because the area held none of the vital interests of Great Britain. If war came, "the inexorable pressure of facts might well prove more powerful than formal pronouncements," and countries other than those original to the war might become involved. Such might be the case with Britain and France because of their "long associations of friendship, with interests

[1] Feiling, *Neville Chamberlain*, 347–48.

closely interwoven, devoted to the same ideals of democratic liberty, and determined to uphold them."[2]

Chamberlain had utilized imprecision to frighten the Germans, whom he did not intend to fight. The subsequent actions of the British government indicated all too clearly the real meaning of his statement. His words would have had greater effect if Britain had possessed the force for war and if Anglo-French military plans had already been completed. There was little extant force to deter the Germans. On March 28, the chiefs of staff reported that Britain was unprepared for war. At all costs, war must be avoided, in order to gain time to rearm because war in 1938 meant defeat for Britain.[3]

A memorandum to the French government further clarified the position of the British government. British obligations to Czechoslovakia were only those of one member of the League of Nations to another. Should war come, little could be done to prevent German conquest of Czechoslovakia, already weakened by the *Anschluss.* Britain could aid only by a blockade, and this would take effect slowly. Britain's obligation to France was in the Treaty of Locarno, a promise of defense against German aggression. No aid was forthcoming in cases not covered by this treaty. Domestic politics and the problems of the commonwealth precluded any further commitments. The London government believed that France should try to "remove the causes of friction or even conflict" by bringing the Czechoslovak government to a settlement of the Sudeten question. The British government would consider consultations between the staffs of the two air forces.

The Czechoslovak government also received a British memorandum on March 24, differing little in content from the memorandum sent to Paris. The British government regretted that they could not accept more "direct and definite" commitments towards Czechoslovakia. "Within limits of their ability," the British government "will do everything to assist the Czechoslovak government, who can

2 *Parliamentary Debates, House of Commons,* Fifth series, Vol. 333, cols. 1399–1407.

3 P. K. Kemp, *Key to Victory: The Triumph of British Sea Power in World War II,* 26. Unfortunately the text of this important document has been omitted from *Documents on British Foreign Policy.* Mr. Kemp was kind enough to supply me with the date.

be assured of their sympathy and good will towards a solution of their difficulties."

The memorandum reflected the views of Halifax who saw no value in "uttering a warning against action which the German government have declared that they do not contemplate." When the French and Czechoslovak governments interpreted the Prime Minister's statements as a warning to Germany that Britain would intervene on the French side, Halifax hastened to disabuse them of this comforting prospect. Chamberlain had not stated a certainty, but only hinted at a probability.[4]

Both Halifax and Chamberlain displayed ignorance of the strategic value of Central Europe by considering that Britain's vital interests did not include Czechoslovakia. They were oblivious to the importance of Czechoslovakia whose capture would give Germany domination of Central Europe. Both men considered their views to be "realistic," given the general state of British and French military unpreparedness.

In Prague, Krofta accepted Chamberlain's statement. Satisfied with British "sympathy and understanding," he appeared ready to rely on the French alliance while hoping for eventual British support. Beneš looked toward British recognition of an identity of interests with the Czechs.[5]

On March 25, Sir Samuel Hoare, a close friend of Chamberlain and the Home Secretary, suggested to Jan Masaryk, as "an old friend," that President Beneš should ask Britain and France to give him their good offices in making satisfactory agreement over the Sudetenland.

Chamberlain's policy was based on the assumption that Henlein, as spokesman for the Sudetens, was acting in complete sincerity. Such was not the case. Henlein sent Ribbentrop the sincere thanks of the Sudetens for the *Anschluss*. He pledged that they would show their appreciation by doubling their efforts in the service of the greater Germany. Because the new increase in the Reich necessitated a reexamination of Sudeten German policy, Henlein asked for an early personal talk. He wanted Eisenlohr present because the German min-

[4] Halifax to Phipps, March 22, 23, April 11, 1938, *DBFP*, Third series, I, 82–88, 140–43. This note was delivered to the Quai d'Orsay on March 24. Halifax to Newton, March 23, April 12, 1938, *ibid.*, 90–91, 150–51.

[5] Newton to Halifax, March 25, 1938, *ibid.*, 102.

ister to Prague had demanded the control of Sudeten policy and censured Henlein and Karl Hermann Frank, his lieutenant, for their insistence on autonomy and racial laws.

Henlein was granted a conference with Hitler on March 28. The *Führer* announced his intention of settling the Sudeten question in the near future. Hitler promised his support to Henlein and proclaimed, "From tomorrow you will be my viceroy! I will not tolerate difficulties being made for you by any department whatsoever within the Reich." Hitler ordered the new viceroy to make unacceptable demands on the Czech government and to visit Britain to insure British nonintervention. Henlein accepted the responsibilities, declaring, "We must always demand so much that we can never be satisfied."

Another conference was held the next day in Ribbentrop's office with Eisenlohr in attendance on "Viceroy" Henlein. Ribbentrop directed that the Sudetens know of German support. The Sudeten leaders would make representations to Prague but avoid entering the Czechoslovak government. The Reich government must not appear to be calling the tune for the Sudeten Germans. Henlein would maintain firm control over the party and keep in touch with other Czechoslovak minority groups. Eisenlohr must co-operate and support Henlein unofficially. The meeting approved a list of demands for the Sudeten Germans that had been drawn up in the Foreign Ministry. These demands included: the cessation of school building for Czech propaganda purposes in Sudeten territory, some profession of Nazi ideology, German officials and civil servants in the Sudetenland, the holding of state and local elections, and the abolition of the hated Czech state police in the frontier areas.[6]

Hitler had taken a major step towards the destruction of Czechoslovakia. Sudeten demands would be subject to periodic review and revision but always upward. By utilizing the minority question, Hitler placed the West at a disadvantage, for there were guilt feelings over the Versailles Treaty. Continually raising Sudeten demands made

[6] Eisenlohr to the German Foreign Ministry, March 17, 18, 1938, *DG,* Series D, II, 169–70, 178–79; Burger to Mackensen, March 18, 1938, *ibid.,* 173–74; memorandum for Ribbentrop, March 28, 1938, *ibid.,* 197; report of Henlein's audience with Hitler, March 28, 1938, *ibid.,* 197–202; Ribbentrop to Eisenlohr, March 29, 1938, *ibid.,* 203–205; Henlein to Ribbentrop, March 17, 1938, *Nazi Conspiracy and Aggression* (hereafter cited as *NCA*), V, 424–25.

the Czechoslovaks appear hardhearted. Psychologically the preparation could not have been better, given the pacifist, guilt-stricken government of Great Britain. Although not similarly guilt-stricken, the new leadership in France would be content to follow the British lead.

On April 8, the Blum government fell after an adverse vote on the finance bill in the Senate. By April 10, Édouard Daladier had formed a cabinet and within two days received the approval of the Chamber and the Senate. The cabinet was more to the right than the Blum government, because the Socialists refused to be represented.

Daladier was far from an amateur in French national politics. He had held posts in twelve cabinets, and this was his third premiership. Born in the department of the Vaucluse, the son of a baker, he had been trained as a history professor. When World War I broke out, he entered the army as a sergeant and eventually received the Legion of Honor, *Croix de Guerre,* three citations for bravery, and a captain's commission. After the war, Édouard Herriot persuaded Daladier to stand for the Chamber of Deputies as the representative for his native department. He won his first election and maintained his seat for the next twenty years. In 1933 he formed his first cabinet, which lasted nine months. His second was formed just before the worst disclosures of the Stavisky scandal in January, 1934; the riots of February 6, 1934, brought an end to this government. When he was immediately driven from office, his career seemed ruined. Finding the only way back to power was to the left, Daladier broke with his old mentor, Herriot, and entered the Popular Front. When Blum formed his cabinet in June, 1936, Daladier once more had a cabinet position as minister for war. Since 1924 he had been recognized as the military spokesman for his party, the Radical Socialists.

Daladier's squat build and thatch of black hair gave him a Napoleonic air and the nickname, "Bull of the Vaucluse"; but, as one French politician observed after meeting him in 1933, "This young bull smells of the stable." There was no question of his basic honesty; on him there was no smell of the tainted money so prevalent in the Third Republic. His outstanding characteristic was the ability to follow the prevailing line of the day, no matter how contrary to his former attitude. To stand well with the voters, he consciously tried to maintain the illusion of the man of the people from the backwoods. He was not a statesman, but a chameleon politician. When sit-down strikes paralyzed France in 1936 while German workers were laboring

39

to build armaments for Hitler, Daladier, then minister of war, kept silent. In 1938, France needed a leader to galvanize the nation into action, instead there was only an Édouard Daladier, politician extraordinary.

Faced with the prospect of choosing a foreign minister, Daladier rejected Paul-Boncour. Daladier disagreed with Paul-Boncour's insistence on the importance of Central Europe, particularly Czechoslovakia. He yielded to hints that the Chamber was cool to Paul-Boncour's policies and might make trouble for the new government. Georges Bonnet was more suitable.

The son of an appellate judge, Bonnet had studied law and had risen to the rank of first lieutenant during the war. After representing France at the Geneva conference in 1922, he was elected to the Chamber in 1924, losing his seat in 1928, but returning in 1929. Daladier brought him into his first cabinet in 1933 as minister of finance. As head of the French delegation at the London Economic Conference in 1933, Bonnet met Chamberlain, who found him "cagey and lacking in frankness."

Bonnet was vain and ambitious. He hoped to be premier someday. There was no doubt of his intelligence and his ability in finance, but his ability in foreign affairs was unknown.

To show that French policy had not changed, Bonnet hastened to meet with Osusky. Although he announced that the departure of Paul-Boncour had altered nothing, Bonnet made no sweeping declaration of French support. Bonnet was determined to avoid anything resembling the blood bath of 1914. He would not take France into war against Germany alone: without immediate support from Britain, France would be committing suicide to fight Reich forces. Not daring to state this publicly, Bonnet hoped to make Britain responsible for the abandonment of Czechoslovakia.

Soon after taking office, Bonnet sent Noël to report on the situation in Prague. Bonnet must have known of Noël's statements at the meeting of April 5, and may have sent him because he did not trust Victor-Leopold de Lacroix, the French minister in Prague. Noël's report left little hope for Czechoslovakia. He found the country disintegrating and Beneš losing more prestige within the nation than without. Beneš admitted that his policy was based completely on France and Great Britain. If they obtained a military agreement with Moscow, he would also; he would always follow their leadership.

Noël candidly revealed the condition of the French air force, deliberately striving to leave no doubt about French weakness.

He advised Bonnet that if the government intended to avoid war, capitulation should also be avoided. He advocated a deadline beyond which France would not aid Czechoslovakia. Noël proposed an honest policy, but Bonnet rejected it, preferring to let Czechoslovakia believe in French help that would never come.[7]

Before Chamberlain made his policy statement, the Czech government began to pacify the Reich. Hodža informed Eisenlohr on March 23 that he had no illusions about British policy and was no partisan of the Russian alliance. The Sudeten German party would be invited to enter the government after the next elections; an amnesty would be granted within four weeks; Sudeten government officials would be transferred out of the Czech areas to the Sudetenland; state police would be barred from frontier territories; and the National Defense Law would no longer apply to Sudeten Germans. Hodža demanded that the Sudeten party reconcile itself to democratic methods. Within this framework, the Sudetens could profess their ideology, give the Nazi salute, and wear the long white stockings which had become a symbol of their movement.

In Berlin, Mastny asked for good relations with Nazi Germany and promised Ribbentrop that his government would do everything possible to remove the causes for misunderstanding. Ribbentrop hedged when Mastny asked him to confirm Göring's promises that "Czechoslovakia had nothing to fear from Germany." When the anxious minister inquired about a new German-Czech treaty, Ribbentrop demanded satisfaction first for the Sudeten Germans.[8]

In early April, negotiations began between Hodža and the Sudeten leaders. In their first meeting on April 3, there appeared to be little ground for mutual agreement. Three days later the Sudeten leaders informed him that his offers were entirely inadequate: a new, radical solution was necessary to solve the problems. The Sudetens must be accepted as a nationality instead of a minority. Then the government must give them self-administration, reparation for the damages suf-

---

[7] Noël, *L'aggression Allemande contre la Pologne*, 198–203.

[8] Eisenlohr to the German Foreign Ministry, March 23, 24, 1938, *DG*, Series D, II, 185–91; memorandum of Ribbentrop, March 31, 1938, *ibid.*, 206–207.

fered in the land reforms, and equal share in the determination of Czech policies.[9]

A meeting on April 11 offered the Sudeten negotiators another opportunity to raise their demands. Sudeten Deputy Ernst Kundt protested over the censorship of Sudeten papers, while German refugee papers accused the Reich of "swindling and fraud at the polls." Hodža promised to rectify the situation; Kundt produced the inevitable memorandum stating that negotiations could not begin unless the proper "preconditions" were in effect. These consisted of measures showing that the government had "the will and power necessary to carry out a fundamental change of system." From time to time the Sudetens would submit suggestions on the preconditions before the negotiations began. All legislation must be stopped or suspended that continued the previous system. Hodža accepted the memorandum, begging not to be pinned down too firmly by claims and forced promises.[10]

The memorandum followed lines used by the Nazis in seizing Austria. By reserving the right to revise the preconditions, the Sudetens could prolong the discussions while throwing the blame on the Czechoslovak government. If all legislation were suspended or stopped, the Sudeten Nazis would be free to make whatever mischief they desired. Attempts to curb them would make Czechoslovakia appear deceitful.

As Hitler examined the situation, the advantages were all on the side of Germany: the necessary resources, an earlier beginning in rearmament, and obsolete equipment in Britain and France. Certainly there would be opposition from Britain and France to his Czech plans, once they became known. Once Mussolini was his ally, Hitler believed that Britain and France would not interfere with his plans for Central Europe. By April the *Führer* ordered an increase in the speed of rearmament and more attention to the secrecy of war planning.

Hitler gave General Wilhelm Keitel, chief of the Supreme Command of the *Wehrmacht*, the first directives for the attack on Czechoslovakia on April 21. He dismissed an attack "out of the blue" because

9 Supreme Headquarters, *Wehrmacht*, April 8, 1938, *ibid.*, 224–25; Newton to Halifax, April 8, 1938, *DBFP*, Third series, I, 125–26.

10 Supreme Headquarters, *Wehrmacht*, April 14, 1938, *DG*, Series D, II, 232–33.

of the effect on world opinion. Hitler ordered preparations for an attack either after a period of diplomatic negotiation or after an incident, possibly the murder of Eisenlohr during an anti-German demonstration. Attack after an incident possessed better possibilities because of sympathetic world opinion: there would be less chance of a breach of security. A period of diplomatic discussion would alert the Czechs to the impending attack. The attacks had to be by land and air simultaneously, breaching the frontier at many points. Motorized columns must move quickly, by-passing Prague if necessary, to convince Britain and France of the hopelessness of the Czech cause. Plans must be ready should France come to the aid of Czechoslovakia. France would not be attacked unless necessary; Hitler did not intend to deliberately start simultaneous attacks in both East and West.[11]

Hitler omitted all reference to the Sudeten Germans. This was not a question of freeing the Sudetens, but of conquering the entire Czechoslovak nation. The Sudeten Germans would fool the West into believing that Hitler occupied himself only with their welfare. Under Henlein's leadership, they would divert the attention of Britain and France from the *Wehrmacht* to the Czechoslovak government.

For his plan to succeed, Hitler needed the friendship of the Italian government. Chamberlain tried to split Italy away from Germany through an agreement of April 13, 1938, settling problems which caused Anglo-Italian tensions. Through this agreement Chamberlain hoped so to improve Anglo-Italian relations that the Rome-Berlin Axis would weaken, but the Italian government kept Germany thoroughly informed. Count Galleazzo Ciano, Italian foreign minister, constantly declared that the negotiations with the British in no way affected the Axis. When France attempted to reach a similar agreement, her diplomats were met with a calculated rebuff.

British officials felt a growing need for pressure on the Czechs. Basil Newton, the British minister in Prague, and Henderson in Berlin pressed for quick action. Newton believed that Germany would take Czechoslovakia next, using Henlein as the Seyss-Inquart of Czechoslovakia. If France and Britain supported Czechoslovakia, there would be no compromise, and war would become more inevitable. No warning would deter the Germans from war, and if

[11] Schmundt notes, April, 1938, *ibid.*, 238–39; memorandum on *Operation Green*, April 22, 1938, *ibid.*, 239–40; Celovsky, *Das Münchener Abkommen*, 157.

war came, "nothing that Britain or France could do would save Czechoslovakia from being overrun." After the war, they could only hope to return to present conditions which were unsatisfactory. Newton proposed that France should be warned that she carried on at her own risk; Britain should not engage in a fresh war to buttress an unsound position. The minority problem was not the root of the matter, he wrote. Czechoslovakia must become a neutral, cutting all her ties to France and Russia.

In Berlin, Henderson had similar opinions. To him, Hitler was "a constructive genius" who never intended to rape Austria as he did. It was time, in Henderson's opinion, to recognize German hegemony east of the Rhine and east to the Russian frontier. Once Hitler solved the Sudeten problem and the Polish Corridor question, he would be "territorially contented." The only solution now was autonomy for the Sudetens and the end of the Russian alliance. Beneš ought to follow British advice and make the best bargain possible with Hitler.[12]

Halifax was concerned because the Czechoslovak government seemed to have given too broad an interpretation to Chamberlain's March 24 statement. Prague did not see the need for drastic concessions. On April 12, Halifax instructed Newton to ask for a meeting with Beneš and to request an account of the recent developments. Newton would then declare that he was speaking on his own authority and anticipating his government's instructions. As instructed, Newton, "on his own authority," warned Beneš to make broad rather than superficial concessions to the Sudetens. Nothing else would satisfy their grievances. Every cause of friction must be removed. Direct negotiations for a comprehensive settlement were necessary, not with Berlin, but with Henlein. The Czech government must not imagine that "Chamberlain's carefully chosen words meant more than they actually said." Beneš replied that a proposal for a nationalities law would be presented to London and Paris shortly, prior to the opening of new negotiations with the Sudeten Germans.

Masaryk brought the proposals for a Statute of Nationality Laws on April 26. Included were: a further liberalizing of the language

12 Newton to Halifax, March 15, April 11, 12, 1938, *DBFP*, Third series, I, 55–56, 138–40, 151–54; Henderson to Halifax, March 24, April 1, 20, 1938, *ibid.*, 97–100, 108–12, 173–76.

laws, protection of nationalities from pressure by the majority nationality, German quota of the national budget in proportion to population, German officials in the Sudetenland, German officials to administer the educational system of the Sudetenland, and the creation of inspectorates to see that "subordinate officials adopt an impartial and courteous attitude."[13]

The proposals were of little value because, following the *Führer's* orders, Henlein had increased his demands at the Sudeten Party Congress at Karlsbad on April 24. Surrounded by hundreds of his party officials dressed in grey uniforms and boots, Henlein had proclaimed new demands, while red and white flags with "SdP" lettered in black waved above the cheering crowds.

If the Sudetens were to be included in the nation, the idea of the Czech national state must be rejected. They could not be considered a minority. Their interests lay in orienting themselves toward the greater German Reich. Henlein requested changes in Czechoslovak foreign policy that would make Czechoslovakia a German satellite. He followed this with his eight famous demands entailing a reconstruction of the Czechoslovak state. There must be establishment, guarantee, and recognition of the Sudeten Germans as a legal entity, equal in rights and status with the Czech people. The Sudeten area must be clearly defined with autonomous administration for every department of government. Within German territory, there must be only German officials. There must be legal protection for those Sudetens who lived outside the autonomous areas. The Sudetens must be relieved of all injustices suffered since 1918, and for these injustices they must receive reparations. Henlein concluded with a demand to profess the Nazi ideology.

If Henlein's eight demands were fulfilled, the results would be intolerable for the Czechoslovak government. A state within a state would be produced, alien in ideology, owing allegiance to a foreign ruler, receiving preferential treatment, and creating a greater threat to the security of the Czech state. The eight demands were an impossible basis for negotiation because the Sudetens would use them as a minimum and seek, wherever possible, to raise them. Could the

[13] Newton to Halifax, April 22, 1938, *ibid.,* 179–80; Halifax to Newton, April 12, 1938, *ibid.,* 149–51; Halifax to Phipps, April 11, 1938, *ibid.,* 140–41: memorandum from Masaryk on nationality policy, April 26, 1938, *ibid.,* 188–95.

Western powers reject these demands and still adhere to the right of self-determination for the Sudeten people? Therein lay the brilliance of Henlein's demands. The speech placed those who opposed the Sudeten demands at a disadvantage. The demand to profess the Nazi ideology made the Sudetens followers of a ruler pledged to unite all Germans in the new Reich. Once that occurred, the defenses of Czechoslovakia would be open to the Nazi hordes.

The Czechoslovak cabinet found the demands for changes in foreign policy impossible to discuss. The government would continue to work on the nationalities statute and negotiate for an agreement within constitutional limits. The police would close their eyes and ears to Nazi activities.[14]

In London and Paris, Henlein's demands only made more urgent a meeting between the British and French ministers. The problem of the Sudetens and Czechs required a united policy.

14 *Survey of International Affairs, 1938*, II, 94–98; *Documents on International Affairs, 1938*, II, 130–38; Newton to Halifax, April 26, 1938, *DBFP*, Third series, I, 186–87, 195–96.

# 6

## The Anglo-French Conference

THE CHANGES in the French government had forced postponement of a much-needed Anglo-French ministers' conference. The *Anschluss* and the subsequent threat to Czechoslovakian independence made the meeting imperative.

The British and French ministers met at No. 10 Downing Street at 10:30 on the morning of April 28. The opening was delayed by a search for Daladier's favorite brand of cigarettes. The chief spokesmen were Chamberlain and Halifax, Bonnet and Daladier: the others present did not take prominent roles in the meetings.[1]

At Chamberlain's suggestion, the agenda was altered so that the military subjects for discussion were placed before the Czech question. Daladier accepted this significant alteration without question.

After discussing relations with Italy, the problem of Abyssinia, and the Spanish Civil War, the ministers turned to the question of military staff consultations. Halifax announced that any staff consultations related only to obligations growing out of the Treaty of Locarno which had no direct relation to Czechoslovakia.[2] Britain's main task would be home defense and the protection of trade routes and Brit-

[1] Those present at the meeting for the British were Vansittart, Cadogan, Sargent, Strang, and Roberts; for the French, Corbin, St. Léger, Rochat, and de Margerie.

[2] Under the Treaty of Locarno (1925), Britain had guaranteed the German-Belgian frontiers and the French-German frontiers.

ish overseas territories. Because of this burden, British help for France would be mainly by sea and air. There was no need for naval consultations at present, Halifax declared. As for the air staffs, consultations would be permitted for the purposes of exchanging information, planning for movement of the R.A.F. to France in wartime, and coordination of both forces in observation and warning systems during war. Daladier accepted the proposals for consultations between the air staffs.

Chamberlain declared that Britain could send France only two unequipped divisions. Daladier asked for two motorized divisions; certainly British industry could equip them. Because of the problems facing France in the Mediterranean, Daladier asked for naval staff consultations. He preferred consultations of all the staffs.

Chamberlain pointed out the weakness in British rearmaments. Factories which would not be fully utilized until war came were not yet completed. Britain had manpower problems. Ignorant of the meaning of "motorized" divisions, he would not commit the government to the dispatch of even two divisions. He saw little value in army staff talks or in naval discussions. The latter might arouse the Italians whom he hoped to detach from the Axis, but eventually he agreed to naval discussions at some future date. Daladier convinced Chamberlain that some staff discussions would be useful to prepare for the debarkation and housekeeping problems when the two hypothetical divisions were dispatched to France.

The first day's meeting did not encourage the French. Chamberlain would not be pinned down to any concrete commitment to aid France with military forces. At most Britain would send only two underequipped divisions, and Chamberlain refused to be held even to that. Daladier did not argue well in trying to force more troops from Chamberlain by asserting that "the French army was certainly in a condition in which it could confront the German army victoriously."

Chamberlain went to great lengths to stress Britain's lack of armaments. He extracted a confession from Daladier that France was weak in armament because of failures in production. The only staff talks of any value related to air, but Chamberlain refused to be committed to the dispatch of a specific number of planes. He would only permit a discussion over the movement of a "British advanced air striking force," whatever that would be. It was a disappointing day for the French, who had sought much and gained little.

Czechoslovakia was the chief subject of the meetings of April 29. Halifax opened with an explanation of the British position. Fearing that one incident in the Sudeten area could precipitate a dangerous crisis, he felt everything must be done to avoid such a threat to British and French security. Halifax considered the risk grave because of the weak military condition of Czechoslovakia, Britain, and France. A British military study after the *Anschluss* convinced the government that the defense of Czechoslovakia was hopeless. Russia had been weakened by the purge. Poland could not be depended upon. The British concluded that under the present circumstances the Germans could successfully use force against Czechoslovakia; even if British forces were victorious, Czechoslovakia could not be re-established on the present basis. However, Germany should not be encouraged to think that she could impose a settlement on Czechoslovakia by use of force. They should make clear to Beneš and his government that a last "supreme effort" must be made to settle the Sudeten question.

Daladier defended Czechoslovakia as a nation that had done more for minorities than any other European nation. Although he agreed to the proposal for a "supreme effort," he was convinced that Henlein was interested only in destroying Czechoslovakia. If they pressed the Czechs for concessions which the Germans refused, then they must support the Czechoslovak government. To Daladier the danger lay outside Czechoslovakia where Europe was faced with a man whose ambitions were greater than those of Napoleon I. He acknowledged that war must be prevented, but only if Britain and France indicated plainly a determination to preserve the liberties and independence of European nations. Daladier refused to accept the British view that the situation was hopeless, for the Czech army must not be despised. The political situation could be saved if they showed determination. France would respect her treaty with Czechoslovakia.

Chamberlain launched his attack by contradicting Daladier: the Czechs were not making concessions to their minorities. Henlein did not intend to destroy the Czech state. This was evidenced by the fact that he had not mentioned the word *"Anschluss"* in his Karlsbad speech. Chamberlain refused to promise Beneš that, if concessions were offered and repulsed, Britain would support him. He would not

49

bluff the Germans because there was no way to save Czechoslovakia. The two governments could not defeat Germany. British public opinion would not permit such a move. Chamberlain doubted that Hitler wanted to destroy the Czechoslovak state.

Bonnet contradicted Chamberlain. Information received in the Quai d'Orsay indicated that those around Hitler wanted to wipe Czechoslovakia from the map, dividing the loot between Hungary and Poland. Given this situation, France could do nothing other than support the alliance with Czechoslovakia.

The discussions were going nowhere. The French could not tie the British down to any commitments. In the late afternoon, the British proposal was accepted. The British government would inform Berlin that it sought a peaceful solution and was going to ask Prague to help; it must know the position of the German government. There was no need for German action. In Prague, both the British and French governments would seek the greatest possible concessions for the Sudetens. Should a peaceful solution not be obtained, Britain would remind Hitler of Chamberlain's March 24 declaration that if France should be compelled to aid Czechoslovakia, Britain could not guarantee to remain an observer of the conflict. This was the only "commitment" Bonnet and Daladier could obtain.[3]

From these talks emerged a basic plan, fathered by Chamberlain and Halifax and followed during the summer. Czechoslovakia was not worth a war and could not be saved anyway. British opinion was reluctant to make the effort; Beneš must be forced to grant concessions to avoid a useless war and save a remnant of Czechoslovakia.

Because France would have to contribute the bulk of troops in any war with Germany, Daladier surrendered to Chamberlain's policies. The Czechs would be forced to make concessions at the expense of the French alliance. The politician in him defeated whatever there was of a statesman. Chamberlain's vague, evasive policy of March 24 prevailed. Through this victory, Chamberlain became the leader of the alliance.

The meeting failed because a strong bond was not forged between the ministers. Bonnet saw how the wind blew and prepared to trim his sails accordingly. Daladier was too weak to fight for the Czech cause. Chamberlain deliberately brought the alliance to the brink of

3 Record of Anglo-French conversations held at No. 10 Downing street on April 28, 29, 1938, *DBFP*, Third series, I, 198–234.

KONRAD HENLEIN, leader of the Sudeten German party,
vowed, "We must always demand so much that
we can never be satisfied."

Milan Hodža, prime minister of Czechoslovakia, 1935–38

rupture; he distrusted Bonnet and found Daladier weak.[4] Because their policy was rejected, the French ministers now determined to let the British government bear the burden of appeasing Hitler. They learned that Chamberlain was using military unpreparedness as an excuse to avoid a war over Czechoslovakia. To the French ministers, their British colleagues seemed to deliberately exaggerate their national weakness in armaments. Such tactics left the French with few illusions over British intentions: the London government would not engage in a war over Czechoslovakia. Chamberlain would use every means to avoid the hypothetical conditions which he had set up in his speech of March 24.

The meeting was a failure because no strong military alliance was forged. Chamberlain agreed to military talks as discussions of what might be done under certain hypothetical conditions. The naval discussions were to accommodate French prestige, not prepare for war.

Here was the moment to face and master the cruel truth of war. Only Daladier seemed to divine the awful danger. Chamberlain would not admit that the only salvation was to prepare for war as quickly as possible. Chamberlain preferred to rearm as a deterrent. It would be almost a year before the cruel truth came to him.

After he returned from London, Daladier asked General Gamelin to indicate possible military action against Germany in a war over Czechoslovakia. The report was vague: after total mobilization and after allotting troops to the Alps and North Africa, France could take the offensive. Any aid to Czechoslovakia was dependent on help furnished by Rumania, Yugoslavia, Russia, Poland, and Great Britain.[5]

The rate of French aircraft production convinced Daladier it was hopeless for France to fight for the protection of Czechoslovakia. When asked by William Bullitt, the United States ambassador, if he had decided to fight in case Germany attacked Czechoslovakia, Daladier cynically replied, "With what?" He confessed that the position of Czechoslovakia had been hopeless since the *Anschluss*.[6]

Already, through a German agent in London, Berlin knew that Daladier would not take any aggressive action. On April 30, the agent reported that Daladier wanted the British to act in Prague and in Berlin to avoid war which he saw coming by summer. War or peace

[4] Feiling, *Neville Chamberlain*, 353.
[5] Gamelin, *Servir*, II, 318–19.
[6] Bullitt to Hull, May 9, 1938, *FRUS, 1938*, I, 493–95.

was now the responsibility of Britain, particularly Chamberlain. The control of French foreign policy had been surrendered to London.[7]

Bonnet returned from London quite delighted because he knew that without British support, France would not keep her promise to Czechoslovakia. That country was to him "a motley of minorities and conflicting interests." If any sacrifices were to be made, Czechoslovakia would make them to appease the Germans.

Bonnet informed Osusky, the Czechoslovak minister, that he "was a friend of Czechoslovakia" and, as minister of foreign affairs, "would fight with all forces to maintain a free and independent Czechoslovakia." Bonnet added, however, that the military situation of Czechoslovakia had been drastically altered by the *Anschluss.* Now that limited help had been obtained from Britain, Czechoslovakia ought to profit by settling the Sudeten question peacefully.

When Bonnet saw the German ambassador, he tried to convince him that the discussions in London had not been aimed at Germany. Bonnet declared his sympathy for German culture and civilization and his "admiration for the rise and achievements of the new Germany which, after the incorporation of Austria, had so splendid and varied a reconstruction program before it." Bonnet begged that Germany not force France to honor her alliance with Czechoslovakia by being violent over the Sudeten question. Both France and Britain would exert all their influence to bring Prague to acquiesce. Any arrangement was better than a world war wherein "all Europe would perish and both victor and vanquished would fall victim to world communism."

Through confidential contacts, the German foreign ministry learned that Daladier was eager that the British convince the Czechs to concede in order that France could gracefully evade the responsibilities of her alliance.[8]

From Halifax on May 2, Jan Masaryk, the Czechoslovak minister in London, learned what his country could expect from Britain. Because of the weak military condition of Czechoslovakia, Halifax ex-

---

[7] Kordt to the German Foreign Ministry, April 30, 1938, *DG*, Series D, II, 252–53. The agent used the cover of a British newspaper reporter.

[8] Wilson to Hull, May 3, 1938, *FRUS, 1938*, II, 47–49; Georges Bonnet, *Défense de la paix*, I, 119; von Dirksen to the German Foreign Ministry, May 6, 1938, *DG*, Series D, II, 257–60.

plained, the Germans could overrun the Czechoslovak defenses quickly. Britain could do little if she entered the war. Czechoslovakia could not be restored until after the end of the conflict and never in her present form. Britain would only inquire in Berlin regarding the conditions satisfactory to the Sudeten Germans. There would not be any guarantee other than Chamberlain's statement of March 24.[9]

Halifax had informed the Germans of the conference more quickly than the Czechs, meeting Theodor Kordt, counselor of the German embassy, after the French departed on April 29. Herbert von Dirksen, the new German ambassador, was briefed by Halifax on May 3. From the Foreign Secretary, the Germans learned that Prague would be pressured to induce Beneš "to show the utmost measure of accommodation to the Sudeten Germans." Britain had made no fresh commitments nor obligations other than those to be found in Chamberlain's statement of March 24.[10]

Following his instructions, Basil Newton, the British minister in Prague, informed Krofta on May 7 that his government wanted every possible step taken to avoid war. After sober examination, the British government had concluded that there was little hope of preventing German military occupation of Czechoslovakia. The war would last a long time; and when peace came, there would still be the question of restoration of Czechoslovakia. If Britain entered the war, she could promise little aid at first. British public opinion would not support a bluff; Britain would not exceed the March 24 declaration of Chamberlain. London wanted speedy negotiations, aimed at a "comprehensive and lasting settlement."

These were gloomy words to Krofta. He argued that the British government overestimated the military difficulties. Probably he felt that the military difficulties had been purposely overemphasized to afford Britain a way out. Following Halifax' instructions, Newton declared that the great gulf between Henlein's demands and the Czech proposals must be bridged by the Czech government.

On May 11, Newton gave the same story to Hodža, whose reaction was more pleasing to Halifax. The Prime Minister accepted the dé-

[9] Halifax to Newton, May 2, 1938, *DBFP*, Third Series, I, 235–38; report of Masaryk, May 3, 1938, *Europäische Politik*, 108.

[10] Von Dirksen to German Foreign Ministry, May 3, 1938, *DG*, Series D, II, 255–56.

*marche* as a "basis for action" and promised that his government would "do everything within their power to ensure appeasement so far as Czechoslovakian power was concerned." Within the next week, he would invite Henlein's representatives to start discussions.

Immediately Hodža let the German minister know that he wanted early confidential talks with the Sudetens. If they were serious, he was prepared to work for practical results, including reconstruction of the state. He would discuss the Karlsbad points and achieve results for every point on which they agreed.[11]

Not until May 17 did Newton deliver the third chapter of his sad story to Beneš, who was less agreeable than Hodža. Although Beneš gave "categorical, formal and sincere assurances" of the need for a quick agreement, he refused to meet with Henlein except to register a decisive success in conciliation. Stubbornly the President stood by the constitution, rejecting all changes that smacked of federalism or autonomy. Beneš damned British policy as an acceptance of "German domination with as good grace as possible," which would make Czechoslovakia a German slave state. He preferred to remain close to Britain and France; if need be, he would cut all ties with Russia. "Czechoslovakia must either accept German domination or continue in intimate connection with Western Europe, guaranteed by France and the object of British interest," he declared. "The domination of Czechoslovakia by Germany would be a first step towards the domination of Europe, and European equilibrium could not be established unless Central European states were able to feel themselves to be as independent as Belgium, the Netherlands, or the Scandinavian countries." Western support of Czechoslovak independence and that of Central Europe would be necessary to prevent Russian penetration, Beneš warned. Western though his inclinations might be, Beneš insisted that he did not want to exclude Russia entirely lest the Kremlin's ruler come to an understanding with Hitler.[12]

Beneš did not follow the script written for him in London. Britain wanted everything done to speed Czech acceptance of Henlein's demands—a procedure to which Beneš objected. He persisted in trying

[11] Phipps to Halifax, May 5, 1938, *DBFP*, Third series, I, 253; Halifax to Phipps, May 4, 1938, *ibid.*, 246; Newton to Halifax, May 8, 9, 11, 1938, *ibid.*, 263–71, 282–83; Halifax to Newton, May 4, 10, 1938, *ibid.*, 241–43, 272; Eisenlohr to German Foreign Ministry, May 12, 13, 1938, *DG*, Series D, II, 274–79.

[12] Newton to Halifax, May 17, 18, 1938, *DBFP*, Third series, I, 307–309, 310–15.

to tie Czechoslovakia closely to France and even to Britain in negotiations with the Sudetens. The British labored to achieve the reverse. Beneš was convinced that Austria fell because of isolation from the Western powers, and he was grimly set on preventing Czech isolation. His cause was hopeless because the British government was as resolutely determined to isolate Czechoslovakia.

Already Chamberlain had created the policy which he would pursue throughout the summer of 1938 and which would culminate in September at Munich. He revealed his ideas in an "off-the-record" talk with newspaper correspondents on May 10 at the home of Lady Astor. Chamberlain believed that Czechoslovakia could not survive in her present form and would be easily overrun in a war with Germany. Even if she were victorious, Czechoslovakia would be forced to give up the Sudetens in the peace. Chamberlain proposed, as his solution, a frontier revision favorable to Germany, placing the Sudetens outside the Czechoslovak frontier. When challenged in Commons about the policy he had outlined, Chamberlain neither admitted nor denied the story. A denial would have risked a quarrel with the newspapers; admission would have damaged the government's position because the threat of war had not yet brought many to accept the necessity for cession of the Sudetenland to Germany. Lady Astor confirmed that there had been such a meeting, but not an interview.[13]

The ticklish phase of the negotiations came with the approach to Berlin. Halifax sent explicit instructions to Henderson to use only general terms when alluding to Anglo-French attempts to promote a comprehensive settlement of the Sudeten question. The ambassador should suggest that Germany influence the Sudetens to be more moderate in their demands. Britain would urge the Czechs to go the limit in concessions, not encouraging them in their treatment of the Sudetens. Germany should make known her desires which Britain in turn would recommend to the Czechs. Should this fail, Halifax intimated to Henderson, the second step would consist of "a kind of warning." Here again, Halifax ordered Henderson to use general terms.

Henderson called on Ernst Woermann, a German undersecretary, on May 7; but, in his eagerness, the British ambassador was far from general. After declaring that the British government wanted a settle-

[13] *Survey of International Affairs, 1938,* II, 113–15; *New York Times,* May 15, 1938; Henderson to Halifax, May 5, 6, 14, 1938, *DBFP,* Third series, I, 255–59.

ment on the basis of a state of nationalities, he begged for German co-operation because Britain supported the Germans against the Czechs. Contrary to his instructions, he went ahead to the second phase of the Halifax plan, warning of the dangerous situation. France had an alliance with Czechoslovakia, unlike Austria, and would consider any solution by force to be a *casus belli*.

Halifax, put out by the violation of his instructions, scolded Henderson. They must not let Berlin know what they said in Prague because "while we are emphasizing in Prague the weakness of the military situation, we hope to make the German government think long before doing anything likely to break the peace." Henderson defended his disobedience as necessary to convince the Germans that Britain was not "merely playing for time till we are militarily better prepared for war." He insisted that Britain could remedy the situation only by "using plain language in Prague, and not by anything we may say in Berlin."

Not until May 11 was Henderson able to talk with Ribbentrop. The Ambassador followed his instructions. Ribbentrop welcomed the British policy towards Prague, but Germany would not disinterest herself from the fate of the Germans. If there were bloodshed, "Hitler would be compelled to take immediate action at whatever risk and cost to themselves and the world." If France declared war, Germany would consider it a war of aggression. However, if the Sudeten question could be settled, Germany would be content. Perhaps they could then discuss the colonies.[14]

Phase one of Halifax' plan had brought only warnings from Ribbentrop. There was no promise nor indication of any advice to Henlein and his followers to moderate their tactics. One idea was agreed on: the Czechs would have to be more accommodating.

To show how reasonable and friendly were the Sudetens, Henlein appeared in London on May 12, in obedience to Hitler's instructions. He had been instructed to proclaim that Prague was the warmonger and that appeasement would be possible only through the implementation of the Karlsbad demands. He must announce that these demands had been unknown in Berlin before he made his speech. Nat-

---

14 Halifax to Henderson, May 4, 5, 11, 1938, *ibid.*, 243–45, 253–55, 281–82; Henderson to Halifax, May 7, 10, 12, 1938, *ibid.*, 260, 273–74, 284–86; German Foreign Ministry to German Embassy in Rome, May 7, 1938, *DG*, Series D, II, 261–62; memorandum of Ribbentrop, May 11, 1938, *ibid.*, 269–71.

urally he would deny that he acted under German instructions. To discourage intervention, he would emphasize the deteriorating conditions within Czechoslovakia.

The Sudeten "viceroy" lunched with Winston Churchill and Archibald Sinclair on May 13. In the afternoon he met Harold Nicolson and other members of Parliament. He met his old friend, Lord Vansittart, in the evening. Vansittart had consulted with Halifax and Chamberlain, who recommended that the meeting take place.

On May 14, Henlein visited Jan Masaryk, accompanied by a bodyguard. The "viceroy" stuck fairly well to his instructions. The Sudeten position was "intolerable"; there must be a quick solution in the direction of autonomy or else some of his followers might press for an *Anschluss*. He was a long-time advocate of conciliation with the Czechs, but the results were so meager. Upon his word of honor he had never received instructions from Berlin, not even so much as a recommendation.

Henlein fooled Vansittart who believed that, as in previous years, he was speaking to "a wise and reasonable man." There is no indication of the effect on Churchill and Sinclair. Masaryk was not fooled. The reports, however, deceived Halifax, who wanted Beneš to know how reasonable Henlein had been on his visit.[15]

The situation seemed little improved when François-Poncet, the French ambassador, called on Ribbentrop, on May 17 to discuss a few points. The Frenchman insisted that, although Britain and France were doing everything to facilitate a solution of the Sudeten problem, there were dangers of a Czech-German conflict. Ribbentrop was infuriated at the implication that France would march in a Czech-German conflict. A war to maintain the state of affairs in Czechoslovakia "in which an unarmed majority . . . was held subject by an armed minority would defy all the principles of democracy so highly prized by France." Any French intervention would be regarded by Germany as a war of aggression against Germany. "The entire German people would rise as one man." Any French attempt to take the side of Czechoslovakia would bring a German riposte; "hundreds

---

15 Memorandum of Weizsäcker, May 12, 1938, *ibid.*, 273–74; Henlein's conversation with Vansittart, May 16, 1938, *DBFP*, Third series, I, 630–33; Henlein's conversations with Churchill and Sinclair, May 15, 1938, *ibid.*, 633–35; Halifax to Newton, May 16, 1938, *ibid.*, 299–300; Winston S. Churchill, *The Gathering Storm*, 285–86.

of thousands of Frenchmen would lose their lives without their soldiers succeeding in setting foot on German soil."[16]

Chamberlain's post-*Anschluss* policy was not successful. Beneš persisted in clinging to Britain and France for security; they could not shake him off. The Germans were more arrogant than ever, preparing for an invasion of Czechoslovakia. Only Henlein's eight demands seemed to offer Chamberlain some possibility of success. Here were concrete demands. Once the Sudeten Germans were appeased by the fulfillment of the Karlsbad demands, a nasty crisis would be avoided. Instead of accepting this opportunity, the Czechoslovak government frightened London and Paris with the crisis of May 20.

16 Memorandum of Ribbentrop, May 17, 1938, *DG*, Series D, II, 284–88.

# 7

## Crisis in May

ALONG THE Czech-German frontier, May was not calm. In the Sudeten-land, Nazis battled with off-duty troops and insulted policemen. Daily, government became a bloody burden for the Czechs. Every incident brought cries of rage from the Nazi press, while the Czech press called for sterner measures to maintain law and order. There was genuine danger that Prague might lose control of the Sudetenland. Already a potential guerilla force, *Freiwillige Schutzdienst,* had been formed to protect Sudeten life and property. Subversive leaflets appeared in the border towns.

On May 17 members of the German Gymnastic Association thronged through the town of Trebnitz shouting, *"Heil Hitler! Sieg Heil!"* The north Bohemian town was 90 per cent Czech; the popu-lation soon intervened. The Henleinists called for reinforcements from a neighboring town. Until early morning, the battle raged as Czechs and Sudetens threw stones and swung any available stick.

Amid the increasing tension, Henlein suddenly broke off negotia-tions with Hodža and departed for Austria on May 19, allegedly, to take his wife on a vacation. That night a crowd from a Henlein meet-ing bearing swastika flags tried to march four abreast through the streets of Prague. A riot inevitably followed.

News of military movements came on May 19. The acting British consul in Dresden reported German troops concentrating in southern Silesia and northern Austria. A British subject from Garmisch claimed that, during the weekend, soldiers in the district moved to the Czech frontier. The French ambassador reported rumors of troop concentrations. From Vienna came reports of German signal units moving toward the Czech frontier.

In Prague on May 20, Krofta phoned to tell Eisenlohr that troop concentrations were occurring in Saxony and in Bavaria. Berlin ordered Eisenlohr to notify the Czech government that the story was "pure nonsense."

Henderson asked Ernst von Weizsäcker, state secretary in the German Foreign Ministry, about the rumors. "Nonsense," was the reply. The State Secretary asked for a report from Keitel, who declared the rumors to be "absolutely nonsense." There were no concentrations in Saxony: only at Königsbrück, because of an annual maneuver, were there more troops than usual.[1]

In the afternoon of May 20, Mastny, the Czechoslovak minister, commented to Weizsäcker that German troops were moving towards the Silesian and Austrian frontiers; S.S. (*Schutzstaffel*) and S.A. (*Sturm Abeilung*) units had been ordered to be ready for May 21–22. Weizsäcker denied the reports.

Later the same evening, Mastny received a rough reception from Ribbentrop. The Foreign Minister blamed Czech provocation for the incidents in the Sudetenland; Germany would not tolerate this. Rumors of troop concentrations were false. The Czechs only sought an excuse for a mobilization. If these were the Czech tactics, then a real German mobilization would occur, Ribbentrop snarled.[2]

In the Sudetenland, rumors spread that Hitler would come on Sunday. Near the border, some warned not to buy Czechoslovak postage stamps because they would be useless after the German invasion. Others insisted Henlein had departed to receive final orders from the *Führer*.

Reports to the Czechoslovak general staff placed the German Seventh and Twelfth Infantry divisions moving in the direction of the Bavarian-Czech frontier. Squadrons of the *Luftwaffe* stationed at Neubrandenburg were in Saxony. German aircraft had flown nine flights over the Bohemian frontier on May 19. Czech agents in Vienna

[1] Henderson to Halifax, May 20, 1938, *DBFP*, Third series, I, 323; Weizsäcker to Ribbentrop, May 20, 1938, *DG*, Series D, II, 296.

[2] Memorandum of Weizsäcker for Ribbentrop, May 20, 1938; minutes of Ribbentrop, May 20, 1938, *ibid.*, 294–95, 298–99.

reported rumors of troop movements towards the Czechoslovak frontiers. The usual barrage of hatred and abuse from the Nazi press was on the increase.

In Prague an immediate mobilization seemed imperative to stop this German provocation which aimed at intimidating the Czechoslovak government until the Sudeten demands were granted or another *Anschluss* occurred. Ribbentrop's angry interview on May 20 with Mastny foretold hostilities.

At a stormy meeting of the Czechoslovak cabinet late on the evening of May 20, the military demanded that five classes of reservists be called to the colors. Cabinet members learned of Mastny's stormy meeting with Ribbentrop and the reports of German troop movements. Hodža and Josef Černy, the minister of the interior, opposed mobilizing five classes because their party (Agrarian) did not want to alienate the Sudetens. The cabinet compromised by calling up one class of reservists and assorted specialists—a total of about 174,000 troops. They sought to avoid provocation while warning the Germans that Czechoslovakia would fight. With troops in the Sudetenland, the Czech government could restore law and order while maintaining a better control over the frontier areas.

At 9 P.M. the cabinet order was dispatched. Throughout the night troops moved to their appointed posts, and by daybreak nearly all were in place.

Because of the troop movements during the night of May 20–21, food was late on the trains into Prague. Throughout the night, heavy police patrols were in the streets. Newspapers were heavily censored when they appeared in Prague on the morning of May 21. By morning the Nazi signs and white stockings had disappeared in the Sudetenland. In the confusion, one Sudeten town thought they were being liberated from the Czechs when the troops arrived. Happily, they broke out the Swastikas and Nazi flags only to welcome Czechoslovak troops!

Now rioting in the Sudetenland could be controlled by the troops. A heavier guard on the frontier could prevent surprise attack. Thus the government assured public opinion that it was alert to the German danger. There would not be another *Anschluss*.

The mobilization was not without Sudeten martyrs. On the morning of May 21, George Hoffman and Nicholas Boehm were traveling

61

from Cheb to Franzensbad on motorcycles. Both had records as violent Nazi extremists; they had probably been drinking. Entering Cheb, they ignored a command to halt. The policeman telephoned a request to stop them when they reached the opposite side of the town. There two policemen tried to block the road, but the cyclists forced them to jump aside by riding straight at them. The Nazis were ordered to halt in Czech and in German, but the commands were ignored. A guard drew his pistol and fired at the tires, but the road dipped, altering his line of fire. The bullet passed through both men. One died instantly, the other in the hospital. The Nazi press now had martyrs, honest Sudetens, out for a motorcycle ride, and slain in a "bestial murder."[3]

The night of May 20–21 passed without a German invasion although *Luftwaffe* bombers were expected hourly over Prague. Morning found Czechoslovak troops at their posts, alert for any German attack.

When questioned by the Germans on May 21, Krofta admitted that the situation was serious but defended the government's action by asserting the need to maintain the authority of the government in the Sudetenland. Hodža was depressed and feared for his life, according to the Sudeten sources. He begged Karl Hermann Frank, deputy leader of the Sudeten German party, to save the situation. "You cannot allow your people to be shot dead by Czech soldiers any longer," Hodža cried.

Josef Černy "broke down completely and wrung his hands," Eisenlohr reported. The Interior Minister alleged that the military had seized control of the government, closed the frontiers, and broken telephone connections without informing his ministry. It was a "military insurrection."[4]

On the morning of May 21, when Henderson called on Ribbentrop, he ordered Henderson not to ask any questions about troop movements because he would not receive any answers. He waved telegrams reporting incidents in the Sudetenland. The German nation would not tolerate such a situation. "The Czechs," he raged,

3 *Survey of International Affairs, 1938*, II, 126–27; *New York Times*, May 22, 1938; Newton to Halifax, May 23, 1938, *DBFP*, Third series, I, 360–61.

4 Eisenlohr to the German Foreign Ministry, May 21, 1938, *DG*, Series D, II, 304–305, 308–309.

"were mad, and if they persisted in their present attitude they would be destroyed." Henderson admitted that the mobilization was "very foolish," but they must be patient. "All would end well," he said, "and Germany would win all along the line." Henderson reminded the irate Foreign Minister of British efforts for peace. Ribbentrop retorted, "The sole result is that in Czechoslovakia they are now starting to shoot down Germans." Henderson insisted that it was "always better for a few men to lose their lives there, bad though that might be, than for millions to perish." Ribbentrop threatened that if Prague found no remedy "the whole German people would rise like one man."[5]

In Berlin the crisis was heightened on May 21 when some of the British diplomatic staff, including the British naval attaché and his family, were returning to Britain on regular leave. For their convenience, an extra coach was added to the train. Soon the French ambassador arrived, breathless, to ask if the entire British colony were leaving. Alarmed by the number of exit visas, Weizsäcker phoned to beg Henderson not to be upset. The ambassador explained the situation and promised to cancel the reservations, a move which the Foreign Office had already ordered.

Rumors spread in London of German troop movements in the direction of the Czechoslovak frontiers. Halifax ordered Henderson to emphasize the responsibilities of the British government if the German government intervened in Czechoslovakia. The British government had the assurances of the Czechoslovak government to work for a peaceful solution and a just settlement. Should a conflict arise, France would be compelled to intervene under her obligations toward Czechoslovakia. "In such circumstances His Majesty's government could not guarantee that they would not be forced by circumstances to become involved also."[6]

When Henderson read his instructions to Ribbentrop, the Foreign Minister directed him to take up the matter in Prague. The threat of Franco-British intervention left the German government "completely cold." If France is crazy enough to attack, there will be a great French defeat and a war to the death with Germany. The ambassador begged

---

[5] Henderson to Halifax, May 21, 1938, *DBFP*, Third series, I, 329–30; memorandum of Ribbentrop, May 21, 1938, *DG*, Series D, II, 311–13.

[6] Halifax to Henderson, May 21, 1938, *DBFP*, Third series, I, 331–32.

for some influence on Henlein. Ribbentrop refused; the matter should be taken up in Prague with Beneš.[7]

By May 21, Bonnet was frantic. Czechoslovakia must not mobilize further without consulting France and Great Britain because German mobilization would bring on that of France. Next, a German ultimatum would make war inevitable. The Foreign Minister dreaded lest "Paris would be destroyed meter by meter by German air attacks." He was horrified that, in a war over Czechoslovakia, "France's only assistance at the outset would be Negrin [Spanish Loyalist premier] and Stalin—a pretty pair!"

Despite his fears, Bonnet issued a statement to the press on the evening of May 21 that a German crossing of the Czechoslovak frontier "automatically" would start a war. France would stand behind her treaty with Czechoslovakia. He tempered his statement with the hope that "Germany will do nothing to put France in the position where her treaty obligations would oblige her to intervene."[8]

May 22 was the first day of the Czechoslovak communal elections. Voting could produce incidents; incidents could bring German intervention. The presence of Czechoslovak armed forces changed the atmosphere. The elections passed quietly, and there were no incidents.

Speaking in Tabor on the same day, President Beneš tried to calm his nation. These were the most anxious moments for Czechoslovakia since the war. He begged his people so to conduct themselves that war could be averted. The nation was strengthening its defenses and would fight to the "last extremity." The treatment of minorities was liberal when compared to other nations in Central Europe; he resented the attacks on this policy, both from within and from without the nation. The government was preparing legislation to improve the nationalities system and make the minorities feel that they were "equals among equals."[9]

Reports coming to London on May 21 from Henderson and Newton were not indicative of peace. Halifax resorted to a personal mes-

[7] Henderson to Halifax, May 21, 1938, *ibid.*, 334–35; memorandum of Ribbentrop, May 21, 1938, *DG*, Series D, II, 315–17.

[8] Phipps to Halifax, May 21, 22, 1938, *DBFP*, Third series, I, 336–37, 340, 343; Bullitt to Hull, May 22, 1938, *FRUS*, 1938, I, 512–15.

[9] *Documents on International Affairs, 1938*, II, 142–44.

sage for Ribbentrop, which Henderson brought to the German foreign ministry on the morning of May 22 and delivered to Weizsäcker. The British Foreign Secretary was doing all possible at Prague to prevent more incidents. Ribbentrop must not expect Britain to stand aside if a European war started. Halifax begged that Germany do nothing to destroy the chance of a peaceful settlement. If war came, "only those will benefit from such a catastrophe who wish to see the destruction of European civilization."[10]

At the same time Halifax cautioned Paris lest his "warning" to Germany be misinterpreted. He thought it "highly dangerous if the French government were to read more into these warnings than is justified by their terms." Britain would come to the assistance of France provided "she were the victim of unprovoked aggression by Germany," but France must not assume that His Majesty's Government would undertake joint military action to protect Czechoslovakia against a German attack. The military situation was so bad that Britain, France, and even Russia could not stop Germany from running over Czechoslovakia. Before the French undertook any action which might provoke Germany to attack France, Halifax asked that Britain express her opinion. Britain was not bound to support France if she went to the aid of the Czechoslovak government. It was unsaid but understood that the British government wanted veto power over French foreign policy.

That evening the British ambassador, Sir Eric Phipps, delivered the message to Bonnet, who agreed wholeheartedly with Halifax' stand. He would gladly place any pressure on the Czechoslovak government which Halifax desired. If the Czechs were unreasonable, the French government would consider herself released from the alliance. Bonnet promised that France would not take any action without consultation with the British government.[11]

Halifax' request to veto French action was a cabinet decision. This demand only hastened the desire of some in the French government to evade the Czech alliance. There was no desire to face Nazi Germany

[10] Minutes by Weizsäcker for Ribbentrop, May 22, 1938, *DG*, Series D, II, 319–20; Halifax to Henderson, May 22, 1938, Henderson to Halifax, May 22, 1938, *DBFP*, Third series, I, 341–48.

[11] Halifax to Phipps, May 22, 1938, Phipps to Halifax, May 23, 1938, *ibid.*, 346–47, 356–57.

alone. The joyful surrender of French foreign policy by Bonnet was a token of French weakness.

Daladier did not hide French weakness when Welczeck called on him, in response to a personal invitation from "a French ex-service man to his German comrade." During the evening of May 22, the pair discussed the dangers of war. Like Halifax, Daladier was fearful of "Cossack and Mongol hordes" pouring into Europe bringing Communism in their wake. "This must be prevented," the premier declared, "even if it entailed great sacrifices." Daladier could not hide his unhappiness over the Czechoslovak alliance which forced him to such a fateful decision. He wanted to know the German point of view on the minorities question. Welczeck denounced the Versailles Treaty and "warmongers in Prague, backed by Russophile elements and international Jewry" for sending *agents provocateurs* into the Sudetenland to cause incidents. The French ex-service man thanked his German comrade for such a "clear and detailed exposé."[12]

By Monday, May 23, the available information indicated that the German army had not moved at all during the weekend. The United States consul general in Vienna visited the entire Czechoslovak-German frontier and saw activity only on the Czech side. The British consul in Breslau toured the frontier, finding nothing unusual. None of the British news correspondents in Germany had information of any troop movements. The French ambassador, François-Poncet, made unsuccessful inquiries about German troop activities. Two British military attachés, with the blessing of Henderson and Weizsäcker, traveled along the frontier and found virtually no military traffic and only normal rail movement. In the German garrison towns, the troops were conspicuous for their small numbers. No armored units were to be seen; some communications units were working. These were strange signs for a nation poised for an invasion.

On the evening of May 23, Henlein, back from his conference with Hitler, met Hodža. The Sudeten *Führer* announced that negotiations would not continue until all the military measures were ended. Hodža refused to accede. Henlein stood fast, upholding orders from Hitler. Both men agreed to keep in contact. This interview with Hodža was Henlein's last personal contact with the Czechoslovak government. Thereafter, he negotiated through his lieutenants.

12 Welczeck to German Foreign Ministry, May 23, 1938. *DG*, Series D, II, 326–BR.

LORD HALIFAX was a member of the inner cabinet that
advised Chamberlain throughout the Czech crisis
and shared the Prime Minister's prejudices
concerning foreign affairs.

BASIL NEWTON, British minister in Prague, repeatedly stated that London wanted speedy negotiations, aimed at a "comprehensive and lasting settlement."

The German denials of troop movements were truthful. Eight to ten divisions moving through Saxony would have been observed by too many people. The German denials were true because the plans were incomplete for the invasion. The Czechoslovak authorities could not know them, as some alleged, because Hitler himself had not even given his final approval.

Such information that came to Prague before the crisis was alarming. Beneš was determined not to be caught off guard as was Austria. While there was time, he would prepare to stand up to German provocation and threats. Disorders in the Sudetenland could produce an incident giving Hitler the needed excuse, reasoned the Czechoslovak authorities. Continual turning of the other cheek only led the Sudeten Nazis to further disorder. The German press had prepared the psychological basis for an attack or an international incident. By May 19–20, all signs pointed to an imminent move against Czechoslovakia.

Reports of German troop movements alarmed the already nervous Czechoslovak general staff. Between old Austria and Germany, military traffic was increasing as Austrian units were brought to Germany for additional training and integrated into the German army. Units in Austria that had completed their training were returning to Germany. The movement of German army units toward the east, amid a violent anti-Czech press campaign, helped start rumors of an invasion. Actually twelve German divisions were in position along the frontier. Czechoslovak agents identified two of these as moving towards the frontier. German aircraft crossed the frontier; the planes came from units newly moved from the interior. The Czechoslovak general staff believed that Germany would effect a concentration of force under the cover of training maneuvers and then launch the attack.

With this information available, Czechoslovak armed forces must mobilize before the German concentration was complete. Time seemed to have run out when Henlein cancelled his talks with the Czech government on May 19 and departed, apparently taking his final report to Hitler. The Sudeten *Führer* would return with the invaders. The Czechoslovak staff could only conclude that mobilization was imperative.

The Germans invented a story that the Czechoslovak military had gone out of control. Certainly the cabinet was under strong pressure from the generals. However, had the military authorities taken control, they would not have been satisfied with mobilizing one class and certain reservists. The near hysteria of Černy was the only possible source of this tale.

During the night of May 20–21, Prague expected a German attack. By morning German denials and lack of any attack indicated the exaggerated danger. Beneš was so certain of the national security that he left Prague for his speech at Tabor. He must have known there was no threat of a German attack.

In this crisis, the Czechoslovak government had shown independence. They tried to be master of their fate by escaping from the control of the great powers. Czechoslovakia looked to her defenses and was ready. From the crisis the Czechoslovak government received experience in calling up troops to man the frontiers and important posts. This experience might save the nation in any future crisis that Hitler could contrive.

The May crisis affected Hitler's planning. He did not decide to destroy the Czechs because of the crisis: that decision had been made months earlier. Field Marshal Wilhelm Keitel sent Hitler the draft of *Operation Green,* the plan for the invasion of Czechoslovakia, on May 20, the day that Hitler's army was reported moving to attack Czechoslovakia.

Because of the May crisis, members of the German general staff had to make basic changes in their planning. No one could deny that Czechoslovakia would fight. The nation was ready, willing, and prepared. Preliminary investigations of the Czech fortifications were not reassuring to the Germans: steel and concrete protected the main blockhouses against bullets of all calibers; machine guns were emplaced to cover all gaps. Blockhouses protected their main cross roads. Because the Czech troops moved swiftly to their appointed stations, surprise must be emphasized in future planning. During training maneuvers, German troops needed additional practice in the capture of fortifications by surprise.

The attitude of the British and French governments meant that Germany's western fortifications needed only to be strong enough to hold them off while Germany threw the main bulk of her forces towards the east. British and French policies did not portend a mighty effort to breach the German fortifications.

In a major conference on May 28 in the garden of the Reichschancery, Hitler announced that it was his "unshakable will that Czechoslovakia shall be wiped off the map." No mention was made of the Sudetens and their problems. He ordered the immediate completion of the German line of fortifications in the west.

The official directive initiating *Operation Green* went into effect on May 30. Then Hitler signed the order but not in a rage over the Anglo-French press reports of the May crisis. He ordered the attack because Czechoslovakia was growing too strong. A little nation threatened his plans of empire. Czechoslovakia must be attacked as soon as German preparations were complete.

The May 30 directive ordered an attack by October 1. Politicians would find favorable circumstances to excuse and justify the attack. The directive showed the effects of the May crisis: emphasis was placed on speed and surprise. If there were a period of diplomatic tension, the attack must be sudden and unexpected before Czechoslovakia could fully mobilize and move troops into the fortifications. A swift attack would make Anglo-French intervention hopeless. Thus Hitler hoped to discourage their desire to aid Czechoslovakia, while avoiding a world war.

The bulk of the German armed forces would be thrown at Czechoslovakia because of the strength of the fortifications. The western front would be lightly held. Supported by the *Luftwaffe,* army assault units would break through the Czech fortifications and encircle to prevent a retreat into Slovakia. Troops would then be transferred to the west if needed.

The *Luftwaffe* would leave a minimum number of squadrons in the west while concentrating on the destruction of the Czech air force and supply bases. The *Luftwaffe* must stop any aid from Russia and France. *Luftwaffe* attacks must immobilize the Czech government and disrupt military traffic. Czech industrial areas would be spared wherever possible: in Bohemia these were often Sudeten centers. The German navy would secure the coasts against surprise attack.[13]

In *Operation Green,* the emphasis on speed revealed the fear of Hitler: a two-front war would bog down the troops. The eastern foe must be destroyed first. France and Britain would be left behind the Maginot Line while Germany digested Czechoslovakia. The May

[13] "Draft for *Operation Green,*" May 20, 1938, "Directive for *Operation Green,*" May 30, 1938, *DG,* Series D, II, 290–303, 357–62; Schmundt File, *NCA,* IV, 309–10, 314.

crisis showed the speed of Czech mobilization. Czech armed forces had learned much. A repetition would give them more experience at German expense. Time was now on the side of Czechoslovakia, not Germany. Germany must hasten her destruction.

Czechoslovakia must not stall the German attack while Britain and France prepared. If Czechoslovakia were completely defeated before aid came, realists in Britain and France would clamor for peace. Why fight for something no longer existing? Why be killed for that which could never again be re-created?

In the directive there was no reference to saving the downtrodden Sudeten people. The emphasis was on speed—speed to crush and defeat Czechoslovakia. In Hitler's public statements, the important question was the settlement of the Sudeten minority problem, but *Operation Green* revealed the truth: he sought the complete military defeat of Czechoslovakia, not the salvation of the Sudetens. They were to be the bait.

The need to destroy Czechoslovakia speedily was the result of the May crisis. Here was a courageous enemy, determined to fight. If the Czechs could prevent it, there would not be another *Anschluss*.

The effect of the May crisis in France did not seem great. No leaves were cancelled; there were no troop movements of any consequence. All of these were unnecessary, the government claimed, because the Maginot Line was permanently manned. Here was an indication of the type of war that France would fight.

The effect on the French Foreign Minister was near hysteria. The mobilization was "a useless provocation to Germany"; it must cease. If "stiff-necked" Beneš refused concessions to the Sudetens, "France would know who was attempting to set fire to Europe and would not be drawn into war to please Beneš." When he saw the German ambassador, Bonnet effusively thanked him for the "dignified and calm restraint" of the German government in making "a contribution toward preserving European peace." He had been on the phone to Prague two and three times a day, demanding that responsible officials be brought to account for the Cheb affair.

Bonnet hoped to obtain 70 per cent fulfillment of the German demands for the Sudetens. He pledged that if the Czechs remained unwilling, the French government "would inform them that under these circumstances they would be obliged to submit their obligations under the alliance to revision." Welczeck saw this as "the proper way to make progress in the Sudeten German question"—force the Czechs to surrender to Nazi demands.[14]

The May crisis brought the British public up short with the realization that there might be a shooting war. There was some hardening in public opinion. At the height of the crisis, the Foreign Office feared war had come. Chamberlain and Halifax interrupted their weekend in the country and returned to London for consultations and cabinet meetings. The crisis increased a feeling among those in high places that war must be avoided although the price would be high.

Chamberlain believed that there had been an attempt at a German *coup d'etat,* but that British warnings had made the Germans decide that the risks were too great. They had lost prestige and had vented their spite in the newspapers. Apparently his reading of the dispatches coming into the Foreign Office had been only cursory.

Halifax resented the Czechoslovak action because the mobilization altered the situation. Mobilization increased Sudeten distrust of Beneš which Halifax felt was justified. He was anxious to impress on the Czechs that their actions were subject to an Anglo-French veto.

Out of the crisis came one proposal which could have helped solve the Sudeten problem if the Germans had been sincere. As a result of a suggestion in the House of Commons, Halifax proposed on May 27 that an international commission, with access to both countries, be appointed to investigate violations of the frontier. German reception was cool.[15] Czechoslovakia welcomed the proposal because it would internationalize the question. No longer would it be simply a question of Czechs versus Sudetens. A third party could be on the spot watching. If the Sudetens and Nazis had been sincere, if aggression had not been Hitler's chief aim, then the commission would have been welcomed. Because of the German attitude, Halifax dropped the idea. Internationalizing the question would have frustrated Hitler's plans.

Halifax feared that the Czechoslovak government would not move fast enough to reach an agreement with the Sudetens. At his instructions, Newton warned Beneš that failure to reach an agreement with

[14] Bullitt to Hull, May 24, 1938, *FRUS, 1938,* I, 517–19; Welczeck to German Foreign Ministry, May 26, 1938, *DG,* Series D, II, 343–44.

[15] Halifax to Henderson, May 27, 1938, *DBFP,* Third series, I, 386; Henderson to Halifax, May 31, 1938, *DBFP,* Third series, I, 417.

the Sudetens "along lines that seemed reasonable here," would have unfavorable reactions in Britain. At Halifax' request, Bonnet threatened Beneš that if negotiations with Henlein failed, "the French government would be driven to reconsider their own position vis-à-vis Czechoslovakia." Both governments insisted that, regardless of the cost, Czechoslovakia must reach an agreement. There was no other way to avoid another May crisis. Next time Hitler might march.[16] These Anglo-French tidings were reported to Berlin.

Though bitter because they had been occupied as if they were enemy territory, the Sudetens were chastened. Before May 20 they thought the government would not restrain their actions. The mobilization checked the spreading anarchy which invited German intervention. No further incidents aroused the populace. The elections were carried out smoothly as scheduled on May 22, May 29, and June 12. In the German areas, the results were not surprising: the Sudeten German party received 91.4 per cent of the votes, engulfing the non-Nazi parties. Elsewhere Beneš' former party (National Social) and Hodža's Agrarian party received votes of confidence. To refute Nazi propaganda, the Communists lost ground.

The May crisis provided the Sudeten leaders with additional demands to be exacted from the Czechoslovak government. Now they planned to complain of elections at bayonet point. Because of the mobilization, they were living under military dictatorship. Until the troops were withdrawn, they would refuse negotiations. Paris and London also joined in the cry for demobilization.

The Czechs would not be easily pushed into demobilization. Hodža would do it after June 12 if the remaining national elections were held peacefully. From London the pressure continued. Prague reluctantly agreed on May 29 to withdraw some troops five kilometers from the frontier and to begin the release of technicians. The majority of the air squadrons were ordered back to their peace time bases on May 31; the government promised that they would not approach nearer than ten kilometers to their own border when on patrol. During the first days of June, more than fifty thousand men were gradually released. Prague promised not to call up reservists after June 12 except for annual training.

Such was the May crisis of 1938. Under the mistaken belief that in-

16 Halifax to Newton, May 31, 1938, Halifax to Phipps, May 31, 1938, DBFP, Third series, I, 418, 419; Bonnet, Défense de la paix, I, 155.

vasion was imminent, Czechoslovakia looked to her defenses and awaited the enemy. Berlin was alerted to a stubborn foe. Paris and London were disturbed by such independence. Both decided to weaken the authority of the Czechoslovak government lest another May crisis lead to war. Should Czechoslovakia again attempt similar action, Britain and France would leave her to her fate. Thus the May crisis undermined rather than strengthened Czech security.

# 8

## Summer Tensions

THE GOVERNMENTS of Great Britain and France longed for any device to settle the Sudeten question. Another May crisis must be avoided lest the Nazi armies march.

Beneš had a thorny problem: how could he satisfy his Western friends and also force the Sudetens to show their hand? So great was the pressure from the West that he protested on June 11 because Great Britain and France believed he was prolonging the negotiations. This slanderous accusation had been authored by the Germans, who knew he was a stumbling block to the advance of Nazi ideology. Alone and faced with opposition from within his own cabinet, he labored to find an answer for the Sudeten question.[1]

On June 8 the Sudeten Nazis produced a fantastic scheme for the organization of the Czechoslovak nation on the basis of minority groups. Each national minority would have the right of self-administration. This power would include control of the municipalities, police, educational system, social services, public buildings, trade, finance, and taxation. Anything remaining would belong to the national state. Each minority group would elect members to a national assembly where they would form a minority bloc or *curia*. Within each minority area, the *curia* would become a governing diet or *Volkstag*. Each *Volkstag* would control the budget for the area, the educational system, and the election of a president. The latter would be a member of the Prague cabinet, but accountable only to his

1 Newton to Halifax, June 13, 1938, *DBFP,* Third series, I, 472–73.

74

minority. The entire national administration would be reorganized. Within the ministries of Justice, Interior, Railways and Ports, Agriculture, and Public Works, national minority sections would be created to manage their minority affairs in their own language. Bureaucrats in the national administration would speak whatever languages were required for the job.

The minority groups included: Poles, Czechs, Slovaks, Sudetens, Ruthenes, Jews, Rumanians, and Russians. Had each been granted these autonomous powers, anarchy would have been the only product. The Nazis could have used this as a device to capture the Sudetenland, forming a state within a state. The rest of Czechoslovakia would have descended into madness, offering Hitler an opportunity to intervene. The Prague government rebuffed the fraudulent offer.

On proposals by the Prague government, progress was slow. Quarrels within the cabinet and parliamentary committees were resolved by laborious compromises. The politicians were reluctant to weaken the state by granting too much autonomy to the *curia*. From London and Paris came orders for swift action.

Late in July the Czech government brought forth two bills on the minority question. A nationalities bill promised equality before the law for all citizens. Government jobs, public services, and schools would be distributed among the minorities according to their numbers. Government contracts would be denied concerns who violated the nationalities law. Autonomous control would be permitted over the schools. A language bill offered official recognition to minority languages even if they were used by less than 20 per cent of the population. Correspondence concerning educational affairs could be carried on in the language used in the particular school. Knowledge of minority languages would be necessary for state employment.

Because the Sudetens did not receive full equality with the Prague government, their leaders spurned the bills. Had they been sincere, the bills would have been the means to solve their ancient quarrel with the Czechs. If enacted into law, these bills would have made Czech treatment of minorities superior to that of neighboring countries. Neither Poland, Hungary, Italy, Yugolavia, nor Rumania offered such advantages to their minorities. Events in July and August ended further discussion of the bills.

To the horror of the London government, another crisis came in mid-July. Reports circulated in Prague of more than normal German troop movements in Austria, but British observers in Germany found nothing unusual along the Czech frontier. From Germany came the news of another Czech mobilization. Machine gun positions were manned; the road system was controlled by the military. Observers found no signs of a Czech mobilization.

How long could such crises continue? A drastic solution was needed. In Henderson's words, "The moment has come for Prague to get a real twist of the screw."[2]

Amid the July crisis, Captain Fritz Wiedemann, Hitler's former company commander, appeared in London. Supposedly the Captain was to prepare the way for an official visit by Göring. Wiedemann's instructions came from the *Führer,* who ordered the Captain to express his anger and chagrin over the May crisis. Wiedemann must declare that Hitler was unmoved by force or threats. The Sudeten question would be solved by peace or war. Throughout the meeting, Hitler insisted, the Captain must be a friendly chap.

On July 17, in a conversation with Halifax, Wiedemann followed his *Führer*'s instructions. Halifax pressed for a declaration that Germany had no intention of using force against Czechoslovakia. Not for a moment, Wiedemann replied, but if incidents continued, Germany would not neglect the Sudetens. The pair parted cordially. Halifax requested Wiedemann to inform Hitler that before the Foreign Secretary died, he wanted "to see, as the culmination of his work, the *Führer* entering Buckingham Palace, at the side of the king, amid the acclamations of the English people."

When Wiedemann reported to Hitler, the *Führer* was involved for two hours with Unity Mitford, an eccentric young English girl who was enamored of Nazism. Hitler gave Wiedemann only five minutes.[3]

Within a week of Wiedemann's visit, Chamberlain asked Ambassador von Dirksen to see him without appointment. The Prime Minister wanted to improve relations with Germany through discussions. The statement in Parliament on March 24 merely confirmed that negotiations in such an atmosphere were impossible. Chamberlain feared a deadlock in the Czech-Sudeten negotiations. Would the Germans please not lose patience? His government had prepared for such a failure and had "measures to persuade the Czechoslovak government to overcome this deadlock." If some Czechs resorted to force, he

2 Henderson to Halifax, July 18, 1938, *ibid.,* 590.
3 Wiedemann Papers, *DG,* Series D, VII, 626–33.

begged Dirksen that his government remain calm and avoid force.[4] Chamberlain's concern was increased by German tactics. In the press and in public speeches, Nazi officials whipped up hatred for the accursed Czechs. In Dessau late in May, Paul Goebbels snarled that there were seventy-five million Germans but only thirteen million Czechs, who acted as though the figures were reversed. Speaking at Stettin on June 12, Rudolf Hess, third deputy *Führer,* denounced the Czechs' inability to insure peace and security within their own frontiers. They were a source of danger for the peace of Europe. Only the *Führer* saved Europe from a war when a sudden mobilization was made without reason. German quiescence must not be mistaken for weakness. In Berlin on June 21, Goebbels declared, "Germany desires peace, but not the graveyard peace which Versailles proposed to organize." Someone in the crowd asked about the Sudetens. Goebbels replied that Germany would not regard their mistreatment calmly forever.[5]

Ribbentrop used the complaint that the Sudetens were negotiating at gun point. With both Britain and France he took the line that neither was vitally concerned with Czechoslovakia. Despite his objections, he offered no solution, leaving Britain and France to seek one satisfactory to the Sudetens.

Henlein spoke out on July 25 as he prepared to leave for the Reich National Gymnastic Festival at Breslau. The Sudetens did not want war, but he could not be responsible for what might happen if there were no agreement by fall. Only full autonomy would be acceptable.

At Breslau the paunchy gymnastic teacher proclaimed that Germans outside the Reich would "render unto the state that which is the state's, and unto the nation that which is the nation's . . . we are and remain German national citizens serving voluntarily under the laws of the German nation. We have become one people, a community of all Germans throughout the world."[6]

Forty thousand Sudetens filed past Hitler on July 31. Suddenly they broke ranks to grasp Hitler's hands. Sudeten girls and women rushed

4 Von Dirksen to German Foreign Ministry, July 22, 1938, *ibid.,* II, 509–10.

5 *Survey of International Affairs,* 1938, II, 160–62; *Documents on International Affairs,* 1938, II, 163–64.

6 *Ibid.,* 172–73.

to lay flowers at the feet of the *Führer*. To Hitler they cried, *"Führer help us! Take us home to the Reich!"*[7]

Information available to the British and French during June and July, 1938, was frightening. Work on the western fortifications along Germany's frontier was being pushed to completion by August 15. Requisitioning procedures were instituted to commandeer supplies. German pilots in Spain were ordered to return home for service. Leaves in the *Luftwaffe* were cancelled. Large stores of oil and gas were accumulated by the *Luftwaffe*. Additional reservists were recalled to the army. All signs indicated a planned attack on Czechoslovakia in the autumn.

The Czechoslovak government seemed too slow in its negotiations. Daily the German attitude grew nastier. Continually Henderson predicted war if there were incidents in Czechoslovakia involving Sudetens. New tactics seemed imperative. Moved by Henderson's reports, without consulting either France or Czechoslovakia, Chamberlain and Halifax decided to send a mediator to Prague.

The decision was made only after much thought and not as the result of a hasty scare. Because old methods were failing, something new was necessary to save peace. Someone in the Foreign Office had proposed a mediator as early as April 30, providing Henlein and Hodža accepted the scheme. Halifax found it a good idea to keep in mind, but the moment had not come then. Such a person would be hard to find.

The idea was discussed once again when William Strang, a Foreign Office official, was sent to Berlin and Prague after the May crisis to obtain firsthand information and give the government's opinions. In Prague, Strang and Newton felt that the British government should send an investigator into the Sudetenland to observe and report on the situation, supplementing the reports of the minister and his staff. He could then make suggestions and be better prepared to comment on London's suggestions. Information gained would be current, enabling Britain to "play the honest broker" if negotiations collapsed. "A senior and experienced consular officer who has not served in either Germany or Czechoslovakia might fill the bill."[8]

By June 18, Halifax had further thoughts about a mediator. If

---

[7] Celovsky, *Das Münchener Abkommen*, 288.

[8] "Notes by Mr. Strang on conversations with members of His Majesty's Legation at Prague, May 26–27, 1938," *DBFP*, First series, I, 403–16.

negotiations broke down, he proposed to ask the Czechs "to accept the services of an independent British expert who would try and reconcile the two parties." Someone would be chosen with "practical experience of administration and minority problems, such as an ex-governor of an Indian province."[9]

A hint of the search for a mediator was dropped in Paris. Because the mediator would get France off the hook, Bonnet was enchanted.

By July 16, Walter Runciman had agreed to accept the heavy task. The news delighted the French leaders when Halifax informed them of the choice during his visit of state with the King and Queen on July 20. Paris would push the Czechs to accept Runciman.

As the British government described Runciman's task, he would be independent of the government while acquainting himself with the problem and the causes of the trouble. He would maintain contact with both sides, and if negotiations broke down he would restore them on the spot. Czechoslovakia should request him. If they refused, London threatened to reveal the proposal, throwing the blame on Czechoslovakia. Once Czechoslovakia accepted, the Sudetens would be approached.

These tidings gave Beneš a shock that lasted two hours. He was aghast at the British threat to Czechoslovak sovereignty. The government might fall; he might be forced to resign. He begged that this be treated as a preliminary sounding.[10]

Hodža, alerted by Beneš, took the news better, promising to convince the cabinet that the mediator was proof of British good will. On July 23, the Czech Prime Minister officially requested someone to help in overcoming the difficulties arising out of the nationalities bill. To salve national prestige, he did not ask for a "mediator."

Bonnet was delighted, A mediator would throw responsibility on Britain. Prague must accept because France was supporting Britain. If Czechoslovakia refused the mediator or his proposals, Britain would announce her unwillingness to fight for Czech domination of the Sudetens. France could follow suit with clean hands. Some in the French Ministry of Foreign Affairs feared that the Sudetens might reject the proposal.[11]

9 Halifax to Newton, June 18, 1938, *ibid.*, 501.

10 Halifax to Newton, July 18, 1938, *ibid.*, 581–83; Newton to Halifax, July 20, 21, 1938, *ibid.*, I, 600–601, 604–608.

11 Report of Osusky, July 25, 1938, *Europäische Politik*, 118.

In Parliament the British government told a different story. Before Commons, Chamberlain denied rumors that "we were hustling the Czech government." The reverse was true: he was trying to prevent hasty action in so delicate a matter. In response to a request from the Czechoslovak government, he had agreed to propose someone with experience and ability to investigate the question in Czechoslovakia and to suggest the means to complete the negotiations. The mediator would be independent, acting only in a "personal capacity." His task would be to inform the public and make the "intractable" issue more soluble. They were fortunate to obtain Runciman, who had "outstanding personal qualifications for the task." The Prime Minister praised him for his experience among "men of all sorts and conditions." He was a man of "fearlessness, freedom from prejudice, integrity and impartiality." Above all, Chamberlain hoped that if they could somehow find a peaceful solution to the Sudeten problem, the way would be open for "a further effort for a general appeasement."

In the House of Lords, Halifax asserted that the government would not be responsible for Runciman's suggestions. The proposal for a mediator had been made in close accord with the French and at the request of the Czechs. After the Foreign Secretary had outlined Runciman's task, the new mediator had replied, " 'I quite understand; you are setting me adrift in a small boat in mid-Atlantic.' "[12]

Avowals to the contrary notwithstanding, Runciman was a British agent. His task was not to insure a just solution, but to force on the Czechs a solution pleasing to the Sudeten Nazis. The promise of independence meant nothing because Runciman reported to Halifax who, in turn, gave the instructions.

Runciman symbolized a change in British policy. No longer were the negotiations to be carried on by a sovereign state. A foreigner instructed by a foreign government would mediate. The British government was taking the direction of policy away from the Czechoslovak government. A process had commenced that would end in the Munich Agreement.

Not until Beneš accepted did the British government approach Berlin. Weizsäcker saw no objection to the plan, but he could not commit the government. Before Henderson reached Ribbentrop, the story leaked to the newspapers. Ribbentrop announced that the Ger-

12 *House of Commons Debates,* Fifth series, Vol. 338, cols. 2950–2959; *House of Lords Debates,* Fifth series, Vol. 110, cols. 1281–1282.

man government could not be committed to the mission. The mission would be treated as a British concern without German approval. Eisenlohr, the German minister in Prague, was instructed to keep Berlin informed of Runciman's plans, but official German co-operation with the mission was forbidden.

Thus did Ribbentrop scheme to thwart the mission. Germany would hinder the negotiations and delay the search for peace. Through regular channels of communication with Berlin, the Sudeten Nazis were ordered to accept the mission. Such guile left Beneš no alternative other than to promise complete freedom for Runciman and to pledge that every facility would be at the mediator's disposal. The President would be happy to meet Runciman.

The independent expert, Walter Runciman, his wife, and party reached Prague on the morning of August 3. The Runciman mission had begun.

# 9

## The Runciman Mission—A Fresh Solution?

WALTER RUNCIMAN was a millionaire with experience in banking, railways, and shipping. He had been a member of Parliament since 1899, had served as president of the board of trade in 1914, and had been in the House of Lords since 1937. With Runciman came Frank T. A. Ashton-Gwatkin, head of the economic section of the Foreign Office; R. J. Stopford, an expert on India and international finance; Geoffrey Peto, who had been Runciman's parliamentary private secretary; and Ian Henderson, a member of the consular service.

Runciman, who still wore stiff winged collars, was a total abstainer. His background was North Country and non-conformist. Naturally he could not speak Czech. He was "as full of facts as a balance sheet." Runciman "seemed to have fallen from a page of Dickens and resented his fall." He had a great passion for classical German music. Soon after his arrival at the Alcron Hotel in Prague, the three-man hotel orchestra mysteriously received large bundles of classical German music.[1]

At the Prague railway station, Runciman was met by the Czech chief of protocol, the Lord Mayor of Prague, Newton, Hodža, and Krofta, representing the Czechs, and by Ernst Kundt and Wilhelm Sebekovsky, representing the Sudetens. Newton made the introductions. Kundt exclaimed, " 'I bid you welcome in the name of the Su-

[1] *New York Times*, April 14, 1938; Robert Coulandre, *De Staline à Hitler*, 155.

deten German people.' " All representatives of the Third Reich were absent.[2]

In the evening of August 3, Runciman met 150 newsmen in the dining room of the Hotel Alcorn. He announced that he had not asked for the job but had been told that his presence would be welcome. He was free from prejudice, without instructions, and acting independently. Through his forty years of experience in politics, he had learned that "permanent peace and tranquility can only be established on a basis of mutual consent." He was "a friend of all and an enemy of none."[3]

On the next day, Runciman and his colleagues called on the Foreign Minister, the Prime Minister, and the President. Czech citizens were impressed by the odd Englishmen who wore top hats in sweltering, midsummer heat.

In the hot afternoon, Kundt led a delegation of the Sudeten German party in a call on Runciman. Kundt welcomed anyone devoted to "unbiased and objective study of the problem." Runciman explained the conditions under which he had accepted the mission: he had been guaranteed his independence and free judgment and had received the consent of both parties. He wanted to study the problem in its entirety, then he would offer his services as mediator and honest broker.

At Runciman's suggestion, the Sudetens returned in the evening to talk with his staff. The Englishmen heard Sudeten tales of discrimination in the allotment of civil service jobs and contracts. Before the night was over, the Sudetens argued the Englishmen into admitting that a state of nationalities would not destroy the Czechoslovak state.

Runciman's first contacts revealed to him the great chasm which he must somehow bridge. Beneš, he reported, did not "show much sign of an understanding or respect for the Germans in Czechoslovakia." Although the President and his ministers were helpful, Runciman was not satisfied fully with their attitude. For Runciman this was a new and wearing experience. Nothing was farther away from the international crisis which he was mediating than the labor disputes and genteel business problems that had been his life.[4]

2 Hencke to the German Foreign Ministry, August 4, 1938, *DG*, Series D, II, 534.
3 Runciman to Halifax, undated, *DBFP*, Third series, II, 50–51.
4 Runciman to Halifax, August 4, 5, 1938, *ibid.*, 50, 56–57.

A collapse of the negotiations threatened on August 9. The Sudetens refused to negotiate with a Czechoslovak committee representing the six ministerialist parties instead of the government. Negotiations resumed when representatives were included from the cabinet and government departments. Another meeting, on August 11, accomplished nothing.

At every opportunity, the Sudeten leaders burdened the mission with their tale of persecution by the cruel Czechoslovak government. Deliberately they crammed the mission with memoranda, articles, and documents, hoping to convince them that the nationality problem was insoluble within the Czechoslovak state. Runciman must believe that the Czechs would not grant honest concessions. The Mediator must place the blame solely on the Czechs: they disturbed the peace of Europe. From Berlin instructions came for the Sudeten leaders to appear to conduct negotiations seriously, both with the Czechoslovak government and with the Runciman mission.[5]

Many of Runciman's weekends in Czechoslovakia were spent in the homes of wealthy Sudetens, who carefully recounted their sufferings in the land reforms. During the weekend of August 15, he visited the estate of Ulrich Kinsky, a member of the Sudeten German party. His host toured the district with Runciman, pointing out Sudeten businesses driven bankrupt by the Czechs. Kinsky omitted factories run by Czechs which employed Sudetens. Runciman was shown a home inhabited by five suffering German families. Someone neglected to mention that the landlord was the local mayor, a good Sudeten German party member.

At Kinsky's estate, a spontaneous demonstration was performed for Runciman's interest. A crowd of Sudetens appeared calling, "We wish to see Lord Runciman!" When he appeared, a piteous cry arose: "Please help us in our need! Give us a just solution, Lord Runciman!"[6]

Back in Prague on August 16, fresh from his weekend in the country, Runciman upbraided Beneš for his failure to appoint German officials. The erring President promised to mend his ways.

The meeting on August 17 of the Sudetens and the Czech ministers

[5] Minutes of Woermann for Ribbentrop, August 14, 1938, *DG*, Series D, II, 561–63; Bürger to the German Foreign Ministry, August 17, 1938, *ibid.*, 577–82.
[6] Ashton-Gwatkin to Strang, August 16, 1938, *DBFP*, Third series, II, 661–63.

brought meager results. They could only agree that Hodža and Kundt should discuss further procedures.

Beneš decided to take an active role in the negotiations. He would expect sincere negotiating by the Sudetens. The Sudetens were thrown off guard; in their panic, they begged Ribbentrop for advice. The Foreign Minister ordered them to stop running to him. Henlein had his instructions. They must always negotiate, avoiding the blame for any breakdown, and demand more than the Czechoslovak government would grant. Beneš' proposals must not be accepted as a basis for negotiation lest the Western press regard them as a magnanimous offer. Let Beneš carry out his proposals, but the Sudetens must still insist on Henlein's Karlsbad points.[7]

As yet Runciman had not met Henlein. The Nazis planned to hold him in reserve for the final negotiations. Runciman's insistence on a meeting with the Sudeten *Führer* was rewarded on August 18 at the *Schloss Rottenhaus,* the home of Prince Max Hohenlohe. There Henlein put forth his case. The German people must protect themselves against a Czech invasion assisted by the Czechoslovak government. Separation, achieved by negotiation, was the only remedy. He had always urged moderation on his people and would continue to keep them in hand, but time was running out. Without something to show for his efforts, he could not restrain the suffering Sudetens. He was an advocate of peace. The Karlsbad points were not his absolute demands. He had no desire to break up the Czech state, for he only wanted autonomy.[8]

A sudden invitation for another meeting with Henlein was answered by Ashton-Gwatkin on August 22. Henlein repeated much of his story: local autonomy through negotiation, withdrawal of the Czech police, end of persecution, punishment for the guilty, prohibition of press attacks, and the transfer of German officers to the German areas. He had no sympathies for the Nazi terror and swore to prevent Jewish persecutions. Germany and Great Britain must be friends. Ashton-Gwatkin asked Henlein to tell Hitler of his experiences with the British and of their desire for peace. Henlein was glad to oblige. The Sudeten leader impressed Ashton-Gwatkin. "I

7 Memorandum by Altenburg, August 18, 1938, *DG,* Series D, II, 586–87.

8 "Notes of a conversation between Viscount Runciman and Herr Henlein on August 18," August 19, 1938, *DBFP,* Third series, II, 656–57.

like him," he wrote. "He is, I am sure, an absoutely honest fellow."[9]

That such a policy would succeed was reinforced by news from London. There Horace Wilson, speaking for Chamberlain, assured Theodor Kordt, counselor of the German Embassy, that only Bolshevism would gain in an Anglo-German war. The government was aware of the precarious position of Czechoslovakia, "an air cushion out of which the air was gradually escaping." London was prepared to do anything to meet German wishes. Once the Czech-Sudeten quarrel was regulated, the way would be opened for German dominance of southeastern Europe. Great Britain only asked that she not be completely debarred from trading in southeastern Europe. Grant her only 20 per cent.[10]

In the meeting of August 24, Beneš proposed three autonomous districts to be governed by the Sudeten Germans, independent budget for the areas, loans from the Prague government, withdrawal of state police, a commission to decide on constitutional changes, and a press armistice. The next day, discussion of Beneš' proposals began. Kundt and Sebekovsky did nothing but criticize. Beneš would not discuss the Karlsbad points because he had taken an oath to uphold the constitution, and his honor demanded that he maintain such an attitude. When Beneš asked for an opinion about his proposals, the Sudeten pair announced that they could not give an official opinion. They must confer with other members of the party.[11]

To London these proposals corresponded largely to the Karlsbad points. Because they seemed a promising basis for negotiation, Runciman pressed Beneš for an early agreement. They must have something—anything—to publish in the next week. Beneš must exceed the limit of concessions.

Beneš handed over his proposals in writing on August 30, with the hope that they represented the start of fulfillment of the Karlsbad demands. He had no objection to an announcement that the Karlsbad demands would be fulfilled. Thus did he "go the limit of concessions to the Sudetens and even beyond," as demanded by Walter Runciman.

[9] Ashton-Gwatkin to Strang, August 23, 1938, "Notes of a conversation between Mr. Ashton-Gwatkin and Herr Henlein at Marienbad on August 22," August 23, 1938, *ibid.*, 657–59, 663–64.

[10] Kordt to Weizsäcker, August 23, 1938, *DG*, Series D, II, 605–609.

[11] Hencke to the German Foreign Ministry, August 27, 1938, *ibid.*, 633–47.

Karl Hermann Frank confessed to his superiors that Beneš' proposals were far-reaching and could not be rejected outright. Kundt saw their realization as the fulfillment of the Karlsbad demands. Because the *Führer's* orders must be obeyed, Henlein found the proposals inadequate in their written form; he doubted if Beneš could be trusted or that the Czech government would give them fair treatment. Kundt, posing as the independent spokesman, formally rejected the proposals. They did not cover all the Sudeten requirements.

Now Runciman claimed that Beneš' written proposals were diluted. Ashton-Gwatkin found them too academic. Neither gentleman realized that generalizations were not so glittering when made precise in writing. Runciman wanted Beneš to combine his concessions with the Karlsbad points, then he could go home. The Mediator was worn out by the incessant meetings, the travels, and the delegations. He could not even take a day off to enjoy partridge shooting, for which Czechoslovakia was so famous![12]

Runciman's criticisms of Beneš' memorandum of August 30 convinced Halifax that Beneš was playing "fast and loose." Drastic action was needed to bring him to heel. Concessions must be published forthwith. Because the Sudetens rejected them, Runciman opposed their publication.

Halifax next pinned his hopes on Henlein's visit to Hitler, who had agreed to receive him if he brought a message from the British. Despite a head cold, the paunchy Sudeten *Führer* agreed to transmit messages from Runciman. To Henlein on September 1, Runciman gave a message for Hitler. He informed the *Führer* that he was trying to reach a settlement at the earliest possible moment on the basis of the Karlsbad points and Beneš' new proposals. Should the two parties fail to reach an agreement, Runciman was ready to produce a scheme by September 15. This message was a mistake. Now Hitler knew that the Karlsbad points would be supported by Runciman. Until September 15, Hitler could order the Sudetens to reject all Beneš' proposals, thus prolonging the crisis.

Other news reaching Berlin from London was reassuring. "Our friend," Horace Wilson, revealed to the Germans that Chamberlain would make every effort to reach an understanding with Germany. Nothing would deter the Prime Minister from advising Czechoslovakia to make fundamental changes in her policy toward Germany.

[12] Newton to Halifax, August 29, 1938, *DBFP*, Third series, II, 183.

Wilson promised that if Germany and Great Britain settled the Czech problem, " 'we shall simply brush aside the resistance that France or Czechoslovakia herself may offer to the decision.' "[13]

Henderson had been called to London on August 24 for consultations. He returned to Germany on August 31 with instructions to make clear to the Germans that no one in Britain "wished to fight for either Czechs or Sudetens." If Germany chose force to solve the question, the situation would be altered—particularly if France chose to honor her alliance.

When the ambassador saw Weizsäcker, he reported that now it was only a matter of forcing "the unreliable Beneš" to make a comprehensive offer to Henlein and tying him down to a public statement so that he could no longer evade the issue. Beneš was now considering really big concessions. "Eyewash," Weizsäcker answered.

When Henderson saw Ribbentrop on September 1, he made it plain that "the Sudeten Germans and the Czechs were a matter of complete indifference to Great Britain." In the British government there was concern over what course France might take because of her honor. French honor had nothing to do with the issue, Ribbentrop snarled. It was an immoral alliance because the Czechs oppressed three and one-half million Germans. Germany's honor was at stake. A French attack would be a "war of aggression," and Germany would react accordingly. Britain must make the French see reason and must not risk her empire "for the sake of a perverted idea of France about her honor."[14]

For Georges Bonnet, August had been a trying month. His mood changed daily from wild optimism that everything would be settled in a matter of hours to extreme depression when he thought that France might have to stand behind her ally. He hoped Runciman could extract France from her dilemma. By early September he knew that Germany was well on the way towards preparing for war. Somehow he had to convince the Germans of the French desire for peace. To Welczeck he complained on September 2 that Germany did not

13 Hencke to the German Foreign Ministry, August 30, 1938, *DG*, Series D, II, 660–61; Runciman to Halifax, August 30, 1938, *DBFP*, Third series, II, 192–93.

14 Henderson to Halifax, September 1, 1938, *DBFP*, Third series, II, 203–206; minutes by Weizsäcker, September 1, 1938, *DG*, Series D, II, 679–80; memorandum by Ribbentrop, September 3, 1938, *ibid.*, 688–89. In his report, Henderson softened Ribbentrop's replies, omitting some parts entirely.

appreciate the attitude of the French government. A full 90 per cent of the French people desired an understanding with Germany. Bonnet and Daladier were sincere admirers of Hitler. "Without bloodshed the *Führer* had prepared the way for the grandiose reconstruction of Germany and carried this out in a fashion which no one would have believed possible before the great war." Such a glorious achievement should be crowned by peaceful revision of the peace treaties and an understanding with France and Great Britain. Thus the *Führer* would become "the greatest statesman of the century." Then Bonnet hoped Hitler would visit Paris. As if an after thought, the Foreign Minister interrupted his monologue to declare that France and Britain would aid Czechoslovakia if attacked during the present negotiations, even the United States and Russia would join the war. The Foreign Minister promised that France would force Prague to give the Sudetens 90 per cent of their demands. Bonnet supported the natural incorporation of the Sudetenland into the Reich, once autonomy had been obtained. These statements, Bonnet claimed, were so important that, in the name of France, he had placed a copy of these among the records of the Quai d'Orsay as a historical document.

Publicly the Foreign Minister sang a different tune. At Pointe de Grave on September 4, 1938, he declared: "France, in any case, will remain faithful to the pacts and to the treaties which she has concluded. She will remain faithful to the engagements which she has taken." But Berlin knew differently.[15]

Halifax asked Bonnet for French support in forcing Beneš to quick concessions because it was time "to twist Beneš' tail." Bonnet was overjoyed to agree. Any solution proposed by Runciman was acceptable; but if Beneš rejected the solution, "the Czechs would have to look out for themselves."[16]

Halifax instructed Runciman to impress on Beneš that he could no longer maneuver for position, "spinning out the negotiations without any sincere intention of facing the immediate and vital issues." Following his instructions, Runciman visited Beneš on September 1 and 2. The Mediator insisted that nothing less than the Karlsbad

---

[15] Welczeck to the German Foreign Ministry, September 2, 1938, *ibid.*, 682–84; *Documents on International Affairs, 1938*, II, 177–78.

[16] Kennedy to Hull, August 31, 1938, *FRUS, 1938*, I, 565–66; Phipps to Halifax, September 2, 1938, *DBFP*, Third series, II, 215–16.

points would suffice. If Britain had to choose between Karlsbad and war, Beneš should not be under any illusion as to what the choice would be.[17]

In Prague, the Sudeten agents had to obey the *Führer*'s orders, given at Breslau during the meeting of July 29–31. They were to " 'hold out and wait.' "[18] On September 2 they rejected most of Beneš' proposals. Insufficient self-government was the excuse. In reply they offered a counter proposal, raising enough questions and conditions to prolong the negotiations and throw the burden back on the Czechs. To Beneš the counter proposals aimed at the destruction of the state. Nevertheless, there was to be another meeting on September 5.

At last Henlein returned from the *Führer* with his message. Ashton-Gwatkin motored to Asch to receive the news from the Nazi Valhalla. In a small house, complete with gardens, Alsatian dogs, a few bookcases, and plaster reproductions of Greek statues, lived the Sudeten *Führer*. He served Ashton-Gwatkin some sherry—which turned out to be cherry brandy. Henlein had seen Hitler on September 1 and 2. Hitler did not want war. When Henlein announced that he hoped to obtain autonomy within Czechoslovakia, Hitler seemed skeptical. The Nazi *Führer* would not set a deadline for the negotiations.

The British were still no nearer a solution. Henlein purposely left them adrift with this noncommittal report, Hitler probably instructed Henlein to continue as he had in the past, always objecting to whatever the Czechs proposed, raising his demands, seemingly never departing from the Karlsbad program, and continually reasserting that Hitler favored peace. Because Beneš would not grant the Sudetens their desires, he would appear to favor war. Once more the Czech government would stand condemned as a tyrant and an aggressor.

Newton, following Halifax' orders, returned to the attack on September 4 with a demand for the Karlsbad program as a minimum. Czechoslovakia, he threatened, would be fought over and occupied: at best, Beneš could only hope for civil war. The British Minister doubted that Czechoslovakia could be re-established in her present form. "Painfully impressed," Beneš objected because no one would tell him precisely the meaning of the Karlsbad program. He

17 Halifax to Newton, August 31, 1938, *ibid.*, 195–96; Newton to Halifax, September 1, 2, 3, 1938, *ibid.*, 202, 207–209, 221.

18 K. H. Frank interrogation, *NCA*, V, 858.

feared lest he sign a blank check. Newton brushed aside these hesitations. Beneš had months to overcome these slight difficulties, but his "attitude suggested that it was hopeless to expect progress."[19]

When Beneš complained to Runciman about Newton's hostility, the independent Mediator joined in the attack. Beneš must make every sacrifice necessary for the salvation of his country. Runciman emphatically declared: "If the British people and government had to choose between Henlein's eight Karlsbad points and war, there is no doubt as to the decision." Runciman next convinced Cardinal Kaspar, Archbishop of Prague and Primate of Bohemia, to send a letter telling Beneš "that in this patriotic Czech Cardinal's view anything is better than war."[20]

For Beneš the worst had come to pass. His Western allies were forcing on him the Karlsbad points. This scheme spelled the end of the Czechoslovakia he had helped to create. He had accepted Runciman to placate his Western allies. In them he had placed all his hopes for Czech independence. Before the security of Beneš' country, his allies placed the appeasement and satisfaction of Sudeten Germans. The Runciman mission had offered Beneš no solution, only the Karlsbad points. If he rejected these, Czechoslovakia would be without friends. Beneš' friends threatened him with defeat and occupation if he did not grant the Sudetens their demands. Appeasement was the order of the day. Beneš prepared to appease.

[19] Newton to Halifax, September 4, 1938, *DBFP*, Third series, II, 226–29.
[20] Runciman to Halifax, September 5, 1938, *ibid.*, 248–49.

# 10

## The End of the Mission

To PREVENT THE ISOLATION of Czechoslovakia, Beneš prepared to appease the Sudetens as Britain and France demanded. On September 4, he called in Kundt and Sebekovsky and ordered them to write down their demands. He would grant them at once. The pair could not trust their hearing. " 'Go on. I mean it. Write!' " Beneš insisted. Taking out his fountain pen, Beneš made them dictate their demands. He signed the paper, promising to fulfill them.[1]

Another Czechoslovak cabinet meeting on the afternoon of September 5 produced proposals, called the Fourth Plan. Hastily assembled in a loose arrangement, these proposals were not a faithful copy of the Karlsbad points, but they were the nearest yet. The Fourth Plan could easily be revised to meet the Karlsbad demands.

Under the new plan, nationalities would be awarded civil service posts and government contracts corresponding to the proportion of the population they comprised. The national budget would be apportioned among the nationalities. Loans would be granted for the depressed areas, with seven hundred million crowns set aside for firms employing German workers in German areas. A committee from each nationality would handle the disbursement of the loans. All past cases of discrimination on the basis of nationality would be reviewed. The German, Russian, Magyar, Polish, and Czech languages would be declared equal.

The nationality area would be divided into cantons or *gaue*. Diets

1 John W. Wheeler-Bennett, *Munich: Prologue to Tragedy*, 91.

or *curiae* would protect the minorities within each canton and control autonomous administration. Special legislation would protect the nationalities, and the diets could protest any infringement. All departments of the central government would have sections for each nationality, staffed by its members. Thus the cantons would receive a large degree of territorial autonomy, but the Sudetens were not recognized as a corporate, legal entity.

The Fourth Plan was vague on the profession of Nazi philosophy, yet it was as far as Beneš could go while keeping Czechoslovakia intact as a state. Assuming the plan had been implemented, the red tape and bureaucratic confusion would have been a nightmare. Linguistic equality would have produced the chaos so desired by the Nazis. Conceivably a problem could arise involving documents in Russian, Polish, Czech, Magyar, and German.

Beneš produced the Fourth Plan to pacify Great Britain and France, who threatened to throw over Czechoslovakia unless the Sudetens were granted the Karlsbad points, but this was an impossible goal because the Karlsbad points were never meant to be achieved. To Runciman and Newton, Beneš declared that the plan was a "capitulation and would, in future years, be regretted by Great Britain and France."[2] His hearers were not interested in such warnings. The cause of Sudeten appeasement must be served.

The Fourth Plan seemed to promise salvation to worried politicians in London and Paris. Sudeten leaders admitted that the Fourth Plan represented acceptance of nearly 95 per cent of the Karlsbad points. Those who had so long posed as martyrs did not know what to do. Kundt saw no alternative but to accept the plan. Otherwise Beneš and the Czech government might prove that members of the Sudeten German party were pretenders for a peaceful solution who plotted to conquer Czechoslovakia for the Third Reich. Kier, a German assigned to give legal advice to the Sudeten party, urged acceptance of the Fourth Plan because it could be utilized to destroy Czechoslovakia.

Conveniently there came an incident at Mährisch-Ostrau, a town in which Czechs comprised about 80 per cent of the population. On September 7, German deputies visited Sudetens imprisoned some weeks earlier for gun running. The local German schoolmaster de-

[2] *Documents on International Affairs,* 1938, II, 178–84; Newton to Halifax, September 6, 1938, *DBFP,* Third series, II, 253–54.

93

cided that the visit was an appropriate time to dismiss his classes. Soon a crowd of shouting Germans gathered outside the jail. Police sought to quell the demonstration because Czechs were thronging to the jail, aroused by the shouts. As the hostile mobs gathered, the deputies emerged from the jail. Now the story becomes blurred. In one account, Deputy Karl May, who had a reputation as a Sudeten tough, seized the bridle of a mounted policeman's horse. The policeman hit him on the shoulder, then arrested him. Another story says the policeman hit May because he was thrashing a Czech. Six Sudetens were arrested. When their identities were known, the politicians were released by the police.

Within hours Sudetens related how their fellow nationals, on an errand of mercy, were "threatened with riding whips, thrashed, and pushed against walls by the horses of the police.[3] Sudeten leaders now had an excuse to suspend negotiations until the incident had been liquidated.

The incident could not have been better timed for the Nazis. British investigators on the spot were of the opinion that it was deliberately staged. Why did the deputies wait until September 7 for the visit when they could have gone earlier? Had the Sudeten Nazis been sincere in their search for a peaceful solution, the Mährisch-Ostrau incident would not have stood in their way. The incident was too convenient to be attributed to chance.

Cessation of the negotiations gave the Sudeten leaders time to consult Berlin, time to extract themselves from their dilemma, and time to find objections to the Fourth Plan. While they waited for the end of the incident, other incidents would be staged to frighten the West.

So disturbed was Halifax that he was ready to make a personal appeal to Hitler, but Runciman dissuaded him. Bonnet was on the verge of collapse. Throughout the night he called Ambassador Phipps repeatedly and dispatched telegrams to London to check on British loyalty. Constantly he phoned Prague. To the West's relief, by September 9 the incident seemed virtually resolved. All the Sudeten demands would be accepted. The policeman who struck May was dismissed, while the police chief at Mährisch-Ostrau resigned, and other policemen were suspended. Negotiations would resume on

[3] *New York Times*, September 8, 1938; *Survey of International Affairs, 1938*, II, 254.

September 13, one day after Hitler's scheduled speech at the party rally at Nuremberg.

Because France was so directly affected by the fate of Czechoslovakia, Bonnet and Daladier could no longer contain their fears. Daladier, "the bull of the Vaucluse," was a worried politician, brave or frightened as the occasion demanded.

Daladier feared Bolshevism after a war, he informed Bräuer, the German chargé on September 7. Soviet Russia would be the victor in a Franco-German war. France completely understood the German demands on Czechoslovakia, the Premier exclaimed. If the demands were met peacefully, there would be no opposition. French people did not hate German people and could be won over to a revision of the Versailles Treaty through a peaceful solution of the Sudeten question.

Twenty-four hours later the Premier uttered martial declarations to the British ambassador. If Germany crossed the Czech frontier, the "French will march to a man." Despite some strikes, the internal situation was excellent. Gamelin was prepared for "limited offensives." Rumania and Poland would grant passage for Russian planes.

There was less of the brave sergeant when Daladier talked with William Bullitt, the United States ambassador. The Premier complained that he was now about to reap a war whose seeds had been sown in that Versailles Treaty. He damned the Czechs for their brutal treatment of the Sudetens.[4]

The French Foreign Minister tried to obtain more explicit promises from the British. Bonnet had information that Hitler's decision to intervene in Czechoslovakia was based on "uncertainty of British policy." Would Halifax please correct this impression. Although he understood the French obligations, Halifax explained that British opinion, both in the government and in the country, was not ready to fight Germany because of Czechoslovakia. He doubted if the British people would fight to prevent Hitler's aiding the Sudetens to establish home rule. After the war, Czechoslovakia could not be completely restored. Why fight for what could neither be defended during a war nor restored after the war? Halifax saw no reason to fight now to

4 Bräuer to the German Foreign Ministry, September 7, *DG*, II, 712–14; Phipps to Halifax, September 8, 1938, *DBFP*, Third series, II, 269–70; Bullitt to Hull, September 8, 1938, *FRUS, 1938*, I, 581–83.

95

avoid future fighting in less favorable circumstances when the war might never come.

Again Bonnet tried to pin down Halifax. How would Britain answer if Germany attacked Czechoslovakia and if France declared: " 'We are going to march, will you march with us?' " Halifax replied that no reply could be made to such a statement in advance of German aggression. The British government could not answer without consulting the Dominions. While Britain would never permit a threat to French security, Halifax could not make a precise statement about future action.

France could not expect firm support from Britain if either Czechoslovakia or France took the initiative in the Sudeten crisis. The French government would not face Germany alone: Britain must be at her side. If Britain refused to fight, then so must France. French foreign policy now became that of Britain, for Bonnet agreed to accept any plan proposed by the British or Runciman. Such would give him a path to avoid fighting.[5]

Confusion over British policy increased when the London *Times* appeared on September 7 with a leader advocating the cession of the Sudetenland to Germany, "in case it might be worth-while for the Czechoslovak government to consider whether they should exclude altogether the project, *which has found favor in some quarters* [italics mine], of making Czechoslovakia a more homogeneous state by the secession of that fringe of alien populations who are contiguous to the nation with which they are united by race."[6] The italicized words implied Foreign Office approval. Such was not the case. The idea came from the pen of Geoffrey Dawson, the editor, who firmly believed that Germany should be given compensation for the Versailles Treaty. Twice Masaryk called at the Foreign Office and received an official denial. That evening the Foreign Office had to issue a statement that the *Times* leader in no way represented the views of the British government. The leader actually had little effect on the events, although some overestimated the damage.

To calm the Czech population, Beneš went on the air in a broadcast on September 10 to explain that the new settlement would improve Czechoslovak democracy. He appealed for confidence and co-

5 Halifax to Phipps, September 7, 9, 12, 1938, Phipps to Halifax, September 10, 1938, *DBFP*, Third series, II, 262–64, 275–77, 287, 303.

6 *The History of the Times*, IV, 930.

operation between Sudeten and Czech. All must avoid incidents and restrict party strife. More than ever before, the nation must unite.

On the next day the Sudetens replied with planned riots. In Eger, they attacked Czechs and German Social Democrats. Eighteen were injured, including thirteen policemen. In Reichenberg, Sudeten Nazis drove the police into the police station. Sudetens besieged a hall where Social Democrats were meeting peacefully. Policemen were summoned from adjacent towns to disperse the mobs.

Even Runciman was subjected to a demonstration. He spent the weekend at the castle of Count Ottokar Czernin von und zu Chudenitz, a former Austrian nobleman. Sudeten Nazis, with members of the *Freiwillige Schutzdienst* in uniform, serenaded the Mediator with the "Horst Wessel Song" and cries of *"Sieg Heil! Heil!"* and "Dear Runciman make us free from Czechoslovakia!" At last, Runciman spoke to the throng. "Men and women of Bohemia," said the Mediator, "you live in a beautiful country—perhaps one of the world's most beautiful. May God grant that this beautiful country have peace and that you will all continue to live in it in unity." The mob replied with cries of *"Sieg Heil! Sieg Heil!"* Once more the "Horst Wessel Song" echoed across the beautiful countryside.[7]

The riots throughout the Sudetenland on September 10–11 revealed the enormity of the crisis. To British and French statesmen it seemed that a powder train was laid. Hitler need only apply the spark at Nuremberg.

To Nuremberg thousands of the Nazi faithful flocked in September, 1938, for speeches and rousing demonstrations of German might. Their glorious *Führer* would provide the climax in a speech on November 12.

Among the spectators at Nuremberg was Nevile Henderson. According to his instructions, he must tell the *Führer* not to underestimate dangers for general peace in Europe. Chamberlain's government counted on German co-operation in obtaining an agreement over the Sudeten problem, while preserving the integrity of the Czech state. Henderson was to remind Hitler how pitiful it would be to spoil good relations when a peaceful solution of the Sudeten question appeared possible.

While the throngs gathered for the Nazi circus, Henderson talked with Göring, Goebbels, Neurath, Weizsäcker, and Ribbentrop. He

7 *New York Times*, September 12, 1938.

97

imagined that through these satraps he could rewrite Hitler's speech. To his hearers, Henderson suggested that Hitler welcome British intervention at Prague. The *Führer* ought to proclaim his zeal to co-operate with Britain in finding a solution similar to the Karlsbad points. The Nazi leaders convinced Henderson that there would be no aggression against Czechoslovakia—unless the "pinpricking" continued. Peace was possible if Beneš satisfied Henlein. On all sides, Henderson was inundated with the Versailles myth in which he fervently believed. Overwhelmed by Nazi arguments, the ambassador begged London to avoid another May crisis lest it "drive Herr Hitler straight off the deep end."

Henderson met Hitler once at a tea for the diplomatic corps. The Ambassador was unable to follow his instructions. Only François-Poncet tried to impress Hitler by asking if he were ready to join efforts for peace. Hitler merely shook hands.

As news of the disturbances following Beneš' speech of September 10 reached London, Halifax was quite distressed. By courier he sent Henderson a message, to be delivered immediately to Ribbentrop at Nuremberg, announcing how "greatly disturbed" was the British government by the riots in Czechoslovakia. If Germany used force, Czechoslovakia would ask France for aid. With France involved, Great Britain would be unable to stand aside. The British government fervently urged the German government "to use every effort . . . to avert a tragic and avoidable disaster."

By telegram Henderson protested the message because Hitler had not yet made up his mind on peace or war. Such a threat was a repetition of May 21 and would "drive him to the very action which we seek to prevent." Convinced by Henderson's pleading, Halifax cancelled the instructions.[8]

Before thousands of cheering Nazis, in a broadcast heard around the world, Hitler replied to the desire for peace on September 12. Czechs were depriving the Sudetens of their vital rights. Conditions in the Sudetenland were intolerable. The misery was "indescribable." Bestial Czechs annihilated and oppressed innocent Sudetens. In Germany these persecuted folk would find help and justice. Hitler reminded the listening world that not forever would he regard calmly

[8] Halifax to Henderson, September 6, 10, 1938, Ogilvie-Forbes to Halifax, September 10, 1938, Henderson to Halifax, September 10, 1938, Halifax to Kirkpatrick, September 9, 1938, *DBFP*, Third series, II, 249–50, 277–78, 282–85.

the oppression of Germans in Czechoslovakia. For these people he claimed the right of self-determination, denied by the Versailles Treaty. The oppression "shall cease" and self-determination should be substituted. Hitler concluded: "The Germans in Czechoslovakia are neither defenseless nor are they deserted, and folk should take notice of that fact."[9] France and Britain, Beneš and the Czechs now had their answer. Hitler's diatribe was but one phase of the campaign against the West; the other followed shortly.

As Hitler's speech ended, bricks and rocks were hurled through the windows of Sudetenland homes and business establishments with Jewish or Czech names. Sudeten thugs plundered the contents. They attacked Social Democratic clubs and workers' clubs. In more than seventy towns, fighting and rioting broke out. Police stations were a favorite target for attacks by Sudeten Nazi bands armed with weapons smuggled into Czechoslovakia from Germany. Swastika banners were hoisted in these towns, and paint brigades obliterated signs in Czech and painted swastikas over them. Throughout the night and into the next day, the terror continued.

In Eger, the Sudetens attacked the local Social Democratic club, but the police drove them off. Then they attacked Jewish and Czech shops. Thousands of Sudetens demonstrated in Aussig, where a Sudeten deputy harangued them and administered an oath of allegiance to the swastika. The roaring mob screamed, "Dear Hitler, free us from Czechoslovakia."

A Sudeten mob seized control of the post office in Habersbirk. After killing three of the policemen, the mob dragged a policeman's wife through the streets.

Hordes poured into the streets of Asch, while the police retreated within their barracks. Henlein's storm troopers set up their own guard around the town.

In Cheb, the Sudeten party had its offices in the Victoria Hotel. When the police came to search the building for arms, the Sudetens opened fire. For three and one-half hours, the fight raged about the hotel. After the police killed the defenders, they discovered a large supply of German-made arms and ammunition.

The Czechoslovak government met the challenge by swiftly restoring law and order. Reservists were called up, and a limited troop movement began in the direction of the Sudetenland. By September

[9] *The Speeches of Adolf Hitler,* II, 1488–90.

15 these forces, augmented by special police detachments, had quelled the revolt, leaving the Sudeten people helpless and frightened.

Insulted by the attempt to keep law and order, the Sudeten German party executive issued an ultimatum at 4 P.M. September 13 with a six-hour time limit. Troops and state police measures must be cancelled. Police powers must be transferred to local officials who would arrange for Sudeten substitutes; then the disorders would cease. If these conditions had been enforced, the Sudetenland would have fallen under the tyranny of Henlein, and his storm troopers would have become the new police.

Hodža offered to capitulate if the Sudetens would send representatives to Prague, prepared to negotiate. Late that night the Sudetens rejected Hodža's terms. Ashton-Gwatkin and members of Runciman's staff set forth that same evening to contact Henlein, who had already crossed into Germany. By 11:30 the next morning, Henlein had recrossed the frontier and met the British at his home in Asch. Henlein rejected Hodža's proposal. Sudeten terms must be accepted unconditionally, then negotiations could begin afresh on the basis of a plebiscite. Henlein had no wish to break off relations with the Runciman mission. It was all the work of the evil Czechs.

After nightfall the Sudeten *Führer* with his closest followers fled into Germany. Secure behind Nazi bayonets, Henlein issued a proclamation claiming that the Sudetens had been forced into the Czechoslovak state against their will. Czechs had refused a just settlement because they sought to destroy the Sudetens. To the world Henlein declared: "We wish to live as free Germans! We want peace and work again in our homeland! We want to return to the Reich! God be with us and our righteous struggle."[10]

In Paris it was "peace at any price." Bonnet was certain that war was only minutes away. Runciman must immediately bring both sides together and announce his plan. If the Mediator wanted the Karlsbad points, France would force it on the stubborn Czechs. He quoted Colonel Charles Lindbergh's statistics that Germany had eight thousand airplanes and could manufacture fifteen hundred a month. British and French towns would be destroyed without any means of retaliation. Neither nation was prepared for war:

[10] Newton to Halifax, September 13, 1938, *DBFP*, Third series, II, 313; memoranda of Altenburg, September 13, 14, 1938, Proclamation of Henlein to the Sudeten Germans, September 15, 1938, *DG*, Series D, II, 751–52, 757–58, 801–802.

they must maintain peace at any price. Bonnet's panic so alarmed Ambassador Phipps that he asked for an interview with Daladier.

The Premier was much changed from the man of September 8 who then declared that "if German troops cross the Czechoslovak frontier, the French will march to a man." With Hitler's cries fresh in his ears, Daladier was loath to march. First, he must be certain about the rights and wrongs of the troubles in Czechoslovakia. Losing his reserve, he broke down. Matters in Czechoslovakia were out of control. A German invasion had to be prevented at any cost lest France be faced with the obligations of her alliance. Runciman must present his plan and get both sides together. If this failed, a three-power conference— Britain, France, and Germany—must be held.[11]

Just as Beneš had surrendered his foreign policy, so now the leaders of France turned to London to save them from their alliance with Czechoslovakia. They presented a picture quite different from that of the men who had stood by Russia loyally in 1914.

In London there was no doubt that the Runciman mission was useless. A new step was needed. France had thrown the burden on Britain, whose government had already seized control of Czech policy through the Runciman mission.

Late in the evening of September 13, the German government was asked if Neville Chamberlain could meet with Adolf Hitler. On September 14, Hitler agreed to see Chamberlain the next day.[12] The Runciman mission was finished.

Runciman left Prague on September 16, his mission ended. His final report on September 21 was written after Chamberlain's first visit with Hitler and shows the influence of Chamberlain and Halifax. After reciting all of the Sudeten woes, he concluded that they were justified in their attitude. For them to turn to the Nazis, he considered natural. He did not ask why, if it were natural to turn to Germany under the Nazis, the Sudetens had not resorted to this movement when the Weimar Republic existed?

Runciman admitted that Beneš' Fourth Plan could be extended to cover the Karlsbad points. Extremists among the Sudeten German party found the plan too favorable and forced the incident at Mäh-

11 Phipps to Halifax, September 13, 1938, *DBFP*, Third series, II, 305–306, 309–12; Bullitt to Hull, September 14, 1938, *FRUS, 1938*, I, 594–96.

12 Henderson to Halifax, September 13, 1938, Halifax to Henderson, September 13, 1938, *DBFP*, Third series, II, 306–307, 314.

risch-Ostrau. Runciman blamed Sudeten extremists for the troubles on September 11, 12, and 13, which led to the breaking off of negotiations.

The Mediator wanted the Czech State Police withdrawn from the Sudetenland—precisely the desire of the Sudeten Nazis. Apparently he did not think that the Sudetens would then resort to violence and murder, which would encourage a German intervention.

Where the Sudetens were in the majority, Runciman advocated immediate transference to Germany. A plebiscite, he thought, would take too much time. In areas where German minorities remained, he advocated a form of autonomy. He would have Czechoslovakia neutralized and guaranteed by the big powers, Great Britain, France, Germany and Italy. Between Germany and Czechoslovakia, an economic treaty should be negotiated.[13]

Runciman lacked any conception of Beneš' problems. The Czech President seemed too clever, too stubborn, too intent on saving his country. Always concessions were required from Beneš, seldom if ever from the Sudetens.

Did he ever suspect that the Sudetens had deliberately tried to overwhelm him with tales of their mistreatment at the hands of the dastardly Czechs? His report intimates no such suspicion. Sudetens had been persecuted because they were Sudetens.

All of the blame must not be carried by Runciman. He was instructed to solve a problem, about which he knew little, within a few weeks. For decades the Hapsburgs had failed to solve the Sudeten problem. Why should a millionaire English shipbuilder succeed where so many had failed? Chamberlain thought he could. The Prime Minister did not realize how the idea of an expert mediator discriminated against the Czechs, nor could he foresee how an English Liberal would grapple with passions carrying Europe to the brink of war.

[13] Runciman to Beneš, September 21, 1938, ibid., 675–79.

# II

## Those Who Waited and Watched

<br>

ATTITUDES, TACTICS, AND POLICIES of other nations all influenced Chamberlain's flight to Hitler. The crisis was not solely a German-Czech quarrel with Britain and France as anguished seconds. Decisions of many nations were important as, one by one, they chose to wait and watch.

Chamberlain's dream of separating Italy from Germany remained unfulfilled. By May, 1938, the intention of Mussolini and Ciano was to remain " 'at order arms' " in a Czech-German war. The Fascist pair proclaimed their loyalty to the Axis, promising assistance and thoroughgoing support.

To *il Duce,* Hitler sent a personal message early in September. Germany must prevent Czechoslovakia from becoming a future threat to Germany, the *Führer* declared. Hitler, while admitting his skepticism over the results of the negotiations between the Czech government and the Sudetens, promised intervention if "intolerable provocation" occurred.

Exhilarated by the confidence bestowed upon him, Mussolini placed his writing talent at Hitler's command. In *Populo d'Italia* Mussolini published an open letter to Runciman declaring that there was no Czechoslovak state. The time was too late for compromise. Plebiscites for all nationalities were the only solution. However, the *Duce* did not mention plebiscites for the German minorities within Italian frontiers.

News of Chamberlain's trip to Germany meant "the liquidation of

English prestige" to *il Duce*. His foreign minister, Count Ciano, swore to remain at Germany's side until the end.

Chamberlain's Italian policy had miscarried. When Count Dino Grandi, the Italian ambassador in London, speaking for Chamberlain, asked Mussolini to intervene and restrain Hitler, the *Duce* replied, "An absurdity of this kind proves that the English are suffering from a displaced uterus."[1]

Hitler could achieve his goals in Central Europe more easily if other nations joined in the assault on Czechoslovakia; German aggression would then seem less obvious. Perhaps France and Great Britain would not criticize if other nations participated in the attack on Czechoslovakia.

When Minister-President Kálmán de Darányi and Foreign Minister Kálmán Kanya of Hungary visited Berlin on November 25, 1937, Hitler indicated where next to turn their attention—Czechoslovakia. The generous *Führer* offered Hungary the eastern half of Czechoslovakia.[2]

When Milan Stoyadinovitch, Yugoslav premier, visited Berlin on January 17, 1938, he promised Hitler never to enter into any pact against Germany. Stoyadinovitch showed sympathy neither for Czechoslovakia nor Austria. They were fair game for Hitler.

On May 4 and 5, when the permanent council of the Little Entente met in Rumania, the Czechoslovak delegate depicted the Little Entente as a force for Hitler to consider. Stoyadinovitch declared, "Germany absolutely desired peace." The Sudeten question was an internal affair, and Czechoslovakia ought to settle the question which could not be a subject for discussion at the meetings of the Council of the Little Entente.[3]

To further weaken the Little Entente, Berlin informed Belgrade and Bucharest that Germany intended to take every necessary measure if Czechoslovakia failed to give complete satisfaction to the Sude-

1 Weizsäcker to Woermann, May 12, 1938, *DG*, Series D, I, 1110; Prince Hesse to *Duce*, August 31, 1938, *ibid.*, II, 671–73; Woermann to Weizsäcker, September 15, 1938, *ibid.*, II, 798–800; *The Ciano Diaries, 1939–1943*, (ed. and translated by Andreas Mayor), 154–56.

2 Memorandum by Meissner, November 25, 1938, *DG*, Series D, V, 200–202; C. A. Macartney, *A History of Hungary, 1929–1945*, I, 203.

3 Fabricus to the German Foreign Ministry, May 6, 1938, *DG*, Series D, V, 274–75.

tens. French intervention would be aggression. Should Czechoslovakia then march, that would also be aggression; the other members of the Little Entente would be free of their obligations.[4]

Late in August, during the state visit to Berlin of Regent Miklós von Nagybánya Horthy, the Hungarian ruler, and his wife, talks with the Nazi masters were stormy. The Germans pressed their guests for support in the war. The Hungarians had to refuse the proffered feast. Although Hitler offered arms, Horthy declined to join the attack. His armies were unprepared and needed more time. Spring would be a better season for war. Horthy dreaded lest British intervention change the conflict into a world war. At this remark, Hitler yelled, "Stupid! Shut up!"

The *Führer* left no doubt of his intention to destroy Czechoslovakia. If the Hungarians wanted to share the prey, they must join the slaughter. He observed, "He who wants to sit at the table must help in the kitchen."[5]

To assuage the Nazi leader's ire, the Hungarian premier promised a German direction-finding station in Hungary to aid German flights over Czechoslovakia. Should German aircraft be forced to land, landing facilities would be offered in Hungary.

Bulgaria strengthened her relationship with Germany through a secret protocol of March 12, 1938. Bulgaria agreed to place orders for thirty million Reichsmarks' worth of war materials. Deliveries would begin within two years, but no payments would be made until 1942.

The May crisis revealed that the official Bulgarian attitude towards the fate of Czechoslovakia was indifference. King Boris III was convinced that Beneš hated Bulgaria; the monarch returned the hatred. Many Bulgarians considered the Czech to be the "Jew of the Slavs." In Bulgaria, Nazi Germany had a good friend.[6]

In the Sudeten-Czech crisis, no country had more to lose than Poland, and no nation thought there was so much to gain. None acted so foolishly as Polish politicians blinded by greed and consumed by hatred. The Franco-Polish treaty was completely bilateral. Both pledged themselves to help if Germany attacked either. Nothing in

---

[4] Shone to Halifax, August 23, 1938, *DBFP*, Third series, II, 135–36.

[5] Macartney, *A History of Hungary*, I, 239–47.

[6] Secret Protocol, Germany and Bulgaria, March 12, 1938, *DG*, Series D, V, 254–55; Rumelin to the German Foreign Ministry, May 31, 1938, *ibid.*, 283–84; Rumelin to the German Foreign Ministry, June 22, 1938, *ibid.*, 286–88.

the alliance related to Czechoslovakia. The Polish government re-membered the Czech seizure of Teschen in 1920 while the Poles were fighting the Bolsheviks. Teschen had been part of the old Duchy of Teschen and the crownlands of Silesia. In July, 1920, the Allied Con-ference of Ambassadors satisfied Czech claims, awarding the western part of the duchy to Czechoslovakia. The memory of this blighted Polish-Czech history and diplomatic relations.

The Teschen area had little strategic value for Poland, but for Czechoslovakia it was a vital communications center. There railway lines crossed from Bohemia to Slovakia. Within Teschen were 120,000 Poles. Bringing them home to Poland would give little help to Poland and seriously cripple Czech unity and security.

Foreign Minister Józef Beck controlled Polish foreign affairs. A close associate of Marshal Józef Pilsudski, Beck became head of the Polish Foreign Office in 1932. A tall, elegant figure, he seemed like something from the Renaissance. Success came to him too soon and too easily; his self-confidence was overpowering and, for him, de-structive.

Beck was cool towards the French arrangements with Poland and Czechoslovakia. He believed that Czechoslovakia would not fight and that Britain and France were unprepared for war. He objected to the Czech alliance with Russia. The Polish minority within Czecho-slovakia was too tempting, and Beck deliberately aided this group, educating and organizing them against Czechoslovakia.

Beck saw the Czech crisis as a struggle between two axes, Rome-Berlin and Paris-London. Poland would not adhere to either bloc. Too positive an attitude toward Czechoslovakia could harm relations with Germany. Early in May, when Paris asked for help, Ambassador Juljusy Lukasiewicz was instructed to say that the Polish attitude towards Czechoslovakia would be dictated by security questions: Poland had no desire to give Czechoslovakia a military guarantee. Poland would not take the initiative in the crisis because of the Czech treatment of the Polish minority.[7]

During the May crisis, Bonnet asked Beck to make demands on Ger-many similar to those made by Britain and France. The elegant Pole refused because such a condition was not within the terms of the

7 Supreme Headquarters, *Wehrmacht*, to the German Foreign Ministry, May 17, 1938, *ibid.*, II, 208–81; Jean Szembek, *Journal, 1933–1939*, 309.

Franco-Polish alliance. For Czechoslovakia there would be no support while the Polish minority suffered brutal treatment at the hands of the Czechs. Czechoslovakia would soon disappear.[8]

French Ambassador Léon Noël was instructed to ascertain the opinions of Marshal Edward Śmigly-Rydz, the Polish commander in chief, who had promised General Gamelin in 1936 that Poland would never oppose France. When asked on June 3, 1938, if Poland would oppose France, the Marshal could not imagine what could produce such a situation. To Noël, the Marshal gave the impression that Poland would be neutral toward Germany in a world war. When she was certain of the outcome, she would join the side offering her the most plunder.[9]

In July, Beck refused to promise in writing that he would abide by Article 16 of the Covenant of the League of Nations. He admitted to Ambassador Noël that "the fate of Czechoslovakia leaves us cold."[10]

The Runciman mission offered new opportunities for Beck's mischief-making. There must be no discrimination in the treatment of the Polish and Sudeten minorities, he informed British representatives. Runciman must investigate the claims of Poles within Czechoslovakia that they were being mistreated.

As the crisis deepened in September, Bonnet tried once more to remind Śmigly-Rydz of promises made in 1936 to Gamelin. In 1938, Śmigly-Rydz had a different version. He had sworn to aid France if she were attacked by Germany. Because such was not the case now, Poland could do as she wished.[11]

The question of Russian passage through Poland to aid Czechoslovakia under the terms of their alliance brought vows of resistance from the Polish government. Russian troops and planes crossing Poland to aid Czechoslovakia meant a declaration of war. Flights of Russian planes for Czechoslovakia in the spring did not bring a declaration of war although Polish fighter planes failed to shoot them down.

The Polish government was reluctant to invite Russian troops into lands once a part of the Russian Empire. Polish military opinion

---

8 Bonnet, *Défense de la paix*, I, 132–43.

9 *Ibid.*, 138–40; Kennard to Halifax, June 4, 1938, *DBFP*, Third series, I, 444–45.

10 Szembek, *Journal*, 324.

11 Bonnet, *Défense de la paix*, I, 204–205.

judged Russia weak. The purges indicated that the nation soon would be rent asunder.[12]

Rumania was not hostile towards Czechoslovakia. Membership in the Little Entente made the nation more friendly. Lack of a minority problem prevented the bitterness that marred relations with other neighbors of Czechoslovakia.

During the May crisis, King Carol II informed Beneš that Rumania would not intervene unless there were a Czech-German conflict. Rumania would march only if Hungary attacked or a world war broke out, compelling intervention through the League Covenant.

Rumanian relations with Germany during the summer were somewhat altered by oil. Germany desperately needed to obtain oil for her air fleets. No scheduled deliveries from the Rumanian oil fields were planned until 1939. To secure the release of oil ahead of schedule, Germany offered twenty-seven 37-mm. antiaircraft guns in July. Rumania agreed in August to release 8,600,000 Reichsmarks' worth of oil or grain. Germany gladly took 60 per cent in oil immediately.[13]

The question of Russian aid to Czechoslovakia was of supreme importance to Rumania. In the spring and summer of 1938, rumors about Rumania's offering passage to Russian troops were common. German diplomats were hard put to keep up with the latest of these.

Some thirty-five Russian planes consigned to Czechoslovakia were flown over Rumania during the spring, unarmed and piloted by Czech crews. The story of the flight brought forth a protest from Beck. Because of Polish pressure, King Carol ordered an attack on future flights of such aircraft, although Rumania lacked the antiaircraft artillery to hit the Russian planes.

Beck forced the Rumanian government to forbid the passage of Russian troops. Nicolae Comnen, the Rumanian foreign minister, promised not to allow a single Russian soldier to pass. If Russia attempted to move through Rumania, the treaty with Poland would go into effect.

The Rumanian attitude was colored by fear that Russian troops, passing through, might forget to leave. Russia claimed Bessarabia and never recognized Rumanian annexation. From a practical point

[12] Kennard to Halifax, June 14, 1938, *DBFP*, Third series, I, 481–84.

[13] Fabricus to the German Foreign Ministry, July 15, August 16, 1938, *DG*, Series D, V, 289–90, 298.

of view, the rail and road connections between Rumania and Russia were not of the best.

Rumania and Czechoslovakia negotiated in late August over the passage of one hundred thousand Russian troops in civilian clothes. The discussions came to nought. Rumania permitted some unarmed Russian planes, without photographic equipment, to fly over late in the summer.

Early in September, Comnen assured the German chargé that no negotiations were in progress with Russia about transporting troops across Rumania. The Foreign Minister explained that Rumania lacked proper facilities to transport Russians through Bessarabia. If a German-Czech war broke out, he expected a world war to follow, benefiting "Bolshevism and international Jewry."[14]

Of the countries who watched the drama in Czechoslovakia, none's reactions were so puzzling as those of the Soviet Union, but the attitude of the Soviet leaders was not so mysterious as it was shrewd and self-seeking. Stalin was convinced that Chamberlain labored to strengthen Germany for the purpose of turning the Nazi armies loose on Russia, but he believed the Prime Minister would fail. According to the Premier, Russia was prepared to stand and defend herself. From the beginning of the crisis, isolation was not forced on Russia but sought by her leaders.[15]

Despite a Russo-Czech alliance, by 1938 there had been no joint military planning. The Czech general staff had lost confidence in the Russian army after the 1937 purge of high army officers, including Marshal Mikhail Nikolaevich Tukhachevski. Soviet charges that the purged were leagued with Nazis and Fascists rendered them suspect to nervous allies. Fearful lest Russian generals might again reveal military information, in January, 1938, the Czechoslovak general staff rejected a Soviet proposal for a joint commission to study defense planning. Such a policy seemed wise the next month when the purgers turned on the Russian navy.

Beneš admitted that military collaboration was needed, but on his own initiative he would do nothing. French permission was necessary. Coulondre, the French ambassador, received permission in May, 1938,

14 Stelzer to the German Foreign Ministry, September 6, 1938, *ibid.*, II, 701.
15 Davies to Hull, June 9, 1938, *FRUS, Soviet Union 1933–1939,* 572.

to take up the question of Franco-Russian military collaboration. He hoped to arrange Czech-French, Czech-Soviet, and French-Soviet discussions. Neither Daladier nor Bonnet showed enthusiasm over the project, fearing domestic political repercussions. Coulondre insisted that this was the only way to assess the value of Russian help. Krofta welcomed this initiative, But Czechoslovakia could do nothing without French permission. If France were silent, Czechoslovakia must be silent. Now that France had spoken, Czechoslovakia would be happy to follow her lead.

Nothing further was heard on the question. The French government feared the reaction of British Conservatives towards aid. Chamberlain's supporters could undermine support for France, leaving France alone with Czechoslovakia and Russia. This thought must have chilled the bourgeois souls of the French politicians. They gave up any thought of military planning, hoping that by summer Runciman could extract them from their dilemma.[16]

The Russian position toward Czechoslovakia seldom varied. Russia would fulfill her treaty obligations to the letter. President Mikhail Kalinin so informed a delegation from Czechoslovakia who were visiting Moscow for the May Day celebration. On May 12, Maxim Litvinov, the commissar for foreign affairs, told Bonnet a similar tale. Bonnet reminded him of the lack of a common frontier with Czechoslovakia. Litvinov shoved the problem back to Bonnet. Russia would not march through Poland and Rumania. France had agreements with them; she ought to find a way across. Furthermore, this was a military affair, and Litvinov was a civilian. Bonnet asked for contacts with the French chargé in Moscow. Litvinov reminded him there could not be discussion of these affairs because in Moscow there were no representatives of the French and Czech general staffs.[17] Kalinin and Litvinov knew that the alliance depended on prior French action. The harder France tried to evade this action, the harder the Soviet leaders could claim that they were standing by their treaty.

By mid-August Russia still publicly trumpeted her intentions to

[16] Memorandum of Alexandrovsky, May 30, 1938, *NDM*, 46–47; Coulondre, *De Staline à Hitler*, 142–46, 153; *Les événements survenus en France de 1933 & 1945*, V, 199; German Foreign Ministry to the German Embassy in the Soviet Union, March 14, 1938, *DG*, Series D, II, 164–65.

[17] Litvinov to Alexandrovsky, May 25, 1938, *NDM*, 39–42; Bonnet, *Défense de la paix*, I, 124–26.

fulfill the treaty with Czechoslovakia to the letter in a war with Germany, provided France had first gone to war. If France did not move, Russia had no obligations to fulfill. Soviet politicians could bluff and bluster, secure in the knowledge that they did not have to move until France marched.

With the Germans, Litvinov became more coy. He explained that the Sudeten problem was an internal Czech affair. The Soviet Union had not interfered nor given advice in the question and would not do so in the future. Litvinov declared to Count Werner von der Schulenburg, the German ambassador, that the Soviet Union had no responsibility for the creation and composition of the Czechoslovak state. That had been done in the Paris Peace Conference which the Soviet Union had not attended. Let the creators of Czechoslovakia protect her: the affair was not for the Soviet Union. Litvinov constantly dodged Schulenburg's question of the form of Russian aid to Czechoslovakia.

Schulenburg and his military attachés were intrigued by Litvinov's evasions. Their study led them to conclude that the Soviet Union would hold back in a German-Czech war and would not attack Germany, although Russia would attempt to stir up trouble against Germany while granting aid to Czechoslovakia. Schulenburg's colleagues were agreed that the Soviet Union would do as little as possible in the war, keeping her army intact. Only Russia would gain in a war.[18]

For Germany the omens were excellent. When the May crisis broke, Russia refrained from announcing her attitude until May 26. Then danger of war had passed. Indications were clear to Nazi diplomats that Russia would not commit herself in a Czech-German war. They noticed Soviet reluctance to give precise announcements on fulfilling the alliance with Czechoslovakia. Schulenburg believed that Russia would remain apart in the crisis, using geography, internal problems, and fear of a two-front war—there had been some fighting in Manchuria against Japanese troops—as excuses.

By the end of the May crisis, Berlin was certain that Russia need not be feared. "Russia hardly exists in our calculations today," Weizsäcker wrote.[19]

[18] Schulenburg to Woermann, August 22, 23, 26, 1938, *DG*, Series D, II, 601–602. 604–605, 629–31.

[19] Weizsäcker to Trautmann, May 30, 1938, *ibid.*, I, 864.

In Britain there was no enthusiasm for the Russian connection. Chamberlain made no secret of his dislike of the Soviet Union and of his conclusion that the purges had weakened Soviet strength. Halifax feared lest war leave the Soviet Union in control of Central Europe. Both men dreaded a split in the Conservative party resulting from close collaboration with Russia. These opinions were duly reported in Berlin.

Surfeited by Russian demands that France be firmer in her dealings with Germany, Bonnet asked Jakob Suritz, the Russian ambassador, "what help the Soviets would give in case of a German attack on Czechoslovakia." The ambassador sought the answer from Litvinov.

Bonnet instructed Coulondre to ask the question in Moscow, because military information indicated German use of force against Czechoslovakia in September. Considering that Poland and Rumania had refused their help, how would Russia aid Czechoslovakia?

When the French chargé, Jean Payart, called for an answer on September 2, Litvinov reminded him that France was obligated to Czechoslovakia irrespective of Russian aid. Soviet help was conditional on prior French aid to Czechoslovakia. Once this condition had been filled, Russia would bring all aid to bear. As for Poland and Rumania, their objections could be overcome by working through the League of Nations under Article 2 of the Covenant. Payart doubted that unanimity could be attained in Geneva. Litvinov brushed this problem aside, contending that "even a decision of the majority would have a great moral effect."

The Foreign Commissar refused to contemplate any offers of concrete help to Czechoslovakia without a meeting of representatives of the armies. Czechoslovakia could not be defended otherwise. Yet Litvinov argued for a three-power declaration on Czechoslovakia, even with the support of the United States.[20]

Despite a return visit on September 5 to clarify some points, Payart failed to obtain an answer to his original question: how would Russia aid Czechoslovakia, given the attitudes of the Polish and Rumanian governments? Instead, Litvinov had thrown in new procedures: League of Nations, joint staff consultations, and three-power talks with the adhesion of the United States—something that was completely impossible.

Coulondre, having returned from his vacation, visited the Soviet

20 Litvinov to Alexandrovsky, September 2, 1938, *NDM*, 62–63.

Foreign Ministry in hopes of clarifying the meaning of the answer given Payart's question. The ambassador hoped for a concrete statement that would demonstrate Russian willingness to help Czechoslovakia. Vladimir Potemkin, deputy commissar for foreign affairs, would only repeat Litvinov's phrases about an appeal to the League of Nations, a three-power conference, and consultation of the military staff before the Soviet Union would fulfill her obligations to Czechoslovakia—and then she would only be willing if France first went to war. The sequence of this reply indicated Soviet feeling: the last thing desired was a fulfillment of the alliance.[21]

At the September meeting of the League of Nations, Bonnet conferred with Comnen, the Rumanian foreign minister. The Rumanian government would not authorize passage of Russian troops. A decision of the League of Nations would not produce any change. Comnen saw no point in further discussions because there was no practical way for Russia to cross Rumania. Rumania lacked direct rail connections, and travel by road would be too time-consuming. He feared that Russia only desired Bessarabia. If Russian planes flew over, they could not be stopped. Bonnet did not press the matter, apparently asking the questions only for the record. Comnen's statements gave Bonnet ammunition to use against those in Paris who counseled resistance to Germany over the Sudeten question.[22]

Bonnet consulted also with Litvinov, whose opinion was little changed. The Commissar wanted an appeal to the League of Nations to facilitate passage of Russian troops through Rumania. Litvinov reminded Bonnet that France must first aid Czechoslovakia. Bonnet countered that the procedure of working through the League of Nations was too lengthy and the outcome too uncertain. Would the League Council act in time? Could the Council persuade Rumania to let the Russians pass? Litvinov retorted that Soviet troops would not cross Rumanian frontiers without the assent of the Rumanian government.[23]

21 Potemkin memorandum, September 11, 1938, *ibid.*, 70–73; Coulondre, *De Staline à Hitler*, 157.

22 Bonnet, *Défense de la paix*, I, 201–202; Celovsky, *Der Münchener Abkommen*, 322–23.

23 Bonnet, *Défense de la paix*, I, 199–201; Celovsky, *Der Münchener Abkommen*, 324. Unfortunately the only full record of this conversation comes from Bonnet.

Bonnet returned to Paris with sad tidings. Russia would help only after discussions and meetings had opened the way through Rumania. Poland seemed determined to prevent the passing of Russian troops through Rumania. While the negotiations continued, French troops would fight: French women and children would die, while the Russians debated in Geneva.

Bonnet was not too unhappy, because he did not want war. Russian involvement would guarantee a world war. There was no certainty that Russia was a worthy ally. Litvinov never gave a direct answer to the original question of Russian aid to Czechoslovakia but only erected additional barriers to intervention.

By September 14, French prospects of an alliance were discouraging: too many waited and watched. Russia was legalistic; Poland and Rumania were defiant; Britain was reluctant. Within France few burned with a zeal to keep the Sudetens within Czechoslovakia. It was no surprise that the French government eagerly grasped at Chamberlain's plan to fly to meet Hitler on September 15.

# 12

## Armies and Plans

WHILE RUNCIMAN PLAYED out his futile role in Prague, German war preparations increased until they could not be hidden. These preparations were a mighty impetus for Chamberlain's trip to Hitler.

Because the May crisis indicated Anglo-French participation in a German-Czech war, further directives for the German forces were necessary. *Operation Red,* involving the *Luftwaffe* in the west, was announced on June 2, 1938. According to this directive, France was expected either to interfere during *Operation Green* or begin fighting immediately in conjunction with Czechoslovakia. British intervention was expected. The *Luftwaffe* would co-ordinate with the army against Czechoslovakia because of the strength of the Czech fortifications and the need for a quick victory. Until more forces were available, war in the west would be limited to denying France freedom of the air. There were no plans for wholesale bombings of French cities, as many feared. During the campaign, if more strength could be transferred to the west, planes would be used on French airfields—not French cities, not the R.A.F., and not on British cities. These were to be spared because Germany lacked high-level, long-range bombers.

By June 18 a new directive from the German High Command showed the effects of Anglo-French diplomacy. "There is no danger of a preventative war by foreign states against Germany," declared the authors of the directive, Lieutenant Colonel Kurt Zeitzler and General Wilhelm Keitel. Hitler would take action against Czecho-

115

slovakia if he were convinced that Britain and France would not interfere. Nevertheless, should they intervene during *Operation Green,* the main blow would still be thrown at Czechoslovakia. In the west, the fortifications would be held until *Operation Green* was concluded.[1]

By August 1 military activities were so great that the German War Office had to admit their existence. They informed the British military attaché that eight divisions would be up to war strength in September. Training exercises would be carried out in the Fifth Army Group in Austria. Reservists would stay on active service four additional weeks after October 1. By August 4 all members of foreign military forces were barred from the western fortifications of Germany.

Henderson reported that in the areas bordering Czechoslovakia, nearly full mobilization was completed. To a limited degree, the entire mobilization machinery was in motion throughout Germany. Additional reservists were called to the colors for training beginning August 15. Members of labor battalions were sent to labor on the western fortifications. The German government excused these activities on the grounds that it was necessary to train entire units of reserves as France had recently done. But practice mobilization could appear provocative to the Czech General Staff, already prone to mobilize for war.[2]

Halifax and Chamberlain, alarmed by reports from Berlin, drew up a memorandum to be sent to Hitler. They begged him to alter military measures lest the Runciman mission be destroyed by the subsequent developments. They referred to the completion of the western fortifications and the mobilizing of German forces, particularly along the Czechoslovak frontier. If the Czechs considered these measures threatening, they might mobilize. Into the Sudetenland would march German troops, a French declaration of war would follow, and French help for Czechoslovakia would bring a German attack in the West.

Following instructions on August 12, Henderson brought the memorandum to Hitler's Reichschancery office. The *Führer* would receive the memorandum the following day. Next the ambassador left a copy

---

[1] *Operation Red,* June 2, 1938, *DG,* Series D, II, 379–83, General Strategic Directive, June 18, 1938, *ibid.,* 379–83, 473–77.

[2] Henderson to Halifax, August 1, 3, 4, 5, 1938, *DBFP,* Third series, II, 26, 27, 41–45, 47–48.

at the Foreign Office, where it was rejected. Henderson failed to see how a communication for the *Führer* could be rejected. Woermann, undersecretary of state, filled with protocol, condemned the memorandum as "contrary to diplomatic usage." A flabbergasted British ambassador could only argue that it was in reply to the Weidemann mission.

German confusion increased after study of the memorandum. Henderson erred by presenting an exact copy of the memorandum, including the title: "Memorandum to His Majesty's Ambassador, Berlin." A close reading of the memorandum revealed that it was intended for Hitler, not for Henderson, and it came not from the British Foreign Secretary but jointly from the British Foreign Secretary and the British Prime Minister. The form was not that of a proper diplomatic note but a personal, man-to-man, appeal to change military measures. Protocol suffered because Henderson failed to deliver the note via the Foreign Office and went first to the Reichschancery; for this error Woermann gave him a suitable scolding. In London, the Foreign Office received similar reproof. When the memorandum at last reached Hitler, he refused to take the desired action. Germany would continue preparing for war.[3]

Halifax requested that Henderson tell German officials that the French government must be informed of the memorandum. The instructions terrified Henderson. Any hint of the memorandum would make it impossible for Hitler to change the military measures. Perhaps if they said nothing, Hitler might heed their advice. "I do not believe that he wants war or that sort of a situation in which it is forced on him." Hitler wanted peace; he had not yet made up his mind for war. This was not the time to lecture him or threaten him. Only those who wanted war would profit: "German and Czech extremists, Communists and other influences and the universal hatred abroad of Nazism." Overwhelmed by Henderson's protests, Halifax promised to say nothing unless the French inquired.[4]

[3] Halifax to Henderson August 11, 1938, *ibid.*, 78–80; Henderson to Halifax, August 13, 1938, *ibid.*, 97–98; minutes of Woermann, August 12, 13, 1938, *DG*, Series D, II, 551–54; unsigned note for Foreign Minister, August 12, 1938, *ibid.*, 560–62; German Foreign Minister to the German Embassy in London, August 14, 1938, *ibid.*, 564–66.

[4] Henderson to Halifax, August 15, 18, 19, 1938, *DBFP*, Third series, II, 97–98, 108–109, 116, 118.

As August passed, British military intelligence discovered signs of more than a practice mobilization. Men of military age were refused permission to leave Germany for Italy. Women shop assistants were ordered to report to the Labor Office for emergency duty. Work on the western fortifications was accelerated. Military traffic from Bavaria to Austria increased abnormally. The Ministry of War refused to answer any further questions of the British military attaché.

By August 21, Henderson had a new tale. At a recent council of his generals, Hitler announced his decision to attack Czechoslovakia at the end of September. Mobilization would be completed by September 15. The main thrust into Czechoslovakia would come from Austria. Because of their lack of war preparations, Britain and France would not intervene. Hitler hoped for a short war, but the population feared a catastrophe. Intervention by Great Britain and France, reported the informant, would "bring the downfall of the regime." Henderson viewed the possibility of Anglo-French intervention as "largely propaganda." However, he admitted that perhaps the remainder of the information should be taken seriously. The puzzled ambassador scarcely imagined how extremely accurate some of his information was.

By August 25 a complete test mobilization seemed underway. Reservists were called up in Bavaria, Saxony, Hesse, Brandenburg, Pomerania, and Austria. By the end of August, twenty-one reserve divisions would be up to full strength. None would be discharged before the end of the Sudeten crisis. As the reservists joined their units, the German War Ministry gave less information. News was scarce from Silesia and Austria where the concentration for an attack on Czechoslovakia would begin.

By the second week in September, London learned of more widespread troop movements. Industry was operating under wartime conditions. Railways were too crowded to accept commercial traffic. Twelve divisions toiled on the western fortifications. Two hundred thousand troops were concentrated within fifty miles of the Czech frontier, and motorized units were within one hundred miles of that same border.

Ambassador François-Poncet reported on July 19 that Hitler had ordered the army to be ready for immediate mobilization by August. A month later, the French ambassador observed that Germany already had the look of war. Workers labored in the fortifications. Food supplies in the west were transferred into the interior; supply depots were created; inventories were made of critical materials.

In mid-August, General Joseph Vuillemin, chief of the French air staff, came to Germany. His hosts graciously showed him the military sights. Their revelations shook him. To Paris, he reported that all French aviation could be destroyed within two weeks. The *Luftwaffe* was superior to the French air force in every category. If war came, he advocated using mediocre pilots while keeping the better ones for the new planes, yet to be constructed.

Vuillemin's frightening report confirmed the fears of Bonnet. He hastened to inquire of General Maurice Gamelin, chief of staff, what counter measures he was taking. Solemnly the General declared: "Our whole system is ready, and it is only necessary to press a button to unleash it."[5]

Lieutenant Colonel Henri Gauché, chief of French military intelligence, was convinced that the German army was actually mobilizing. His sources informed him that men were being replaced by women in factories. All signs indicated that Germany was preparing for immediate war.

At last the French army began to move. Reserve units were called up by September 9. Troops, finishing their training in September, were ordered to stay with the colors. Men who had just completed their training in the Maginot Line were recalled to active service. On September 11, Gamelin informed the German military attaché of his order banning leaves. The General explained that reservists were being recalled and the first emergency measures taken. If Germany took additional steps, so would France.

What of Gamelin's plans? Daladier questioned him on the subject on September 12. The Premier was interested in the method by which help would go to Czechoslovakia. Solemnly the General asked for confidence in final victory because Germany would not be defeated before Czechoslovakia lost most of her territory. The restoration of the conquered Czechs would depend on the peace treaty. Gamelin proposed to wear down the Germans by frontal attacks between the Rhine and the Moselle. It would be a repetition of the campaign along the Somme in 1916 when Sir Douglas Haig lost twenty thousand men before lunch on July 1. Gamelin expected little help initially from Russia. Daladier interrupted to remind Gamelin of the

[5] Gamelin, *Servir*, II, 341.

expected heavy air attacks on French cities, particularly Paris.[6] Prospects of such slaughter made the French government reluctant to engage in another war with Germany. The generals could offer only bloody frontal attacks while the Luftwaffe dominated the skies. Czechoslovakia could not be protected from invasion. No other country would stand resolutely beside France. Why then oppose a solution of the Sudeten question based on self-determination? Daily the desire increased to avoid an unnecessary war. Hourly a desire grew to make concessions and to force them on Czechoslovakia. These desires were swiftly reported in Berlin.

While Western leaders fretted, Germany prepared for war. Early in August the Germans began to reconnoiter potential landing fields in the Sudetenland. Orders were sent out to antiaircraft batteries to fire on Czech aircraft flying over Germany.

For two days Hitler consulted with his generals and found some cool to the idea of war. General Gustav Anton von Wietersheim feared that the west wall could only hold out for three weeks. Hitler retorted that it would hold for three years. Clearly Hitler intended to settle the Sudeten affair without military interference from the British and the French. He had learned of French reluctance to fight for Czechoslovakia. Early in August he knew of the British intentions. Henderson declared publicly that Britain would not risk one sailor or airman for Czechoslovakia; any reasonable solution would be accepted. From the Runciman mission, Hitler learned of British reluctance to use force.[7]

By August 30, Hitler and his generals had agreed on the timing of X-Day. The army needed three days' warning before the invasion began. The armed forces had to know well in advance of X-day in order to camouflage their advance measures. An incident would set Operation Green in motion, and there must not be any conspicuous departure of Reich Germans from Czechoslovakia before the incident. After the incident, the swiftest possible action must follow. There would not even be time to warn diplomats in Prague.

6 Bonnet, Défense de la paix, I, 176–80, 225; Gamelin, Servir, II, 341–42, 344–47; Campbell to Halifax, August 30, 1938, DBFP, Third series, II, 190–91; Bräuer to the German Foreign Ministry, September 11, 14, 1938, DG, Series D, II, 740–41, 762–63.

7 Memorandum of Heyden-Rynsch, August 6, 1938, ibid., 536.

On September 3 the *Führer* conferred at the Berghof with General Walther von Brauchitsch, commander in chief of the army, and Keitel. Brauchitsch reported that by September 28 combat units would be ready for the incident. Once X-Day was known, divisions concentrated for maneuvers would swing towards Czechoslovakia.

When Brauchitsch brought up the basic plan for invasion, Hitler was unhappy. As proposed by the general staff, the Second Army in Silesia, commanded by General Gerd von Rundstedt would invade Czechoslovakia from the north. From the south, the Fourteenth Army under General Wilhelm List, would strike north from Vienna, joining up with the Second Army inside Czechoslovakia. The Tenth Army under General Walther von Reichenau, concentrated north of Nuremburg, would move east while the Twelfth Army under General Wilhelm von Leeb would strike north towards Prague. On the western front, an Army group under General Wilhelm Adam would hold off the Anglo-French armies. In this group were the First Army under General Ludwig Beck, defending the Rhineland; the Fifth Army under General Curt Liebmann, watching the Low Countries; and the Seventh Army in the south along the Rhine, under General Seutter von Lötzen. The Third Army under General Georg von Küchler in East Prussia would keep watch over Poland, along with the Fourth Army under General Kurt von Hammerstein in Pomerania. In the air the *Luftwaffe* would turn all its planes against Czechoslovakia, leaving only a thin defense in the west.

Hitler insisted that the Czechs would stop the Second Army, under von Runstedt, and a second Verdun would follow. This was Hitler's nightmare. The Fourteenth Army coming from the north would be too slow. Opposite the Tenth Army on the western frontier of Czechoslovakia were few concrete fortifications. He decided to increase the motorized units in this army to give it more punch. When joined with the Twelfth Army, it would be too strong for another Verdun.

The *Führer* issued orders to further strengthen the western fortifications and increase the artillery facing the Maginot Line. Before the day ended, Hitler decreed a complete blackout on all military information for foreign military attachés within Germany.[8]

The argument over planning continued. Another conference came on September 9 and 10, at Nuremberg. Speaking for the generals, Franz Halder explained *Operation Green* as planned. The main effort

[8] Notes by Schmundt, September 3, 1938, *ibid.*, 686–87.

Reproduction of map showing the German plan for
the invasion of Czechoslovakia.

was still contemplated in the Second Army area because the Austrian Frontier was expected to be held more strongly. There the Twelfth and Fourteenth armies must co-operate to prevent the creation of a redoubt in Bohemia and Moravia; the Fourteenth Army would link up with the Second Army in a pincers movement. Strong fortifications and poor roads would hamper the Tenth Army.

Hitler rejected the argument. He considered the area facing the Second Army so important that the Czechs must have reinforced it since March, 1938. The pincer movement with the Fourteenth Army was good, but he detected uncertainty about success. An attack, partially successful, was his great fear. Should the pincers fail, the Tenth and Twelfth armies would smash through to Prague. If both succeeded, Hitler prophesied the end of Czechoslovakia.

Hitler ordered the strengthening of the Tenth Army with motorized divisions taken from the Second and Twelfth armies. The Generals accepted the former Austrian corporal's plan.[9]

Hitler's plans were not perfected without opposition. General Ludwig Beck, army chief of staff, had welcomed Hitler's coming to power. By 1938, Hitler's tactics with the army and his foreign policy were alarming to Beck. In a series of memoranda, the chief of staff protested against a war at that time. While admitting that Czechoslovakia needed to be reduced in size, Beck feared Britain and France, supported by Russia and the United States of America. Germany was isolated and could not hold the western front against the French who would have three times as many divisions on the front line five days after the beginning of the war. The German army would not be ready until 1941.

Beck proposed that the generals stage a *coup d'état* against those who had Hitler's ear. Beck would keep Hitler in office but reform the nation. At a meeting of the generals on August 4, Beck presented his views; he appeared to have their agreement, but most of these generals feared Hitler, who had given them jobs, prestige, and higher pay. There was no decision for action. Through von Brauchitsch, Hitler learned of Beck's actions. His position in the army was weakened. Hitler began to by-pass him; there was no relenting in Hitler's drive for war. Beck resigned on August 18.

Only General Adam loudly opposed *Operation Green*. A Bavarian, one of the senior generals in the army, Adam was not beloved of the

---

9 Notes by Schmundt, September 9–10, 1938, *ibid.,* 727–30.

Nazis. When the command of the western front was entrusted to him, he found little there to cheer his spirits, judging the fortifications so weak that the French could easily break through. The aged general did not shrink from informing Hitler of these weaknesses when the *Führer* toured the western fortifications in late August. Criticism of one of Hitler's pet projects brought only scorn. At the end of the tour, Hitler sneered: "The man who does not hold these fortifications is a scoundrel." To General Adam he declared: "I only regret that I am the *Führer* and Reichschancellor and cannot be the supreme commander on the western front!"[10]

Chamberlain and the British Foreign Office were not in complete ignorance of the objections of German army officers to war. A man who called himself Herr von Kleist came to London by plane August 18 as an emissary of the moderates among the German generals and sought to obtain information to convince Hitler that Britain would intervene if Germany attacked Czechoslovakia. Ewald von Kleist was a member of the old pre-Hitler Conservative party, a gentleman, and an old opponent of Hitler. Von Kleist came as one "with a rope around his neck" to warn Britain.

In his talks with Vansittart and Sir Winston Churchill, von Kleist reported that war was certain. Hitler alone had made the decision without pushing from extremist Nazis. Without exception all the generals opposed war. Before they were forced to march they needed help and encouragement from outside Germany. War could be stopped by September 15. Von Kleist wanted to check Hitler by calling his bluff: Great Britain would intervene. Chamberlain's statement of March 24 was not enough. Through speeches British statesmen should appeal to those in Germany who opposed war, stressing the possible horrors and bloodshed. Once the generals resisted, the Nazi government would fall within forty-eight hours.

Churchill gave von Kleist a letter warning that a crossing of the Czechoslovak frontier would bring world war with Britain marching with France. Once begun, Churchill prophesied a long and bloody struggle. He reminded von Kleist of the March 24 statement of the Prime Minister in the House of Commons. Von Kleist returned to

10 Jodl Diary, in *The Trials of the Major War Criminals Before the International Military Tribunal, Proceedings and Documents* (hereafter cited as *TMWC*), XXVIII, 375.

Germany on August 23 without seeing either Halifax or Chamberlain. The letter from Churchill came to rest in the files of the German Foreign Ministry. On September 2 another emissary, Lieutenant Colonel Hans Böhm-Tellelbach, came from the generals. He talked with Vansittart and the head of the press department of the Foreign Office, repeating the warnings of von Kleist with little effect.

Chamberlain saw Vansittart's account of the meeting with von Kleist, who reminded the Prime Minister of Jacobites at the Court of Louis XIV, intriguing to bring war between France and England. "I think we must discount a good deal of what he says," Chamberlain wrote, still believing that Hitler had not yet made up his mind on war. But the Prime Minister wondered if there was some truth in von Kleist's story.[11]

Von Kleist's trip did provide one warning, if it might be so described, from Sir John Simon, chancellor of the exchequer, speaking on August 27 at New Lanark. Simon was not averse to peace with nations of differing political systems. War was not inevitable, and all nations ought to strive to remove the causes of war. The government was toiling to strengthen "the foundations of peace" and to achieve "the adoption of argument and reason in the settlement of international differences," but where British interests were involved, the nation and the Empire would fight. Simon reminded his hearers of the statement of the Prime Minister on March 24 regarding Czechoslovakia. There was nothing to add. The British government was convinced that given goodwill on both sides, a peaceful solution could be found to the Czechoslovak-Sudeten quarrel.[12]

A last attempt to get through to Chamberlain came from Theodor Kordt, counselor of the German Embassy in London, and a member of the group in the German Foreign Ministry who were cool towards Hitler's brashness and timing, but not his goals. Horace Wilson was so impressed by the revelations that he hurried Kordt through a garden door to No. 10 Downing Street where he talked with Halifax on September 7. Those for whom Kordt spoke believed a clear state-

[11] John W. Wheeler-Bennett, *The Nemesis of Power: The German Army in Politics, 1918–1945*, 410–14; memorandum of Vansittart, August 18, 1938, *DBFP*, Third series, II, 683–86; Chamberlain to Halifax, August 19, 1938, *ibid.*, 686–87; Churchill's conversation, *ibid.*, 687–88; Churchill to von Kleist, August 19, 1938, *ibid.*, 688–89.

[12] Halifax to Newton, August 27, 1938, *ibid.*, 172–75.

ment by Sir Edward Grey in July 1914 would have had great influence on the Imperial German government. A public announcement that an attack on Czechoslovakia would make war with Britain inevitable would stop Hitler and Ribbentrop. Should Hitler persist in seeking war, the generals would oppose him with force. Halifax politely agreed with Kordt that war over the Sudetenland would be a crime and promised to inform Chamberlain, but already the Prime Minister was thinking about flying to meet Hitler and personally learn his terms.[13]

Chamberlain was wise to treat the generals' tales with care. The German army had never opposed Hitler. One of its leaders, Kurt von Schleicher, had considered helping Hitler to power. Could this be an attempt to lower Britain's guard?

These generals objected to war only because they felt unprepared. Assuming strong Anglo-French intervention, their position seemed hopeless. Fully prepared, they would face any foe. They did not dislike war; they feared defeat; they had no objection if victory were certain. They had no qualms about attacking Czechoslovakia for territory that had never been German. A victorious war would further their careers; defeat meant another Versailles Treaty or worse if Britain and France attacked from the west. The generals were ignorant of the diplomatic information coming to Hitler, indicating that Britain and France had no wish to march on Germany.

Theodor Kordt and his brother Erich, who was close to Weizsäcker, were of a similar opinion. Weizsäcker tried, in a halfhearted way, to convince Ribbentrop that war should be postponed while economic penetration brought Czechoslovakia under Hitler's control. Ribbentrop disdained the idea. They also objected to Hitler's methods but not his goals, preferring a bloodless *coup d'état* in the fashion of the *Anschluss*.

For Chamberlain to have entrusted the security of Great Britain and France to these men was folly. What guarantee had he that, upon the issuance of a declaration to fight, German generals would leap to overthrow Hitler? Would a handful of German diplomats, whispering in corners, emerge heroic German leaders? Could Britain and France threaten war and expect a coup of Hitler's generals to save them? Why must Britain and France do Germany's work? Let the German generals and diplomats overthrow their beloved *Führer*.

13 Erich Kordt, *Nicht aus den Akten*, 280–81.

126

Suppose Chamberlain threatened war and the generals' revolt was quashed or they failed to revolt? Could he take such a risk? What guarantee had he that German generals would overthrow their paymaster? Could Chamberlain risk war merely on the word of Germans who had followed their *Führer* devotedly for five years? For a businessman of Chamberlain's training, the answer was plain: the security of Great Britain and the peace of the world could not depend on the word of such men.

As Chamberlain's plane flew toward Munich on September 15, the German armies continued their final preparations for war. If the conference with Hitler failed, the armies would strike on X-Day. Hitler was prepared for war, a handful of generals notwithstanding: Neville Chamberlain could not call the *Führer's* bluff, because Great Britain and France were unprepared.

# 13

## The Ides of September

CHAMBERLAIN'S DECISION to fly to Germany was the result, not of panic, but of thought based on available information. All signs indicated Hitler's resolve to seize Czechoslovakia by force, if necessary, unless someone produced a satisfactory answer for the Sudeten-German question.

Chamberlain was not one to accept war unless it were forced on him, and he was resolved to keep Great Britain out of war by all possible means. Recently he had read Harold Temperley's book, *Life of George Canning.* Canning insisted that Great Britain ought not to threaten war unless she could carry out her threats. "We are certainly not in a position," Chamberlain wrote, "in which our military advisors would feel happy in undertaking to begin hostilities if we were not forced to do so."[1] The memorandum of March 28 from the chiefs of staff was much on his mind. The Prime Minister opposed those who wanted to fight Hitler now rather than later and to begin a war that might never come. The story of Sir Edward Grey and 1914 was ever in his thought. Once committed to war, there would be no return to peace.

During the summer of 1938, Chamberlain had sought to reach Hitler through the usual diplomatic channels, for he was convinced that knowledge of Britain's attitude was withheld from him. He feared that radicals would push the *Führer* into war, believing that Britain would not intervene; Czechoslovakia would then resist;

[1] Feiling, *Neville Chamberlain,* 360–61.

France would support her and drag Great Britain into the conflict. If Chamberlain could present the truth to Hitler, perhaps another world war could be avoided.[2]

The solution was a man-to-man meeting, common among businessmen, to which Chamberlain was well accustomed. He broached the idea first to Henderson and Halifax in late August; it took away Halifax' breath, for within the inner cabinet Hitler was known as "the madman." Henderson wanted to use it only as a last resort. The inner cabinet—Hoare, Simon, and Halifax—approved of the trip on September 10.

On September 13, Germany and Czechoslovakia seemed on the brink of war. Throughout the day, reports of violence and riots came from Prague. In the afternoon Henderson telegraphed for immediate action because it was only a matter of time before Hitler would march. "Severest pressure" must be placed on Beneš to force concessions for peace. If that failed, Henderson insisted that Britain act alone.[3]

In Paris, September 13 had been a day of bitter wrangling in a cabinet divided over supporting Czechoslovakia. Bonnet was so frightened that he wanted anything but war, because "we cannot sacrifice ten million men in order to prevent three and a half million Sudetens joining the Reich." To Georges Mandel, colonial minister, Daladier declared that he would not "sacrifice the entire youth of France merely to whitewash the criminal errors that had been committed by you and your friend Clemenceau and the other members of the Big Four during the Paris Peace Conference." The Premier proposed to Chamberlain by telephone late on September 13 that Runciman publicize his plan for the Sudeten German question or attempt personal mediation. If these failed, Daladier suggested a three-power meeting be held by Germany, France, and Great Britain. He asked Chamberlain for any other proposals; he did not ask that Chamberlain fly to meet Hitler alone.[4]

Chamberlain determined on the dramatic move to avert war. The political risk was great, but he could not forgive himself unless he

---

[2] Kennedy to Hull, August 30, 1938, *FRUS, 1938*, I, 560–61.

[3] Bonnet, *Défense de la paix*, I, 231–32; Phipps to Halifax, *DBFP*, Third series, II, 313–14.

[4] Phipps to Halifax, September 14, 1938, *ibid.*, 323; Bullitt to Hull, September 15, 1938, *FRUS, 1938*, I, 600–602.

tried. He rejected the idea of an invitation for Hitler to come to London lest he be given the more dramatic role. Instead the Prime Minister would fly to Germany and confer with Hitler hoping that the trip would shock public opinion and strengthen German moderates who would then turn Hitler towards peace. To make the trip was right, he thought, because "the only alternative was war and I would never take that awful responsibility upon my shoulders unless it were forced upon me by the madness of others."[5]

Somehow he hoped to persuade Hitler that he could fulfill his often declared aim, the strengthening of Anglo-German understanding through the settlement of the Czech question. When Hitler demanded action, Chamberlain would suggest Runciman as arbiter of the Sudeten question. The Prime Minister would compel Beneš to accept this arbitration.

During the evening of September 13, Chamberlain telegraphed Hitler that because of "the increasingly critical situation," he proposed to fly at once to see him. He was ready to depart on September 14; he asked Hitler to suggest a time and place for the meeting.

On the morning of the fourteenth, Henderson delivered the telegram to Weizsäcker, who immediately telephoned Ribbentrop. Hitler was delighted. "I was astounded," he confided later.[6] At 2:40 P.M. Ribbentrop phoned from Munich that Hitler would be pleased to receive the Prime Minister and his wife, if he so desired. London learned of Hitler's favorable reply late in the afternoon.

Chamberlain sent the message without consulting the French, Czechoslovak, or British cabinets; they learned of the message after the telegram had been dispatched. Thus the responsibility for what followed belonged to Chamberlain. He did not intend to capitulate forthwith to Hitler's demands, as some have argued. In his heart he believed this was the path to peace for millions of innocent people. By this method he would clarify the position of Great Britain and avoid confusion over his government's views. In 1914, Sir Edward Grey had failed to clarify British intentions; it must not happen again.

In Britain, the news of the trip met with almost universal rejoicing. Tension lifted; reason would triumph over force; millions would

5 Feiling, *Neville Chamberlain*, 359, 363–64.
6 Alan Bullock, *Hitler: A Study in Tyranny*, 415.

Ernst von Weizsäcker, state secretary in the German
Foreign Ministry, branded rumors of German
troop concentrations in May, 1938,
as "nonsense."

DURING THE TENSE SUMMER OF 1938, members of the Sudeten
Free Corps trained for the struggle to rend the
"*Sudetendeutsche*" from Czechoslovakia and
unite it with Hitler's Third Reich.

*The National Archives*

live out their lives peacefully. Poet Laureate John Masefield, wrote in the *Times*:

> Neville Chamberlain
> As Priam to Achilles for his Son
> So you, into the night, divinely led,
> To ask that young men's bodies, not yet dead,
> Be given from the battle not begun.

The British cabinet learned of the proposed flight on the morning of September 14. The news was received with silence; one by one the ministers gave their enthusiastic approval. "Well," said Chamberlain, "I take it that it is agreed."[7]

When Daladier learned of Chamberlain's trip late in the afternoon of September 14, he was piqued that he had not been invited; he had rejected other invitations to visit Hitler because he felt that a British representative should be present. Bonnet was gleeful because he wanted the British more deeply involved in the crisis. He promised to advise his government to accept anything Chamberlain proposed whether the Czechs liked it or not. Important French political figures hastened to call at the British embassy to express their thanks for Chamberlain's trip. Most of official Paris was greatly relieved because they hoped that Chamberlain would extract them from the dilemma of abiding by their alliance while trying to avoid war.

In Prague the news of the trip spread fear. The cabinet had not been consulted as should have been their right. From London, Masaryk warned Prague that Czechoslovakia might have to pay the price of the "senile ambition of Chamberlain to play the peacemaker in Europe."[8]

The Czechoslovak government had not been consulted because Chamberlain was convinced that Beneš was the bar to any settlement with the Sudetens; he would only have balked at any proposal for personal negotiation. Because Daladier and Bonnet also blamed Beneš for a lack of solution, they raised no objections to Chamberlain's snubbing of their ally.

The night of September 14-15 was one of rejoicing in London as crowds flocked to Whitehall shouting: "Good old Chamberlain!"

[7] *New York Times,* September 15, 1938.
[8] Masaryk report, September 15, 1938, *Europäische Politik,* 127.

At Heston Airdrome on the morning of September 15, Chamberlain was met by reporters, photographers, and a cheering crowd, crying: "Good Luck! God speed you!" To the reporters, Chamberlain explained that he was meeting Hitler because the situation was one in which discussions would be "fruitful." His policy was always to seek peace. Hitler's acceptance of a personal, man-to-man meeting led the Prime Minister to hope that the visit would "not be without result."[9]

Dressed in a stiff-winged collar, grey silk tie, and clutching an umbrella, the sixty-nine-year-old Prime Minister climbed into a silver Lockheed monoplane for the first long-distance airplane ride of his life. The plane flew off into a cloudless sky at 8:36 A.M. With Chamberlain went Horace Wilson—"our outspoken enemy," wrote Masaryk—and William Strang, head of the Central Department of the Foreign Office—"a decent man," Masaryk reported.

At 12:30 P.M. the plane reached Munich where Chamberlain was met by Ribbentrop, Nevile Henderson, and officials from the German Foreign Office. Ribbentrop asked if Chamberlain had a good flight. "Well it is the first I have ever made," the Prime Minister answered, "so that I can't judge whether it was good or not. The sun was shining when we left England. It was only when we got over the Continent that the clouds began."

Chamberlain was impressed by the friendly crowds as he was driven through the streets of Munich to the railroad station where he boarded a special train for Berchtesgaden. Throughout the trip, at every crossing, people waved and cheered. Chamberlain lunched with Ribbentrop; they were served a meal of trout, roast beef and Yorkshire pudding, cheese, cakes, fruit, sherry, Rhine wine, German red wine, and port. Their conversation included fishing, the scenery, the weather, and the German highway system.

At Berchtesgaden, the party was taken by car to the Berghof, Hitler's private residence, on the side of a mountain. Hitler and General Keitel received the Prime Minister and escorted him into a huge room, where one wall was a window with a view of the mountains. The view was as dreary as prospects for peace: rain poured and winds howled ominously as the statesmen prepared to settle the fate of Czechoslovakia.

While Hitler and Chamberlain had tea, they made small talk

[9] *New York Times*, September 16, 1938.

about the scenery, the bad weather, the size of the room. When tea was finished, Hitler asked about the procedure. Prompted by Henderson, Chamberlain requested that the two leaders meet privately with only an interpreter present. Henderson wanted to exclude Ribbentrop, believing that the Foreign Minister was desirous of war and would harm the discussions. Ribbentrop had his revenge by refusing to give the British a copy of notes of the talks made by Paul Schmidt, the interpreter.

Hitler led the way through a hall, decorated with pictures of nudes, into a smaller room with only three chairs, a table, sofa, a stove, and two bottles of mineral water. There, with Schmidt interpreting, the pair talked for three hours.

Chamberlain stated that his purpose in making the trip was to strengthen Anglo-German relations by a direct exchange of views and to clarify perplexing problems. Hitler replied that he was aware of the significance of the journey. From his youth, he wanted Anglo-German co-operation; the war of 1914–18 had been a great shock.

Chamberlain explained that he wanted to utilize the first conversation for an exchange of general ideas. Instead of a general survey of Anglo-German problems, Hitler launched on a rambling tale of the Sudeten question whose solution could not wait. Those Germans living in Czechoslovakia who desired to return to the Reich must be enabled to do so. Hitler vowed that he would face the risk of a world war to bring the Sudetens home from Czechoslovakia. He would not yield on this question. He would chose his own time for a swift solution. "The Czechoslovak question would then, of course, be the last major problem to be solved."

Now Chamberlain understood that Hitler was intent only on having the Sudetens home within the Reich. He asked the *Führer* if Czechoslovakia would not still be a "spearpoint in Germany's flank" after the Sudetens returned to the Reich. Hitler replied that such would be true as long as Czechoslovakia maintained her alliances with other countries. Chamberlain proposed that this be overcome by the rump of Czechoslovakia ending the alliance with Russia.

Chamberlain, ever a practical soul, saw difficulties in bringing the Sudetens home to the Reich. If only areas with populations that were more than 80 per cent German were transferred to Germany, other Germans would still remain within Czechoslovakia. Hitler replied that the entire section where Germans were in a majority must

133

be turned over to the Reich; the minorities could be sent back later. He reiterated the need to make haste because the Sudetens were being persecuted: whole villages had been evacuated, the Czechs had used gas, and ten thousand refugees were already on German soil.

Chamberlain proposed that an appeal be made to both sides for peace while mutual discussions were carried on. Hitler rejected an appeal for peace. The Czechs were cruel and cowardly at heart. Once more he proclaimed that he would settle this question quickly, by war if necessary. Chamberlain became excited. If Hitler were determined to use force, his trip was a waste of time. Under the circumstances he would return to London because anything else was pointless if Hitler were determined to settle the question by force. Hitler retorted that he would settle the question speedily.

Chamberlain did not break off the discussions but asked for some kind of an armistice. The *Führer* replied that if the British would accept the principle of the cession of these areas on the basis of self-determination, it would be possible to pacify the Sudetenland. Hitler reminded Chamberlain that the right of self-determination had been invented to justify the changes created by the Treaty of Versailles. Chamberlain was delighted that "they had now gotten down to the crux of the matter at last." He must consult the French and Lord Runciman, but personally he recognized the principle of the detachment of the Sudeten areas. The implementation of the principle presented difficulties. He must, however, report to his government and secure their approval. Before parting, Hitler promised that if it were possible, he would not set the German military machine in motion unless "a completely impossible situation should arise."[10]

The Prime Minister had been jolted by Hitler's attitude. The situation was more critical than Henderson's reports had led him to imagine. Chamberlain had no doubt that his visit had saved Europe from war. He believed that his practical measures had brought the discussions down to the crux of the matter: Hitler would be satisfied if the Sudetens were safe within the Reich.

Chamberlain came away believing that he could depend on Hitler

[10] Chamberlain's notes of his talk with Hitler, September 15, 1938, *DBFP*, Third series, II, 338–41; Feiling, *Neville Chamberlain*, 366–68; memorandum of a conversation between Hitler and Chamberlain, September 15, 1938, *DG*, Series D, II, 786–98; Ward Price, *Year of Reckoning*, 254–69; Paul Schmidt, *Hitler's Interpreter*, 90–94.

as a man of his word although he disliked him personally, finding him hard and ruthless. He was astounded that a man in Hitler's position believed the stories that were fed to him. Chamberlain did not realize that Hitler was an actor who could feign great indignation over Sudeten agonies conjured up by Goebbels. The Prime Minister thought he had struck the right note of frankness, and now that Hitler knew the truth, perhaps peace would be possible.

Chamberlain revealed to Hitler his willingness to reduce Czechoslovakia to a German satellite. He did not care whether the Sudetens were in Germany or Czechoslovakia so long as there was peace. He was willing to make a bargain, but was Hitler willing to do the same? Apparently Chamberlain thought he was.

Chamberlain's plane arrived in London in the afternoon of September 16. The Prime Minister was met by cheering crowds, shouting, "Good old Neville!" Stepping up to a microphone, Chamberlain informed his hearers at the airfield that he had a frank but friendly talk with Hitler. "I feel satisfied now that each of us fully understands what is in the mind of the other." He had to report to the cabinet, and in a few days he would pay a return visit to Hitler, who promised to come halfway to meet Chamberlain and spare "an old man another long journey." The happy throng broke into cheers. As Chamberlain's car left the airport, there were cries of "Bravo! Well done Neville!"

That evening Chamberlain reported to the inner cabinet and talked with King George VI. Outside Buckingham Palace, crowds waited to cheer the frosty Prime Minister who was fast becoming popular.

On September 17, Runciman described his unsuccessful mission to the cabinet. Chamberlain followed with an account of his trip. He seemed satisfied with the reception given him in Germany. He could not conceal his pleasure over a report that Hitler felt the Prime Minister was "a man." He stressed Hitler's refusal to compromise and repeated Hitler's demand for self-determination. The Prime Minister expected the cabinet to accept this principle because Hitler demanded a swift solution.

There were two long cabinet meetings, indicating a division in the cabinet. According to one rumor, Halifax, Malcolm MacDonald, the colonial secretary, and Duff Cooper, first lord of the Admiralty, opposed the cession because of other minorities in the area. Hoare, Simon, and Sir Kingsley Wood, secretary for air, objected to any commitments beyond the Rhine. In the afternoon meeting, Duff Cooper spoke up against permitting one power to dominate the Continent because war might then result. The meeting ended about 5:30 P.M. without any agreement.[11]

In Paris, Georges Bonnet had eagerly informed Phipps on September 16, before he knew the results of Chamberlain's visit, that the French government would accept any plan advocated by either Chamberlain or Runciman and impose it on Czechoslovakia. If the Czechs proved defiant, Bonnet promised to inform them that France was leaving them to their fate. Of course, he added, if Germany attacked Czechoslovakia, France would abide by her alliance.

Refusing to accept these brave words on their face value, Phipps warned Whitehall that even if the Germans invaded Czechoslovakia, France would not automatically spring to the defense of Czechoslovakia. Instead, the French government would examine the circumstances under which the war began with great caution.

Daladier was bitter because he had not been given information on the talk at Berchtesgaden. He wanted an invitation to a consultation in London, but Chamberlain apparently expected to use Ambassador Phipps to inform the French. Hints from Paris brought an invitation for the Premier and Bonnet to come for consultations on September 18.

Before he left Paris, Daladier called in his generals. What could the French army do alone without British support? The generals were agreed that after a few days of fighting, Germany could wipe out Czechoslovakia. The armies of France needed two to three weeks before they could launch a frontal assault on Germany. Russia would play only a secondary role. An effective offensive would be launched only if a coalition could be formed, but no one wanted to join a coalition.[12] With his cabinet split, his generals frightened, his foreign minister willing to accept anything, Daladier was ill-prepared for a strong stand against yielding to Hitler's wishes.

11 *Survey of International Affairs, 1938*, II, 334–37; *New York Times*, September 17, 18, 1938; Duff Cooper, *Old Men Forget*, 229–30; Feiling, *Neville Chamberlain*, 367–68; Kennedy to Hull, September 17, 1938, Wilson to Hull, September 17, 1938, *FRUS, 1938*, I, 608–12; "Notes by Sir Wilson on Conversations during Mr. Chamberlain's visit to Berchtesgaden," Halifax to Newton, September 19, 1938, *DBFP*, Third series, II, 351–54, 407.

12 *Les événements*, I, 33.

In the churches of France and Great Britain, September 18 was a day for prayer that war would be averted. All day people filed past the Tomb of the Unknown Soldier in Westminster Abbey; many paused to kneel and pray for peace.

Chamberlain and Halifax met Daladier and Bonnet at Croyden Airfield. After conferring with Charles Corbin, the French Ambassador, the Frenchmen went to No. 10 Downing Street to meet with the English statesmen. In Whitehall, extra police struggled to handle the crowds, including anti-Nazi demonstrators who demanded "No concessions to Hitler! Stand by the Czechs!"

Chamberlain opened the meeting by announcing that the government of Czechoslovakia had decided to mobilize but would await the results of the meeting. Then Chamberlain recounted his meeting with Hitler. The Prime Minister had received the impression Hitler "could be relied upon unless something quite unexpected occurred." To avoid a catastrophic war, they must immediately seek self-determination: to choose any other policy meant that Hitler would march. Chamberlain then asked for the French opinion, hoping to pass on the burden of decision. Daladier refused, claiming he needed time to deliberate on the problem.

The Prime Minister explained Runciman's views: the Mediator had reported that any scheme of mediation was without any chance for success. Runciman believed that the only possible solution was some plan based on acceptance of the principle of self-determination. Chamberlain reminded the French of their different position because they were bound by treaty obligations. Were they still prepared to resist Hitler?

Daladier objected to the policy of self-determination lest it open up Central Europe to Hitler. German minorities in Slovakia, Rumania, and Poland could use the right of self-determination to demand autonomy and then annexation. Instead of fostering peace, the door would be opened to dissensions and finally to a world war.

Chamberlain countered that Hitler did not want acceptance of the right of self-determination to be applied everywhere. The *Führer* was interested only in using this principle to solve the Sudeten German question. Daladier reported that, once admitted in the Sudetenland, the principle could be used by other minorities to destroy Czechoslovakia. Chamberlain confessed that he anticipated similar demands from Poland and Hungary, but he was not worried.

Striving to force the solution on the British, Daladier asked if they proposed the acceptance of the principle and method. Chamberlain reminded the Premier that German military preparations had continued since his visit to Hitler. In the light of these conditions, what did France propose as an alternative to self-determination?

Daladier vowed that France would not desert her ally if Germany attacked while the negotiations were in progress, but neither the French government nor the French people wanted a war that could bring only general destruction. Despite the observations of Runciman, Daladier was not convinced that it was impossible for Sudeten and Czech to live side by side. He wanted some alternative to a plebiscite, so fraught with danger to the peace of Europe; therefore, he preferred to hear the British conclusions because they had had more time to consider the situation.

Next Halifax endeavored to corner the Premier. The Foreign Secretary fully appreciated the French desire to honor their obligations to Czechoslovakia; however, by reason of their special arrangement with Czechoslovakia, the French government ought to advise if self-determination should be considered. Halifax realized the dangers and pitfalls involved in the principle of self-determination, but Chamberlain had concluded that Hitler would have peace only on this basis. Halifax reminded the French that there was no way to protect Czechoslovakia. In the peace conference after the war, statesmen would not create Czechoslovakia as she now existed. They must face hard facts and seek means to save Europe from war by considering the only condition upon which Hitler would accept peace.

Chamberlain at last came to the point which he had hoped that the French would admit first. There was no alternative proposal: they accepted either self-determination or war. It behooved the French government to advise the Czechoslovak government regarding this choice.

Daladier was reluctant to concede all Germany's demands lest further demands follow with accompanying concessions. He and his colleagues had come to London to seek means of preserving peace without destroying Czechoslovakia. They must prevent France's being forced into war because of her obligations and yet preserve as much as they could of Czechoslovakia. The diplomats adjourned for the midday meal.

When the meeting resumed, Daladier announced that after consultation with the other members of his delegation, they rejected a plebiscite for self-determination because such a solution would not solve the Sudeten problem but only initiate the disintegration of Czechoslovakia. Driven to make a proposal, Chamberlain advised a cession of Sudeten territory to the Reich, with proper safeguards for minorities and with provisions for transference of populations. Daladier seized upon the suggestion, declaring that the Czechoslovak government had already intimated that they would resist a plebiscite by force. He thought that with "friendly pressure" the Czechoslovak government might accept the proposal, but they would ask for guarantees. Chamberlain suggested that it be made to appear as if the Czechoslovak government had chosen this alternative in preference to plebiscite: this would create a more favorable reaction from the British public. He proposed that areas in which Germans comprised 50 per cent of the population be ceded to the Reich and that the actual delimitation be carried out by an international commission.

Chamberlain was reluctant to guarantee the rump of Czechoslovakia because this country was far away, and Britain had no army to aid her. The British guarantee would be valuable only for its deterrent power. Would the French consider a neutral Czechoslovakia similar to Belgium? Bonnet objected to the distance argument, claiming that the main value of the guarantee would be moral. Halifax insisted that Britain would have to be consulted regarding Czechoslovak foreign policy because it was impossible for the control of British foreign policy to be in the hands of another country. Daladier feared that France would lose an important element in her security system if even the rump of the Czechoslovak state were neutralized. Chamberlain argued that Czechoslovakia was a potential liability to France; France would gain if she were free of her responsibilities towards Czechoslovakia. Daladier contended that a British guarantee of Czechoslovakia would help France prevent German domination of Europe, a goal which he believed Hitler to be seeking.

The meeting adjourned at 5:00 P.M. and resumed at 7:30 P.M. Chamberlain announced that after consultation with the British delegation, they were agreed on a guarantee of Czechoslovakia. The French should consider a draft regarding the guarantee, which would be circulated, and resume the discusison after supper.

When the meeting resumed at 10:30 P.M., Daladier announced French acceptance of the draft. Once more Chamberlain urged speed;

he did not wish to postpone his meeting with Hitler beyond September 21. Daladier promised an answer by midday; he would bring "the strongest pressure" to bear on Beneš to accept the proposal. The meeting ended at 12:15 A.M. on September 19.

In a telegram to the Prague government, the British and French governments declared that further maintenance of the Sudetens within Czechoslovakia imperiled the peace of Europe. Sudeten areas in which Germans made up over 50 per cent of the inhabitants should be ceded directly to the Reich. Frontier adjustments and population transfers would be handled by an international commission, on which Czechoslovakia would be represented. The British government was prepared to join in an international guarantee of the new frontiers against unprovoked aggression; the guarantees would be substituted for existing treaties with Russia and France.[13]

Thus did Chamberlain's views seem to prevail over the French. The French capitulation was more apparent than real, for Daladier had been informed by Bonnet of Beneš' willingness to cede certain "salients" to Germany. Bonnet did not quite tell all of the truth. On September 15, Beneš had intimated to de Lacroix that in 1919 he had thought of the possibility of excluding some areas in Bohemia. Such a cession had no relation to the present negotiations, the President cautioned. Beneš begged de Lacroix not to give Paris the idea that he wanted to cede part of the Sudetenland. De Lacroix, when reporting the conversation to Bonnet, asked that the statement be treated confidentially. When Bonnet next told the story, there was a change: Beneš proposed a cession of territory. Certainly this moved Daladier to accept the British plan, much to Bonnet's delight.

The idea of cession had been reported to London from two sources in Prague before the meeting with Daladier and Bonnet. Someone in the Czech Foreign Office, perhaps Hodža, had inferred that if a cession of Sudeten territory were necessary for peace, perhaps areas near the frontier could be ceded if they did not harm the security of the state. From the Czechoslovak general staff came a hint that the exclusion of such territory from Czechoslovakia would raise no great

13 *New York Times*, September 19, 1938; "Record of Anglo-French Conversations held at No. 10 Downing Street on September 18, 1938," *DBFP*, Third series, II, 373–400; Halifax to Newton, September 19, 1938, *ibid.*, 404–406; Bonnet, *Défense de la paix*, I, 237–39.

opposition and might even be welcome in certain quarters.[14] All thought in terms of slight frontier adjustments, but not of a massive cession, tearing asunder the nation, and leaving it prey to the Nazi terror. These tales, brought to eager ears in Paris and London, facilitated the Anglo-French plan to cede territory with a 50 per cent Sudeten population.

The discussions reveal that both parties thought first about avoiding war and secondly about Czechoslovakia. Daladier had better insight into the subsequent course of events, but Chamberlain could not be convinced. Neither side displayed nobility in its haste to thrust the responsibility for the decision on the other. They failed to invite either Beneš, who could have flown there, or his representative Masaryk, because now both sides were persuaded that Czechoslovakia was the chief hindrance to peace.

From the outset Chamberlain had the advantage over the French, who impressed him "as coming over with their tongues out looking for some way to save themselves from war."[15] Had the French rejected the proposal, Chamberlain could have washed his hands of the crisis, leaving them to face Germany. When Chamberlain informed Parliament of the offer, spurned by the French, he would have been acclaimed for his service in the cause of peace. Daladier would have found his cabinet splintered and the nation hostile at his failure to make a deal in the interest of peace. Because he wanted Great Britain tied to the French cause, Daladier was probably not too unhappy that Chamberlain had taken the responsibility for a proposal which Daladier could second at Czech expense. Chamberlain knew, and Daladier proved by his conduct, that France would accept any deal Chamberlain could make with Hitler no matter what Beneš might say or do. Cession of parts of Czechoslovakia was the price of peace.

At 10:00 A.M. on September 19, the French cabinet heard the reports of Bonnet and Daladier. The Premier presented Chamberlain's warning that unless there were aggression against France, British aid could not be expected, and it would be of little immediate value. Daladier explained the proposal for cession, clinching his

14 *Les événements*, II, 267; Newton to Halifax, September 16, 1938, *DBFP*, Third series, II, 358, 364–65.
15 Kennedy to Hull, September 19, 1938, *FRUS, 1938*, I, 621–22.

argument with the tale of de Lacroix, embroidered by Bonnet, that Beneš was willing to dispose of some "salients" with a total Sudeten population of nine hundred thousand. The Premier advised his colleagues to accept the proposal because France would have to fight alone for at least a month. They could not help the Czechs because Germany could send over four thousand planes against twelve hundred French planes. When the troops attempted to break through the Siegfried Line, there would be enormous losses. Guy la Chambre, minister for air, echoed the views of General Vuillemin: it would be absurd to send such a feeble air force against the *Luftwaffe*. Bonnet announced that France had never been in such a poor diplomatic situation. He alleged that Czechoslovakia had been forewarned, because he always told Osusky that France would not intervene without Great Britain, no matter what the cause of war. Russia would not join with France to stop Germany.

When Camille Chautemps, vice-president of the council of ministers, demanded the Czechs be warned that if they refused the proposal, they could not count on French help, the uproar was so great that Daladier promised to discuss the question later. Thus he implied that no pressure would be used to force the Czechoslovak government to accept the proposal. With this promise in mind, the cabinet accepted the plan unanimously. Those ministers—led by Paul Reynaud, minister of justice, and Georges Mandel, colonial minister —who did not favor the proposal approved the Anglo-French plan only because they expected that Czechoslovakia would reject the proposal, forcing the French government to abide by the treaty of alliance.[16]

Bonnet had no intention of letting this happen. When he saw the American ambassador after the cabinet meeting, he swore that if Czechoslovakia refused the proposal, "France positively would not march in support of Czechoslovakia." As for Beneš, Bonnet said, "He cannot refuse. We will not let Beneš, in order to maintain the domination of seven million Czechs over three and one-half million Germans, drive forty million French people to their deaths, and he knows it."[17]

16 Jean Zay, *Carnets secrets de Jean Zay (de Munich à la guerre)*, 3–7; Bonnet, *Défense de la paix*, I, 243–44; *New York Times*, September 20, 1938; Anatole de Monzie, *Ci-devant*, 31–32.

17 Bullitt to Hull, September 19, 1938, *FRUS, 1938*, I, 620–21.

After the meeting, Bonnet informed Osusky of the plan, explaining that France had to take into account the peculiar position of Great Britain, who had no arrangement with Czechoslovakia. Bonnet alleged that there had been a veritable "battle" in London to avoid a plebiscite. The proposal was the lesser evil for a nation so menaced as was Czechoslovakia. As he emerged from the Quai d'Orsay, Osusky blinked back the tears. To waiting newsmen, he murmured, "My country has been condemned without a hearing."[18]

In Czechoslovakia the wave of violence in the Sudetenland unleashed by Hitler's speech on September 12 had now subsided, leaving the Sudetens confused and angry with their leaders who had fled to the Reich. Because war in their homeland seemed so near, Sudeten ardor for rioting cooled.

Hitler did not aid peace when he ordered the Gestapo to arrest as many Czechs, living in Germany, as Sudetens were under arrest in Czechoslovakia. Reprisals would be carried out in equal number if any death sentences were imposed by the Czechoslovak government.

German diplomatic missions were instructed to find out who could receive and transmit money for the German government during wartime. The German legation in Prague was ordered to begin the gradual evacuation of wives and children of the staff. British citizens began to leave Berlin.

Both German and Czechoslovak armies continued to mobilize. The Czechs repeated their tactics of May 20, occupying frontier areas. Hitler ordered all Sudetens with military experience into the Sudeten Free Corps. On September 19, the corps came under the control of the German High Command. Ordered to make their first attack on the Czechoslovak frontier, they were promptly repulsed. Bands of Sudeten refugees could not invade their homeland: only Hitler's armies were powerful enough to gain such a victory. To avoid this, Great Britain and France hastened to force the Czechoslovak government to cede the Sudetenland to the Reich.

18 *New York Times*, September 20, 1938.

143

# 14

## The Ultimatum

IN THE AFTERNOON of September 19, Newton and de Lacroix presented the Anglo-French proposal to Beneš. The presence of the Sudetens within the Czechoslovak state imperiled Czechoslovakia and European peace. Maintenance of peace and security in Czechoslovakia required immediate transfer of the Sudetenland to the Reich. In view of objections to the plebiscite, Czechoslovakia might prefer direct transfer of areas in which the population was more than 50 per cent German. The British and French governments wanted the frontiers adjusted by an international body with Czechoslovak representatives. Should the Czechoslovak government agree to this proposal, the British govenment would join in an international guarantee of the new frontiers against unprovoked aggression, substituting this for the existing treaties. Chamberlain needed an immediate reply to take with him to his next meeting with Hitler.

The proposal shocked Beneš: it was worse than he had expected. As a constitutional president, he must refer the proposal to his government and to parliament. Beneš complained that after all the Czech efforts for peace, they were being abandoned. Not so, Newton countered; here was a guarantee from the British government. The choice was either to lose everything acquired in 1918 or retain an area where Czechs and Slovaks would be in the majority. It was not a final solution, Beneš argued, but only a stage towards eventual German domination. At last the diplomats withdrew.

Beneš faced a terrible choice. To accept the proposal would open the door to further German demands. To reject meant war without Anglo-French help. As president, dared he risk the lives of his people? Within the time limit laid down, he could do little other than accede or reject. Calling parliament would have given time to maneuver and gain sympathy, but this was denied Beneš. Thus the Anglo-French proposal became an ultimatum.

When members of the Czechoslovak cabinet met with Beneš in the afternoon of September 19, they were stunned by the ultimatum. A decision did not come easily. The generals warned of the extreme danger in facing Germany alone: to some, fighting alone was synonymous with suicide. Throughout the night the cabinet wrestled with their reply.

About midday September 20, London and Paris heard that the Prague cabinet was considering an appeal for arbitration. Newton and de Lacroix cautioned the Czechoslovak Foreign Office that such would be folly, leading to war.

Late in the afternoon, the cabinet decided on rejection with an appeal to arbitration. They believed that some of the British cabinet were not in complete agreement with the proposals. There was hope that the French cabinet might fall, giving way to those Frenchmen who would stand by the alliance. Paul Reynaud, Georges Mandel, and Auguste Champetier de Ribes were in contact with Prague by telephone, urging the Czechoslovak government to stand fast against the ultimatum.

At 7:45 P.M. that evening, Krofta handed Newton and de Lacroix the Czechoslovak reply. He explained that it was impossible to accept proposals to dismember Czechoslovakia: arbitration was preferable. Newton replied that refusal of the Anglo-French proposal meant the destruction of Czechoslovakia. De Lacroix joined in warning Krofta that his government risked world war.

In the notes handed to Newton and de Lacroix, the Czechoslovak government objected to not having been consulted by Britain and France before the proposals were drafted. For the government to cede territory without calling parliament would destroy the constitution. Cession of the Sudeten areas would paralyze Czechoslovakia economically, create an unpleasant strategic problem, and end in absolute dominance by Germany. The proposals would not solve the minority question because some Sudetens might prefer to remain within Czechoslovakia. The treaty of arbitration was still in force; the

Czechoslovak government requested the application of this treaty.[1] While de Lacroix was drawing up the telegram reporting the Czech refusal of the Anglo-French proposals, Hodža telephoned, asking to see him. When de Lacroix arrived at Hodža's office, the Prime Minister inquired if Czechoslovakia could count on French aid. For a moment, de Lacroix could not speak. He was without instructions but expected that his government would answer negatively. Hodža, after confessing to a similar belief, asked de Lacroix to learn the exact attitude of his government. In such a vital affair of state— the breaking of an alliance—the Czechoslovak government and army needed exact information. If France refused to join forces with Czechoslovakia because of her relations with Great Britain, Beneš must take immediate action. The cabinet must be summoned to consider so drastic a development.

Hodža sought to learn precisely French intentions. The question of French loyalty was vital because the Czechoslovak cabinet had rejected the Anglo-French proposals believing that France would remain a faithful ally. If France were to be disloyal, the Russian alliance would be ended; Czechoslovakia would be isolated, without an ally, and surrounded by greedy neighbors.[2]

That same evening, Bonnet received a telegram from de Lacroix at 8:20 P.M. announcing the rejection and requesting arbitration. At 8:30 P.M. in another telegram, he asked that the influence of the French general staff be exerted on the Czechoslovak general staff to convert Prague to the plan. About 9:30, de Lacroix telephoned to advise Bonnet that the request for arbitration was not definite; an important telegram was on the way. Bonnet called Daladier to the Quai d'Orsay. He alerted the cipher section to give the Prague telegram priority. At 9:50 the message came through. If Hodža could inform Beneš that, in a war between Germany and Czechoslovakia over the Sudetenland, France would not fight, the cabinet would be summoned. "The Czechoslovak government needs this pretext if

1 Hubert Ripka, *Munich: Before and After*, 71–72; Alfred Fabre-Luce, *Histoire secrète de la conciliation de Munich*, 56–57; de Lacroix to Foreign Ministry, September 20, 1938, *Les événements*, X, 272; Newton to Halifax, September 19, 20, 1938, *DBFP*, Third series, II, 411–12, 414–17, 420, 426–27; Phipps to Halifax, September 20, 1938, *ibid.*, 419; note from the Czechoslovak government to the British legation in Prague, September 20, 1938, *ibid.*, 434–36; Halifax to Newton, September 19, 1938, *ibid.*, 404–406, 412.

2 See Appendix.

The Runciman·mission symbolized a change in British policy
toward the Czech crisis. Here, industrialist Walter
Runciman (left) confers with Prime Minister
Hodža in Prague, August 5, 1938.

WALTER RUNCIMAN (LEFT) AND FRANK T. A. ASHTON-GWATKIN
return to London after the Mährisch-Ostrau incident
brought the Runciman mission to convenient ruin.

they are to accept the Franco-British proposals," Hodža informed the minister. Army chiefs declared that to fight alone would be suicide. The hasty decision not to fight was the only way to save the peace. Hodža wanted a reply that night.

After Daladier reached the Quai d'Orsay, he conferred with Bonnet over an answer for de Lacroix. Daladier rejected Bonnet's suggestion to call a cabinet meeting, for it was about 11:00 P.M.; some of the cabinet members were out of the city. Had there been a meeting, the cabinet would probably have been badly split, forcing Daladier to resign—a fate he abhorred. In the ensuing crisis, France would have been unable to stand by Czechoslovakia: Bonnet would have achieved his goal.

Bonnet and Daladier drafted the reply for the Czechoslovak government, with the advice of two career diplomats, Alexis St. Léger and Jules Henry. Though they might wish to, they could not pass this task on to London, for they already knew London's answer.

Early in the morning of September 21, the telegram was dispatched to de Lacroix. France, in agreement with Britain, had instigated the only possible procedure to prevent the dread German invasion of Czechoslovakia.

> By rejecting the Franco-British proposal, the Czech government takes the responsibility of deciding on the use of force against Germany. It alone breaks the Franco-British solidarity which has just been established and by this action it removes all practical effectiveness in any French assistance. . . . Czechoslovakia assumes then a risk from which we have in conscience tried to extract her. She ought to understand herself the conclusions that France is correct in taking if the Czechoslovak government does not accept immediately the Franco-British proposal.

Nowhere did Bonnet and Daladier say explicitly that France would not fight, but the meaning was obvious. Speaking for the French government and without consulting either the cabinet or parliament, they had broken an alliance. Responsibility rested with Georges Bonnet and Édouard Daladier.[3]

That same night the British government took an identical step.

[3] Les événements, XI, 268–72, 275; Ripka, Munich, 88–89; Celovsky, Das Münchener Abkommen, 362–63; Newton to Halifax, September 20, 1938, DBFP, Third series, II, 418: Bonnet, Défense de la paix, I, 248–50.

Newton proposed an ultimatum to make the Czechs give in because some were so committed to resistance that only an ultimatum would bring capitulation. Taking up this suggestion, Halifax replied at 1:20 A.M. on September 21, instructing Newton to join with de Lacroix in demonstrating to the Czechoslovak government that its reply was not an answer to the crisis. The Czech reply must be withdrawn because acceptance of the Anglo-French proposal was the only way to avoid attack. Lacking acceptance of the proposal, Chamberlain would have to cancel his visit: the German government would surely refuse arbitration. The Czech government was free to take whatever action it thought appropriate. Halifax did not have to add that Britain would then wash her hands of the whole affair.

At 2:00 A.M., Newton and de Lacroix read their telegrams to Beneš. De Lacroix concluded with the warning: "If the Czechoslovak government does not accept unconditionally the Anglo-French plan, it will be held solely responsible for any war which may ensue, and France will take no part in it." Both ministers demanded that Czechoslovakia agree without reservations or face Germany alone. Their governments would not accept any conditional answers. Beneš was frantic. With a map, he indicated the dangers in transferring territory which would narrow the frontier between German Silesia and Austria. Vital railway lines would be affected; German refugees would settle in Czech territory, perpetuating the minority problem. The ministers demanded acceptance without reservation.

Beneš could not bring himself to face the obvious: Czechoslovakia was being deserted. He argued that he had never intended to provoke war, nor did he mean to drag France and Britain into war. Never had he been under the influence of the Soviet government, nor had he considered its wishes in his negotiations. He anticipated internal disturbances; he was dubious about controlling them.

It was past 3:00 A.M. Wearily Beneš conceded the Anglo-French statements were "a kind of ultimatum and indeed only such an ultimatum could justify him and his government in accepting Anglo-French proposals without obtaining beforehand sanction of Parliament." Newton and de Lacroix confessed that it was an ultimatum. Beneš promised a reply by midday.

Once more Beneš wrestled with the fate of his nation which he felt had been "disgracefully betrayed." The cabinet met at 6:30 A.M., joined later by parliamentary representatives of the government

148

parties. Because of opposition, the meetings continued throughout the day.

Learning of the delay, de Lacroix and Newton reiterated the demand for an affirmative reply by noon, or their governments would no longer be responsible for the fate of Czechoslovakia. In the afternoon both ministers presented written notes, confirming the demands they had made on Beneš in the early morning hours. Beneš requested a written declaration that, if he accepted the Anglo-French proposals and Germany attacked, Britain and France would come to the defense of Czechoslovakia. It was now too late to lay down such conditions, Newton replied. Let Beneš express "a wish" for such a declaration. The President did so, but the wish was later ignored.

At 5:00 P.M. Krofta handed Newton and de Lacroix his government's reply. Forced by circumstances, pressures, and the Anglo-French ultimatum, the Czechoslovak government accepted the proposals with the expectation that both governments would safeguard the vital interests of Czechoslovakia while the proposals were being effected. The Czechoslovak government expected a guarantee against German invasion until the territory was transferred and the new frontiers fixed by the international commission.

Those who feared war could now be soothed; the stubborn Czechs had seen reality; self-determination would triumph; the Sudetens would go home to the Reich; Hitler's rages would subside; those who believed in the Versailles myth could rejoice. The French government had been delivered from the peril of keeping an alliance. Now, more than before, the fate of Czechoslovakia was in the hands of the British and French leaders, particularly Chamberlain.

Prague hoped that Britain and France would stand behind the guarantee, but the conditions of the guarantee were undefined. Should Czechoslovakia object to the frontier drawn by the international commission and Germany launch an attack, would Britain and France keep their word? The procedure for drawing the frontier and completing the transfer was poorly defined. The Prague government was refused time to negotiate these proposals. An ultimatum directed them to tear asunder their country as though defeated in war and to accept a vague promise of future security.

By afternoon the news of the capitulation was abroad in Prague. Stalwart men sobbed openly; telephone operators refused calls in French and English. Aroused by the insult to their nation, crowds came into the streets, parading, demonstrating, and shouting threats at the government: "Down with Hodža! Away with Beneš! Long live the Army!" When the throngs massed before the official residence of Beneš, General Jan Syrovy, inspector general of the Army, addressed them, asking for confidence in the government, whose reasons they could not know. The crowds moved off, singing the national anthem. Hodža's cabinet resigned the next day, and a new government was formed, headed by General Syrovy.

On the same day, Beneš went on the radio to quiet the population. He explained that changes were taking place not only in Czechoslovakia but in all parts of Europe. The nation must face the changes with calmness and unity. He said:

> I have never feared, and I do not fear for the future of our nation. I have a plan for all circumstances, and will not allow myself to be led astray. . . . I see things clearly, and I have my plans. . . . Have no fear for the nation and the state. The nation has deep roots. Czechoslovakia will not perish.

Later these words would haunt him, but for the moment they soothed an anxious people. He believed that ultimately Great Britain and France would see the error of their ways; then they would be steadfast in their support for Czechoslovakia.[4]

Why did Beneš capitulate and bear the reproach to his grave? Why did he not fight as some demanded? In 1943, Stalin asked, "And why didn't you fight in September, 1938?" Beneš had tied his policy to Britain and France. When they thrust him away, he was isolated from every power. Germany, Poland, and Hungary seemed ready to pounce; Russian aid was a chimera. What right did he have to gamble the lives of his people, their children, and unborn generations? If Czechoslovakia fought alone, she might be overwhelmed by another defeat as great as White Mountain in 1620 when the Hapsburg forces destroyed Czech independence for three hundred years. Perhaps he could save a remnant of his people until the Nazi scourge was gone. That Czechoslovakia would be engulfed by the Nazi conquest so soon and for so long, he could not forsee. He thought that Britain and France would be loyal to their guarantee.

4 Ripka, *Munich*, 80, 103, 105, 108–109; Sydney Morrell, *I Saw the Crucifixion*, 195–203; Newton to Halifax, September 20, 21, 1938, *DBFP*, Third series, II, 425, 437–38, 440–42, 444–45, 449–50; Halifax to Newton, September 21, 1938, *ibid.*, 437–38.

Russian behavior was instrumental in forcing Beneš to capitulate. On September 19, he put two questions to Sergei Alexandrovsky, the Russian minister in Prague. "Will the U.S.S.R. in accordance with the agreement render immediate effective assistance if France remains true and also renders assistance?" He asked if the U.S.S.R. would help through the League of Nations, utilizing Articles 16 and 17 of the Covenant. Beneš stressed that the Anglo-French proposal would be rejected, and France would be asked if she intended to renounce her obligations. Beneš' second question was an oblique way of asking whether the Soviet Union would support Czechoslovakia if France declined to fulfill her obligations and rejection of the proposals brought on war.

Moscow's reply was delayed until after Beneš had agreed to the Anglo-French ultimatum. Alexandrovsky replied on September 21 in the affirmative to the first question. As to the second question, in case of German aggression against Czechoslovakia, the Soviet Union would request Czechoslovakia to turn to the League of Nations where a majority vote would satisfy the Soviet Union in her decision to aid Czechoslovakia. Beneš replied that the second answer meant little in view of the slow Geneva procedure. Later in the day, when the decision to accept the Anglo-French proposals was well-known, Alexandrovsky returned to announce that if Czechoslovakia presented Germany at Geneva as an aggressor, then the Soviet would be authorized to help. There was no Soviet promise to stand beside Czechoslovakia regardless of French action.

In Geneva, speaking before the general assembly of the League of Nations earlier on September 21, Litvinov proclaimed that the Russian War Ministry was ready to meet with representatives from the French and Czech war ministries; the question should be raised under Article 11 of the Covenant to mobilize public opinion; there ought to be a meeting of the great powers of Europe and anyone else who was interested in drawing up a collective note. Russia was prepared to render aid in accordance with the terms of the Soviet-Czech pact.[5]

[5] Celovsky, *Das Münchener Abkommen*, 374–77: Andrew Rothstein, *The Munich Conspiracy*, 121; Alexandrovsky to Commissariat for Foreign Affairs, September 19, 1938, *NDM*, 86–88; Potemkin to Alexandrovsky, September 20, 1938, *ibid.*, 90; Hencke to German Foreign Ministry, September 19, 1938, *DG*, II, 838; Edward Taborsky, "Beneš and the Soviets," *Foreign Affairs*, Vol. XXIX, (January, 1949), 304–306; *Soviet Documents*, III, 303.

Litvinov's performance was potent Russian propaganda but worthless in easing the Czechoslovak agony. He neglected to tell his audience that France must first fulfill her obligations under the pact. Because he knew this would not happen, he could promise Russian help with the world listening. His other suggestions were either too slow or involved nations who had no wish to battle Germany over the Sudetenland.

Beneš was reluctant to embrace Soviet help because many in his government opposed such a step, particularly the Agrarian party. If he spurned the Western proposals and turned to Russia, the West would consider him an instrument of Bolshevism. He would not be a Kremlin stooge like the Czech Communist, Klement Gottwald, who urged him to fight, alleging that Stalin would help if Czechoslovakia first resisted Germany. To follow such advice would make Beneš and his people ever more dependent on Russia, while Great Britain and France would abandon Czechoslovakia as they had abandoned the Loyalist government of Spain.

Beneš' decision to submit to the Anglo-French plan was influenced also by the conduct of the Poles, Hungarians, and the Slovak minority. On September 16, Beck instructed his agents, in London, Paris, Rome, Belgrade, and Bucharest to demand the same concessions for the Polish minority in Czechoslovakia as were given to the Sudetens. If the Sudetens were granted self-determination, the Poles must have the same. On September 17, the Polish frontiers were manned by troops. When Beck learned of the Anglo-French plan for a revision of frontiers without a plebiscite, he had his agents again demand the same for the Poles in Teschen.

Hitler revealed new plans to the Polish ambassador on September 20. He preferred to occupy the Sudetenland by force; however, if his conditions were accepted, he would have to abide by them only because of German public opinion. If his proposals were declined, Hitler was prepared for armed action to annex the Sudetenland. If he were asked to guarantee the frontiers and freedom of the rump of Czechoslovakia, he would do so only if Poland and Hungary made a similar guarantee and their demands were met. If war came between Poland and Czechoslovakia, Hitler promised that Germany would side with Poland. He preferred that the Poles commence fighting only after the Germans took the Sudeten mountains, in order to shorten the battle.

On September 21 the Polish government officially demanded from Czechoslovakia the same treatment Germany had received. If Germany obtained land, Poland must have land. If Beneš resisted Germany, he could expect an attack from the north.[6]

On September 20, Prime Minister Imrédy and Foreign Minister Kánya were received by the *Führer*, who was resolved to settle the Czech crisis at the risk of a world war. All of the Sudetenland must become part of the Reich; Britain and France would not intervene; Czechoslovakia must be destroyed. "It was quite impossible," he asserted, "to tolerate the existence of this aircraft carrier in the heart of Europe." At the next meeting he planned to present his demands to Chamberlain with brutal frankness, hoping for rejection and disturbances within Czechoslovakia to give him a pretext for invasion. He directed Imredy to demand a plebiscite in the territories claimed by Hungary and to refuse any guarantee of the new Czechoslovak frontiers. Imredy vowed to comply with Hitler's orders.

The Hungarian government had been fearful that Yugoslavia might object to an increase in Hungary at the expense of Czechoslovakia. Fears of Yugoslav support were needless; on September 21, Yugoslav Premier Stoyadinovitch expressed doubts that the provisions of the Little Entente were binding now that Czechoslovakia was ready to cede territory.

Already on September 20 the Slovaks, prompted by the Germans, had demanded autonomy. From Rumania came no message of loyal support for her ally. All indications were that Rumania would be neutral; Berlin was assured that such was the case.[7]

The knowledge that no nation would support Czechoslovakia impelled Beneš to submit to the Anglo-French ultimatum. Nowhere was there a word of encouragement, no pledge of armed assistance,

[6] Wühlisch to German Foreign Ministry, September 16, 1938, *DG*, Series D, II, 811; Molkte to German Foreign Ministry, September 20, 1938, *ibid.*, 849–50; Woermann to Ribbentrop, September 21, 1938, *ibid.*, 861–63; Lipski to Beck, September 20, 1938, *Documents Relating to the Eve of the Second World War*, I, 176–84; Bonnet, *Défense de la paix*, I, 256–57.

[7] Schulenburg to the German Foreign Ministry, September 19, 1938, *DG*, Series D, II, 847–48; Hencke to German Foreign Ministry, September 20, 1938, *ibid.*, 852–53; Imredy to Hitler, September 20, 1938, *ibid.*, 850–51; minutes by Erich Kordt, September 21, 1938, *ibid.*, 863–64.

but only demands for territory, only cries to tear asunder Czechoslovakia. Hitler and his allies were of one mind: dismember Czechoslovakia. Against such an array, Beneš could not prevail.

# 15

## Godesberg

AFTER THE ANGLO-FRENCH ULTIMATUM had been accepted, Chamberlain asked Hitler to resume the talks at Godesberg on September 22 at 3:00 P.M. Although Hitler accepted the proposal, he ordered the preparations for war to continue and preparations to begin for the peaceful penetration of the Sudetenland.

For the West on September 22, the news was grim. During the night of September 21–22, Sudeten Nazis had seized Czech towns. Along the Czech-German frontier, thirty German divisions were in position, moved up under the guise of peacetime maneuvers. Prague requested full mobilization because Germany would attack sometime before September 23. London and Paris advised Prague to abstain from mobilization while negotiations were in progress.

There were no indications that Hitler dreaded Russian intervention because German divisions in East Prussia were below strength, lacking modern weapons and tanks. In the eastern skies the planes of the *Luftwaffe* were absent. There seemed little that Czechoslovakia could do to offset the impending German invasion.

While his plane warmed up for the flight to Germany, Chamberlain informed newsmen that a peaceful solution of the Czechoslovak problem was essential for Anglo-German understanding—"the indispensable foundation of European peace." He declared: "European peace is what I am aiming at, and I hope this journey may open the way to get it."

His plane reached the Cologne airfield at 12:27 P.M. Ribbentrop,

Hitler's bodyguard, a brass band, the *Gauleiter* of Cologne, and a host of minor officials met the Prime Minister's plane. Chamberlain emerged hatless but with umbrella in hand. Surprised by his reception, he flapped his right hand in a half Nazi salute. As he drove away from the airfield, German citizens, out on their lunch hour, and children, given a holiday from school, cheered the bewildered but smiling Englishman. At Bonn, Chamberlain's car crossed the Rhine and then drove on to the St. Petersburg Hotel in Godesberg. There the British delegation found a magnificent suite of rooms prepared for them. Fruit, cigars, and cigarettes had been supplied, as well as samples of the products manufactured by the hotel owner: eau de cologne, hair lotion, shaving soap, bath salts, and hair pomade.

At 4 P.M., Chamberlain and his delegation crossed the river by ferry, escorted by police launches. The British entered the lobby of the Dreesen Hotel, crowded with a glittering array of Nazi satraps. To cries of *"Der Führer kommt,"* Hitler appeared, preceded by an S.S. guard. He chatted for a few moments with Chamberlain, asking questions about the journey and the hotel accommodations. Then Hitler led Chamberlain into a conference room, with windows looking out on the Rhine and the distant mountains. The room had a large table covered with green baize; Hitler sat at the head with Chamberlain on his right, and Paul Schmidt, the interpreter, and Ivone Kirkpatrick on his left. Kirkpatrick, head of chancery in the Berlin embassy, had been brought to the conference by Chamberlain to provide a British account of the meetings and to check on Schmidt's translating. There was silence for a moment, then Hitler gestured to Chamberlain to begin.

Like an efficient executive, Chamberlain reported on his recent diplomatic activity. He had convinced the French and Czech governments to accept self-determination, because Hitler wanted a quick solution; they had all agreed that the Sudetenland should be ceded to the Reich. An international commission would draw the frontier; those territories in which Germans comprised 65 per cent of the population would be returned to the Reich. Germany would take over public buildings at agreed valuation and assume a proportionate share of the Czechoslovak public debt. The British government would join in guaranteeing Czechoslovakia against becoming a victim of unprovoked military aggression.

Chamberlain finished, proud of his achievements of the past few days. Hitler asked if these had been submitted to the Czechoslovak government; Chamberlain assured him they had. *"Es tut mir furchtbar leid, aber das geht nicht mehr,"* Hitler announced. "I am very sorry," he said, "but these [proposals] cannot be maintained." As the words were translated, Chamberlain started, his face flushed with anger.

Hitler reverted to an old theme, the Versailles myth. Czechoslovakia was an artificial being, based only on political considerations. Great wrongs had been done to the Sudetens, the Slovaks, and the Poles. Now Hungarian and Polish representatives would not agree to their nationals' remaining under Czech rule. Their demands had his sympathy; until their claims were settled, there would be no peace.

For him as a German the problem was urgent. Delay was impossible; the question must be settled completely by October. Because of the unstable political conditions within Czechoslovakia, no one knew what the future might bring. Now there was a Czech cabinet crisis; Bolsheviks were fighting to seize control; a total of 480,000 refugees had flocked to Germany since 1918; Sudeten, Slovak, Hungarian, and Polish soldiers deserted from the Czechoslovak army; daily there were shooting affrays along the frontier. If this continued there would be a regular frontier war.

Chamberlain was hurt and angry. Hitler disappointed him because he had told him to arrange for the settlement on the basis of self-determination, with only the procedure left for discussion. Without the shedding of a drop of German blood, the Prime Minister had brought the French and Czechs to accept the *Führer's* desires. He had jeopardized his political career; today he had been accused of selling out the Czechs; he had been booed when his plane left England. He only wanted "to show the world that the orderly operation of treaty revision could be achieved by peaceful means. Agreement had been reached in principle." What proposals did Hitler have?

Thus Chamberlain threw the question back to Hitler to avoid breaking off the negotiations and placing the onus for war on the shoulders of the west. Hitler wanted a frontier line based on language drawn at once; the Czechs must withdraw their army, police, and all government officials behind the line. The German army would occupy the area enclosed within the line. He would hold a plebiscite on the basis of the 1918 population, excluding all the Czechs that had moved in since and permitting all of the Germans who had emigrated to vote. After the plebiscite, the frontier could be adjusted by a frontier commission. The Czechs could not have any indemnification for state property; destruction or removal of property by the Czechs would be a breach of the agreement. Hitler would accept a nonaggression treaty after the Polish and Hungarian claims had been met. The *Führer* asserted that the remainder of Czechoslovakia did not interest Germany.

Hitler required the immediate release of Germans serving in the Czech army and police. Chamberlain was agreeable, but he found it difficult to fix a frontier which projected far into Czechoslovakia and would be considered unfair by the English public. Hitler grew more angry at the old man's arguments. "If English public opinion took that view," he yelled, "it was because their information was based on the Czech maps used in England." The plebiscite would prove that the German map was fair, and it would show the world how many Germans lived in Czechoslovakia against their will. Once more he stated two solutions: a peaceful one with a national frontier or a military solution with a strategic frontier.

Chamberlain found this incredulous because war meant loss of life. If Hitler could obtain his wishes peacefully without loss of life, why did he seek the reverse? Alert to avoid a break over the use of force, Hitler replied that he preferred a good understanding with the English rather than a good strategic frontier with the Czechs.

In response to a request by Chamberlain for more information on the language frontier, the meeting adjourned to another room to view the maps. Here the argument went on. Chamberlain pressed Hitler for more details on his plan, but Hitler roared that after their conduct for the last twenty years, the Czechs had no reason to complain. There must be speed, for if Prague became Bolshevik, or if hostages continued to be shot, he would at once order his troops to march on Czechoslovakia.

Chamberlain begged Hitler to intervene with the Sudetens while the British intervened at Prague. With reluctance the *Führer* consented to try to reach the Sudetens although it would be a terrible strain on his nerves to withhold orders from his troops in view of Czech provocation. No military action would take place. (Indeed, his plans were not yet complete). Chamberlain and Hitler finished talking for the evening; they agreed on further conversations the next day.[1]

By shrewd use of the Versailles myth and the alleged Sudeten suffering, Hitler kept Chamberlain on the defensive. The demand for speed made peace dependent upon a quick Czech surrender. Because Hitler's arguments were short on logic, they confused Chamberlain. Stubbornly the Prime Minister hammered away at the need for an efficient, peaceful method of cession. Several times the talks veered to the brink of war, but one or the other fended off the collision. Hitler could not have a break down in the talks when he appeared to be the one who could not be appeased. He wanted others to reject his conditions, leaving him free to invade Czechoslovakia. At no time was there any quibbling over the sacrifice of Czechoslovakia.

About 7:15 P.M. the conference broke up. Chamberlain and his party drove down to the ferry, amid cries of *"Heil* Chamberlain!" Disturbed at the direction of the discussions, Chamberlain hurried up to his suite in the St. Petersburg Hotel. By the next day he had made up his mind not to resume the discussions but to send Hitler a letter.

To clarify the negotiations, Chamberlain explained in his letter that he was prepared to place Hitler's proposals before the Czechoslovak government. The military occupation, however, would be impossible because French and British opinion would condemn it "as an unnecessary display of force." The Czechoslovak government would not consider it to be in accord with the Anglo-French plan. When German troops entered the Sudetenland, Czechoslovak forces would do likewise. "This would mean destruction of the basis upon which you and I a week ago agreed to work together, namely, an orderly settlement of this question rather than a settlement by use of force." Alternatives could be found to Hitler's proposed occupation. In some areas, Sudeten Germans could maintain law and order; there would be no need for a German occupation. If his suggestion were accepted, Chamberlain would seek the views of the Czechs and urge them to withdraw their forces, leaving the maintenance of law and order to the Sudeten Germans.[2]

The negotiations were apparently deadlocked, yet Chamberlain

[1] Minutes of conversations between Chamberlain and Hitler at Godesberg, September 22, 1938, *DG*, Series D, II, 870–79; *DBFP*, Third series, II, 463–73.

[2] Chamberlain to Hitler, September 23, 1938, *DG*, Series D, II, 887–88.

had not broken them off. His letter displayed a willingness to go a long way towards granting Hitler his desires. For the Czechs in the Sudetenland, his solution meant a reign of terror. He was agreeable to a cession of the Sudetenland if it were peaceful, orderly, and free from the threat of force.

While he awaited a reply to his letter, Chamberlain lunched, regaling his hearers with tales of his early days in Birmingham and a discussion of the theater. On the opposite side of the Rhine, his letter produced hurried consultations. About 3 P.M., Paul Schmidt emerged from the Dreesen Hotel carrying a letter from Hitler while newsmen followed his progress with field glasses. Ignoring their questioning in the hotel lobby, he went to the British suite. After an hour spent in translating the letter and answering Chamberlain's questions, Schmidt was sufficiently fortified with a couple of drinks to run the gauntlet of waiting newsmen once again. He returned to the anxious *Führer*, who wanted to know Chamberlain's reactions. Schmidt could only report that Chamberlain displayed little excitement and promised a reply by letter.

In his letter, Hitler repeated the tale of the frustrated attempts by the Sudeten Germans to end their suffering at the hands of the Czechs. Again Hitler rehearsed the Allied failure to keep Wilson's Fourteen Points and allow the Sudetens to belong to Germany. They must be returned by the right of self-determination, enforced by the German Reich. To enable changes in the frontier, he would permit a plebiscite under international commission or a German-Czech commisison. He would even withdraw German troops from the disputed territory during the plebiscite if the Czechs did the same. Entrusting the maintenance of order to the Sudeten Germans he considered impossible because of past opposition to their political organization.

If the principle that the Sudetenland belonged to the Reich was sincerely accepted, no reason existed for postponing action. Similar conditions applied to the other oppressed nationalities within Czechoslovakia. If Germany could not have the rights of the Sudetens recognized by negotiations, other means would be used. His meaning was clear: either grant his demands or face war.

The British delegation rejected the possibility of a rupture because that would throw the onus on them, leaving Hitler free to shout his grievances. If a rupture came, Chamberlain lacked a written

160

statement of Hitler's demands; without such a document, Hitler could say whatever he liked. Wilson and Henderson were dispatched to the Dreesen Hotel with another letter from Chamberlain. The Prime Minister explained that in his role as "intermediary" he must now present Hitler's proposals to the Czechoslovak government. He requested a memorandum containing these proposals and a map indicating the areas to be transferred: then he would return to England and report to his colleagues and the French government.[3] British fears of a rejection of this request were ended by a telephone call from Ribbentrop that Hitler would be pleased to discuss a memorandum with Chamberlain later in the evening.

In the Dreesen Hotel the drafting of the memorandum was not easy. According to the memorandum, suffering by the Sudeten Germans made the separation of the Sudetenland an urgent matter for the peace of Europe. The frontier should be delimited according to the wishes of those involved. While the plebiscite was being prepared, disturbances must be prevented. Attached to the memorandum was a map indicating areas the German troops should occupy. Hitler demanded that Czech troops and police begin evacuation on September 26 and complete it by September 28. The area would be handed over without destroying or injuring any of the industrial plants, military installations, wireless stations, or rolling stock. No foodstuffs, cattle, or raw materials were to be removed; the area would be handed over in its present condition. All Sudeten Germans in the Czech military and police forces would be discharged and all German political prisoners freed. A German·Czech commission would manage the plebiscite held in areas designated on the map before November 25. All persons residing in the area on October 28, 1918, or born there prior to that date had the right to vote.

The memorandum was not as important as the attached map, where a line delineated the occupation for German troops. Thousands of Czechs were to be included in the occupied area while many Germans would remain in unoccupied territory. Within the occupied area lay important Czech industries and vital rail centers. In the north and south, the frontier line cut far into Czechoslovakia, tearing the nation almost in two.

These Godesberg demands did not all originate with Hitler. On

[3] Hitler to Chamberlain, September 23, 1938, *ibid.*, 889–91: Chamberlain to Hitler, September 23, 1938, *ibid.*, 892.

September 15, Henlein had proposed German occupation of areas in which Germans comprised over 50 per cent of the population, omitting a preliminary plebiscite. Two Sudeten deputies came to the Foreign Office on September 17, acting under orders from Henlein, and objected to a preliminary plebiscite for the Sudeten area. They proposed that a zone be designated and transferred to the Reich, then a decision could be made on the method of dividing the area. A map showing the suggested line was prepared and sent to Hitler.

Henlein made this proposal because of the failure of the Sudeten attack following Hitler's speech on September 12. By his sudden flight to the safety of the Reich, Henlein had weakened his cause among the Sudeten Germans. He might lose an honest plebiscite. The new proposal would give Hitler's forces a foothold in Czechoslovakia in case open conflict came, and the Czechoslovak forces would have less time to act if attacked. Germany could thus begin to attack Czechoslovakia from Czech soil.

Some of Hitler's demands had come from the German High Command, whose suggestions had been sent to him before he met Chamberlain. If the Czechs agreed to cede the Sudetenland, the High Command advised Hitler to demand withdrawal of Czech troops from the ceded area; surrender of arms and fortifications in the ceded area; discharge of Sudetens in the Czech armed forces and police; ceding of specified area for purely military purposes; the cessation of all military intelligence activities directed at Germany; the release from prison of all Sudetens convicted of espionage; prohibition against destruction of all military installations in the ceded areas as well as all rolling stock, radio transmitters, and public utilities; demobilization of the armed forces and destruction of all fortifications in the unoccupied area of Czechoslovakia.[4] Enough of these demands were incorporated into the Godesberg memorandum to sap Czech defensive strength.

Not until 10:30 P.M. was the British delegation invited to receive the memorandum. When they arrived at the Dreesen Hotel, the

4 Memorandum of Altenburg, October 17, 1938, German Foreign Office Microfilm, reel 2443, frame 23927; Henlein to Hitler, September 15, 1938, DG, Series D, II, 801; Chief OKW memorandum September 21, 1938, NCA, III, 347–49; British Delegation, Godesberg, to Newton, September 24, 1938, DBFP, Third series, II, 495–96.

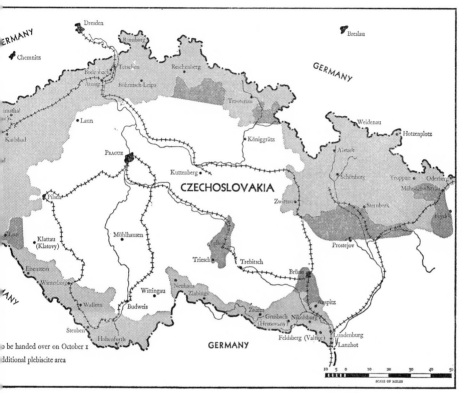

Reproduction of map attached to the German memorandum
at Godesberg, September 23, 1938.

Based on a map in *Documents on British Foreign Policy, 1919–1939.*

163

lobbies were almost empty; the bodyguard was gone. Heinrich Hoffman, Hitler's official photographer, recorded the gathering; then they moved off to the lounge. Included in the meeting now were Henderson, Ribbentrop, Wilson, Weizsäcker, Schmidt, and Kirkpatrick.

Hitler was a smiling host as he presented the memorandum, declaring that the Sudeten question was for the Germans "not only a national question of life and death, but also a question of national honor." A solution to this question could well be a turning point in Anglo-German relations.

Chamberlain also wanted a peaceful solution that would become a turning point in Anglo-German relations, but at Berchtesgaden, Hitler had accepted self-determination with only method and procedure to be settled. Now Hitler refused to consider the Prime Minister's proposals and demanded immediate cession and occupation.

Hitler retorted that this problem had lasted for twenty years and necessitated a quick solution. He had never thought that Chamberlain would mediate, and he had anticipated settling the question in a different manner. Some in Germany wanted to destroy the Czechoslovak state entirely; that the memorandum did not adopt these views could be attributed to Chamberlain's suggestions.

Chamberlain complained that Hitler was gambling away the prospects of peace to avoid a few days' delay. Hitler demanded to know what the Prime Minister meant. Chamberlain referred to the demand in the memorandum that the evacuation begin on September 26; this was impractical. "The whole thing was in terms of dictation, not in terms of negotiation."

A message brought to Ribbentrop was read to the group: Beneš had ordered general mobilization. The dining room was quiet. "In that event," said Hitler, "things are settled." Hastily Chamberlain argued that they were not settled; Czech mobilization was only a precaution, not an offensive measure. Germany had also mobilized. Hitler retorted that the mobilization meant that Czechoslovakia would not cede territory. The memorandum was his last word; he had to take certain military measures because of the Czech mobilization. In that case, answered the Prime Minister, there was no further purpose in negotiations. "He would go home with a heavy heart, since he saw the final wreck of all his hopes for the peace of Europe.

164

But his conscience was clear; he had done everything possible for peace."

The Prime Minister promised to transmit the memorandum to Czechoslovakia if Hitler would not invade Czechoslovakia. Hitler assured him that he would not invade Czechoslovakia during the negotiations.

Chamberlain complained that, in form, the memorandum was an ultimatum and not a document of negotiation. Hitler replied that the document was headed "Memorandum," and not "Ultimatum." Chamberlain was impressed by contents because the language was that of a conqueror dictating his will to the vanquished. Hitler and Ribbentrop inquired about his objections. He objected to the word "demand." Putting on his spectacles, Hitler looked at the memorandum and agreed to change the word. Chamberlain did not want a Czech-German commission but an international commission. Hitler changed the wording to read "a Czech-German commission or an international commission." In response to Chamberlain's protest, Hitler changed the time limit for Czech evacuation of the Sudetenland to October 1—the date called for in his plans. Chamberlain objected to the occupation of areas that were not predominantly German. Could not Hitler have his troops occupy only those areas with German population of 80 per cent? Hitler replied that his generals wanted troops in all of the Sudetenland. Occupation of only part of the area would hamper troop movements, for roads and railway lines passed through areas where Germans were not in the majority. What protection would Hitler give to the Czechs in the occupied area and to the Germans who opposed cession? Hitler swore that he would only prosecute murderers and Communists. Chamberlain ended the discussion with a promise to transmit the proposals to the Czechs.

As the Prime Minister left the hotel, he bade Hitler farewell exclaiming that between them a feeling of confidence had grown in the last few days. He hoped that the present trouble could be overcome, and then he would discuss other problems with Hitler in the same spirit. Hitler declared once more that "the Czech problem was the last territorial demand which he had to make in Europe."

When Chamberlain returned to his hotel, waiting newsmen asked if the situation were hopeless: he replied: " 'I would not like to say that. It is up to the Czechs now.' " Later in the morning of September 24, he returned by air to London.[5]

For Britain and France the Godesberg meeting was a warning of Hitler's goals. Here he had revealed his intention to incorporate Czechs into the Reich, disregarding self-determination. Instead of negotiation over the transfer of land, people, and properties, he demanded a hasty occupation that would breed dissatisfaction and offer him further cause to harass the Czechs. He followed his earlier advice to Konrad Henlein in demanding more than the Czechs would give. By these tactics he made the Czechs appear to be warmongers while uniting his people. The British and French would have to fight a war against the Godesberg demands.

Chamberlain saw only that Hitler advocated a method fraught with danger. He could not see that Hitler wanted all of Czechoslovakia although his desires had been partially revealed. Certainly Chamberlain would have been delighted if the Czechoslovak government had accepted the Godesberg program without too much tumult, but the Czechs had other ideas.

While Chamberlain had conferred with Hitler at Godesberg, reports of violence along the Czech-German frontier poured into London and Paris. Halifax realized that a new situation was developing. That Germany was deliberately seeking an excuse to launch an attack could no longer be denied. Late in the afternoon of September 22, Daladier agreed with him that they ought to withdraw their objections to Czech mobilization: otherwise they would "incur a terrible responsibility."

After consulting with Hoare and Simon, Halifax proposed to advise the Czechoslovak government that the British and French governments would no longer take the responsibility of preventing mobilization. Chamberlain, however, disagreed, instructing Halifax and the French to suspend the advice until further discussions with Hitler the next day. He feared that news of the mobilization would disrupt the negotiations, making Hitler appear the injured party.

By midday September 23, Paris and London learned of the impasse

5 Price, *Year of Reckoning*, 291–92; Schmidt, *Hitler's Interpreter*, 96–102; Ivone Kirkpatrick, *The Inner Circle*, 113–19; R. W. Seton-Watson, *Munich and the Dictators*, 24; notes of the conversations between Hitler and Chamberlain in Godesberg, September 23–24, 1938, DG, Series D, II, 898–908;*DBFP*, Third series, II, 499–508.

at Godesberg. Once more Halifax asked if he could advise the Czechs, but Chamberlain refused until he had received Hitler's reply to his letter.

In the afternoon, learning of the contents of Hitler's letter, Halifax informed the Czechoslovak government that the British and French governments no longer opposed mobilization. Later in the afternoon, Chamberlain sent a similar message.[6]

Members of the new Czechoslovak government met at the presidential palace on the evening of September 23. By 6:15 P.M., France and Great Britain had given a sovereign government permission to mobilize. At 10:30 P.M. the Prague radio announced the order for the mobilization of all classes under forty years of age. The announcement ended with the cry, "Our cause is a just one!"

The proclamation of mobilization was greeted with cheers in Prague as men and women poured into the streets. Cars were commandeered to take men to railway stations. Processions of singing, shouting Czechs escorted some to their destinations. Suddenly the lights of the lovely city were dimmed. By the next day one and one-half million men were under arms. Offices needed for the prosecution of the war were handed over to the military. Antiaircraft batteries were deployed around the city; a guard was placed over the railroad. Communist newspapers were suspended. Foreigners and Czech reservists who were forty years of age and older flocked to volunteer for military service. Czechoslovakia was preparing for war.

[6] Halifax to Phipps, September 22, 23, 1938, *DBFP*, Third Series, II, 457–62, 480–81; 488; Phipps to Halifax, *ibid.*, September 22, 23, 1938, 459, 481: British Delegation, Godesberg, to Halifax, September 22, 23, 1938, *ibid.*, 462, 488; Halifax to Newton, September 22, 23, 1938, *ibid.*, 460–61, 483; Viscount Templewood, *Nine Troubled Years*, 309.

# 16

## And After Godesberg . . .

ON THE EVENING of September 24, Chamberlain outlined Hitler's position to the cabinet. The Prime Minister would accept his demands and advise the Czechs to do likewise. A suggestion for adjournment to study the Godesberg demands brought a protest from Duff Cooper, first lord of the Admiralty. The Germans were not convinced that Britain would fight; only an immediate declaration of full mobilization would persuade them. Already the chiefs of staff had judged immediate mobilization "vital and important." Chamberlain interrupted in anger; the chiefs of staff were assuming the danger of war with Germany in a few days; this was not necessarily so. Duff Cooper begged that preliminary measures be taken to protect the Suez Canal. Chamberlain refused. Leslie Hore-Belisha, secretary for war, wanted some mobilization—the only argument Hitler could understand. Antiaircraft and searchlight units could be deployed without a general mobilization. Frightened lest such measures drive Hitler to war, Chamberlain refused again.

Another meeting of the cabinet on the morning of September 25 was the scene of an argument over aid to France, with Hore-Belisha insisting on support of Czechoslovakia despite the unpreparedness of the armed forces. The meeting ended without a decision.

In an afternoon meeting, Chamberlain announced that Daladier and Bonnet were coming the same day for a conference. Cooper complained over the lack of decision; because others were not as alarmed as he over the paralysis, he would resign. Fearing the cabinet would be weakened by the resignation of the First Lord of the Admiralty, Chamberlain persuaded Cooper to reconsider. The meeting broke up without any agreement on policy regarding either the Czechs or the French.[1]

During the afternoon of September 25, Jan Masaryk brought the Czech reply to the Godesberg demands. The German demands were an ultimatum to the defeated rather than a message to a sovereign nation prepared to sacrifice for the peace of Europe. The Godesberg demands exceeded the Anglo-French plan of September 18 and deprived Czechoslovakia of every safeguard for her national existence. Large areas of the Czech defense system would be ceded and German troops admitted before new defenses could be organized. Masaryk informed Whitehall:

Against these new and cruel demands my government feels bound to make their utmost resistance and we shall do so, God helping. The nation of St. Wenceslas, John Huss and Tomáš Masaryk will not be a nation of slaves. We rely upon the two great western democracies, whose wishes we have followed much against our own judgement, to stand by us in our hour of trial.

Chamberlain then gave Masaryk a new plan for an international conference, including Germany, Czechoslovakia, and other powers, to consider the Anglo-French plan and the best method of placing it in operation. Masaryk replied on September 26 that the proposal was acceptable but in the conference his government would discuss the unworkable features in the Anglo-French plan. They wanted a binding guarantee against aggression during negotiations; their troops would remain in the fortifications. Chamberlain was amazed at such stubbornness. His attitude moved Masaryk to bewail the "bad luck that this stupid, badly informed, little Englishman is prime minister."[2]

The French cabinet considered the news of Godesberg in the afternoon of September 25. Daladier announced that the plan was unacceptable; he would accept either an international commission or a plebiscite but not the latter under threat of German guns. He would

1 Cooper, *Old Men Forget,* 234–37; R. J. Minney, *The Private Papers of Hore-Belisha,* 144–47.

2 Masaryk to Halifax, September 25, 26, 1938, *DBFP,* Third series, II, 518–19, 550–51; report of Masaryk, September 26, 1938, *Europäische Politik,* 132.

not go beyond the Anglo-French plan of September 18 and proposed a "symbolic and a progressive occupation," which was approved by the cabinet. They favored an international commission working while the occupation occurred. If Hitler resorted to force, Daladier promised to call the Chamber of Deputies into session. The Premier would make every possible concession, but in the face of an unprovoked aggression, the engagements with Czechoslovakia would come into play.

Bonnet gave the cabinet his version of the telegram to de Lacroix during the night of September 20–21. He protested the stories about his pressure on Prague. The meeting broke up in a heated argument over French obligations to Czechoslovakia with some arguing that France was only obligated to take the matter to Geneva, not to go to war. In a driving rain, Daladier and Bonnet drove to the airport with their aides. During the flight to London, all was silent on the plane as they meditated and studied their papers.[3]

At 9:25 P.M. on September 25, the French ministers accompanied by Corbin, Alexis St. Léger, Charles Rochat, Jules Henry and Roland de Margerie came to No. 10 Downing Street. There Chamberlain had assembled Halifax, Simon, Hoare, Vansittart, Horace Wilson, Alexander Cadogan, permanent undersecretary of state for foreign affairs, E. E. Bridges, secretary to the cabinet, and William Strang and F. K. Roberts from the Foreign Office.

Chamberlain gave his account of the meetings with Hitler at Godesberg. Daladier replied with the announcement that the French government rejected Hitler's right to take Czech territory by force and his demand for a plebiscite in purely Czech areas. Disturbed by such resolution, Chamberlain explained that Germany only intended to preserve law and order until a plebiscite could be held and the final frontier determined. The area handed over to Hitler would not be final until a definite frontier was decided after a plebiscite. The only difference between the Anglo-French plan and Hitler's Godesberg demands was that an area would be occupied by German troops. Should the eventual frontier exclude this area, Hitler would withdraw his troops. Chamberlain asked for French proposals.

Daladier wanted the Anglo-French plan of September 18; if Hitler refused then each knew his duty. Chamberlain was not satisfied.

3 Zay, *Carnets secrets*, 11–17.

170

Should Hitler's memorandum be refused, he would march into
Czechoslovakia. What then would be the French attitude? Hitler
would have provoked the aggression, Daladier replied, but Chamberlain was suspicious. Would France declare war? Daladier retorted,
"In the event of unprovoked aggression against Czechoslovakia,
France would fulfill her obligations." Chamberlain inquired about
the French plans, assuming it was impossible to give Czechoslovakia
direct aid. Daladier expected that France would help by bringing
Germany's forces on herself.

Sir John Simon took up the prosecution. Did Daladier contemplate an invasion of Germany? Daladier referred Sir John to General
Gamelin, who was not present. Although he was "only an ordinary
public man" who was not playing strategist, Sir John asked if the
French intended to man the Maginot Line or to declare war and
take offensive action? Daladier replied that such would depend on
many things. Would the French air force be used over German territory? Daladier had considered its use. How did they intend to use it?
His anger rising, Daladier rebutted that, after concentrating troops,
an offensive would be launched against Germany, and it would be
possible to bomb industrial and military centers. For the Premier
these strategic details were not as important as the moral obligations
of France: he would not accept Hitler's desire to destroy Czechoslovakia and dominate the world.

Sir John asked what would Daladier do if Hitler's plan were rejected? The Premier proposed to create an international commission
and then to arrange for a rapid German occupation with a Czech
withdrawal.

Chamberlain thought the plan reasonable but Hitler would reject
it. What they would do if faced with a swift German invasion in two
or three days? Daladier had advocated offensive operations against
Germany by land and air, but the British government had received
alarming reports on the condition of the French air force and the
capacity of the French industries to maintain supplies. What would
happen when bombs rained down on French industry? What assurances had Daladier about Russia? Britain had only disturbing news.
The French press indicated that France was pacifist. Chamberlain
wanted precise information on these points.

The angry Premier retorted that French opinion was indicated by the million Frenchmen who had manned the Maginot Line. They must face facts: after Czechoslovakia, Hitler would turn to Rumania, then Turkey, followed by France, and perhaps even Ireland.

Daladier confessed that the French air force was inferior to the *Luftwaffe*. Nevertheless, after mobilization the French air force could hold its own with Germany in total number of airplanes. They were evading the main question: "Mr. Chamberlain had indicated that Herr Hitler had spoken his last word. Did the British government intend to accept it?"

Sir Samuel Hoare took up the prosecutor's role. Within a short time Czechoslovakia would be overrun. How could they prevent this? Daladier would not answer. Instead he asked three questions: Would the British government accept Hitler's plan? Did they contemplate bringing pressure on the Czechoslovak government to concede even though they knew the Czechoslovak government would die rather than accept this plan? Should France do nothing?

Chamberlain replied that it was up to the Czechoslovak government to accept or reject Hitler's proposals. The British government would not exert any pressure on the Czechoslovak government. The French government must decide for itself on future action.

The Prime Minister asked if Gamelin could not come over the next day; Daladier agreed that it could be arranged. Chamberlain then excused himself for a meeting with the cabinet.

While the French ministers waited, the British cabinet met to hear the report of a tired Prime Minister. Chamberlain informed them that while the French had been evasive, they had promised to fulfill their obligations to Czechoslovakia. As a final effort, Chamberlain announced to the cabinet that he was sending Sir Horace Wilson to Hitler with a letter asking for an international commission to settle the details of the transfer. Should Hitler refuse, Wilson was to announce that France would fight for Czechoslovakia and Britain would support her. The casual announcement was accepted without objection. Hore-Belisha insisted on more precautionary measures such as the mobilization of antiaircraft batteries. His request was ignored.

The meeting with the French resumed at 12:35 A.M., but the exhausted statesmen agreed to adjourn until the next morning.

At the French embassy, Daladier and Bonnet received a telegram from the minister of the interior reporting that there were not enough gas masks for the population; the British government must supply at least one million. Their hosts informed Daladier and Bonnet that one million could not be supplied because there were not enough for the British population.

Chamberlain had questioned Daladier closely on the French attitude towards war because the information coming to the Foreign Office indicated lack of unity. Newspaper opinion was running strongly against war. According to Joseph Caillaux, president of the finance commission of the Senate, that body would vote against war, and only a small majority of the Chamber would approve war. Pierre Flandin, leader of the French Left Republican party, called at the British embassy to declare that all of the peasants opposed war. If there were heavy bombardments, he prophesied demands for an early peace and Communist regimes in the cities. Phipps reported, "All that is best in France is against war, almost at any price." Without initial victories, the best and worst in France would blame Great Britain for urging them to fight in a losing battle.

On the morning of September 26 when Gamelin met with Chamberlain, the General announced that, although France would mobilize five million soldiers, at the beginning of the war only one hundred divisions could be put in the field. Freedom for maneuver would be provided by the Maginot Line. Germany's fortifications were incomplete: the High Command was fearful of war; there was a lack of properly trained German reserves; in a long war the Reich would have supply troubles. France would suffer from the attacks of the *Luftwaffe,* but with firm morale she would hold out until her armies obtained the victory. Czechoslovakia, with thirty to forty divisions, could save her army if she retreated. She would give a good account of herself in the war.

When Gamelin met with Thomas Inskip, minister for co-ordination of defense, the service ministers, and their chiefs of staff, they tried to pin him down to an estimate of the duration of Czech resistance. At first he insisted that it depended on Polish action; later he admitted that the Czechoslovak army could hold out only for weeks but not for months. He expected no effective help from Russia because of Polish and Rumanian opposition to the passage of Russian troops. There was only a slight possibility that Rumania would permit the passage of Russian planes. He revealed nothing of his plans for the French army. He could not conceal his fear of German air attacks on French cities in retaliation for Anglo-French raids on Germany. Gamelin proposed a declaration not to attack the civil population; air forces would not go beyond the battlefield and would avoid attacks on towns within the battle area. His plans and ideas impressed Sir John Slessor as "optimistic to the point of lunacy."

On September 26, Chamberlain opened his first meeting with Daladier and Bonnet by stating that Hitler's final intentions would be known that night through his speech at the Berlin *Sportpalast*. Czechoslovakia was determined to resist, and the French government would fulfill their obligations. The British government would not go back on public statements that they would assist France rather than see her overrun or defeated by Germany. Lest any chance for peace be omitted, Chamberlain was sending Sir Horace Wilson to see Hitler that same day with a personal message: the content could not then be disclosed.

Both parties agreed on a joint *démarche* to Poland asking for an attitude of benevolent neutrality towards Czechoslovakia. In return Czechoslovakia "might be prepared to agree to the cession to Poland of Teschen." The meeting ended after a press communiqué had been prepared.

In these meetings, the British sought to trap the French into admitting their unpreparedness and confessing that war over Czechoslovakia was out of the question. Daladier would not be decoyed into such a confession, but he saw that British sentiments lay not in stout opposition to Hitler's plans of conquest, but in searching out French weakness and excuses to avoid war.

At the British cabinet meeting which followed the departure of Daladier and Bonnet, Chamberlain announced that the French leaders had definitely promised to fight; they had been assured of British support. There was no dissent from the cabinet. In an afternoon meeting, decisions were swiftly reached on measures of defense. At 6:00 P.M. a state of emergency was proclaimed by Orders in Council. The fleet was mobilized. Orders went out for the summoning of coastal defense units and antiaircraft batteries in the Territorial Army. Great Britain was preparing for war.[4]

[4] Record of Anglo-French conversations, September 25, 26, 1938, *DBFP*, Third series, II, 520–41; Phipps to Halifax, September 24, 25, 1938, *ibid.*, 508–10, 513–14; Halifax to Phipps, September 27, 1938, 575–76; Bonnet, *Défense de la paix*, I, 268–

174

Chamberlain dispatched Horace Wilson to Hitler with a private letter on September 26. The Prime Minister told the *Führer* that the Czechoslovak government had rejected the Godesberg memorandum and had complained that the memorandum exceeded the Anglo-French proposals and weakened Czechoslovakia. Because the Czechs accepted the Anglo-French plan, Chamberlain could see no reason for Hitler's complaint that German rights could not be secured through negotiation. He implored Hitler's consent to a meeting of German and Czechoslovak representatives to settle the transfer of territory; if desired, Chamberlain would have a British representative present. Chamberlain believed that such a conference would assure a cession "in an orderly manner with suitable safeguards."

Chamberlain also gave Wilson a secret message for Hitler in his own handwriting. The Prime Minister stated that, according to Daladier, if Hitler's armies crossed the Czechoslovak frontiers, French armies would attack Germany. If this occurred, "Great Britain would enter the war at once on the side of France with all her forces."

At 5:00 P.M. on September 26, Hitler received Wilson, Nevile Henderson, and Ivone Kirkpatrick. Deep in a black mood, Hitler was little interested in the Prime Minister's letter and handwritten message. Wilson declared that the Godesberg memorandum had shocked British public opinion. Hitler snarled that it was no use talking further. With a request that he please listen, Wilson continued with his tale. The Prime Minister had succeeded in bringing the cabinet, the French government, and the Czechoslovak government to accept the Berchtesgaden demands. Hitler interrupted, demanding immediate settlement. Patiently Wilson explained that although Hitler's insistence on speed was appreciated, his method had shocked British opinion.

Schmidt, Hitler's interpreter, began to translate Chamberlain's letter. At the statement of the Czechoslovak rejection, Hitler jumped up and started for the door, yelling, "There's no point at all in going on with negotiations!"

Wilson implored the *Führer* to hear the rest of the letter. Hitler shouted that he would not tolerate twenty thousand refugees daily. His wrath ill-concealed, Hitler slumped in a chair; Schmidt con-

70; Gamelin, *Servir,* II, 350–55; Cooper, *Old Men Forget,* 237; Minney, *The Private Papers of Hore-Belisha,* 148–49.

tinued. But Hitler broke in again. When it was time to give Germany something, there were delays. They treated Germany like "niggers," and even worse than a Turk. "On the first of October I shall have Czechoslovakia where I want her!" he raged. If France and Britain wanted to attack, let them. He did not care.

Wilson pleaded that Chamberlain was appealing to Hitler. Let him appeal to Beneš, Hitler snarled. Henderson promised that the British government would insure that the Czechs turned over the territory. Schmidt started again. When he came to Chamberlain's proposal for a conference of German and Czech representatives, Hitler exclaimed, "Incredible! Amazing!"

At last the reading was finished. Hitler ordered that Czechoslovakia send a representative to put the Godesberg demands into effect, not to negotiate a settlement. Ignoring plaintive objections from Wilson, Hitler roared on. He would not let Beneš lead him around by the nose. Wilson pleaded for a Czech representative to come to Berlin. Hitler wanted someone prepared to accept the Godesberg memorandum completely. There must be an affirmative reply by 2:00 P.M., September 28. There was no need for further talk; it was time for action.

The conference broke up as Hitler damned the Czechs, berated Wilson and Chamberlain, and vowed to have the Sudeten territory by October 1. Sir Horace Wilson bade him good by, promising to call upon him in the morning.

To Halifax, Wilson reported that it had been a "very violent hour."[5]

Invasion of Czechoslovakia would involve the French air force, whose future was not promising, according to a letter on September 26 from General Vuillemin, chief of staff, to his superior, Guy la Chambre. The General reported that in a war France would be at a great disadvantage because the air force lacked reinforcements. He would be unable to make up the casualties suffered in the early weeks of the war. Except for Paris, the remainder of France would be defenseless before the onslaught of the *Luftwaffe*. French bombers

[5] Schmidt, *Hitler's Interpreter*, 102–103; Kirkpatrick, *The Inner Circle*, 122–24; notes of conversation between Wilson and Hitler, September 26, 1938, *DBFP*, Third series, II, 554–57; Henderson to Halifax, September 26, 1938, *ibid.*, 552–53; Chamberlain to Hitler, September 26, 1938, *DG*, Series D, II, 944–45; Bullitt to Hull, September 26, 1938, *FRUS, 1938*, I, 667–69.

could attack only a short distance inside Germany during daylight. Vuillemin dreaded the repercussions from German bombing of French urban areas.

His fears were not groundless, for in Paris there was slight enthusiasm for war. The people were resigned but scarcely resolute. No one wanted to risk his life for Czechoslovakia. On September 26 the longing for peace was growing; most Frenchmen were willing to have the Anglo-French proposals implemented.

Daladier was strengthened by the London trip for at last he had Chamberlain's promise to support France if Germany attacked. To Bullitt he appeared again the courageous poilu, resolved to mobilize all France if Hitler should mobilize and to attack Germany if Czechoslovakia were invaded. Although the war would be long and horrible, he was certain that France would triumph. He swore never to allow Poland or Hungary to destroy Czechoslovakia, yet he still hoped for a conference, summoned by President Roosevelt "to organize genuine peace in Europe."

Bonnet wanted peace at any price. Early on the evening of September 26, he asked Phipps to inquire in London if France mobilized and proceeded to war on Germany, would Britain mobilize when France did so? Would Britain introduce conscription? Would the British pool their economic and financial resources with those of France? Now that war seemed inevitable, he sought to know what help could be expected from the British. Perhaps here he might find some way to keep France from war.

Not until the evening of September 28 did Phipps bring the answer to Bonnet's questions. Regarding mobilization, Britain was calling up defensive units of the auxiliary R.A.F. and mobilizing her fleet. Britain would not mobilize her land forces. As for conscription, Halifax referred the French to the conversations of April 28, 1938, when Chamberlain had rejected conscription and promised only two underequipped divisions. Halifax observed that the pooling of economic resources raised a constitutional issue that Parliament would have to decide.[6]

Bonnet was not surprised at these answers. Here was no stirring

<hr />

[6] Les événements, II, 313; Bullitt to Hull, September 26, 1938, FRUS, 1938, I, 666–69; Phipps to Halifax, September 26, 1938, DBFP, Third series, II, 546–47, 558–59; Halifax to Phipps, September 28, 1938, ibid., 602; Bonnet, Défense de la paix, I, 272.

call to allied unity such as Churchill raised in 1940. Policy would be hesitant and halfhearted. Bonnet was strengthened in his desire for appeasement.

While Bonnet had awaited the British reply, Hitler had given the world new threats. On the evening of September 26, fifteen thousand Germans jammed the Berlin *Sportpalast* to hear the *Führer's* new pronouncements. Once more Hitler reviewed the story of his frustrated attempts to achieve peace. He sketched the terms of the Godesburg memorandum, defending them as only "the practical execution of what Mr. Beneš has already promised." Now Beneš alleged that he could not give up this area. "On October 1 he will have to hand over to us this area."

Hitler assured Chamberlain that once this territorial problem was solved, he would want nothing more for Germany in Europe. Once the Czechs solved their minority problems, "then I have no further interest in the Czechoslovak state."

"We want no Czechs!" Hitler yelled. His patience was ended; the final decision was in Beneš' hands.

As Hitler sat down, Goebbels jumped up, yelling: "One thing is sure: 1918 will never be repeated!" A wild look crossed Hitler's face. Leaping to his feet, fanatic rage gleaming in his eyes, he made a great sweep with his right hand, brought it down on a table, and screamed "*Ja!*" Then he collapsed into a chair. Now Chamberlain had the answer to his letter.

Hitler's speech brought a statement for the press from Chamberlain. He found it unbelievable that people who disliked war must "be plunged into a bloody struggle over a question on which agreement has already been largely obtained." Hitler, said he, had no faith that Czechoslovakia would carry out her promises. Chamberlain's government was ready to see that the Czech promises were carried out promptly if the German government would use discussion instead of force. He begged Hitler not to reject the proposal because it would satisfy German desire without bloodshed.[7]

The next morning, September 27, Daladier gave his cabinet the latest information on Wilson's talks with Hitler and revealed Chamberlain's message to Hitler promising support for France. For the

[7] *Speeches of Adolf Hitler*, II, 1512–25; William L. Shirer, *Berlin Diary: The Journal of a Foreign Correspondent, 1934–1941*, 141–42; Chamberlain's statement to the press, September 26, 1938, *DBFP*, Third series, II, 559–60.

IN THE SUMMER OF 1938, HORACE WILSON described Czechoslovakia as "an air cushion out of which the air was
gradually escaping." Here, Wilson (foreground)
talks with Count Dino Grandi, the Italian
ambassador in London.

*U.S. Information Agency*

A TALL, ELEGANT FIGURE, JÓZEF BECK seemed like something
from the Renaissance. He admitted to French ambassador Léon Noël that "the fate of Czechoslovakia leaves us cold."

*U.S. Information Agency*

future, Daladier proposed to seek conciliation but to increase mobilization.

Bonnet objected to further mobilization lest Germany be angered. He urged only indirect aid to Czechoslovakia because France was unprepared to give direct assistance. Never before had there been such a bad diplomatic situation: Germany, Italy, Poland, and Japan were antagonistic toward France; France had to fight on three fronts; Britain would send, at most, two divisions, some planes and the fleet; Russian help was doubtful. He demanded that Parliament be summoned and reminded them of General Vuillemin's warning: the air force would be destroyed within two weeks. Bonnet called on Guy la Chambre for support. The Minister for Air preferred to speak before the committee on national defense.

Angry voices objected to Bonnet's remarks. Reynaud protested, "If Hitler knew what the Minister for Foreign Affairs has just said, the loss of Czechoslovakia would certainly be a sure thing!" A few ministers took Bonnet's side against other yelling ministers.

Daladier appeared dumfounded at Bonnet's antics. Seizing a pen, Daladier began to write out his resignation, but he was easily persuaded to stop. The meeting ended in supreme confusion.

Because Daladier seemed intent on supporting Czechoslovakia, Bonnet tried to change the Premier's mind once more in the afternoon. France was weak; war would only help fools. If victorious, would they still keep the Sudetens within Czechoslovakia? The Premier would not be swayed: France would support Czechoslovakia.[8]

When Wilson returned to see Hitler at noon September 27, the *Führer* was in a worse mood than before. Wilson tried to set things aright with complimentary references to the speech at the *Sportpalast*. Could he take back any message for Chamberlain? Hitler had none except thanks for Chamberlain's efforts. Wilson explained that Chamberlain would inform the Czechoslovak government of the situation, and they would decide. Hitler roared that they could either accept or reject.

Wilson became more solemn. Speaking quietly, he explained that many Englishmen hoped for an agreement between Germany and Great Britain. Current events would have great effect on future Anglo-German relations. If the Czechs rejected the memorandum,

[8] Georges Suarez and Guy Laborde, *Agonie de la paix, 1935–1939*, 114–17; Zay, *Secrets carnets*, 18–21; Pierre Lazareff, *De Munich à Vichy*, 67–69.

where would the conflict end? Total destruction of Czechoslovakia would be the first end, Hitler interrupted.

Wilson ignored him and plodded on. If France engaged in hostilities with Germany, Britain would feel obliged to aid her. Hitler and Ribbentrop interrupted; this would only happen if France attacked. Hitler could not see any British obligation to attack Germany if France did so.

Patient Sir Horace started to repeat his statement slowly: if Czechoslovakia refused and Germany attacked, France would fulfill her treaty obligations. Again Hitler interrupted, "Which means that France must attack Germany!" Sir Horace insisted that he was only using Daladier's words. Hitler repeated his charge: if France attacked Germany, Britain would support France, and there would be war within six days. Unless his memorandum were accepted, he would smash the Czechs. "If France decided to attack Germany, then England would have to attack Germany!" he yelled. Sir Horace denied the charge. Again Hitler repeated: he would smash the Czechs, France would attack Germany, then England would attack Germany. Wilson insisted that "we must find a way to avoid war." There was one way, Hitler screamed, make the Czechs stop their "frivolous" game and fulfill their obligations. The conference had ended. War seemed certain.

Wilson reported on the interview immediately by telegraph. As he told the story, he asked Hitler if there were anything that Chamberlain could use at the "eleventh hour" to achieve peace. Hitler desired that Chamberlain bring pressure to bear on the Czechs to accept the Godesberg demands. Wilson described Hitler as listening "quietly" to the final warning. The *Führer* had replied, "I do not intend to attack France. It therefore means that France will attack Germany, and England, also, will attack Germany." When Wilson repeated the warning of British support for France, Hitler and Ribbentrop declared their intention not to attack France.[9]

By means of these threats, Hitler had placed Chamberlain and Halifax in a position they did not relish: they became the aggressors. Not until September 28 did they know exactly what Hitler had said in the interview with Wilson. At hand, however, was Wilson's tele-

[9] Henderson to Halifax, September 27, 1938, *DBFP*, Third series, II, 561–64; notes of conversation between Wilson and Hitler, September 27, 1938, *ibid.*, 564–67; *DG*, II, 963–65.

gram that Hitler would remain on the defensive, Hitler's speech that he wanted no more Czechs, and a report from Henderson of a talk with Göring on September 26 that Germany would remain on the defensive in the west. To succor Czechoslovakia, Britain and France must invade Germany. When German armies defended themselves, the Western forces would become aggressors. Chamberlain was convinced of the justice in the Sudeten complaints. Should the British government reply to a cry for self-determination with an invasion?

Hitler's announcement of his intention to remain on the defensive in the west was unexpected. A sudden, massive bombing, turning all of Paris and London into a bloody, smoky shambles, had been anticipated at the same time as a powerful thrust by the *Wehrmacht* against the Maginot Line. Now Hitler's armies would remain on the defensive and force Chamberlain to wage offensive war—a role for which he was wholly unsuited.

At 1:00 P.M., September 27, Hitler ordered the first assault units to their stations for attack on September 30 at 6:15 A.M. *Luftwaffe* attacks should commence as soon as the weather permitted. To prevent any leaks, final mobilization measures would be carried out without special orders to the Nazi party and the police. If the enemy knew that the attack was scheduled for a certain hour, they might decide to fight instead of surrendering. Later in the day, Hitler ordered five more regular divisions mobilized for duty in the west with the nine divisions, frontier guards, and labor battalions already assembled there.[10]

Even as Europe tottered on the brink of war, both sides maneuvered to make the other appear the aggressor. Both were thinking of other nations who watched from afar and sought shelter from the impending conflict.

[10] Schmundt memorandum, September 27, 1938, *NCA*, III, 350–52, 379.

# 17

## Nuetrals and Knaves

As EUROPE DREW NEAR the brink of war, nations sought shelter from the approaching conflict. Holland, Luxembourg, Norway, and Sweden proclaimed their neutrality. Dictator Francisco Franco, helped to power in Spain by Germany and Italy, hastened to seek neutrality. Members of the British Commonwealth were reluctant to fight; they favored pressure on Czechoslovakia to cede the Sudetenland. There were signs that war over such an unpopular issue might demolish the Commonwealth.

Like the Commonwealth countries, the United States had taken little action in the Czechoslovak crisis. Isolationists had frightened the government away from strong action. Secretary of State Cordell Hull would exchange information, confer, and perhaps "proceed on parallel lines" with other nations, but always he reserved full freedom of action when the United States appeared on the verge of commitment to any forceful line of action.

Hitler's agents reported that there were "no military preparations whatever in the United States of America." High officers of the armed forces and politicians were determined not to side with Great Britain and France. American conduct was guided by an overwhelming desire to have peace at any price.

Old hands in the State Department alleged that the British and French schemed to trick the United States into statements of opinion in order to shift the responsibility for their action on to American shoulders. On this score, Joseph P. Kennedy, the United States ambassador to Great Britain, was considered quite susceptible: the Machiavellian Foreign Office was always trapping the naïve millionaire.

Reports on the Godesberg talks forced Roosevelt to ignore the isolationists and the State Department. He ordered a statement drafted for dispatch to Hitler and Beneš. The message was sent on September 26. Should war come, the President wrote, millions of lives would be lost, economies destroyed, societies ruined. The American people wanted to live in peace. They hoped the negotiations would continue to a successful conclusion. Roosevelt appealed to the leaders not to break off talks because once broken off "reason is banished and force asserts itself."

Daladier, Chamberlain, and Beneš sent their personal thanks for this message. Chamberlain proposed to express his gratitude by a personal broadcast to the American people on September 27. Dreading isolationist rage, Roosevelt preferred to receive his thanks through other media.

The message of the greatest importance came last. Hitler disclaimed all responsibility if future developments brought a conflict. He rehearsed once more the story of the Sudeten question and thrust the blame on Wilson, the League of Nations, and the Prague government. Remembering that Americans were sympathetic to stories about refugees, Hitler wrote that there were 214,000 Sudeten refugees inside Germany and "countless dead, thousands wounded, tens of thousands of people detained and imprisoned" in Czechoslovakia. For these reasons he had determined to give the Sudetens the help of the German Reich. His Godesberg memorandum aimed only at just fulfillment of the Czech promises; this could no longer be postponed.

Roosevelt decided to try again on September 27. He asked Daladier and Chamberlain about a meeting of directly interested powers in a neutral country and a direct appeal to Hitler. Daladier was delighted with the suggestion because if Hitler rejected the appeal, he would weaken his support among the Germans; if he accepted, peace would be saved. Chamberlain was tired and bitter when he received the news; he expected Hitler to march into Czechoslovakia the next day. If Roosevelt wanted to say something, this was the only thing that might help.

At 10:18 P.M., September 27, Roosevelt's message went off to the *Führer*. The President stressed the present problem, not errors and

183

injustices of the past. Because agreement in principle was already reached, negotiations should continue; they could be expanded into a conference of all nations directly involved. If Hitler accepted, millions would recognize his service to humanity. The United States would not assume any obligations in the negotiations.

Roosevelt's message reached Berlin at 9:45 A.M., September 28. No reply was ever made by the German government. By mid-afternoon the Munich Conference had been called for the following day.[1]

At the time Roosevelt's efforts were much commented upon in London and Paris. He has since been blamed for the appeasement of Hitler at Munich. Some have accused him of originating the plan for the Munich Conference. Actually, other factors and forces produced the conference: the idea of such a meeting had already been discussed in Paris and London.

Hungary had a more direct interest in the Czech crisis than the United States. She craved Ruthenia, Slovakia, and all the Magyar-inhabited areas of Czechoslovakia. Unfortunately the Hungarian army was unfit for offensive operations and had ammunition for only thirty-six hours of combat. Nevertheless, almost two hundred thousand troops were under arms, concentrated near the northern and western frontiers.

On September 22 the Budapest government requested from Prague treatment for Hungarian nationals in Czechoslovakia similar to that accorded the Sudetens. Prague replied on September 26 that the Hungarians would be accorded minority rights within the framework of the Czechoslovak state. To increase the pressure, the Hungarian Foreign Ministry grumbled to French and British diplomats that if Germany marched into the Sudetenland, Hungary and Poland would occupy their minority areas. From Poland came firm assurances of support.

On September 28, the Hungarian government grew bold enough to demand equal treatment; any discrimination would be an un-

1 Thomsen to German Foreign Ministry, September 24, 1938, *DG*, Series D, I, 922–23; Hitler to Roosevelt, September 27, 1938, *ibid.*, 960–62; telephone conversations, Welles and Kennedy, September 27, 1938, *FRUS, 1938*, I, 678–79; Roosevelt to Hitler, September 26, 27, 1938, *ibid.*, 686–88; *The Memoirs of Cordell Hull*, I, 574; *The Moffat Papers: Selections from the Diplomatic Journals of Jay Pierrepont Moffat, 1919–1943* (ed. by Nancy Harvison Hooker), 202–203, 205–206.

friendly act. Peace would be insured only if Hungarian claims were settled at the same time as the German demands.[2]

Unlike Hungary, Poland was determined to wrench territory from Czechoslovakia. After the conversation of Ambassador Lipski with Hitler on September 20, Colonel Beck knew that German support had been promised; he could now present his demands to Prague. On September 21 he required that Polish peoples in Czechoslovakia receive treatment analogous to that given the Sudetens; Teschen must be ceded. At the same time he denounced the Polish-Czech treaty of 1925 relating to the treatment of Polish minorities in Czechoslovakia.

The only hope for Czechoslovakia was to hold Poland to neutrality by promising to cede the Teschen territory. On September 26, Beneš asked the president of Poland to accept the principle of rectification of the frontiers through the usual channels without foreign interference. In another note, Krofta proposed negotiations to reach an understanding. The British and French governments hinted that if Poland guaranteed her benevolent neutrality, Czechoslovakia might agree to cede Teschen.

Beck, who wanted to play the role of a statesman of a great power, rejected the offer. Prague must cede immediately those areas in Teschen with Polish majority; Polish troops would occupy the areas indicated on an attached map; plebiscites would be held in areas where the Poles were not in the majority.

When news of these demands reached London, Halifax instructed Newton to advise the Czechoslovak government "to abandon without delay all diplomatic maneuvering" and agree to negotiate the cession of the areas inhabited by a Polish majority. Prague did not hasten to comply because the Polish area contained a strategic railway center at Oderberg. Thinking the cession would set a bad precedent, Beneš agreed to cede some areas only after appropriate negotiations. He knew that Poland could not be depended upon to help Czechoslovakia in any German aggression because the loot was too tempting on the other side.

London and Paris were of little help. Halifax would only caution

[2] Knox to Halifax, September 21, 26, 1938, *DBFP*, Third series, III, 11-12, 36-37; memorandum of Sargent, September 22, 1938, *ibid.*, 19-21; Newton to Halifax, September 28, 1938, *ibid.*, 43; Hencke to the German Foreign Ministry, September 26, 1938, *DG*, Series D, II, 956-57.

Warsaw not to "take any rash and irrevocable steps," and to continue negotiating with Prague. The French government found the Polish alliance a useful excuse to avoid pressure on Warsaw.[3]

Polish troop concentrations on the Czech frontier led Krofta to ask Moscow to remind Warsaw that the Polish-Russian non-aggression pact would be invalid if Poland attacked Czechoslovakia. On September 23, Potemkin informed the Polish chargé that if Polish troops crossed the Czech-Polish frontier, Russia would renounce her non-aggression pact with Poland. The Polish government replied that measures had been taken in defense of Poland which were the exclusive concern of the Polish government: Poland did not have to give an explanation to anyone. Colonel Beck sneered that the Russian threat was merely a "propaganda gesture." Because he had little respect for Russian military power, he ignored the threat. He could well do so because Potemkin's statement omitted any reference to the Mutual Assistance Pact with Czechoslovakia which required French support before Russian. Renunciation of the non-aggression pact would have placed Russia under no obligation whatsoever. To Czech listeners, it sounded as though Russia would fight Poland in the event of Polish invasion of Czechoslovakia.

Before the Assembly of the League of Nations on September 23, Litvinov spelled out Russian obligations: if France remained indifferent to the fate of Czechoslovakia, Russia was not pledged to intervene. If France did follow such a policy, the Soviet Union could aid Czechoslovakia by a voluntary decision or by a decision of the League of Nations, but nothing required unilateral aid from the Soviet Union. Litvinov explained that Czechoslovakia had not raised the question of help independent of France "out of practical considerations." He was referring to Poland and Rumania, the convenient barriers to Russian aid to Czechoslovakia.

Litvinov insisted that the Anglo-French ultimatum implied a renunciation of the Mutual Assistant Pact with Russia. After accepting the Anglo-French ultimatum and its implications, Prague had asked

3 Popée to Krofta, September 21, 1938, in L. B. Namier, *Europe in Decay: A Study in Disintegration*, 286–87; Mosciki to Beneš, September 27, 1938, *ibid.*, 290–21; Kennard to Halifax, September 22, 26, *DBFP*, Third series, III, 16, 38–40; Halifax to Kennard, September 26, 30, 1938, *ibid.*, II, 545, III, 53; Halifax to Newton, September 27, *ibid.*, 40; Newton to Halifax, September 28, 30, 1938, *ibid.*, 42–43, 49–50.

if the Soviet Union would still be bound by the pact if Czechoslovakia decided to go to war. Litvinov proclaimed that the Soviet Union would fulfill the obligations to Prague under the terms of the pact which first required France to grant assistance to Czechoslovakia.

If the Soviet Union had been sincere in its protestations of support for Czechoslovakia against Nazi Germany, this would have been the opportunity and the audience in which to rally the anti-Nazi forces. Instead Litvinov retreated behind the pact, calling for France to commence hostilities before Russia. His government would not defend Czechoslovakia against Nazism.

Shortly after Litvinov finished his speech, two members of the British delegation, Lord De La Warr and R. A. Butler, cornered him. They were acting under instructions from Halifax to seek his government's intentions if Germany attacked Czechoslovakia. They asked him to develop his ideas further, a task which he did not relish. They were extremely interested in learning "at what point [the] Soviet government would be prepared to take action."

Litvinov repeated his tale that only if France assisted Czechoslovakia would Russia march. Of course he did not add his personal opinion that France would take no action. His listeners asked if he would raise the Czechoslovak question at the Assembly meeting. Would Russia take action while the question was being discussed at Geneva? Litvinov hedged, alleging that they "might desire to raise the matter." Instead, he welcomed conversations between Great Britain, France, and Russia away from Geneva, with Rumania and other interested small powers attending. Such a meeting, he said, would show the Germans that they meant business. At that time he would be prepared to discuss military questions about which he now knew little because he had been away from Russia so long.

Litvinov had already proposed a similar meeting and been rebuffed. He knew this proposal would meet a comparable fate and that such a meeting would not produce swift action. He knew also that only force and the determination to use it would show Germany that they meant business. When his meeting convened, perhaps Czechoslovakia would then be no more, and the Mutual Assistance Pact could vanish. Should France actually fight, he could use the need for such conversations to delay Russian participation until Czechoslovakia was gone.

To his audience, Litvinov imparted secret information. His government had informed Poland that the non-aggression pact with Russia would lapse if Poland attacked Czechoslovakia, and then "Russia would take action." He lied. There had been no statement about Russia's taking any action against Poland. Nevertheless, Russia had to appear loyal to the pact with Czechoslovakia and eager to meet the foe.

On September 24, Gamelin informed Moscow of the size of German troop concentrations on the Czechoslovak frontiers. The Soviet air attaché, General Vasilchenko, was instructed to declare that thirty Russian divisions were drawn up along the western frontiers and that aviation and tank units were ready. The attaché was unable to inform Gamelin directly because the general had gone to London on September 26 for a meeting with the British; the news was forwarded to him there. Prompted by this news and at the urging of Winston Churchill, Halifax issued a statement to the press the same afternoon. He declared that Chamberlain had been trying to settle the Czechoslovak question peacefully; the German claim to the Sudeten areas had been conceded. If a German attack was made on Czechoslovakia, "the immediate result must be that France will be bound to come to her assistance, and Great Britain and Russia will certainly stand by France."

Halifax hoped to encourage France and indicate to Hitler the unity of Britain, France, and Russia, but neither France nor Russia wanted to be so united. Bonnet doubted that the statement was authentic; Daladier declared that it came from someone of little authority; the French Foreign Ministry announced that the statement was false. Moscow ignored the statement entirely although here was the basis for action that Litvinov had suggested on September 23 to the British delegation in Geneva.[4]

The other highway for Russian aid to Czechoslovakia was Rumania, who still pursued neutrality. The Bucharest government begged that Hungary not attack Czechoslovakia lest the Little Entente

4 Litvinov's speech, September 23, 1938, *Soviet Documents on Foreign Policy*, III, 304–305; Potemkin's statement, September 23, 1938, *ibid.*, 305; United Kingdom delegation, Geneva, to Halifax, September 24, 1938, *DBFP*, Third series, II, 497–98; Halifax' press statement, September 26, 1938, *ibid.*, 550; Alexandrovsky to People's Commissariat for Foreign Affairs, September 22, 1938, *NDM*, 112; Churchill, *The Gathering Storm*, 308–10; André Simone, *J'Accuse: The Men Who Betrayed France*, 267–68; Camille Bloch, "La politique de l'U.S.S.R. pendant la crise de Munich (mars–septembre, 1938)," *Études d'histoire moderne et contemporaine*, Vol. I (1947), 203–204; Molke to German Foreign Ministry, September 24, 1938, *DG*, Series D, II, 922.

pact come into operation. As for a Polish-Russian war, Rumania would take the side of Poland.[5]

All of these nations in their own way were responsible for what followed. Poland and Hungary were eager to devour Czechoslovakia now that Hitler had given them opportunity. Russia watched the tortures of her allies while mouthing pious calls for conferences which would never occur. Despite Roosevelt's good intentions, the United States was a helpless giant, deliberately self-paralyzed. The assorted neutrals and the Commonwealth countries imitated the priest and Levite in the parable of the Good Samaritan: they preferred to look away and pass by on the other side. Czechoslovakia was bereft of friends as she drew near the brink of war.

[5] Minutes for Ribbentrop, September 26, 1938, *ibid.*, 936; Fabricus to the German Foreign Ministry, *ibid.*, 980–81.

# 18

## At the Brink

THE EPIDEMIC of war fever continued. In London a state of emergency was declared by Orders in Council. Antiaircraft units of the Territorial Army were called to active duty on September 26. All officers and men of the R.A.F. were recalled from leave. Regulations for blackout were issued. The unemployed dug trenches in public parks. Messages were flashed on motion picture screens in London urging parents to have their children fitted for gas masks. Already food hoarding had begun.

Jews fled from Czechoslovak towns along the German frontiers. Anti-Nazis could not sell their homes in the Sudeten areas. "We will get all this without paying a cent for it just as in Austria," yelled Sudeten Nazis. Rail transportation to Germany practically ceased; Czechoslovak troops began to blow up bridges.

Nearly one million men were under arms in France. Men and women streamed away from the German frontier. All carrier pigeons in the border areas were ordered killed lest German spies use them; pigeon bodies were to be presented at the town hall. But in aircraft factories, French workers still labored only a forty-hour, five-day week.

Chamberlain, however, continued his search for ways to peace. Hitler had sworn to remain on the defensive, forcing Britain to the attack—a loathsome prospect to Chamberlain. Czechoslovakia seemed ready to fight, but it was not so with France. No neutral, no Commonwealth member, not even Russia would defend Czechoslovakia.

Should millions of British and French now die to deny the Sudetens their right of self-determination? The horrors of Paschendale, the Somme, and Verdun gave the answer to Chamberlain, but peace was possible only if someone gave way. For Chamberlain, that would be Czechoslovakia.

At 5:45 P.M. on September 27, Chamberlain telegraphed Beneš that no power could prevent the conquest of Bohemia unless the German demands were accepted by 2 P.M., September 28. He would not tell Beneš what to do, but Chamberlain wanted him to have this information. He instructed Newton to explain that the British government believed Hitler's Godesberg demands were unreasonable; however, Chamberlain had a new proposal which would achieve the transfer to Germany while providing safeguards for the Czechs. Unless this new proposal were accepted, the Czechoslovak government must expect "invasion and dismemberment" with terrible casualties and without any assurance that Czechoslovakia would be restored to her present form after the war. Before Newton could see Beneš, telegrams were dispatched at 6:45 P.M. to Berlin, Prague, and Paris with the new proposal.

In his new plan, Chamberlain assured Hitler that his worries over fulfillment of Czechoslovak promises could be set at rest. Now he would deal with the British and French governments, not with Czechoslovakia. Because it was impossible to perfect arrangements for an occupation by October 1, Chamberlain proposed a timetable: German troops would occupy Asch and Egerland on October 1, except for the Czechoslovak fortifications. On October 3, Czech, German, and British plenipotentiaries would meet in the Sudetenland to arrange for the withdrawal of Czech forces, the safeguarding of minority rights, and the preparation of instructions for an international boundary commission. Membership of the commission would include Germans, Czechs, and British who would hold their first meeting on October 3. On the same day, observers from the British legion, a veterans organization, would enter the Sudetenland. By October 10, if possible, German troops would enter the area that had been arranged by the plenipotentiaries. If arrangements were not completed by October 10, the Germans would complete their occupation no later than October 31. The plenipotentiaries would decide on any further changes in the frontiers. Negotiations between Great Britain, France,

Czechoslovakia, and Germany must begin immediately for the demobilization of Czech forces, the revision of Czechoslovak treaties, and the preparation of a joint guarantee.

Chamberlain's proposal was little more than an easing of the Godesberg terms. Czechoslovakia was to be placed in a minority position, and outvoted two to one by the plenipotentiaries. France had been shoved aside to a boundary commission. Russia was not even mentioned although she had a treaty with Czechoslovakia. This was clearly a private deal, to be arranged by efficient statesmen. Here, the Munich Agreement was foreshadowed.

To avoid any chance that Hitler could cry aggression and disrupt this plan, later the same evening, France was asked to avoid any offensive action without first consulting with the British government. Bonnet was delighted to follow such a policy. Halifax insisted on this assurance because the British military attaché in Berlin had reported from personal observation that he had found Czechoslovak army morale low and concluded that resistance would be feeble. Should the peace efforts fail, Czechoslovakia would be quickly overrun. They would be faced with a *fait accompli*: Czechoslovakia would be no more. If Hitler remained on the defensive, France and Britain would then become aggressors seeking to tear the Sudetens away from the Third Reich.[1]

Bonnet had been thinking along somewhat similar lines. In a morning conference with Ambassador Phipps, he suggested that areas of the Sudetenland be evacuated by the Czechs and occupied by the Germans on October 1. He wanted an international commission to begin immediate delimitation of a definite boundary as soon as possible.

When Chamberlain's plan came, late in the evening, Bonnet received it coolly because he did not think that it went far enough. His government would await the results of the German reaction, and if rejection came, he would propose the plan upon which he was then working.

Weizsäcker received the plan with a complaint that it was out of date. He did not think that Hitler would consider it: the only chance for peace was Czechoslovak acceptance of the German plan at once.[2]

[1] Halifax to Newton, September 27, 1938, *DBFP*, Third series, III, 570; Halifax to Henderson, September 27, 1938, *ibid.*, 572–73; Halifax to Phipps, September 27, 1938, *ibid.*, 575–76; Phipps to Halifax, September 27, 1938, *ibid.*, 582.

[2] Bullitt to Hull, September 27, 1938, *FRUS, 1938*, I, 680–81; Phipps to Halifax,

Czechoslovak objections to the timetable proposed by Chamberlain did not reach London until the evening of September 29. Czechoslovakia could not evacuate, demobilize, nor abandon fortifications until the frontiers had been delimited and guarantees secured. Once these conditions were met, the Czechoslovak government promised to accept a final date for cession.

When these complaints reached London, work was well under way for the Munich Conference. Halifax asked the Czechs to refrain from raising objections and thereby rendering Chamberlain's task more difficult. They were to leave Chamberlain "a wide discretion and not to tie his hands at the outset by making absolute conditions."[3]

Before the replies to Chamberlain's proposal of September 27 reached London, a letter arrived from Hitler at 8:40 P.M. which only strengthened the Prime Minister's resolution to proceed with his timetable. Although moderate in tone, the letter was intended as propaganda because Hitler asked the British government to include it in a forthcoming white paper.

The *Führer's* letter was in answer to Chamberlain's note of September 26. Hitler argued that Czechoslovakia erred by feeling that the Godesberg terms would destroy her national existence, abolish her political and economic independence, and create panic among the population. The final settlement would depend on a free plebiscite and negotiations by a German-Czech commission. His demand for immediate occupation was to insure that the Czechs would not delay. The loss of the Czechoslovak fortifications was regrettable, but Hitler would not wait for years until new ones were constructed. German occupation within specified limits could be guaranteed by the French and British governments. Hitler was prepared to give a formal guarantee for the remainder of Czechoslovakia. The economy and independence would not be harmed because it was "a well-known fact that Czechoslovakia, after the cession of the Sudeten German territory, would constitute a healthier and more unified economic organism than before." Czechs in German-occupied territory would not be treated as Sudetens had been treated by the Czechs. Hitler concluded

September 27, 1938, *DBFP*, Third series, II, 582–83; Henderson to Halifax, September 28, 1938, *ibid.*, 584–86.

[3] Newton to Halifax, September 29, 1938, *ibid.*, 618–20; Halifax to Newton, September 29, 1938, *ibid.*, 614–15.

that the Czechoslovak government was only using the occupation to mobilize British and French support for a world war.

When these lines were compared with Hitler's other statements, they implied a new, conciliatory attitude. Here was an offer that made the Godesberg demands seem mild. Here was no war cry, only a call for peace. Here was a promise of independence and security for the remainder of Czechoslovakia. Was this an assurance that Hitler would not destroy Czechoslovak independence and seek only self-determination? Gone was the ranting and the cursing of Beneš; there remained reason, or so it would seem to any who yearned for peace at any price.

The letter was deliberately worded to furnish historians and politicians with proof that Germany would not be guilty of starting the conflict. The onus of the decision for peace or war was thrown on London and Paris: Hitler's last offer would sound very peaceful. The message was intended to weaken the resolve of Britain and France while rousing the German people to wage war in behalf of a just cause. Again the British and French were thrown on the defensive in the propaganda battle.

The letter was not the result of disgust with the warrior spirit of the German people. Some writers argue that Hitler had been much influenced by the apathy of German citizens who watched parading troops on the afternoon of September 27 without any show of emotion. The sight of the listless citizens so affected Hitler that he drafted the letter to Chamberlain. There is little proof for this argument. German preparations for war did not slacken. Had Hitler given the order, German citizens would have marched as loyally as they did in September, 1939, and in June, 1941. The letter was only propaganda. It was to be Hitler's final offer before hostilities came.

Chamberlain spoke to the nation that night in a broadcast which revealed his feelings. Instead of a call to arms in defense of a just cause, he complained: "How horrible, fantastic, incredible it is that we should be digging trenches and trying on gas masks here because of a quarrel in a faraway country between people of whom we know nothing. It seems still more impossible that a quarrel which has already been settled in principle should be the subject of war."

He explained that with time, arrangements could be reached for a peaceful transfer of territory. But it was unreasonable for Hitler to demand immediate occupation of Sudeten areas without providing for the safeguard of those who were not Germans and had no desire

194

GEORGES BONNET (LEFT), French foreign minister, tries to learn of
Russia's intentions from Maxim Litvinov, the shrewd commissar
for foreign affairs. "Don't tell me about our [Russia's] treaty
with Czechoslovakia. . . . Read the text again . . . and you
will see that . . . we are obliged to come to the aid of the
Czechs under the League of Nations machinery and
then only if France has assumed her obligations."

*U.S. Information Agency*

GEORGES BONNET, ÉDOUARD DALADIER, AND ALEXIS ST. LÉGER leave No. 10 Downing Street after a meeting with British ministers on September 26, 1938, to discuss Chamberlain's talks with Hitler at Godesberg.

to go home to the Reich. If it would be useful, Chamberlain was prepared to make another trip to Germany. Despite sympathy for Czechoslovakia, he complained, "We cannot in all circumstances undertake to involve the whole British Empire in war simply on her account." If war came, it must be over a larger issue than that of the Sudeten-Czech quarrel. He closed with a promise to work for peace to the last moment.

Here he spoke, not just to the British nation, but to Hitler, hoping he would hear and heed. Chamberlain had no wish to battle over the Sudeten-Czech problem; to him it was not worth a world war. If Hitler would not be so unreasonable about the occupation of the Sudetenland, peace would be assured.

Later the same evening there was a gloomy cabinet meeting. Reports from Australia and South Africa revealed reluctance to do battle for Czechoslovakia. Wilson reported on the failure of his mission; his advice was to tell the Czech government to evacuate the Sudetenland.[4]

In Paris there was no cry for unity against the Nazi foe. Leading politicians rejected aid to a nation whom France was pledged to protect. Without a united cabinet and faced with strong opposition from both Right and Left, Daladier did not know what to do. He admitted that Hitler wanted to dominate all of Europe, yet he dreaded to challenge him because of the Bolshevist threat. Although France would be victorious, he told William Bullitt that Communist regimes would appear all over Europe and Napoleon's prediction that " 'Cossacks will rule Europe' " would come true.

Growing opposition indicated to Daladier that if he asked Parliament to vote him additional powers, the opposition from both Left and Right would overthrow his cabinet. His career, slowly rebuilt since his fall from power in 1934, could be ruined forever. He desired to keep himself in power; thus, he was not hostile to Bonnet's plan.

The night of September 27–28 was a busy one in the Quai d'Orsay. Bureaucrats, politicians, and journalists wandered in and out without anyone's questioning their presence. Outside a crowd awaited tidings of peace or war.

Inside Bonnet drafted instructions for François-Poncet. If Germany rejected the British plan, he was to propose that Germany occu-

[4] Hitler to Chamberlain, September 27, 1938, *DG*, Series D, II, 966–68; *DBFP*, Third series, II, 576–78; Neville Chamberlain, *In Search of Peace*, 173–75; Cooper, *Old Men Forget*, 239–40.

py the most important parts of the Sudeten territory by October 1. If such a plan were acceptable to Hitler, France would do everything to make the Czech government accept; once war began, this would be impossible. Conflict had no real goal because the Czechs had already agreed to cede. François-Poncet was to assure Hitler himself that his essential demands had been met and that France would persuade the Czechoslovak government to agree to the evacuation by October 1. Bonnet purposely gave Beneš no hint of his proposal.[5]

France had now reached the brink of war, but her government chose to force an ally to surrender rather than plunge Europe into a general war. Great Britain was likewise on the brink of war. A decision for peace or war had to be made the next day—September 28.

[5] Phipps to Halifax, September 27, 1938, *DBFP*, Third series, II, 568; Bullitt to Hull, September 27, 1938, *FRUS, 1938*, I, 686–88; Bonnet, *Défense de la paix*, I, 281–84.

# 19

## War or Peace?

By THE AFTERNOON of September 28, war seemed inevitable. Over eighty thousand Czech soldiers were in the field; Prague was ringed with antiaircraft batteries; trenches had been dug; blackout was in effect. Along the disputed frontier, fighting was in progress; small German forces had swarmed across the frontier and seized some border towns.

In England, plans were completed to remove stained glass windows from Canterbury Cathedral. Cemetery vaults in London's East End were opened for air raid shelters. Officials prepared to move the collections from the British Museum, the Tate Gallery, and the Tower of London. Gasoline stations began to ration gasoline. Applications for marriage licenses increased. Stationery stores exhausted their supplies of forms for wills. The unemployed dug trenches in parks and cricket greens. Antiaircraft guns in Whitehall snarled up parking. German and Austrian servant girls hastily departed.

In Paris, pictures in the Louvre were packed away. Supplies of gas masks and suitcases ran short. Trains were packed with those fleeing from a city soon to be in rubble. House painters began to camouflage factories and railroad stations.

There was little excitement among the throngs in Berlin. Troop movements increased throughout the city. In the Wilhelmstrasse, officers scurried about looking more important than ever before.

At 8:30 A.M. on the morning of September 28, following his instructions, François-Poncet telephoned Weizsäcker and asked for a personal audience with Hitler; the ambassador indicated the major points in Bonnet's plan. If Germany were agreeable, France would "demand acceptance from the Czech government." Should the Czechs refuse the plan, conclusions could be drawn which the ambassador did not need to mention. As for Chamberlain's plan, François-Poncet considered it useless.

While he awaited an answer, François-Poncet phoned Henderson who promised to inform Göring and ask that his influence be exerted. At François-Poncet's orders, his military attaché visited the chief of staff of the army with a warning of responsibility if François-Poncet were not received by Hitler.

About 10:20 A.M. in Rome, Lord Perth, the British ambassador, called on Count Ciano. Perth brought a proposal approved by London, which he had suggested twenty-four hours earlier. The ambassador requested that Mussolini induce Hitler to accept Chamberlain's pledge to guarantee that the Czechs would carry out their promises regarding the Sudetenland. Perth added that only Mussolini could bring Hitler to accept a peaceful solution; if he failed, there would be a European war. The announcement that Britain and France were seriously preparing to fight Germany staggered Ciano. He gasped, "There is no time to be lost; it is a question of hours not days." He darted away to confer with Mussolini.

Soon Mussolini was on the telephone calling his ambassador in Berlin, Bernardo Attolico. The *Duce* ordered him to ask for an immediate interview with Hitler and a twenty-four-hour postponement of the attack on Czechoslovakia to give him time to re-examine the situation and seek a peaceful solution. "The point of difference is very small," Mussolini said. "Tell the Chancellor that I and Fascist Italy stand behind him. He must decide. But tell him I favor accepting the suggestion."[1]

Mussolini had no desire for a European war that might involve Italy; his armies were prepared only for battle against barefooted Ethiopian tribesmen, not against modern European nations. That Britain, France, and Czechoslovakia would resist had not entered his mind. With Hitler victorious in Central Europe, Mussolini knew he

[1] Perth to Halifax, September 27, 28, 30, 1938, *DBFP*, Third series, II, 561, 588–89, 602–603, 641–65; *Ciano's Hidden Diary, 1937–1938*, 165; Allen W. Dulles, *Germany's Underground*, 46.

would become his vassal; if Hitler were defeated, the victors could ignore Mussolini.

At 10:30 A.M. in Berlin, Henderson called at the French embassy to confer with François-Poncet. Their conversation was interrupted by a message that Hitler would see François-Poncet at 11:15 A.M. Before Henderson left the French embassy, he was handed a new proposal from Chamberlain to be delivered to Hitler.

By the morning of September 28, Chamberlain had read the reports from Berlin, certainly noting Weizsäcker's coolness, for he was considered a moderate, interested in peace. Chamberlain now had the full text of Hitler's letter of September 27, throwing the responsibility for war on London and Paris while offering to soften the Godesberg demands. During the night harsh advice had come from Henderson: "Compel Czechoslovakia to yield by informing her at once before mid-day September 28 categorically that if she does not do so, we shall not support her."

The time for decision had come. Chamberlain sent a personal message to Hitler. The Prime Minister had read the *Führer's* letter and felt "certain that you can get all essentials without war and without delay." Chamberlain was ready to come to Berlin with Czechoslovak, Italian, and French representatives to negotiate; within a week, agreement could be reached. The British and French governments would undertake to make Czechoslovakia carry out the decisions of the conference. The final sentence threw the burden of responsibility back on Hitler: "I cannot believe that you will take the responsibility of starting a world war which may end civilization for the sake of a few days' delay in settling this long standing problem."[2] Paris and Rome received copies.

When François-Poncet reached the Reichschancery, feeling was tense; officers rushed about, excited, worried, and confused. Tables were laid to feed the commanders of the invasion units, a banquet before the battle. Hitler was nervous and wandered about haranguing whoever would listen. Occasionally he stopped to confer with Ribbentrop, Keitel, or Göring.

François-Poncet was received by Hitler about 11:15 A.M. while Ribbentrop hovered behind the *Führer*. François-Poncet took the initia-

2 Henderson to Halifax, September 28, 1938, *DBFP*, Third series, II, 586–87: Halifax to Henderson, September 28, 1938, *ibid.*, 587.

tive, knowing that his government had at last made up its mind, and explained Bonnet's plan, using a map to outline the areas to be ceded. He warned that the war would not be localized; everyone in Europe would be caught up in the conflict. Hitler ranted about the Czechs, calling them " 'Mongols and not Slavs!' " The ambassador brought him back to the important problem: Hitler was arousing the world with the threat of war. Ribbentrop interrupted to announce that Germany could withstand any coalition. Ignoring him, François-Poncet suggested that French troops should be sent into the Sudetenland to maintain order while the problem was settled.

One of Hitler's adjutants came in to announce that Attolico waited with a message from the *Duce*. Hitler excused himself, saying that he had to answer a telephone call. Outside, Attolico rushed up exclaiming, "I have an urgent message from the *Duce, Führer!*" Mussolini was with him to the bitter end, but he wished Hitler to delay hostilities for twenty-four hours until a message from Chamberlain could be studied. Mussolini would telephone at noon for the answer. Hitler hesitated then said, "Tell the *Duce* that I accept his proposal." Hitler returned to François-Poncet, giving him the impression that Mussolini had been on the telephone, and the ambassador took up his argument once more. Hitler's mind was no longer on the conversation. He terminated the interview with a promise of reply to the French proposal in the afternoon.[3]

Hitler had accepted the postponement so gracefully and quietly because the attack was not to begin until 6:15 A.M., September 30. Apparent postponement would prove his interest in a peaceful solution.

At noon Mussolini phoned Attolico to say that Chamberlain proposed to liquidate the situation within a week by a conference in Berlin; he would guarantee the execution of the solution. To the *Duce* this was such a "grandiose victory" for Hitler that there was no point in starting hostilities. Attolico scurried to the Reichschancery and delivered his message. Hitler was mystified because he had not yet received Chamberlain's latest proposal. Back to his embassy raced Attolico to find a copy of the Chamberlain proposal. There he found

3 Minutes of Weizsäcker, September 28, 1938, *DG*, Series D, II, 988–89; Schmidt, *Hitler's Interpreter*, 105–108; André François-Poncet, *The Fateful Years: Memoirs of a French Ambassador in Berlin, 1931–1938*, 266–67; Bonnet, I, *Défense de la paix*, I, 283–86: Wilson to Hull, September 29, 1938, *FRUS, 1938*, I, 698–99.

a message from Mussolini stating the *Duce* was ready to participate in a conference if Chamberlain attended.

Henderson brought Chamberlain's proposal for a summit conference at 12:30 P.M. Hitler refused definite reply until he had conferred with Mussolini. He was dissatisfied with the British time table because it implied that the Czechs would not have completely evacuated their area by October 10. That was only another loophole for Czech evasion. For military reasons, he found the French proposal unacceptable. He only wanted the principle of Czech cession. Instead of seeking a world war, the Czechs ought to keep their promise to cede the Sudetenland. If they did not cede by 2:00 P.M., September 29, and send representatives to discuss their plans, he would mobilize.

Hitler was called away from Henderson to see Attolico, but now Hitler was no longer mystified by the Italian ambassador's actions. Provided Mussolini were present as the Italian representative, Hitler promised that he would meet with Chamberlain. He dictated his minimum demands to Attolico, who then hastened back to the embassy to communicate with the *Duce*. At 2:40 he returned to announce that Mussolini would come to the conference.

At 3:15 P.M. Henderson phoned London to report that Hitler had invited Chamberlain, Mussolini, and Daladier to meet him in Munich the next morning. A few minutes earlier Paris had learned the same news from François-Poncet.[4]

During the morning of September 28, Chamberlain's confidant, Horace Wilson, joined in the diplomatic activity. To Fritz Hesse, the press attaché at the German embassy, he explained that the British government was ready to agree to everything that Hitler desired if he would change the form of his demands. It was impossible for a government to advise acceptance of the present form. Once he gave way on the form, the British government would "push through all [the German] demands with the Czechs and French." Nothing would be more welcome in Britain than for the Czechs to capitulate by themselves. Sir Horace explained that Chamberlain had not closed the door on further negotiations as he would show in his speech that afternoon in the House of Commons.[5]

---

[4] Wilson to Hull, October 21, 1938, *ibid.*, 727–29; Henderson to Halifax, September 28, 1938, *DBFP*, Third series, II, 597–99; Cadogan's note, September 28, 1938, *ibid.*, 593–94.

[5] Hesse to Ribbentrop, September 28, 1938, *DG*, Series D, II, 989–90.

In Westminster the House of Commons met as usual in the afternoon of September 28 with opening prayers. At 2:55, Chamberlain rose to address a packed house. Solemnly he declared, "Today we are faced with a situation which has had no parallel since 1914." Then he turned to restate the Versailles myth: the mistakes of treaty makers had produced Czechoslovakia and her minority problems; if the treaty had been revised, the present troubles would not be upon them.

He explained that when the deadlock came in July between the Sudetens and the Czechoslovak government, he feared that Germany might intervene forcefully. Britain could not threaten war because there was no treaty with Czechoslovakia, and the government refused to accept such a liability. The country would not have followed the government into war to prevent the Sudetens from obtaining autonomy. Likewise, the government refused to stand aside and let the crisis erupt into war.

Then Chamberlain launched into a narrative of the tribulations of the summer: Runciman's mission, German military preparations, a warning to Berlin, increased tensions, Ribbentrop's discourtesies, Simon's New Lanark speech, pressure on Prague to make concessions, the Fourth Plan, the Mährisch-Ostrau incident, Henderson's warnings to the Nazis at the Nuremberg Party Rally, Hitler's speech of September 12, Chamberlain's visits to Hitler, the Anglo-French plan, the Godesberg meetings, Wilson's talks, and finally Hitler's letter of September 27.

Chamberlain found modifications of Hitler's earlier intentions in the letter, fresh assurances about restricted troop movements, and a proposed plebiscite. To the House, Chamberlain said, "I believe that he means what he says." Then he read his message to Hitler and Mussolini with the news that Hitler had agreed to postpone mobilization for twenty-four hours.

While Chamberlain was talking in a quiet, matter-of-fact way, almost as if waiting for something to happen, an envelope was handed to Halifax, who was sitting in the gallery. After reading the contents, he slipped out. Next Lord Dunglass, Chamberlain's private undersecretary, entered the House and handed two sheets of paper to members who passed them from hand to hand until they reached Sir John Simon. He read them and then tried to get Chamberlain's attention. When the Prime Minister finally paused, Simon shoved them into his hand. He read the sheets, then turned to Simon and asked, "Shall I tell them now?" "Yes," Simon replied. To a quiet House, Chamberlain said, "I have now been informed by Herr Hitler that he invites me to meet him at Munich tomorrow morning. He has also invited Signor Mussolini and M. Daladier. Signor Mussolini has accepted and I have no doubt M. Daladier will also accept. I need not say what my answer will be." Someone cried: "Thank God for the Prime Minister!" He asked that the debate be adjourned for a few days, "when perhaps we may meet in happier circumstances."

The Mother of Parliaments lost her dignity as cheers and applause broke out; members slapped each other on the back; cheers came even from the Opposition benches. The Opposition leader, Clement Atlee, wished the Prime Minister Godspeed. Anthony Eden was silent; Harold Nicolson remained seated. The cheers were an indication of nerves keyed to grim tidings of a war no one wanted. Few expected what would come forth from Munich. They only knew that war had been postponed, and for that they rejoiced.

Jan Masaryk, as he rode back from the Houses of Parliament with the American ambassador, said, "I hope this does not mean they are going to cut us up and sell us out!"

From Washington came a message to Chamberlain: "Good man." Signed, "Franklin D. Roosevelt."

All night crowds surged past No. 10 Downing Street, shouting: "Good old Neville!" At last the Prime Minister came to the door and spoke: "I think you can all go to bed and sleep quietly tonight. It will be all right now."

"The feeling of relief in Paris tonight is comparable to the feeling of relief when the news came that the armistice had been signed," Ambassador Bullitt reported to Washington. Bonnet was supremely confident that the conference would settle the Czech question without war. Concerning Daladier's mood that night, there is no record.[6]

Mobilization measures in Czechoslovakia were nearly complete. Already units were concentrating along the German frontier. If the French would begin their attack early, the four Czech armies could move quickly enough to prevent Hitler's armies from overrunning Bohemia and Moravia.

6 *Parliamentary Debates, House of Commons,* Fifth series, Vol. 339, cols. 26–28; *New York Times,* September 29, 1938; Kennedy to Hull, September 28, 1938, *FRUS, 1938,* I, 692–93; Hull to Kennedy, September 28, 1938, *ibid.,* 688; Bullitt to Hull, September 28, 1938, *ibid.,* 691–92.

That evening Beneš learned officially of the Munich meeting. Chamberlain assured him that he would have "the interests of Czechoslovakia fully in mind." The Prime Minister intended to "find accommodation between the position of the German and Czechoslovak governments by which arrangements may be made for an orderly and equitable application of the principle of cession to which he [Beneš] has already agreed."

Beneš begged Chamberlain to do nothing that would worsen the Czech situation as planned in the Anglo-French proposals which he accepted and intended to put into operation. "I ask Mr. Chamberlain very earnestly for help because it is our real desire to contribute to peace. I beg, therefore, that nothing may be done in Munich without Czechoslovakia's being heard." He instructed Masaryk to ask that a Czechoslovak representative be at the conference to plead the Czechoslovak cause and supply any needed information. The message was delivered to Chamberlain, who promised to bear all of it in mind.[7]

The news of the Munich Conference was greeted with annoyance in Moscow. Potemkin denounced the meeting as a rebirth of the Four Power Pact from which Russia had been excluded. Russia wanted the Czech dispute solved by a general conference in which Soviet representatives would participate. Potemkin had small concern for the fate of Czechoslovakia because he was angered that Russia had been treated like a small power and excluded from consultations on an area dear to Russian foreign policy. For the record, Moscow's policy left her free of blame in the Munich crisis: France would not fight, so Russia would not. Excluded from the conference, Moscow could turn this to her subsequent advantage.[8]

The most famous summit conference since 1919 had been arranged, and Hitler's armies would not begin war on Britain, France, and Czechoslovakia. Why had Hitler consented to this conference? Why did he consent to negotiate instead of invading Czechoslovakia?

Hitler's acceptance of the conference has intrigued historians. They have credited a variety of reasons for his apparent change of policy, forgetting that he often played by ear and could improvise policy if opportunity made it appear profitable. They have based his accept-

[7] Halifax to Newton, September 28, 1938, *DBFP*, Third series, II, 599, 601; Newton to Halifax, September 28, 1938, *ibid.*, 604; Masaryk to Harvey, September 28, 1938, *ibid.*, 606–607.

[8] Memorandum by Schulenburg, September 29, 1938, *DG*, Series D, II, 998–99.

ance of the conference on: Mussolini's fear of war, apathy of the German public for war, Hungarian reluctance, British and French preparations for war, reluctance of the German generals, need for more preparation, and other similar factors. These may have had some influence, but they must not be exaggerated.

The story of the apathy of the German people is not unexpected because they were surprised that war was so near. Threats against the Sudetens had become normal fare, but going to the brink of war was something they had not really expected from the *Führer* of the Third Reich.

Hitler did not journey to Munich because of fear of an officers' coup. He knew the caliber of these men too well. The tale of the German generals has been told elsewhere and does not need to be repeated except that there is slight contemporary evidence that they were seriously intent on overthrowing him when the Munich Conference aborted their plans. After 1945 they seemed too eager to seize on the Munich Conference as an excuse to blame Chamberlain because they did not stop Hitler.

Hitler agreed to a conference because war did not seem necessary. No valid political goal could be won by starting an invasion because Hitler had been promised the fulfillment of nearly all his desires. Daily the differences between Hitler's demands and the Anglo-French proposals had grown smaller. If these powers aided him in weakening Czechoslovakia, why should he refuse their help? If his wishes were not satisfied at the conference, his armies were still poised for invasion.

Chamberlain's offer of September 28 to come again for a talk, plus the attitudes of Daladier and Mussolini, showed Hitler that there was no cause for war. Everyone except the despised Czechs was willing to grant his demands. Britain and France even promised to force the Czechs to accept whatever plan was adopted. To make war under these terms would be foolhardy and a needless sacrifice of troops. Victory at the conference table would swell his prestige within Germany. The German people would have marched to kill Czechs if he had so ordered, but they would be happier if Hitler brought them victory without war.

Only Czechoslovakia opposed his policies, but this nation was no longer a threat, thanks to Hitler's isolation techniques. No nation, not even the Czech allies, France and Russia, would succor her in her time of need.

No one of importance had suggested resistance except the Czechoslovak government, whose representatives had not been invited to the conference. Everyone present would be committed beforehand to supporting Hitler's terms. Already Chamberlain and Bonnet were outbidding each other in the loot to be taken from Czechoslovakia and given to Hitler. Why battle over this? Hitler had little to lose and much to gain by the Munich Conference.

# 20

## The Munich Conference

THE RESPONSIBILITY for the Munich Conference belongs to many. The idea was not snatched out of nowhere in last minute desperation. Many had considered a conference of the heads of state as the supreme, ultimate tactic; most thought of it as an infallible method for achieving peace.

A four-power conference to settle the Czech-Sudeten question had been spoken of in European capitals since early spring. When Strang had passed through Prague on his tour in May, the possibility had been mentioned in his discussions at the British legation. François-Poncet had been interested in the project since early June, and Bonnet took up the idea with Welczeck later in the same month. By late July, Henderson advocated a four-power conference. In mid-August, von Dirksen noticed "some talk in London of a four-power conference." Even Ribbentrop had inquired if Runciman's report could become the basis for such a conference. The topic became the subject of discussion among the military attachés in Prague by late August. At the same time Ambassador von Dirksen reported Chamberlain's interest in Anglo-German discussions of the Czech question to be attended by France and Italy, but not Czechoslovakia. By the second week in September, Alexis St. Léger, secretary-general at the French Foreign Ministry, favored the immediate summoning of a four-power conference. Bonnet asked for Halifax' views on the subject on September 13; at the same time, Daladier stated that he was agreeable to a high-level conference.

All of the discussion over such a conference had occurred before Chamberlain's first trip to Germany. That event made the meeting inevitable because he had taken diplomacy out of the hands of the professional diplomats. Chamberlain, the head of a government, was dealing with the question, and prestige alone necessitated participation by the other heads of government. Events after September 15 only quickened the calling of a four-power summit conference.

At 6:30 P.M., September 28, Mussolini and Ciano boarded the train in Rome for the trip to Munich. Hitler and Ribbentrop, with generals in attendance, joined the Italians at Kufstein about 9:30 A.M. Like an officer on maneuvers, Hitler unfolded a map, not of Czechoslovakia, but of France, and indicated to Mussolini where he intended to launch his attack—in the vicinity of Aix-la-Chapelle. He was certain that the Siegfried Line would hold, despite the worries of his generals, because he would destroy the Czech army before the British and French could complete their mobilization. On he ranted: he would not cede to the democracies lest Germany's future be ruined. "The only way to avoid giving them the advantage is to attack when they seem disorganized." There was no mention of the coming conference; Hitler sounded as though war had already broken out. He criticized the weaknesses of the Maginot Line. As the train neared Munich, Mussolini asked about German demands on Czechoslovakia. Ribbentrop handed him some demands that had been drawn up in the Foreign Office. If France and Britain would force Beneš to accept these demands, Ribbentrop explained, the Reich government would conclude an agreement.

Oblivious to Mussolini's interest in the memorandum, Hitler rambled on about the morale of the democracies, their hatred for Germany, and their desire to strangle Germany. By now, the train was passing through the suburbs of Munich; subdued crowds watched its arrival and the journey of its passengers to the *Führerhaus* for the conference.[1]

In London that same morning, as his plane prepared to leave Heston Airdrome, Chamberlain declared to the reporters and members of the cabinet: "When I was a boy I used to repeat 'If at first you don't succeed, try, try, try again.' That is what I am doing. When I come back I hope I may be able to say, as Hotspur says in *Henry IV*

1 Filippo Anfuso, *Du Palais de Venise au lac de Garde*, 69–71.

[*Part I,* Act I, scene 5, line 11], 'Out of this nettle, danger, we pluck this flower, safety.' "[2]

His plane left for Munich at 8:35 A.M. as dignified cabinet ministers wildly waved farewell. With him went Horace Wilson, Ashton-Gwatkin, Strang, and Sir William Malkin.

When Chamberlain's plane touched down at 11:05 A.M., he was met by the usual guard together with Ribbentrop, Henderson, and General Franz Ritter von Epp, the governor of Bavaria. A huge crowd thronged around his hotel, cheering the Prime Minister to the strains of "Doing the Lambeth Walk."

Daladier arrived a few minutes later, accompanied by Alexis St. Léger and Rochat, the director of public affairs in the Quai d'Orsay. They were met by François-Poncet, Ribbentrop, Weizsäcker, and the guard of honor.

Shortly after noon, the principals assembled in the *Führerhaus* for the conference. There had been no preliminary discussion among the western statesmen, but Hitler and Mussolini had been together for hours; Chamberlain and Daladier entered the conference completely unprepared for any joint action.

The conference had been hastily planned; there was no agenda, nor was there any ink in the inkwells. The discussions wandered from one topic to another until someone produced a new memorandum, and the politicians seized on a fresh subject for their study. Schmidt, the interpreter, Hitler, Ribbentrop, Weizsäcker, Chamberlain, Horace Wilson, Daladier, St. Léger, Mussolini, and Ciano were present for the first session which lasted until 3:00 P.M. When the conference resumed about 4:30 P.M., the doors were thrown open, and various people strolled in to listen and watch like visitors at a zoo.

The principals' attitudes were contrasting. Daladier was quiet and moody; to one observer he seemed about to vomit. Göring and Hitler were particularly attentive to Daladier; Hitler even discussed the war of 1914–18 with him. Chamberlain was businesslike and legalistic; he insisted on property details which infuriated Hitler. He indicated no distaste for the proceedings because here was a job to do, and he would jolly well do it. Hitler found the conference frustrating: it did not go as he had wished; it was not a repeat performance of his browbeating of Kurt von Schuschnigg, the Austrian chancellor, in February, 1938.

2 *New York Times,* September 29, 1938.

His irritation at the form of the proceedings was ill-concealed. To some he gave the impression that the Western statesmen knew his opinion; they could take it, or leave and have war—for which he was prepared. Mussolini could not hide his joy in the conference. Satisfied that there would not be any war endangering his Fascist state, he had a delightful time.

The necessity to translate into English, French, or German delayed the conversations. Paul Schmidt, Hitler's interpreter, found his patience rapidly exhausted as one after another broke into his translation with a new idea. Exasperated by his charges' antics, like a German schoolmaster, Schmidt finally ordered them to keep quiet and wait until he could translate.

The conference began at 12:45 P.M. with a statement from Hitler thanking the participants for their attendance. To place everyone in the proper frame of mind, he once more rehearsed the Sudeten question, calling attention to Czechoslovakia as a threat to peace, the floods of refugees, and the need for swift action. Chamberlain thanked Hitler for the invitation and expressed the hope that these discussions would give Europe "new breathing space." The Prime Minister understood the need for acting quickly; he appreciated Hitler's desire to restore order in the Sudetenland; he was certain that with the proper spirit results could be obtained. Daladier added his thanks.

Mussolini joined in the call for speed. "It was better to come to an agreement this very day, as an adjournment of only twenty-four hours would produce new unrest and new mistrust." The *Duce* just happened to have a proposal for the conference. He produced a memorandum which became the basis for discussion in the conference. Because no one else had a counter proposal, Chamberlain and Daladier accepted the memorandum.

The document has a confused history. Certain proposals originated in the German Foreign Office on the morning of September 28; Göring, Neurath, and Weizsäcker had a hand in drafting these, and they were shown to Hitler for his approval and then given to Attolico for transmission to Mussolini on the same day. Hitler dictated an outline of these proposals to Attolico on the morning of September 28. A list of demands was handed to Mussolini in the train on the way to Munich by Ribbentrop. Mussolini now produced this list at the conference without objection from Hitler. When Ribbentrop handed the list to Mussolini before the meeting, it was probably arranged then

**Chamberlain stands with Halifax** and other cabinet members before departing from Heston Airdrome for Munich on September 29: "When I come back I hope I may be able to say, as Hotspur says in *Henry IV*, 'Out of this nettle, danger, we pluck this flower, safety.'"

CHAMBERLAIN was met in Munich by the usual honor guard together with Joachim von Ribbentrop, Nevile Henderson, and General Franz Xaver von Epp. Here, Chamberlain leaves the airport between Ribbentrop (on the left) and Henderson.

*The National Archives*

that Mussolini, as a mediator, would propose these demands as a basis for discussion.

The document required evacuation and cession of the entire Sudetenland beginning on October 1. Britain, France, and Italy would guarantee that the evacuation would be completed by October 10 without any destruction of existing installations. An international committee would lay down the conditions for the evacuation; international forces would occupy disputed territories until a plebiscite had been held; an international committee would determine the demarcation of the final frontier.

Chamberlain and Daladier requested the presence of a Czechoslovak representative in the next room, but Hitler brushed aside their request; there must be swift action. Daladier voiced agreement with Hitler: if the Czech representative's presence meant delay, he would forego that in order to settle the question speedily. Neither Chamberlain nor Daladier would make an issue of the matter because each one dreaded delay.

Chamberlain raised points that he wished to have clarified. Would cattle be retained in the ceded area and farmers expelled without their cattle? Hitler snarled that the Czechs were driving away German cattle. It was more important that here was a problem for the major European powers to settle. Chamberlain agreed that it was the right and duty of the powers to settle the question and insure that the Czechs did not repudiate their promise, but he wanted a recess to allow further study of the document.

The meeting adjourned about 3:00 P.M. for a short lunch and for further study of Mussolini's memorandum.

The first round of the conference was clearly Hitler's for his emphasis on the need for hasty action and his threat of war if there were delay had broken the resistance of Chamberlain and Daladier. They had not come there to object but to agree; if a Czechoslovak representative would drive Hitler to war, they would drop their request. Once the Czechs were accepted as the cause of the trouble and the Sudetens as the suffering ones whose deliverance must come swiftly, nothing was left but to work out the details according to Hitler's demands.

During the break in the conference, the British delegation revised the German proposals to include a preamble explaining that the four powers held themselves responsible for fulfillment of the agreement.

A second article specified that the Czechoslovak government would be responsible for preventing damage to property.

Both the British and French delegations had retired to their hotels during the luncheon period. Chamberlain invited the French to confer with them at the Regina Hotel, but Daladier never answered the invitation. The meeting resumed at 4:30 without the British and French having agreed on any joint strategy.

At the second session, Mussolini proposed that his memorandum be discussed point by point. At last there was something concrete for discussion. No one objected to the beginning of the evacuation on October 1. Hitler pushed acceptance of the second point, four-power guarantee of evacuation by October 10 with installations undamaged. He wanted the stages of the evacuation outlined on a map and handled by a commission with a Czech representative. If this procedure were accepted, he even promised to be generous regarding the frontier question.

Chamberlain was worried about a British guarantee before he knew the Czech attitude. For Daladier the Czech attitude was no longer troublesome; the Czechs had already agreed to evacuate and this agreement must be adhered to; they must not even wait for the Czechs to erect new defenses in their territory. He expected trouble in the problem of language enclaves when they began to delimit the frontier. Here he wanted geographic and economic problems to be considered. Hitler retorted that such a course would be dangerous because that was the very method used in the founding of the Czechoslovak state; then an economic state had been formed rather than a national state.

The discussion was confused on the meaning of the guarantee for the new state. No solution could be reached; the issue was referred to a drafting committee.

Mussolini, seeking to enlarge Italian prestige in southeastern Europe, introduced a minorities clause calling for analogous treatment for the Polish and Magyar minorities with the implication that force would be used if needed. The British and French delegations rejected it for a milder clause which was incorporated into the final document.

Hitler introduced German proposals for evacuation and occupation of the Sudetenland that were surprising to the British delegation because of their moderation. These proposals were turned over to a drafting committee which labored to reduce the disorder in them.

The meeting adjourned for dinner. Hitler invited Chamberlain and Daladier to enjoy a banquet, but they had no appetite.

During the adjournment, the British delegation sent the drafting committee a proposal for settlement of the financial and currency problems by a German-Czech commission. The Germans wanted none of this; it was referred back to the full conference. When the British returned after dinner, the Germans expressed their disagreement with the proposal; the only copy of the draft had somehow been lost. The British were satisfied, finally, with a vague reference made in a supplementary declaration.

About 10:00 P.M members of the drafting committee brought in the results of their work. These were discussed, corrected, typed out in four languages, and signed by the four statesmen early in the morning of September 30.[3]

What had they signed? As diplomatic instruments go, it was short. In the preamble, the four governments accepted the fact that the cession had already been agreed on: they were now setting forth terms and conditions for cession which they guaranteed would be fulfilled; Czechoslovakia would not be allowed to evade compliance. Evacuation would commence on October 1 and end on October 10. Installations were not to be destroyed, and the Czechs would be held responsible. An international commission with representatives from Great Britain, Germany, France, Italy, and Czechoslovakia would settle the conditions for the evacuation. Occupation of the Sudetenland would be accomplished in four stages, outlined on an attached map, and completed by October 8. By October 10 the international commission would have decided on the remaining area for the Germans to occupy. The commission would also fix the conditions and areas for plebiscites and the areas to be occupied by the international force and would decide on the final frontier. The right of option would be permitted within six months. The Czechoslovak government had four weeks to release all Sudeten Germans from the armed forces and the jails. No provision was made for the release of Czechs seized as hostages or kidnapped by Sudeten Nazis and held in Hitler's prisons.

[3] Feiling, *Neville Chamberlain*, 375–77; Schmidt, *Hitler's Interpreter*, 108–12; *Ciano's Secret Diaries*, 167–68; memoranda on Munich Conference, September 29, 1938, *DG*, Series D, II, 1003–1008, 1011–14; Wilson's notes on the Munich Conference, September 29, 30, 1938, *DBFP*, Third series, II, 630–35: Bullitt to Hull, October 3, 1938, *FRUS, 1938*, I, 711–12. This last dispatch contains Daladier's impressions of the conference.

In an annex to the Agreement, the British and French governments announced their offer to guarantee the new frontiers against "unprovoked aggression." Germany and Italy would guarantee the frontiers after Polish and Hungarian minorities were satisfied. The state secretary of the German Foreign Ministry and the British, French, and Italian ambassadors in Germany would form the international commission. The Czechoslovak government would nominate a representative. In an additional declaration, the four powers agreed that if the problems of the Polish and Hungarian minorities were not settled within three months by agreement, there would be another meeting of the four heads of government.

In a supplementary declaration, the four agreed that all questions growing out of the transfer would be settled by the international commission. Such a vague clause satisfied Chamberlain, a former chancellor of the exchequer, who was worried about compensation for Czech property, cows, and furniture.[4]

The Munich Agreement gave the international commission wide latitude to interpret the Agreement, thus making the composition of the commission very important. Careful examination of the nations represented on the commission would have indicated that Hitler had won another round.

The terms of the Agreement were not as vicious as the spirit. By threats of force and marching troops, Britain and France had been brought to the conference table to divide up the territory of an independent nation, undefeated in battle. Czechoslovakia had not been given any opportunity to state her case; it was worse than the *"Diktat"* of Versailles. Then Germany had at least been able to object in writing; this course was denied Czechoslovakia in 1938. The vague clauses of the Agreement offered opportunity for interpretation beneficial to Germany. Worst of all, there was no real guarantee in the Agreement, only a statement of intentions.

For the moment, the Munich Agreement had prevented war. Hitler would have those people and lands he had claimed. Henlein's Karlsbad program had been more than fulfilled; Czechoslovakia had lost an important section of her territory, no longer would

---

4 Munich Agreement, text, *DBFP*, Third series, II, 627–29. The editors of these documents did not find a signed copy of the Agreement in the Foreign Office archives.

Reproduction of map appended to the Munich Agreement
delineating the proposed stages through which German
occupation of Czechoslovakia was to progress.

Based on a map in *Documents on British Foreign Policy, 1919–1939.*

215

this nation pose a threat to Germany. Whenever Hitler gave the order, his forces now could swiftly extinguish the life of the Czech nation.

Yet he was dissatisfied: he had not been able to crush the Czechs for all the world to admire while shuddering at his power. Chamberlain and Daladier had cheated him by using the conference to make his aggression appear palatable and legal.

Hitler had expected that through the conference he could assert his predominance until no power dared withstand his threats. Hitler hoped to rant and rave while the Western statesmen cowered in the corner until they signed the documents and scurried home. His failure to dominate the conference rankled long within his bosom. He did not expect that Chamberlain would emerge from the Munich Conference as the high priest of peace, popular even among the German population. Later he complained that Chamberlain had stolen his pleasure in the conference.

While the conference had been in progress, the Czech representatives had arrived. Hubert Masařík, Krofta's private secretary, had flown to Munich in the afternoon of September 29. He was escorted by the Gestapo to the Regina Hotel. With difficulty he finally reached Ashton-Gwatkin by telephone and arranged for a conference early in the evening. When he telephoned the French delegation, they refused to see him.

At 7:00 P.M. a nervous Ashton-Gwatkin met Masařík. The Englishman refused to explain the plan for Czechoslovakia, but Masařík had enough hints to realize that Czechoslovak interests were being annihilated. Using a map, he tried to explain to Ashton-Gwatkin the vital interests of Czechoslovakia. The Englishman was sympathetic but argued that the Czechs did not realize how difficult the situation was for Britain and France: it was so hard to negotiate with Hitler. As soon as he could, Ashton-Gwatkin left the Czech.

At 10 P.M., Horace Wilson left the conference to meet with Masařík, who had now been joined by Mastny, the Czech minister in Berlin. Wilson outlined the areas for occupation on a map; he rejected or ignored the objections of the Czech diplomats. Wilson left the pair with Ashton-Gwatkin, whom they tried to convert to their cause. Again he reminded them of the difficulties of negotiating with Hitler. When they demanded firmness from the West against Hitler, he replied: "If you do not accept, you will have to settle your affairs all alone with the Germans. Perhaps the French will put it more amiably, but I assure you that they share our views. They will disinterest themselves."

When the conference finally ended and the documents were all signed, someone had to inform the Czechs. Each of the signatory nations would transmit formal notice to the Czechoslovak government. France, however, was a military ally; someone suggested that Daladier personally take the Agreement to Prague. The "Bull of the Vaucluse" was frightened; he did not dare face the taunts of the Czechs alone. He preferred to see Masařík and Mastny in Chamberlain's company.

The Czechs were ushered in to receive their sentence. Daladier curtly handed a copy of the Agreement to Mastny, who was in tears. While Mastny tried to read the Agreement, Masařík sought an interpretation of the clauses. What was "predominantly German character"? Daladier sat silent. St. Léger explained that this would be calculated according to plans already accepted by the Czechoslovak government. Would the changes in the frontier made by the international commission take into account the vital interests of the Czechs? Daladier was silent. Only to a limited degree, replied St. Léger. In response to a query from Mastny on the voting powers of the Czechoslovak representative serving on the international commission, Chamberlain promised that the Czech member would have the same voting privileges as the other members. Would an answer be expected from the Czechoslovak government about the Munich Agreement? Daladier was silent. At last St. Léger answered that none was expected because the plan was considered by the four statesmen to have already been accepted by the Czechoslovak government. The Czechoslovak government had until 5:00 P.M. that day (September 30) to send a representative to the first meeting of the international commission. Chamberlain added his assent and insisted that Mastny meet with the international commission.

The meaning was clear to Mastny and Masařík: there was no appeal from the *"Diktat"* of the Munich Conference. Throughout the discussion of the Czech sentence, Daladier was silent and morose. Chamberlain was courteous but yawned in the faces of the Czechs. Finally the pair departed with their sad message; Mastny took a copy of the Agreement back to Prague that same night.[5]

[5] Kirkpatrick, *The Inner Circle,* 129–30; Hubert Masařík's memorandum of his visit to Munich, September 29–30, 1938, *Documents and Materials Relating to Eve of the Second World War,* I, 264–67; Ripka, *Munich,* 224–27.

While waiting for the drafting committee to finish its work, Chamberlain asked Hitler if they could have another private talk. Hitler agreed, and they met later, after the signing of the Agreement, in the *Führer's* private apartment with only Paul Schmidt present. The talk was Chamberlain's own idea; he had consulted neither his cabinet nor Daladier, who left Munich without knowledge of the talk.

Both men announced their satisfaction with the results of September 29–30. Once more Hitler brought up the oft-told tale of three and one-half million Sudeten Germans who would suffer no more at the hands of the dastardly Czechs. Chamberlain trusted that if "the Czech government might be mad enough to refuse the terms and attempt resistance . . . there would be no [German] bombardment of Prague or killing of women and children by attack from air." Hitler promised to "try to spare the civilian population and to confine himself to military objectives. He hated the thought of little babies being killed by gas bombs."

Chamberlain was most thankful for this kind promise and turned the conversation to Spain. He reported on his conversation with Mussolini, to whom he had suggested a four-power conference to settle the Spanish Civil War. Mussolini was tired of Spain, Chamberlain announced, as Hitler roared with laughter; the *Duce* bemoaned the loss of fifty thousand men when Franco continually threw away chances for victory. Soon he intended to withdraw many of his troops and was willing to consider Chamberlain's suggestion.

Hitler reported that Germany had no territorial ambitions in Spain, only the desire to fight Bolshevism; he would be delighted to withdraw "the few German volunteers" when others did the same. He would consider a four-power conference to settle the matter.

Chamberlain next suggested the abolition of bombers by agreement with Russia excluded. Hitler countered that to be effective it must be an international agreement with Russia included. Years ago he had proposed the abolition, but he would make no promise to do that in 1938.

Turning to international trade, Chamberlain sought from Hitler some indication that the Munich spirit would bring relaxation in trade in southeastern Europe, where Britain had been squeezed out. Hitler would discuss that problem one day, but there was not enough time that night.

At last Chamberlain came to the purpose of this meeting. It would be unfortunate if nothing more than the Czech question were settled. Would it not be helpful to Britain, Germany, and to the world if they issued a statement to show their agreement on Anglo-German relations and to help stabilize peace? He just happened to have a prepared statement (in two typed copies) which he wanted Hitler to read and to consider signing. By now the tired *Führer* would sign anything to get away from this Englishman. *"Ja, ja,"* he said. "Yes, I will certainly sign it; when shall we do it?" "Now," answered the delighted but tired Chamberlain. The two leaders signed the document, then parted never to meet again.

On the surface, the signed statement seemed innocuous if not pious. Both men viewed the Munich Agreement and the Anglo-German Naval Agreement of 1935 as symbols of national desire never to war again on each other. Both resolved that the method of consultation would be used to settle questions affecting the two nations. Both determined to remove all sources of discord and "thus to contribute to assure the peace of Europe."

Before the meeting, Chamberlain had directed Strang to draft a statement on the future of Anglo-German relations. Chamberlain made minor corrections and rewrote the second paragraph which introduced the Anglo-German Naval Agreement as a symbol of future relations. Strang objected to this mention of the agreement because it was not worthy of pride. Chamberlain was not interested because he believed that this was the type of agreement they should reach with Germany. Strang suggested conferring with Daladier, who was still in Munich, but Chamberlain refused. He knew Daladier would have resented the reference to the Anglo-German Naval Agreement which allowed Germany to break the naval clauses of the Versailles Treaty without French approval.[6]

The statement was in line with Chamberlain's whole life, personality, beliefs, and experience. Here was the culmination of man-to-man diplomacy at the highest effective level, a private agreement with the man who mattered, without diplomats or Foreign Office bureau-

[6] Notes of conversation between Chamberlain and Hitler in the *Führer's* flat in Munich in September 30, 1938, *DBFP*, Third series, II, 635–40; *DG*, Series D, IV, 287–93; Feiling, *Neville Chamberlain*, 367–77; Schmidt, *Hitler's Interpreter*, 112–13; Lord William Strang, *At Home and Abroad*, 146–47.

We, the German Führer and Chancellor and the British Prime Minister, have had a further meeting today and are agreed in recognising that the question of Anglo-German relations is of the first importance for the two countries and for Europe.

We regard the agreement signed last night and the Anglo-German Naval Agreement as symbolic of the desire of our two peoples never to go to war with one another again.

We are resolved that the method of consultation shall be the method adopted to deal with any other questions that may concern our two countries, and we are determined to continue our efforts to remove possible sources of difference and thus to contribute to assure the peace of Europe.

*September 30, 1938*

THE STATEMENT SIGNED BY HITLER AND CHAMBERLAIN
September 30, 1938.

*The National Archives*

crats interfering. Chamberlain had signed a contract believing that Hitler's word could be trusted and taking seriously the *Führer's* declarations that he wanted no more Czechs. To a man of his training, this was a holy instrument, not to be taken lightly.

By "consultations" Chamberlain must have meant the private meetings that he had with Hitler at Berchtesgaden and Godesberg. He believed that these had ushered in a new era of diplomacy ending months of delay by Beneš and his Czechs. Chamberlain intended that these should be a series of these high-level conferences to end discord and remove anything irritating to Hitler. In these searches for appeasement, France and Italy might be included. He chose the Munich Agreement and the Anglo-German Naval Agreement as the symbols of the new spirit, the "spirit of Munich."

What was this spirit? To Chamberlain it was the practice of private meetings between Hitler and Chamberlain, without Mussolini and Daladier. Under these conditions the pair would iron out their mutual troubles. Like two corporation presidents, they would arrange a cartel for the peace of the world, avoiding ruinous competition or war. If the old man wanted to go through this silly ritual, Hitler would oblige him. Hitler interpreted this statement as giving him the domination of continental Europe, particularly in the east. As a symbol, the Munich Agreement implied that Germany had all of Eastern Europe as her sphere of interest. Britain would not interfere.

Unwittingly Chamberlain had trapped Hitler; the peaceful old gentleman had fooled the cunning dictator, bestowing on him one of his worst defeats. Hitler had pledged himself to consult first with Chamberlain before he seized any more territory; this was never his intention. Properly applied, their bilateral agreement would mean that Hitler could not make any move without first consulting Chamberlain. Chamberlain did not realize how cunning his trap was; he had led Hitler to make an error—a fatal one.

In isolationist Washington, some wit could not refrain from composing a poem in honor of the Munich Conference:

> *Meine Herren* and *Signori*
> Clients of the British Tory
> Kindly note that No. 10
> Requests your patronage again.
> Opening as from today,

As Chamberlain et Daladier.
Messrs. Hoare, Laval successors
For doing business with aggressors.

Frontiers promptly liquidated;
Coups d'etat consolidated;
Pledges taken and exchanged;
Acquisitions re-arranged.
Loans on Fascists risks advanced;
Nazi enterprises financed.
European intervention
Given personal attention.
Have you problems of partition?
Let us send a British mission.
Breaking with Geneva's firms
We offer Nazi favored terms.
Let us lend, to back your name,
England's honorable fame.
For the dirty deals both great and small
Our representatives will call.
Orders carried out with speed;
Satisfaction guaranteed.
We obsequiously remain,
Daladier and Chamberlain.[7]

[7] *The Moffat Papers* (ed. by Nancy Harvison Hooker), 219–20. This work was copyrighted in 1956 by the President and Fellows of Harvard College, and the poem is reprinted here by permission of the publisher, Harvard University Press, Cambridge, Massachusetts.

# 21

## ~Mourning and ~Celebration

CZECH ACCEPTANCE of the Munich Agreement had to be obtained before peace was assured. Chamberlain immediately instructed Newton to urge Beneš to accept the plan that had been drawn up "with a view to avoiding conflict." Beneš must be reminded that "there is not time for argument: it must be plain acceptance." De Lacroix received similar instructions.

At 6:15 A.M., September 30, the German chargé handed Krofta the decision of the Munich Conference, together with an order for the Czechoslovak representative on the international commission to appear in Berlin at 5:00 P.M. that same day.

Beneš called a full cabinet meeting for 9:30 A.M. There the future of Czechoslovakia was debated in bitter anguish. French, British, and Italian ministers followed the instructions of their governments and called at the Foreign Office to demand a swift decision in favor of the Munich Agreement.

Before the cabinet met, Beneš called in the Russian minister, Alexandrovsky. Czechoslovakia was faced with either rejecting the Agreement, which meant war with Germany while Britain and France looked on, or capitulation to the terms of the Agreement. Beneš asked to be informed of the Soviet attitude towards these alternatives as quickly as possible; he would like a reply by 7:00 P.M. Prague time. Alexandrovsky's telegram with this important request was not handed in until 11:45 A.M. He alleged that a delay in transmission prevented

dispatch of the telegram until 5:00 P.M. Never was a delay so convenient. By noon the Czechoslovak cabinet had decided on capitulation,
and Beneš informed Alexandrovsky that the request was canceled.

Beneš canceled the request because he knew that if France did not
fight, Russia had no obligation to defend Czechoslovakia; Litvinov
had made this very plain. Beneš had not hidden his fears, even from
Alexandrovsky, that in depending on Russian aid alone, the Czech
*bourgeoisie* would be committing suicide. This must have been mentioned in the cabinet meeting. Worst of all, Beneš, a man of the West,
would be taking his country into the Communist camp where the democracies would shun him. He was well aware of the Spanish tragedy
when France refused to grant aid to the Loyalist government because
of the insignificant help given by the Soviet Union. Beneš dreaded
isolation from the West; he knew it would mean that Czechoslovakia
would become a Russian satellite. If he threw his country into the
arms of Russia, there was no certainty that Russia would or could
save Czechoslovakia; such a move would make Hitler's invasion a
crusade against Communism. All of Czechoslovakia would become a
Communist protectorate.

A study of the Munich Agreement and the report of Mastny, who
had returned to Prague, showed Beneš that if a war came, Czechoslovakia would bear the responsibility for causing the conflict. The
Munich Agreement thrust all the responsibility on Czechoslovakia
for the preservation of peace. Any decision for war belonged now to
Czechoslovakia. Through the Munich Agreement, Hitler, Daladier,
Chamberlain, and Mussolini were leagued together in behalf of peace.

If Beneš had decided on war with or without Russian support,
Czechoslovakia would be anathema to the West and become a warmonger, perhaps a Communist one. Resistance to Germany could
involve Poland and perhaps Hungary. All signs indicated that Britain
and France would stand aside and watch the destruction of Czechoslovakia. Czechoslovakia would be wiped out and vanish as had Poland in 1795. His decision, and that of the cabinet, was plain but
agonizing: accept the Munich ultimatum, hoping that a remnant
might be saved.

At 12:30 P.M. the ministers of Britain, France, and Italy filed into
the foreign office to hear the official answer from Krofta: Czechoslovakia would capitulate. De Lacroix expressed Daladier's regrets but
added that the cession was necessary. Newton claimed that "Cham-

berlain had done all he could." The Italian said nothing. Grimly Krofta replied:

I do not intend to criticize, but this is for us a disaster which we have not merited. We surrender, and shall endeavor to secure for our nation a peaceful existence. I do not know whether your countries will benefit by these decisions which have been made at Munich, but we are certainly not the last: after us, there are others who will be affected and who will suffer from those decisions.

In the evening, General Syrovy announced the decision to the nation. "We are deserted," he said. They had to choose between losing part of the nation and the death of the entire nation. Without any assistance, their choice was obvious.[1]

The news that a conference had been called at Munich without Poland wounded Beck's vanity; he had not been accorded the prestige due him. Poland had been treated as a small power. Poland would show the world that she could accomplish in twelve hours what had taken Hitler three months.

In answer to Beck's request, the German government promised benevolent neutrality in the event of hostilities. Should Russia intervene, which Beck did not expect, Ribbentrop promised to re-examine the situation. Beck dispatched an ultimatum to Prague on the evening of September 30. Evacuation of the Teschen area must begin by noon, October 1; the remaining areas would be evacuated by October 10. No one offered to defend Czechoslovakia; France could not fight one of her allies. A British proposal to mediate was rejected by Beck. Again Beneš had no alternative other than to bow to the ultimatum.[2]

Soviet officials acted properly indignant over the Munich Conference and Agreement. Potemkin fumed over the news of the conference, alleging that it was a revival of the Four Power Pact. He insisted

[1] Ripka, *Munich*, 230–33; Chamberlain to Newton, September 30, 1938, *DBFP*, Third series, II, 629–30; Newton to Halifax, September 30, 1938, *ibid.*, II, 640–41; minutes of Ina, September 30, 1938, *Documents and Materials Relating to the Eve of the Second World War*, I, 268–70; Alexandrovsky to People's Commissariat for Foreign Affairs, September 29, 30, October 1, 1938, *NDM*, 124–28, 103–31.

[2] Newton to Halifax, September 30, October 1, 1938, *DBFP*, Third series, III, 54–55, 64, 68–73; Halifax to Kennard, October 1, 1938, *ibid.*, 59–60; Molkte to the German Foreign Ministry, October 1, 6, 1938, *DG*, Series D, V, 78–79, 85–88.

to Schulenburg, the German ambassador, that the Czechoslovak dispute should be settled by a general conference along the lines set forth by President Roosevelt. Such a conference would have settled little if it had been held; of this fact the Russian government was well aware. Of course Roosevelt had never suggested such a general conference, but that mattered little to Moscow.

German diplomats reported nothing unusual in Moscow during the crisis of late September. While other nations took preliminary steps towards mobilizing some of their armed forces, Russia felt so secure that nothing was done.

Moscow was silent during the crisis with only *Izvestia* complaining that the Soviet Union had been excluded. Even Litvinov disappeared from view in Paris, emerging only on October 1 when the crisis was past. He reappeared to spend a lunch hour berating Bonnet for the French attitude. Chamberlain should not have made his trips to see Hitler, but "these mistakes were as nothing, however, compared to the enormity of what had passed at Munich." Hitler had bluffed them completely; he had never meant war; if Britain and France had been firm with Hitler, with the help of Russia, they could have forced him to back down.[3]

This was the first time that Litvinov offered to help Britain and France stand up to Hitler and make him back down. Always he had taken the line that Russia would fulfill her alliance, which required France to help Czechoslovakia first. Once he was certain that his offer would not be accepted and that all danger was past, Litvinov was generous in offering help against Germany.

Perhaps there was some disappointment in Moscow not to have been treated as a major power. However, this was a slight inconvenience if Russia could avoid responsibility for the Munich Agreement. The fact that no invitation to Munich came produced only relief in Moscow. No government was ever so delighted to have been excluded from a summit conference.

In Munich, Chamberlain was cheered by crowds every time he left the *Führerhaus*. Germans pressed around his automobile trying to shake his hand, their faces beaming with the joy of peace.

3 Phipps to Halifax, October 1, 1938, *DBFP*, Third Series, III, October 1, 1938, 67–68; Bullitt to Hull, October 3, 1938, *FRUS, 1938*, I, 83–84; memorandum of Schulenburg, September 29, 1938, *DG*, Series D, II, 998–99; Tippelskirch to Schiep, October 3, 1938, *ibid.*, IV, 602–604.

# THE MEN OF MUNICH

Édouard Daladier premier of France, 1938–40.

Neville Chamberlain, prime minister of Great Britain, 1937–40.

*"The men I got to know in Munich are not the kind that would start a new world war."*

---

# THE MEN THEY BETRAYED

Eduard Beneš, president of Czechoslovakia, 1935–38.

Kamil Krofta, Czechoslovak foreign minister.

*"We surrender, and shall endeavor to secure for our nation a peaceful existence.... There are others who will be affected and who will suffer from those [Munich] decisions."*

Photographs Courtesy U.S. Information Agency

DURING THE CRISIS Colonel General Hermann Göring, commander in chief of the *Luftwaffe,* Ciano di Cortellazzo, Adolf Hitler, and Benito Mussolini parade through Munich.

*The National Archives*

On September 30, Chamberlain returned to a cheering Britain. Along the five-mile route from Heston Airdrome to Buckingham Palace, crowds pressed up to his car, banging the windows and thrusting their hands into the automobile to touch their Prime Minister. In Buckingham Palace, King George VI thanked him for his accomplishment in the cause of peace. Outside crowds stood in pouring rain to catch a glimpse of Chamberlain, who was forced to appear on the balcony with the King in response to their cheers. Such excitement had not been seen since the announcement of the Armistice in 1918.

Back in Whitehall, traffic had to be diverted because of those who crowded into Downing Street hoping to catch a glimpse of Chamberlain and his wife upon their return from the Palace. After he entered No. 10, the crowds continued to cheer for "Good Old Neville!" Stepping to an open window, Chamberlain uttered words that haunted him to his grave. "My good friends," he said, "this is the second time in our history that there has come back from Germany to Downing Street, peace with honor. I believe it is peace for our time." The crowd roared their assent; they wanted his words to come true. "Go home," he concluded. "Get a nice, quiet sleep."

Chamberlain had gone without sleep for many hours during the crisis. By September 30, as he later confessed, he was on the verge of a nervous breakdown. Tired, worn out by nervous tension, he did not realize the danger in these words spoken to a happy throng. He never regretted the Munich Agreement, but he must have cursed his promise of peace.

The cabinet met at 7:20 P.M. while the happy throngs still shouted the Prime Minister's praises. He explained the difference between the terms of Godesberg and Munich; some questions followed, and once more congratulations—from all but one. Duff Cooper, first lord of the Admiralty, announced his resignation. A writer, soldier in World War I, a man with much promise of an even greater career ahead of him, chose to step aside. Cooper disliked the terms and feared for the future; he believed that the Prime Minister's talk of peace "for our time" would retard the rearmament drive. Chamberlain smiled at his pessimistic colleague, promising to discuss it later. They did talk over the problem the next day, but Cooper resigned anyway.

Letters of thanks poured in from old and young, famous and unknown, Englishmen and Germans, archbishop and king. Dutchmen shipped him gifts of tulips; someone asked for a piece of his umbrella to be made into a Greek icon. Flowers, poems, umbrellas, and fishing rods were bestowed on the now popular Prime Minister in deep gratitude for a new era wherein mankind would at last have peace. To Halifax he muttered on September 30 amid the cheers of the crowd, "All this will be over in three months."[4]

In his heart, Édouard Daladier knew what the Munich Agreement meant for the security and prestige of France. When he came to the Regina Hotel after the conference to congratulate Chamberlain, newsmen asked him if he were satisfied with the Munich Agreement. He started to make a statement, but the words would not come. Without a word, he stumbled away.

Daladier returned to Paris expecting political attack without mercy, perhaps even physical assault. He had betrayed an ally, and for this reason his career might be ruined forever.

At Le Bourget Field a noisy, happy crowd awaited his arrival. As the plane landed, they rushed forward, shouting, just as they had welcomed Lindbergh in 1927. Daladier, frightened by the clamor, hesitated to descend in the face of the throng. Turning to Gamelin who had met the plane, he remarked plaintively: "It is not brilliant, but I have done all that I could. How will they take it?" Gamelin replied: "Ah, monsieur President, you will be well received!" Then the Premier realized that the throng was cheering him. "Idiots," he snapped, "they do not know what they applaud."

Should he tell them the truth as a statesman or capitalize on the Munich Agreement for political profit? Daladier, the politician, could not resist the temptation; he chose profit over truth. To newsmen he declared:

> The negotiations certainly were difficult, but I have the deep conviction that the accord which was concluded was indispensable to the maintenance of peace in Europe.
>
> I am also certain today that thanks to the desire to give mutual concessions and the spirit of collaboration which animated the action of the four great western powers, peace is preserved.

Together with a beaming Bonnet, the Premier rode through the streets, lined with hordes of French men, women, and children, wav-

4 *New York Times,* October 1, 1938; Schmidt, *Hitler's Interpreter,* 113–14; Cooper, *Old Men Forget,* 242; Feiling, *Neville Chamberlain,* 377–82.

ing the tricolor, laughing, and crying out their thanks for the peace he had brought back.

To those of his cabinet who met him at the Ministry of War, Daladier explained: "I do not think that in the situation in which we found ourselves we could have done anything else." Later in the afternoon, he met with the cabinet at the Elysée Palace where he defended Munich as a compromise between Hitler's Berchtesgaden terms and those formulated at Godesberg. He buttressed his explanation with Göring's statement that his planes could have destroyed the Czech fortifications within a week. The cabinet gave his work unanimous approval.

In the French provincial towns subscriptions were started to give country homes and works of art to Chamberlain, Halifax, Bonnet, and Daladier. The *Petit Parisien* started another subscription for a book of gold in which would be inscribed the names of thankful Frenchmen; soon more than a million signatures poured in. All the great cities of France sent their thanks to Daladier for the Munich Agreement. Small French towns solemnly changed street names to "Rue Neville Chamberlain," or "Avenue Édouard Daladier."[5]

Germany was delirious over the Munich Agreement. Peace had been assured; there would be no war, and Germany would have the Sudetenland. Many Germans celebrated the Munich Agreement with a gigantic hangover.

In his memoirs, Weizsäcker described September 30 as the last happy day of his life. To German embassies and legations he announced, "For the first time in history it has been possible to arrive by peaceful means at a frontier revision in the spirit of the peoples' right to self-determination."

General Alfred Jodl, writing in his diary, was perhaps more truthful than the diplomat. The General observed, "Czechoslovakia as a power is out. . . . The genius of the *Führer* and his determination not to shun even a world war have again won the victory without the use of force."

When Hitler returned to Berlin on October 1, every street between the railroad station and the Reichschancery was jammed with a happy throng. Following their orders, employers had given a holi-

5 *New York Times*, October 1, 1938; Shirer, *Berlin Diary*, 145; Gamelin, *Servir*, II, 359; Lazareff, *De Munich à Vichy*, 71; Bonnet, *Défense de la paix*, I, 293–99; Zay, *Carnets secrets*, 24–26.

day to their workers to welcome home the victorious *Führer*. School children were released to swell the reception. At the railroad station Hitler was greeted with a blare of bands; one of these was composed of three hundred uniformed Italian Fascists. When his car reached the Reichschancery, three Sudeten women presented flowers, and another Italian band boomed forth joyful tunes.[6]

In defeated Czechoslovakia, there was no rejoicing. Crowds wandered about Prague crying in helpless fury and singing in their anguish the Czech national anthem, "Where Is My Homeland?" To the army, hitherto undefeated, came orders to withdraw from their lines. Back they trudged, a once proud army, armed with excellent equipment, led by good officers, but now without morale. Through the rain they trudged, neither singing nor shouting. Thronging behind the soldiers came the refugees who did not want to go home to the Reich. These Jews, Czechs, and Germans had been forgotten by the peacemakers of Munich. Now their fate was only the concentration camps of Hitler's "thousand year Reich." No preparations had been made for their coming; there was fear that they would cause unemployment. They were thrust back into a "no man's land" before the oncoming German troops and their jackals, Henlein's Free Corps. Germans in particular were sent back lest they create another minority problem. Many chose suicide rather than return to their homes. The ink was scarcely dry on the Munich Agreement when the Sudeten Nazis began to slaughter Czechs in the Sudetenland.

At last Hitler entered the Sudetenland on October 3. His reception was not as noisy as that in Vienna; the crowds were small; the towns insignificant; the weather was wet and grim. His speeches were poor because he lacked the mighty mobs to excite him. The crowds tried to show their enthusiasm by pelting their new *Führer* with flowers; when rose thorns scratched his face, all flower-throwing was ordered to cease. In Asch, where many Czechs had been murdered in the name of Hitler, an archway adorned with flowers proclaimed: "Sudetenland welcomes its Liberator."[7] The Sudetens had come home to the Reich.

[6] Weizsäcker circular, October 3, 1938, *DG*, Series D, IV, 18–19; Ernst von Weizsäcker, *Memoirs*, 158; Jodl diary, *NCA*, IV, 368; *New York Times*, October 2, 1938.

[7] Morrell, *I Saw the Crucifixion*, 288–304; Henderson, *Eyewitness*, 240; Whitaker, *We Cannot Escape History*, 145–46; Newton to Halifax, October 2, 3, 1938, *DBFP*, Third series, III, 74, 82–85; *New York Times*, October 2, 4, 1938.

# 22

## The Spirit of Munich

FOLLOWING THE SIGNING of the Munich Agreement, Western statesmen welcomed a new mood in Europe, the spirit of Munich. To them it meant a new era of peace because a method had been found to settle international disputes and because all of Hitler's desires had been fulfilled.

Chief among these statesmen was Neville Chamberlain, who extolled the results of the Munich Agreement and the new spirit when Parliament considered the Agreement in a four-day debate, beginning on October 3. Chamberlain argued that the Munich terms were better than those of Godesberg because an international commission would draw the frontier line, administer the plebiscites, and determine the conditions of evacuation. The Munich Agreement was not an ultimatum but a peaceful settlement under supervision of an international body. His Anglo-German agreement was more than a pious expression of opinion.

Chamberlain warned the House of Commons: "Lasting peace is not to be obtained by sitting still and waiting for it to come. It requires active, positive efforts to achieve it." Despite those who might accuse him of "facile optimism" and being too ready to believe every word the dictators spoke, he recognized that paradise would not come in a day. "We have only laid the foundations of peace. The superstructure is not even begun." He cautioned that they could not relax their rearmament program merely because they had signed the Munich

Agreement. "Disarmament on the part of this country can never be unilateral again."

Then followed attacks on his policies. His critics, headed by Clement Attlee, leader of the Labor party, found no balm in Munich. Attlee denounced the Agreement as a victory of brute force: Chamberlain had brought them to the brink of war. He believed that a "firm declaration by Britain, France, the Union of Soviet Republics and any other interested state would have halted aggression." To Archibald Sinclair, leader of the Liberal party, it was a travesty of self-determination. Leo Amery described the Munich Agreement as a triumph of "sheer, naked force, exercised in the most blatant and brutal fashion." For Viscount Cranborne it was "one of the most humiliating episodes in our history." Winston Churchill condemned the Agreement as a "disaster of the first magnitude." Harold Nicolson saw the guarantee as the most "farcical piece of diplomatic hypocrisy that has ever been perpetrated."

Chamberlain's defenders took up the battle in his behalf. Colonel Sanderson Allen argued that Britain had not undertaken to protect Czechoslovakia; therefore, there had not been any betrayal. William Mabane saw the Agreement as the saviour of civilization. Lieutenant Colonel Sir Thomas Moore believed that if war had come, they would not have been fighting for democracy because Czechoslovakia was not a democracy. Edward Burgin, minister of transport, claimed that by September 22, Czechoslovakia had been breaking up from within and that Chamberlain was a realist who saw that no Allied army could reach Czechoslovakia; the nation could never have been restored. Sir John Simon admitted that the Agreement had been obtained under threat of invasion, but was not this better than war? He argued that each member must ask himself if he would have rejected the Munich terms for war had he been prime minister. Sir Samuel Hoare emphasized that regardless of who was the victor in war, Czechoslovakia would have been destroyed and never restored. He believed that Germany would carry out the conditions "in a fair and reasonable manner."

Neither the defenders nor the critics saw that the Sudeten-Czech problem was older than the Hapsburg Empire, far older than the Versailles Treaty. Both sides seized upon the Versailles myth to bolster their arguments. The Government benches were greatly affected by the horrors of 1914–18; their relief was unmistakable. To them

Czechoslovakia was not worth a war, because they accepted Runciman's report that the Sudetens were so unhappy. The critics were not agreed on exactly what would be a good alternative. The Laborites could not decry the military weakness because they had contributed to it with righteous fervor. They could only urge collective security, which they did not define, or insistence on aid from Russia, which was a myth.

Chamberlain was not swayed when he finished the debate on October 6. He refused to make the people fight and die for a cause unless convinced that the cause was worthwhile. His efforts at Munich had saved the Czechs from annihilation and given them a chance for a new life with "a neutrality and security comparable to that which we see in Switzerland today." He asked the House not to read too much into his words about peace "for our time" because of his fatigue at the time they were uttered. There was good in the crisis, he declared, because it had revealed the strength and weaknesses of the nation's defenses. He closed with a request for the House to show unanimity in the succeeding division. The House divided 366 to 144.

In the House of Lords, the debate was not so bitter. Halifax took great care to contrast the Godesberg terms unfavorably with those of Munich. With the guarantee he found that Britain was able to give Czechoslovakia full protection against unprovoked aggression, now that a restless minority had been removed. He repeated that no matter how much force had been used, "nothing could have saved Czechoslovakia from destruction." When the war would end "no body of statesmen drawing the boundaries of a new Czechoslovakia would have redrawn them as they were left by the Treaty of Versailles." Nevertheless, he warned that British diplomacy was only commensurate with its armed strength which required a rapid and efficient increase.

Perhaps the most ecstatic comment on Munich came from Earl Baldwin of Bedley, the former Conservative prime minister. As he listened to the debate on September 28, his mind went back to 1914 and the speech of Sir Edward Grey. When Chamberlain read the telegram from Hitler, the earl was strangely moved. "It was just as though the finger of God had drawn the rainbow once more across the sky and ratified again His Covenant with the children of men."[1]

[1] *Parliamentary Debates, House of Commons,* Vol. 339, cols. 40–554; *House of Lords,* Vol. 110, cols. 1297–1414.

For Chamberlain, the spirit of Munich meant a fresh opportunity to work with Germany, to achieve a complete appeasement through agreements on other subjects. If they could be achieved with accompanying relaxation of international tensions, then the sacrifice of Czech security would have been worth while.

Because of his background, Chamberlain thought that the spirit of Munich could be enhanced by solving economic questions. In accordance with his desires, Sir Frederick Leith-Ross, an economic adviser, approached the Germans in October, 1938, with a request for more economic co-operation among the Munich powers.

In November, Ashton-Gwatkin hinted at the granting of larger credits to Germany, an agreement on markets and prices for British and German industry, and greater allocation of foreign currency to help Germany pay for her imports. He assured his hearers that Germany could have economic dominance in the Balkans.

At the insistence of the Board of Trade, a delegation from the Federation of British Industries asked the Germans for an agreement on markets and prices in return for tariff changes. When the negotiators met in December, 1938, the Germans were bowled over by the British eagerness to come to terms. An agreement on export quotas in European coal industry was reached on January 28, 1939, after the ministry of Mines restricted demands of the British mining industry. Coal disputes with the Germans must not disturb the spirit of Munich.

Ashton-Gwatkin visited Berlin in February, 1939, to inquire about German interest in economic co-operation. The results of his visit were meager. Ribbentrop used the occasion to warn the British once more to stay out of Central Europe.[2]

Another purpose of Ashton-Gwatkin's trip was to lay the groundwork for the visit of Oliver Stanley, president of the Board of Trade, to Germany on March 17, 1939. From this visit great results were anticipated in London, but events in Prague and Berlin in March prevented the trip.

Chamberlain had expected much from these activities, but little was forthcoming. He thought in nineteenth-century terms—almost

2 Conversation of Wienke and Ashton-Gwatkin, November 6, 1938, *DG*, series D, IV, 323–25; German economic mission to the Foreign Ministry, November 9, 1938, *ibid.*, 329–30; von Dirksen to the Foreign Ministry, October 19, 1938, January 28, 1939, *ibid.*, 314–17, 394–95; Ashton-Gwatkin's report, March 5, 1939, *DBFP*, Third series, IV, 597–601.

Marxist—that once economic relations were favorable, confidence would be restored and a secure peace established. Hitler was not thinking of the spirit of Munich in terms of economic adjustment with Great Britain.

Despite his enthusiasm for Anglo-German friendship, Chamberlain wanted to rearm, not for world war, but in order to bargain from strength in the future. He knew that in the past he had been forced to bargain from weakness. He and Halifax were aware of the terrible gaps in British defenses revealed by the September crisis. These must be filled. They urged France to hasten her rearming in order to "render any attack upon them hazardous."

Chamberlain did not hesitate to call for rearmament in speeches praising the Munich Agreement, but Hitler knew that a rearmed Britain might curtail his aggression. This was not his interpretation of the spirit of Munich. German newspapers were ordered to criticize British speeches on the need for rearmament. The German embassy in London hired extra correspondents to file stories damning British rearmament, with the hope that public opinion could thereby be split. These correspondents were to attack rearmament as subverting the spirit of Munich.[3]

In France the first pronouncement on the spirit of Munich came in the debates in the Chamber of Deputies. These were listless and uninspired; only a few speakers explained the votes of their parties.

Daladier's arguments were a mixture of half-truths, omissions, and revelations of the total lack of French leadership. He claimed that he and Bonnet had advised the Czechoslovak government to make "just and rapid concessions within the structure of the State." He took credit for Chamberlain's trip to Berchtesgaden. He even claimed that at Munich "perhaps for the first time in the history of the world everything was publicly undertaken and discussed before the people." The tricks of secret diplomacy had been avoided. Daladier accepted the invitation to go Munich because "it was a question of saving peace." By their "frank conversations" in Munich, they had "provoked in four countries a plebiscite of peace." He finished with vague references to the need to raise national production and a need for spiritual transformation.

3 Henderson to Halifax, October 12, 1938, *ibid.*, III, 158–59; Ashmann to von Dirksen, October 17, November 8, 1938, *DG*, Series D, IV, 313, 327; Weizsäcker to von Dirksen, October 17, 1938, *ibid.*, 311–12.

Only Henri de Kerillis offered a strong attack on the Agreement, with a few weak echoes from the Communists. When the Chamber voted on the Munich Agreement, Daladier won an even greater victory than Chamberlain: the vote was 535 to 75.[4]

Unlike the British government, Daladier deliberately chose not to release any documents on the crisis, thereby keeping his critics even more in the dark. Thus disarmed, they lacked effective means to challenge him.

Daladier's tragedy was that he knew the real meaning of the Munich Agreement. The politician within his soul would not let him tell the truth to France; instead he used the Agreement for his own political advantage. To Bullitt, he claimed that Chamberlain had been taken in by Hitler. He described the Prime Minister as "an admirable old gentleman, like a high minded Quaker who had fallen among bandits." Daladier confessed that within six months France and Britain would be faced with fresh German demands. He realized "fully that the meeting in Munich was an immense diplomatic defeat for France and England."

Unfortunately for France, he did not express these sentiments publicly for the education of the voters. To do so required more nerve than Daladier possessed. Because he preferred to be premier rather than a mere deputy, Daladier kept his silence on the danger to French security in the Munich Agreement, but he snatched every opportunity to profit from the Agreement.

Daladier and Bonnet indicated to the Germans their desire to continue the spirit of Munich. Both men disliked the private agreement between Hitler and Chamberlain although they tried to cover up their chagrin. Accordingly, they were delighted when François-Poncet reported on October 19, 1938, that Hitler was inclined to a Franco-German accord in the spirit of the Munich Agreement. He would accept an accord recognizing the frontiers of France and Germany and promising not to change them. An agreement could also be reached for mutual consultation on all questions which could affect Franco-German relations.

François-Poncet had suggested this agreement which fitted into Hitler's ideas. Another bilateral agreement might help to split the

[4] *Journal Officiel, Débats parlementaries*, Chambre des Deputies, October 4, 1938, 1526–43.

Western allies, while keeping the French from taking action when Hitler tried his next aggression.

By November 5, Ribbentrop had sent a rough draft of an agreement, acting under Hitler's express orders. Bonnet was delighted with the draft, for it meant to him friendship between France and Germany, "the fulfillment of his life's dream." While he anticipated the signing, the Germans took their time, dragging out the negotiations until early December.

On December 6, Ribbentrop and Bonnet signed the declaration in Paris pledging that both governments would do all in their power to assure the development of "peaceful and good neighborly relations." According to the declaration, there were no outstanding territorial questions between France and Germany; their common frontiers were final. Both pledged to keep in contact on problems affecting both nations and to confer if these problems led to international difficulties.

Czechoslovakia was not mentioned. In conversations with Bonnet, however, Ribbentrop brought up the Czech question. "Germany," he stated, "regarded this part of Europe as being definitely within her sphere of influence." There must not be a repetition of another Runciman wandering into the East at the behest of Chamberlain, Ribbentrop announced. Germany would not tolerate French military alliances in the East. Bonnet did not object, but swore that the Munich Agreement had changed everything. He asked for the German opinion on the guarantee of Czechoslovakia but said little further when Ribbentrop indicated dislike for the matter.

Despite Bonnet's pleading that he did not promise a free hand to Germany in the East, the facts are against him. There are no contemporary statements indicating that Bonnet told Ribbentrop that Germany must stay out of the East. By saying nothing, Bonnet implied that the East belonged to the Germans.[5]

The true meaning of the Munich spirit was reflected in the work of the international commission whose members included: Henderson, François-Poncet, Attolico, Mastny, and Weizsäcker, who was chair-

5 François-Poncet to Bonnet, October 19, 20, 1938, *Le livre jaune française* (Ministère des Affaires Étrangères: hereafter referred to as *Livre jaune*), 23–30; Bonnet to François-Poncet, October 21, 1938, *ibid.*, 31; text of Franco-German Declaration, December 6, 1938, *DG*, Series D, IV, 440; Schmidt memorandum, December 6, 1938, *ibid.*, 417–77.

man. Henderson caused some trouble for the Germans because he insisted on taking the Munich Agreement seriously. François-Poncet could do little because his superiors wanted to placate Germany. He was ordered to "do nothing to spoil the effects of Munich." Attolico was a cipher. Mastny was always outvoted.

The commission appointed three sub-committees to deal with problems relating to the Munich Agreement. Sub-committee A, composed of military attachés, handled the technical problems of the evacuation and occupation of the Sudeten area. These included the interval between the armies, mine fields, road blocks, and fortifications. The attachés handled their assignment with efficiency and dispatch, usually agreeing to whatever Colonel Walther Warlimont, Jodl's deputy, demanded. Whatever the attachés could not settle was referred to the international commission where the German suggestion was always approved.

Subcommittee B handled financial and economic questions, but most of these were taken from its consideration through direct negotiations between the Czech and German governments. The subcommittee's chief work was to reach a formula defining the installations in Sudetenland which could not be removed and to determine the condition in which the ceded areas would be surrendered by the Czechoslovak government.

Subcommittee C struggled with the most important problem for Hitler's future aggression, that of plebiscites and frontiers. Here the Germans scrambled to make their influence felt, at one time sending in seventeen generals, who disrupted the meetings because the chairman was awed by the presence of so much rank. Often with Germans, Sudetens, and Czechs screaming and shouting, order could be restored only by a German officer silencing them by barking out parade ground commands.

Hitler ordered the German members to secure as much of the Godesberg line as possible. His agents also were to be talked out of plebiscites for the German areas composing the rump of Czechoslovakia. Thus would he have German minorities within Czechoslovakia to cause trouble in the future.

The German members of Subcommittee C tried to seize the initiative with a demand for the Godesberg line but the Italian, French, and United Kingdom representatives fended them off temporarily.

The work of the subcommittee came to a standstill on October 3 in

238

determining the line to be occupied between October 7 and 10, known as Zone V and unmarked on the Munich map. According to paragraph 4 of the Munich Agreement, this zone would be of "predominantly German character," but the meaning of this phrase was not defined by the Agreement. The Czechs, seconded by the French, Italian, and British representatives, defined the phrase as meaning areas in which Germans comprised 75 per cent of the population. The generals and the Sudetens opposed this interpretation.

When the subcommittee members were given large-scale geographical maps for their work, on the German copies someone had already marked the Godesberg line and the ethnographic frontier of 1919, based on the 1910 census. The Czech delegates produced a map on which a line had been marked according to the 1930 census. The German generals rejected it and announced that "predominantly German character" meant a German population of 51 per cent.

When the subcommittee reported to the international committee late on October 3, they were instructed to draw the frontier for Zone V on an ethnographic basis. No indication of what constituted such a basis was given to the subcommittee. On October 4, the subcommittee tried to draw such a frontier but lacked any criterion for determining it. The Germans demanded the 1910 census because this was the nearest to 1918. The Czechs wanted to use the 1930 census since it was nearest to 1938; they contended that the 1910 census was based on spoken language and that many Czechs had said at that time that they spoke German.

That evening the matter was referred to the full international commission. Mastny was adamant: his instructions permitted no compromise; he was ready to break off negotiations. Henderson was without instructions. François-Poncet proposed that figures for 1910 and 1921 be compared, using two-thirds as the percentage to indicate predominance of German character. Neither Czech nor German would accept the proposal.

During the night Ribbentrop called in François-Poncet and shouted that Hitler accused the British and French of going back on the Munich Agreement. If the Czechs did not accept 51 per cent as showing German predominance and the 1910 census by noon October 5, German troops would be ordered to occupy the Godesberg line.

Before all of the representatives had their instructions, Weizsäcker rushed them into a meeting on October 5. Only François-Poncet had definite instructions to accept Hitler's ultimatum lest the Munich Agreement be nullified. Henderson and Attolico followed suit, accepting the 1910 census and 51 per cent as indicative of German predominance.

After the meeting, Henderson received instructions that both Chamberlain and Daladier accepted Hitler's interpretation of the census and percentage. Faced by the unanimity of the Munich powers, the Czechoslovak government capitulated.

Already the Germans made no secret of their desire for the line of military occupation to be the final frontier, without plebiscites and the accompanying nuisance of foreign observers. Plebiscites could force alterations in the frontier that would unsettle the planning of the German generals. A new Czech government took office on October 6, and the members were determined to do the Germans' bidding in regard to plebiscites. Gradually the other representatives came around to the German desire. On October 13, following Hitler's orders, Weizsäcker proposed that the occupation line of October 10 become the frontier; Mastny seconded, and the others approved.[6]

Self-determination, which had been Hitler's issue since April, had been discarded. The final frontier was that desired by the German generals, not a line approved by plebiscites corresponding to the wishes of the population involved. Not even the Sudeten population had been consulted. The desires of Hitler and his generals were accepted in the spirit of Munich.

For the government of the rump of Czechoslovakia, future policy must be in accord with Germany; all who represented the old way must go. The first to leave was Beneš who resigned under German threats on October 5 and for his own safety left the country on October 22. When he reached Paris, Daladier refused to see him. Sick, near collapse after his ordeal in September, Beneš reached London where he was ignored by the Chamberlain government.

Czech foreign policy was now in the charge of František Chval-

6 Minutes of the meetings of the international commission, September 30, October 1, 3, 4, 5, 6, 13, 1938, DG, Series D, IV, 2–4, 9–15, 22–24, 27–29, 34–35, 41–43, 63–67; Henderson to Halifax, October 5, 7, 12, 14, 1938, DBFP, Third series, III, 91–94, 99, 120, 122–23, 128–36, 161–67, 175–78, 615; Makins to Strang, October 8, 1938, 1938, ibid., 116–17; Kordt memorandum, October 2, 1938, DG, IV, 15–16, memorandum, October 3, 1938, ibid., 19–20; Protocol of October 5, 1938, ibid., 32–33.

kovsky, formerly minister to Italy. He hastened to assure the German chargé, Andor Hencke, that his government had nothing in common with France and only desired the closest relations with Nazi Germany. "What Germany had demanded and received at Munich had been just. . . . The chief blame for recent developments lay with the strong Jewish influence in Prague."

Hitler granted the representative of his new satellite an audience in Berlin on October 14. There Chvalkovsky promised a complete change in Czechoslovak policy and begged for German good will. The *Führer* offered two alternatives: realize that Czechoslovakia was now within the German sphere, cease to be an enemy towards Germany, and then be able to organize the country as the people of Czechoslovakia desired; or act as an enemy and suffer the consequences, for he could not tolerate such a threat to Germany's flank; he would take forceful action. Hitler reminded Chvalkovsky that there must be a satisfactory solution of the Hungarian demands. There was no need to consider strategy in ceding Czech territory; it meant little now. Nor was there any need for a large army because Czech security lay in German friendship. Here was Hitler's view of the spirit of Munich.[7]

Hungary was not yet in firm possession of her slice of Czech territory. Because Germany had her loot, and even Poland had been satiated, Hungary pushed for cession. Britain and France remained outside of the negotiations.

In mid-October negotiations broke down because the Czechoslovak government would not cede immediately everything demanded by the Budapest government. The Hungarian government dispatched an agent to beg that Hitler use force to compel the Czechs to cede the disputed area. He instructed Ribbentrop to pressure the Czechs. To the Czech foreign minister, Chvalkovsky, on October 14, Ribbentrop showed a map with a frontier line already drawn. The hint was enough, and the Prague government reopened talks with Budapest. Because of certain towns which the Czechs wished to keep, Hungary would not negotiate. Both parties appealed to Germany and Italy to arbitrate.

On November 2 in Vienna, the Czechs and Hungarians presented their cases to Ciano and Ribbentrop, who gave their decision at 7:00 P.M. that evening. Neither Czechs nor Hungarians were pleased. The

[7] Hencke to the German Foreign Ministry, October 10, 1938, *ibid.*, 51–52; memorandum by Schmidt, October 14, 1938, *ibid.*, 69–72.

new frontier was drawn along ethnic lines and caused much suffering because economic factors were overlooked. Over one million Slovaks and Ruthenes became Hungarians with no chance to protest.

In the spirit of this document, Chamberlain expressed only satisfaction that the problem had been solved peacefully and that no action would be necessary from the British government. From France there was silence.[8]

The final frontier between Germany and Czechoslovakia had not yet been drawn. The need was great because German forces crossed the line often during October in more than 300 places and did not withdraw. The German delegation followed Hitler's personal orders at the meeting of the German-Czechoslovak frontier commission on November 10, 1938. Baron von Richthofen curtly announced that Germany would not retreat from any area that had been occupied: the Reich government had further claims to put forward; an attached map indicated these claims. They would "be carried out as soon as possible." As for Czech claims, they had caused the German government much surprise: they would disrupt the decisions of October 5. Within two days, the German government must have its answer.

When the Czech minister, Mastny, later protested the ultimatum, Woermann gave him no mercy. He said, "The German demands admitted of no bargaining, and the Czechoslovak government would be well advised to accept the demands in the form in which they were presented." On November 11 the Prague government accepted the ultimatum. Ribbentrop informed the Czechs that their acceptance of this ultimatum did not end further frontier demands from Germany, nor did it mean that Germany would entertain any requests from Czechoslovakia.

The Czech government was presented with another ultimatum, an answer in a "positive manner" to the German demand for free access to an auto highway stretching from Breslau to Vienna with obvious military advantages to Germany. The Czechs submitted to their overlords. The land for the highway was placed at the disposal of the

8 Hencke to the German Foreign Ministry, October 2, 3, 26, 1938, *ibid.*, 16–17, 25–26, 112–13; Ermannsdorff to German Foreign Ministry, October 13, 1938, *ibid.*, 67; conversation of Hitler and Darányi, October 14, 1938, *ibid.*, 73–77; memorandum of conference, November 2, 1938, *ibid.*, 118–27; Newton to Halifax, October 15, 1938, *DBFP*, Third series, III, 74–75, 184–85.

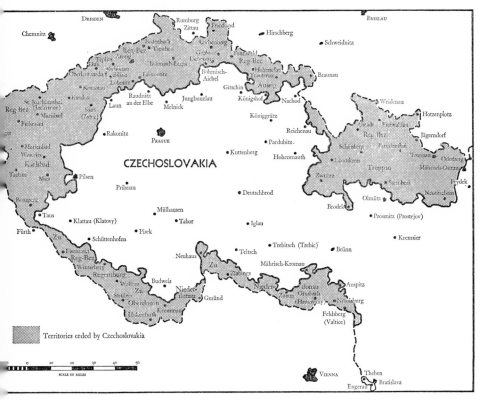

Map showing territories finally ceded by Czechoslovakia to Hitler.

Courtesy the *Macmillan Company, London*

German government. They were also granted extraterritorial privileges including security, passport, customs, and traffic control.

Despite the crisis, the alarms, fears, and terrors of September, Germans remained within Czechoslovakia. Hitler had insisted that they must all come home, but he "forgot" an estimated 478,589. How should they be protected? He decided on a minorities declaration instead of a treaty lest the latter give the more than 676,000 Czechs within Germany rights that Berlin wanted only for the Germans within Czechoslovakia. On November 20 the Czechs again signed as desired. A mere declaration governed the minorities. By leaving a substantial minority within Czechoslovakia, Hitler retained a nucleus for future crises.

On November 21, the international commission met for its ninth session with Karl Ritter of the German Foreign Ministry in the chair. He announced that the task of delimiting the German-Czech frontier was completed. The Czech delegate confirmed the announcement. Ritter bemoaned the grievous sacrifices made by Germany, for it had been painful to leave so many good Germans within Czechoslovakia. The Italian and French ambassadors together with the British chargé joined in thanks that the frontier had been settled by direct negotiation[9] and that war had been avoided.

The spirit of Munich was also apparent in the handling of the guarantee question upon which Chamberlain and Halifax had based much of their defense of the Munich Agreement. After the final frontier had been accepted on November 21, 1938, the Czechoslovak government asked for the settlement of the guarantee. Following his instructions, Hencke informed the Czechs that there was no connection between the frontier settlement and a four-power guarantee.[10] The question was now up to Britain and France.

When the British and French leaders met in Paris on November 24, 1938, the Munich Agreement was almost two months old. In discussing the Czech question, the promised guarantee was brought up.

[9] Ogilvie-Forbes to Halifax, November 21, 22, 1938, *ibid.*, 234–36, 241–42; minutes of meeting, November 10, 1938, *DG*, Series D, IV, 139–40; memorandum of Woermann, November 11, 1938, *ibid.*, 143; memorandum of Altenburg, November 13, 17, 1938, *ibid.*, 145–47, 152; Hewel memorandum, November 19, 1938, *ibid.*, 163; memorandum of Ritter, December 3, 1938, *ibid.*, 163–66; memorandum of Twardowski, November 11, 1938, *ibid.*, 140–41.

[10] Hencke to the German Foreign Ministry, November 23, 1938, *ibid,* 166–67.

Halifax proposed a joint guarantee instead of a collective one. If there were unprovoked aggression against Czechoslovakia, each power would decide whether to invoke the guarantee. It would come into force only by decision of at least three of the four powers. To Bonnet's objection that the value of the guarantee would be reduced, Chamberlain retorted that a collective guarantee was dangerous because France and Britain would have to go to war over acts committed by Germany and Italy. He contended that the interests of Italy and Germany did not necessarily coincide in Central Europe. A guarantee by the British government alone was not worth much.

Daladier objected to the collective guarantee, feeling that the four Munich powers had promised individual guarantees in the Agreement. Chamberlain categorically refused individual guarantees lest Britain have an obligation to fight alone in Central Europe. Halifax feared that if there were individual guarantees, the Czechoslovak government might seek French and British support of a policy contrary to German wishes. Once Germany were provoked, there would be nothing that Britain and France could do to help Czechoslovakia. Under these circumstances, it was impractical for Britain and France to implement individual guarantees: it would be humiliating for them to make promises that they could not fulfill. Halifax challenged Daladier to solve this practical problem. The French Premier capitulated and accepted the British conditions for a type of collective guarantee to perpetuate the spirit of Munich.[11]

When Bonnet posed the guarantee problem to Ribbentrop in December, the German Foreign Minister was not enthusiastic. German-Czech relations must be placed on a completely new basis. A "four-power guarantee" now consisted of maintaining friendly relations between Czechoslovakia and Germany.

When Chamberlain and Halifax visited Rome, the guarantee issue was raised by Chamberlain on January 12, 1939. The *Duce* was cool, insisting that first the Czechoslovak internal problems must be settled, Czech neutrality must be definite, and the Czechoslovak frontier must be demarcated on the ground, not merely on maps. Only then could the guarantee be considered.[12]

[11] Anglo-French conversations, November 24, 1938, *DBFP*, Third series, III, 285–311.

[12] Conversation of Chamberlain, Halifax, Mussolini, and Ciano, January 12, 1939, *ibid.*, 524–29.

If Chvalkovsky hoped to discuss the guarantee when he appeared before Hitler at Berlin, on January 21, 1939, he was quickly dissuaded. Hitler launched into a tirade on the sins of the Czechoslovak government and complained because the followers of Beneš had not been cleaned out but continued their nefarious work. "Czechoslovakia must in all things be allied with Germany," he declared. The Czechoslovak army must adapt itself to the changed conditions by a reduction in size. "No power in the world would send even one soldier to save Czechoslovakia." Jews were still poisoning Czechoslovakia; the problem had to be solved.

Chvalkovsky complained that he had nowhere to send these accursed people. If they were placed in concentration camps, English ladies visited them and then made nuisances of themselves with petitions. Chvalkovsky begged the *Führer* "to say a good word to the Czechoslovak people. That might work wonders." Hitler ignored the pleading Czech and bestowed upon him his best wishes for a very happy future.

After he left the *Führer*, Chvalkovsky had to undergo further condemnation from Ribbentrop, Chvalkovsky pleaded that he had had only three months to rectify the sins of twenty years of Beneš' government.

The harassed minister hurried home to report to Prague where disappointment was great because only a few additional demands had been expected. The Czechoslovak cabinet hastened to act upon Hitler's orders. Because of the swift pace of the changes, the joke went the rounds in Prague that Chvalkovsky was "learning shorthand to be able to keep up with the dictation more quickly."[13]

In identical notes, the British and French governments raised the question in Berlin on February 8. The time had come to settle the guarantee. What were the views of the German government?

Hitler helped in drafting the reply which came on March 3. A guarantee by France and Britain would only increase Czechoslovak hostility towards Germany because the Czechs would have someone to take their side. Past guarantees led the Czechs to believe that they could disregard the rights of their national minorities, which had caused the recent crisis. Fresh guarantees would bring on new conflicts and pre-

13 Memorandum by Hewel, January 21, 1939, *DG*, Series D, IV, 190–95; memorandum by Schmitt, January 23, 1939, *ibid.*, 195–202; Schleinitz to the German Foreign Ministry, February 17, 1939, *ibid.*, 213–15.

vent appeasement of internal Czech troubles. Because this area fell within the sphere of German interests, Germany would await "clarification of the internal development of Czechoslovakia and the improvement of that country's relations with the surrounding states."[14]

Such a guarantee would have been undesirable because Hitler would have been tied, even in a joint guarantee. Czechoslovakia would have become a protected neutral instead of a vassal. As a guaranteed neutral, the Czechoslovak government would have legal grounds to resist Hitler's demands.

Thus the guarantee of Czechoslovakia, so prominent in the defense of the Munich Agreement, would not be implemented. The only international protection for Czechoslovakia was denied her. France and Great Britain seemed happy to be rid of the guarantee. Where now was the spirit of Munich, so lively and promising on September 30? It was dying.

[14] Verbal note from the British Embassy, February 8, 1939, *ibid.*, 207–208; Henderson to Halifax, March 3, 1939, *DBFP*, Third series, IV, 171–73.

# 23

## The Conquest

Before the spirit of Munich had begun to ebb, Hitler resolved to liquidate Czechoslovakia. He considered the Sudetenland occupation only a partial solution. From the beginning he had been unhappy with the Munich Agreement. He would not have another conference with Western statesmen butting in. The army would be prepared for a swift intervention when a convenient excuse developed. Chamberlain would not cheat him out of this chance to humiliate the Czechs and show the world his power and might. All signs since the Munich Conference indicated little objection to his wishes.

On October 10, Hitler approved orders for demobilization of some German troops, but enough would be ready for intervention in Czechoslovakia whenever an opportunity arose. Keitel reported that five additional divisions and one tank unit would be needed; these could be brought up within five days. The *Luftwaffe* did not need additional reinforcements. The army needed only six days to reach a state of readiness; the *Luftwaffe* needed twenty-four hours.

With this knowledge, Hitler laid his plans. On October 21 he directed that the *Wehrmacht* prepare to liquidate the remainder of Czechoslovakia. At any time, the *Wehrmacht* must be ready to smash the Czechoslovak government should an anti-German policy be pursued. Preparations must begin for a surprise attack that would make organized Czech resistance impossible. The speed of the attack must leave the West with nothing to defend. In the September crisis,

248

Britain and France indicated that they saw no reason to fight for Czechoslovakia after it had disappeared.

To aid his plans, Hitler insisted that his negotiators secure the frontier demanded by the general staff. For this reason the German officers had dominated and harangued the meetings of the commission dealing with the Czech-German frontier. Wherever necessary, German troops simply pushed into Czechoslovakia to seize the desired areas.[1]

For British and French governments the task of fathoming Hitler's intentions during the winter of 1938–39 was difficult. By November, London had news of some move to be made in the spring of 1939, but the direction was unknown. Ogilvie-Forbes, the British chargé in Berlin, heard rumors of a move into the Ukraine. Paris heard similar rumors of a move but in the direction of Memel. The sources of Colonel Mason-Macfarlane, British military attaché in Berlin, led him to the conclusion that mobilization would begin in February with action eastward at an early date. He found the possibility remote that Hitler might occupy the rest of Czechoslovakia. In January, Mason-Macfarlane reported quickened military activity; German officers were so overworked and tired that they declined party invitations. Troop concentrations increased in Austria and southeastern Germany.

From other sources came stories that Hitler was planning to move towards the west before attacking in the east. Another story, probably planted by Nazi agents, related to a sudden air attack on Britain followed by invasion. On February 5, 1939, one of the French embassy staff in Berlin received a hint that he ought to prepare for the inevitable dismemberment of Czechoslovakia.

When Sir Nevile Henderson returned to Berlin after medical treatment in London, he produced a new interpretation for the future. Hitler did not contemplate any adventure at the moment; all stories to the contrary were false. In his heart, Hitler now wanted

---

[1] High Command to Schmundt, October 11, 1938, *NCA*, III, 370–71; Keitel to Schmundt, October 11, 1938, *ibid.*, 372–74; Hitler's speech, November 23, 1939, *ibid.*, 573; directive of Hitler, October 21, 1938, *DG*, IV, 99–100; supplement, December 17, 1938, *ibid.*, 185–86; memorandum by Hewel, October 24, 1938, *ibid.*, 109–10; memorandum by Martius, November 3, 1938, *ibid.*, 132–33; circular of Weizsäcker, October 10, 1938, *ibid.*, 52.

only to be respectable. Writing on March 9, Henderson insisted that Hitler preferred consolidation of his past gains. Rumors of an attack on Holland or Switzerland were "very premature." Germany's immediate objectives were to secure Memel, Danzig, and some colonial holdings and to subordinate Czechoslovakia to Germany. "We may dislike the latter, but geographically speaking it is inevitable."

In his speech to the *Reichstag* on January 30, 1939, Hitler informed Britain and France that Germany had given self-determination to ten million people in an area where Britain and France had no business. "In the future," he declared, "we shall not tolerate the Western states' attempting to interfere in certain matters which concern nobody but ourselves in order to hinder national and reasonable solutions by their intervention."[2] This was not an illogical conclusion if the Munich Agreement were interpreted as a renunciation of Western interest in Eastern Europe. Chamberlain, Halifax, Daladier, and Bonnet would have been happy to give up interest in Czechoslovakia if peace would result. Instead a new crisis over Slovakia loosed a storm and roused their interest in an area Hitler considered his own.

Within Slovakia there had been an autonomist movement since 1919, represented chiefly by the Slovak People's party. Participants in the movement opposed a homogeneous Czechoslovak nation and fought the centralism of Prague, demanding their own diet and an executive for Slovakia within the framework of the Czechoslovak republic. Existence of the decentralized, federal republic they sought would have weakened the political influence of the Czechoslovak nation.

By 1938 the Slovak People's party veered towards totalitarian methods and ideas, mouthing platitudes of allegiance to Czechoslovakia only to escape charges of treason. On February 8, 1938, Sudeten German leaders, led by Karl Hermann Frank, met with Monsignor Andrej Hlinka, a Roman Catholic clergyman and the long-time leader of the Slovak People's party. Hlinka promised to ally with the Sudeten Nazis in working against the Prague government. His chief goal was an independent Slovak nation. Thereafter the Slovak

2 Ogilvie-Forbes to Halifax, December 6, 29, 1938, January 26, 1939, *DBFP*, III, 386–87, 544–51, IV, 18, 22–24; Halifax to Mallet, January 24, 1939, *ibid.*, IV, 4–6; Henderson to Halifax, February 18, March 9, 1939, *ibid.*, 120–22, 210–17; Coulondre to Bonnet, March 14, 1939, *Livre jaune*, 80–83; *Speeches of Adolph Hitler*, II, 1572.

autonomists' activities were more closely aligned with those of the Sudeten Nazis. The Slovaks were happy to follow the urging of the Sudetens and presented demands to Prague on September 20, 1938, for Slovak autonomy. These demands helped force Beneš' acceptance of the Anglo-French ultimatum on September 21.

After the Munich Agreement, the Slovak People's party seized control of the government in Slovakia, profiting from the paralysis of the Prague government. An autonomous government was formed in Bratislava with Father Josef Tiso as premier. Hlinka had died on August 16. Assuming dictatorial powers, the government followed Nazi and Fascist examples, abolishing rights and liberties. The Prague government admitted five Slovak ministers to the cabinet and granted Slovakia a diet. A Fascist army with Fascist salute and black uniforms named Hlinka Guard was formed. Soon it was busily engaged in slugging Jews and Czechs, chasing them out of their homes, and creating a reign of terror.

Both the German Foreign Office and the German High Command were agreed that an autonomous Slovakia within a weak Czechoslovakia would be the best solution for German plans. There would be an excellent opportunity to use "self-determination" as an excuse for intervention.

On October 19, Father Tiso, who still supported autonomy, and his deputy, Ferdinand Ďurčansky, visited Ribbentrop. Tiso sought to enlist German support against Hungarian demands for Slovak territory. Ribbentrop promised German co-operation with Slovakia. Tiso explained to Ribbentrop that if Prague did not adhere to the agreement on autonomy, complete separation would follow. Ďurčansky made no secret of his itch to form an independent Slovakia.[3]

With the support of Ribbentrop and Göring, the Slovak separatists pushed on with plans to destroy the Czechoslovak state. Hitler, however, did not feel that anything should be attempted by Germany and ordered the separation question dropped on November 17. Bela Tuka and Franz Karmasin, the leaders of the Sudeten Germans in

3 Jozef Lettrich, *History of Modern Slovakia*, 11–142; High Command to Foreign Ministry, October 6, 1938, *DG*, IV, 40; Woermann memorandum, October 7, 1938, *ibid.*, 46–49; memorandum of Göring and Ďurčansky talk, October 17, 1938, *ibid.*, 86–93; note of Woermann, November 11, 1938, *ibid.*, 142–43; memorandum of Brückmeier, November 17, 1938, *ibid.*, 151.

Slovakia, were received by Hitler on February 12, 1939. Tuka erupted with praise for "my *Führer*" who had been the first to acknowledge the dignity of the Slovak people. The Slovaks, Tuka gushed, wanted to fight to preserve European civilization under the leadership of the *Führer*. Hitler was unhappy over the "Beneš mentality" which he saw daily growing within the Czechs. They were insane to seek hope in Europe for the fulfillment of their ideas of revenge. He would guarantee an independent Slovakia any time, but he "could not guarantee Czechoslovakia today."[4]

Later in the month, Tuka and Ďurčansky went to Vienna for a conference with Wilhelm Keppler, a member of the German ministry of Foreign Affairs, Artur von Seyss-Inquart, the Reich governor in Vienna, and Josef Bürckel, the Austrian *Gauleiter*. They agreed on the dispatch of terrorists armed by the Gestapo to Slovakia to destroy law and order; they laid plans for an independent Slovakia with German aid. German arms were smuggled into Slovakia for use against the Prague government.

By early March relations between Prague and the Slovak government were rapidly deteriorating. The Tiso government demanded a separate army and a loan from Prague, but German economic control of Slovakia was growing. The Prague government insisted on conferences over the subject during the first week in March.

Czechoslovakia had made no preparations to repulse any Slovak drive for independence. The Czechoslovak army had been reduced to 120,000 men. Some of them were a new class of recruits and others were needed for labor service and recruit training.

Negotiations in Prague between the Czechoslovak government and the Slovak representatives broke down on March 9. The Slovaks did not deign to conceal their German support and, in particular, their assurance from Göring of German economic aid should Slovakia proclaim her independence. Chvalkovsky hastened to inquire from Andor Hencke, the German chargé, regarding the wishes of Hitler about Slovak independence. "If Berlin wanted an independent Slovakia, then Prague would somehow have to reconcile itself to this solution," Chvalkovsky announced. Hencke would only declare his ignorance of Reich plans regarding Slovakia. German-Czechoslovak relations were governed by the Munich Agreement. Beyond this, he

[4] Conversation between Hitler and Tuka, February 12, 1939, *ibid.*, 209–13.

knew nothing.[5] Whether Hencke knew of Hitler's plans mattered little because his answer was perfect for Nazi plans.

During the night of March 9–10, President Emil Hácha dismissed Tiso and appointed Josef Sivak, minister of education, as his successor. Sivak refused; on March 11, Karol Sidor became premier. The appointment was not appreciated in Berlin for he was known to be cool towards German protection from the Czechs.

German agents hastened to demand that Sidor proclaim the independence of Slovakia, but he refused. Slovak Fascists and Sudeten Nazis, armed by the Gestapo, seized public buildings in Bratislava. A German delegation led by Seyss-Inquart appeared on March 12 but failed to force Sidor to declare Slovak independence under German protection.

Because Sidor still would not accommodate the Germans, a propaganda campaign was launched from Vienna against him; an attempt to assassinate him failed. Daily terrorism in Slovakia increased at German orders.

During the night of March 12–13, Tiso was routed out of bed by Gestapo agents and told to fly to Berlin for a conference with Hitler. When he reached Berlin in the evening of March 13, he was immediately taken to Ribbentrop. Slovak hesitancy over independence amazed Ribbentrop. They must not let this opportunity slip through their fingers.

Tiso was received by Hitler at 6:40 P.M. while General Keitel and General Walther von Brauchitsch, commander in chief of the army, looked on. Hitler launched into a tirade about the ungrateful Czechs who did not appreciate his generosity in not mutilating them in September; Czechs had been accepted within the Reich but scores of Germans within Czechoslovakia had been fired from their jobs and made the victims of discrimination. It had become intolerable; now the Beneš spirit had revived. There had been incidents on March 12 in Czechoslovakia involving Germans. Hitler did not explain that the incidents had been deliberately provoked.

The Slovaks had disappointed Hitler. Because he thought they wanted independence, he had offended the Hungarians to keep Slovakia out of their clutches at the Munich Conference. Now the Sidor government rejected independence. If he had known this

5 Hencke to the German Foreign Ministry, March 9, 1939, *ibid.*, 230–31.

earlier, he would have let Slovakia fall to Hungary. If Slovakia wanted independence, he would support her and even guarantee her efforts. If Slovakia refused separation from Prague, he would leave her to her fate.

Tiso was grateful for the *Führer's* words; the Slovaks could be depended upon. First he must consider these weighty words with his colleagues; however, Hitler could be assured that "they would prove themselves worthy of the *Führer's* benevolence and interest in their country."[6]

Tiso called Sidor, telling him to convoke the Diet the next morning at 10:00 A.M. Ribbentrop had a prepared copy of a law in Slovak proclaiming Slovak independence. Tiso, however, refused to sign the law without the approval of the Slovak Diet. Ribbentrop delivered an ultimatum: Tiso must give an affirmative answer before 1:00 P.M.

The next morning, the Slovak cabinet accepted Hitler's demands unanimously. When the Diet met, Sidor presented the resignation of his cabinet. Tiso reported on his trip to Berlin; the Diet gave a unanimous vote for independence. Now Hitler had his excuse to move.

On orders from Berlin, Hencke ceased to have any relations with the Prague government on March 13. Members of the legation were not to communicate with the Prague government in any way. In Berlin the Czech minister was cut off from all official contact with the German government. Desperate Prague officials had no recourse other than to request an audience with Hitler. The request was granted for an audience for President Hácha and Chvalkovksy on March 14.

Because of his heart condition, the ailing President had to travel by train. With his daughter and Chvalkovsky, he was received in Berlin with full honors befitting a head of state and escorted to suitable rooms in the Adlon Hotel.

Hácha thought that he had been called merely to settle the matter of Slovak independence, but at the railroad station he learned that already the frontier had been crossed, German troops had occupied Mährisch-Ostrau. Full-scale invasion was scheduled for 6:00 A.M. the next morning.

Hitler received Hácha at 1:15 A.M., March 15, in a dimly lit room which served to make the atmosphere more sinister. The President made his confession to the *Führer*. He had only been a humble official

[6] Memorandum of conversation, Hitler and Tiso, March 13, 1939, *ibid.*, 243-45.

254

in the Vienna administration and had deliberately refrained from mixing in politics. He had been appointed to the presidency of the administrative court and had still not dabbled in politics. He had little connection with the government. He had met President Masaryk only once a year at the judges' dinner and Beneš even less often. With Beneš his relations had not even been friendly. The task of president had been thrust upon him as a patriotic duty.

For Hácha, the destiny of Czechoslovakia lay in Hitler's hands. Czechoslovakia was more akin to Germany than to Slovakia. The dismissal of the Slovak government had been in accordance with constitutional practices. He was glad to be rid of Slovakia. The future position of Czechoslovakia demanded good relations with Germany. A majority of the nation agreed with him although there were some exceptions. His country should not be blamed because there were still a few supporters of Beneš; every means was being used to quiet them.

Hitler apologized for making the sick President take such a long trip; however, he thought the trip would benefit Czechoslovakia because in a short time Germany would intervene. Germany, Hitler explained, had no hatred for Czechoslovakia, but Czechoslovakia insisted on a different attitude beginning in 1936 when she promised support for France should she fight Germany. The rump of Czechoslovakia existed only because he had warded off Hungary. France and Britain could not protect Czechoslovakia.

Hitler had warned Chvalkovsky about the Beneš spirit, but no improvement had followed. Everywhere he looked the old ways persisted. In a few years, Czechoslovakia would be where it had been six months earlier. Now he had given the order for the invasion of Czechoslovakia and its incorporation into the Reich. At 6:00 A.M. the German army would invade from all sides. The *Luftwaffe* would seize all the Czech airfields. If there were no resistance, Hitler promised autonomy and a limited measure of national liberty. If battle came then the concessions would be withdrawn. He sympathized with the Czech people, but this was a turning point in history. Allowing an unresisted invasion would be the last good turn that Hácha could render the Czech people. "The hours were passing. At six o'clock the troops would march in. For every Czech division there was a German division."

An old man, sick in heart and soul, dumbly accepted the *Führer's* orders. "Resistance is folly," mumbled Hácha. But how was the Czech army to be disarmed? Only four hours remained until the invasion. Hitler bade him confer with his companions and call Prague because the German military machine could not be stopped. Hácha begged for some other way to disarm the Czech army. Hitler would not change; only a German army could disarm the Czech army.

Chvalkovsky and Hácha withdrew, followed by Göring and Ribbentrop. On the table lay the documents for the Czech signatures, thoughtfully prepared by the German Foreign Ministry and the High Command. Hácha and Chvalkovsky tried to avoid signing, arguing that they lacked the authority. They would be forever cursed by their nation. Relentlessly Göring and Ribbentrop pursued them around the table shouting for them to sign and thrusting pens into their hands. Unless they signed, bombs would fall on Prague. Hácha fainted, and Hitler's doctor, Morell, was called to revive the President. It could develop into a nasty situation if he were to die in their hands.

Finally a phone connection was made with Prague for Hácha to confer with Rudolf Beran, the premier. Instructions were given to avoid all resistance; the invaders must be permitted to come in peacefully. Suddenly the line went dead; Hácha again fainted. Ribbentrop was violent, screaming that he would fire the personnel of the telephone companies. At last the connection was restored, and Hácha completed his message.

Two beaten men were herded back to the waiting *Führer*. Their surrender was announced. Happy Hitler expostulated on the coming glories of "coexistence" now that Czechoslovakia would be imbedded in the Reich. Czechs could live happily as Czechs, and Germans would live happily as Germans. In the coming economic union, Czechoslovakia would benefit from increased orders placed in her factories. The Czechs would receive more rights than were ever accorded the poor Sudeten Germans.

Three documents were thrust before the Czechs. The first was a declaration which they signed with Hitler and Ribbentrop, stating that they had discussed the events in Czechoslovak territory with "complete frankness." Their unanimous conviction was to use all efforts to safeguard peace and order in Central Europe. The President of Czechoslovakia "confidently placed the fate of the Czech people and country in the hands of the *Führer* of the German Reich."

The *Führer* would take the Czechs under the protection of the Reich and guarantee an autonomous development suited to their character. Hácha and Chvalkovsky next signed a promise that a military memorandum would be implemented. Then they affixed their signatures to a military memorandum drafted by the High Command on March 11. All troops would remain in their barracks and lay down their arms; all military transport would cease, including aircraft; anti-aircraft guns would be dismantled and stored away; there would be no destruction of airfields; public life and the economic life would continue without disruption; there would be no public criticism; all military resistance would be destroyed; military aircraft that left fields would be shot down; airfields taking defensive measures would be bombed.[7] The Munich Agreement had been destroyed.

On March 14 the news came to Prague that Slovakia was now independent. A few Nazi bullies appeared on the streets but there were no Communist mobs as the Nazi papers claimed. Czech citizens hurried home from their jobs, ate supper, went to their beds and slept soundly. They awoke on March 15 to find the independence of their country gone. Many did not know what had occurred until they left their homes for work and passed German troops in the city. Some hurried down side streets, unable to bear the shame and bitter humiliation. Others stood their ground, cursing and spitting at the Nazi invaders. Already the Gestapo was hard at work, raking in a rich harvest of anti-Nazi refugees, including Sudeten Germans who had supported the Social Democratic party. Ambulances were hurrying to take those who had sought suicide as their only way of escape from Hitler's "coexistence."

In the early hours of March 15, Hungarian troops helped wipe out Ruthenia, the eastern remnant of Czechoslovakia. Hitler had invited the Hungarians to seize this strategic area. Admiral Horthy accepted the loot with joy.

By the evening of March 15, Hitler was in Prague within the ancient walls of Hradschin Castle, seat of the kings of Bohemia and

---

[7] *Wehrmacht* to the Foreign Ministry, March 11, 1939, *ibid.*, 234-35; memorandum of conversations between Hitler and Hácha, March 15, 1939, *ibid.*, 263-69; declaration of March 15, 1939, *ibid.*, 270-71; Schmidt, *Hitler's Interpreter*, 122-25. In 1942, Hitler confessed that the fog was so thick at 6:00 A.M., March 15, that the planes of the *Luftwaffe* could not have flown against the Czechs. See *Hitler's Table Talk, 1941-1944*, 204-205.

the residence of the president of Czechoslovakia. There Hitler signed a proclamation the next day ending the independence of Czechoslovakia. As a basis for "the future coexistence" of Bohemia and Moravia, they were incorporated into the Reich with a Reich protector as head of state to guard the interests of the Reich.[8] Old Baron Constantine von Neurath, received the new office. His secretary of state was Karl Hermann Frank, who made the Czechs recognize their new masters.

Thus did Czechoslovakia sink into the long night of Nazi barbarism.

[8] Hitler's proclamation, March 16, 1939, *DG*, Series D, IV, 283–86.

# 24

## Reaping the Whirlwind

FOR THE BRITISH AND FRENCH, the effect of the occupation was devastating, because they had expected so much from the Munich Agreement and were so ill-prepared for the sudden crisis. By March 6, Newton reported signs of a growing crisis over Czech-Slovak relations because of failure in discussions over finances and loyalty of the Slovak government. Paris and London knew, on March 10, that Tiso had been dismissed by Hácha. In Berlin, Henderson observed growing interest in the newspapers over the Czech-Slovak question, but he concluded that Hitler had not made up his mind yet. On March 12 and 13, Paris and London received grim tidings of troop movements across Germany and Austria towards the east. Newton reported forays into Bratislava by German gangs and Hlinka Guards.[1] Paris and London were now faced with a fresh crisis where they had expected none.

The Foreign Office believed that if Hitler were convinced action was essential in Czechoslovakia, no British action short of war would be effective. Because Germany had always claimed that Czechoslovakia was of no concern to Britain, protest could only be made if Germany resorted to territorial aggression. Britain would then be bound by her offer of a guarantee, but France would not support such a position. Effective action was impossible without France. The Chamberlain-Hitler declaration of September 30 related only to

[1] Newton to Halifax, March 6, 12, 1939, *DBFP,* Third series, IV, 183–84, 229; Henderson to Halifax, March 13, 1939, *ibid.,* 232, 234–35.

259

questions that concerned both countries; Hitler never considered Czechoslovakia one of these. France would meet the same objection if she used her December 6 accord. It was the opinion of the Foreign Office that Great Britain had no basis whatsoever for taking any action.[2]

When Henderson inquired on March 14 about the type of action Germany was considering in the Czech question, Weizsäcker brushed him off with an assurance that "the German government wished to arrange matters in a decent way."

Von Dirksen telegraphed the same day that all was well in London. The British government regarded the settlement of relations between Slovakia and Czechia as an internal concern of the Czechoslovak state. He advised that if it were made to look like self-determination, there would then be greater understanding from the British public.[3]

In France, unconcern was widespread. On the evening of March 13, Bonnet and Gamelin dined at the British Embassy; they were calm and unworried. Both admitted that the Czech-German situation should be watched carefully, but the less they interfered the better. The troubles between Czech and Slovak only proved to Bonnet that "we nearly went to war last summer to boost up a state that was not likely to live."

Later in the evening Bonnet received different tidings from Coulondre: Bohemia and Moravia were to be annexed; an ultimatum would be sent to Prague, but the answer would not affect the outcome. Bonnet saw no reason to intervene, but he did not like such behavior. He instructed Coulondre to protest the German actions as contrary to the Munich Agreement, but not in a formal way. He should merely seek information to interpret the action in Slovakia. At the same time he could indicate serious thought over any German troops entering Czech territory because such action would cause anxiety over the German attitude towards the rest of Europe.

Before Coulondre reached the German Foreign Ministry on March 15, German troops had entered Prague. When he was permitted to see only Weizsäcker, Coulondre followed his written instructions but then voiced his shock at the occupation contrary to the Munich

2 Memorandum, March 13, 1939, *ibid.*, 238–41.

3 Henderson to Halifax, March 14, 1939, *ibid.*, 244, 250–51; Weizsäcker memorandum, March 14, 1939, *DG*, Series D, IV, 253–54; von Dirksen to the German Foreign Ministry, March 14, 1939, *ibid.*, 258–59.

Agreement and the accord of December 6. Weizsäker cut him short. He was not to give any lectures on the Munich Agreement. The Agreement meant the maintenance of peace and French disinterest in Eastern Europe. Weizsäcker alleged that the decomposition of Czechoslovakia was provoked by circumstances and the Prague government. In Bohemia and Moravia, German blood was flowing. Berlin had to potect the German minority. Coulondre was not convinced that the Hitler-Hácha agreement was unrelated to the troop movements. Weizsäcker, overflowing with sincerity, declared that after two hours of conversation with Hitler, in full awareness of his incapacity to prevent return of the Beneš elements, Hácha had signed the accord and placed the fate of his country in the *Führer*'s hands. Coulondre wanted to debate the invasion of Bohemia and Moravia, but Weizsäcker dismissed him with advice to read the text of the accord and return to his embassy where he would probably find fresh instructions.

By the evening of March 14, Halifax had some inkling of the German demands on Prague. Henderson was instructed to deliver a note explaining that the British government had no desire to interfere in affairs of other governments with more direct concern. However, they were concerned over the "success of all efforts to restore confidence and a relaxation of tension in Europe." Any action in Central Europe would be deplored which set back the development of this general confidence.

When Henderson handed in the note on March 15, all was finished for Czechoslovakia. He announced that the visit to Germany by the president of the Board of Trade was inopportune for the time.

In the afternoon of March 15, Ambassador von Dirksen appeared in the Foreign Office with the text of the Hitler-Hácha agreement. He told of Germans suffering at the hands of persecuting Czechs. All of the trouble was caused by the Versailles Treaty, the unconstitutional action of Hácha against the Slovaks, the growing anarchy in Czechoslovakia, and the survival of the Beneš mentality.

Halifax did not conceal his unhappiness at the blow to the spirit of Munich. He thought such questions should be settled by consultation. Hitler had stated that he had no more territorial ambitions, but now the world had seen contradictory action. No one felt that the assurance of the German government was worth much. The conclusion must be drawn that Germany had no desire for good relations and sought "to establish a position in which they could by force dominate Europe and, if possible, the world." To Berlin, Ambassador von Dirksen reported that he sensed "a feeling of supressed fury" within Halifax.[4]

At noon the same day, Welczeck appeared at the Quai d'Orsay to inform Bonnet of the events in Czechoslovakia and to notify him of the Hitler-Hácha agreement. Bonnet was hurt. The Germans had ruined his work for peace. It was the "heaviest blow yet struck against the friends of peace in Europe who, in the teeth of the storm and the crash of the waves, had stood out for the liberation of the Sudeten Germans." He had expected stabilization in central Europe, but now assurances had been ignored and the Czechs had been incorporated. "The peace and appeasement policy of the 'men of Munich' had suffered a lamentable disaster," Bonnet complained. "And now in every country warmongers who would lead Europe toward catastrophe were bound to gain the upper hand."[5]

During the day Bonnet resorted to one action: Hervé Alphand, director of commercial accords, was ordered to break off negotiations with the Germans.

In the House of Commons that same afternoon, Chamberlain defended his policy poorly. Because his story of events in Berlin came from German sources, he announced that Hácha "placed the destinies of the Czech people and country with confidence in the hands of the German Reich." The four-power guarantee of Czech frontiers was not yet in force, but it related only to unprovoked aggression of which there had been none. Again he defended the Munich Agreement, insisting that it was better than threatening war or standing aside and letting events take their course. The settlement was not final, but he could not believe "that anything of the kind which has now taken place was contemplated by any of the signatories to the Munich Agreement at the time of its signature." The manner and method of changes in Czechoslovakia were not in accord with the Munich Agreement. The Germans now occupied territory of people

[4] Halifax to Henderson, March 14, 15, 1939, *DBFP,* Third series, IV, 250, 270–72; von Dirksen to the German Foreign Ministry, March 15, 1939, *DG,* Series D, IV, 281–82.

[5] Phipps to Halifax, March 14, 1939, *DBFP,* Third series, IV, 243; Weizsäcker memorandum, March 15, 1939, *DG,* Series D, IV, 273–74; Welczeck to the German Foreign Ministry, March 15, 1939, *ibid.,* 282–83.

with whom they had "no racial connection." Nevertheless, the government would not be deflected from the aim of promoting peace and substituting discussion for the use of force.[6]

Even before Chamberlain had spoken, his ambassador in Berlin had telephoned with new information. Hitler had refused any discussion with Hácha, "and the whole proceedings constituted nothing but an ultimatum, under threat of aerial bombardment of Prague." Here was the key to Halifax' change in attitude when he talked with Ambassador von Dirksen later the same afternoon.

Information continued to come into Whitehall illuminating the occupation and revealing its running counter to the spirit of Munich. Thus when Chamberlain journeyed to Birmingham on March 17 to speak before the Unionist Association, he had more information to assess the crisis, so devastating to his hopes of appeasement.

That evening he confessed to his audience that when he made his statement in Parliament two days earlier, he lacked full information on the crisis. Some thought that he did not feel strongly on the subject; he would correct that mistake. First he had to defend the Munich Agreement as a means of averting war. Without it "hundreds of thousands of families would to-day have been in mourning for the flower of Europe's best manhood." Nothing that anyone could have done would have saved Czechoslovakia from destruction. After the war the treaty makers would have rejected reconstructing her as had been done by the Treaty of Versailles.

In the speech he gave one of the clearest statements of his meaning of appeasement. Peace would follow if no power dominated Europe, if each could have facilities to develop resources, secure a share of international trade, and improve the material conditions of its own people. Then with good will and understanding, mutual differences could be resolved by discussion without the use of force. He had gone to Munich to ascertain if Hitler was interested in such a course. Hitler had assured him that the Sudetens were his last territorial demand. Upon this basis Chamberlain hoped to begin his appeasement policy. Now it had all been undone. He had been entitled to consultation if Hitler thought the Munich Agreement should be revoked. "Instead of that he has taken the law into his own hands."

In deepest disappointment, he asked his audience: "What had become of this declaration of 'no further territorial ambition'?" He

6 *Parliamentary Debates, House of Commons,* Fifth series, Vol. 345, cols. 435–38.

rejected German stories that disorders within Czechoslovakia threatened the security of her powerful neighbor. The question came to mind: "If it is so easy to discover good reasons for ignoring assurances so solemnly and so repeatedly given, what reliance can be placed upon any other assurances that come from the same source?" Would there be other attacks on small states? "Is this, in fact, a step in the direction of an attempt to dominate the world by force?" It was a new Chamberlain speaking. He would sacrifice almost anything for peace save "the liberty that we have enjoyed for hundreds of years, and which we will never surrender." He declared: "No greater mistake could be made than to suppose that, because it believes war to be a senseless and cruel thing, this nation has so lost its fibre that it will not take part to the utmost of its power resisting such a challenge [of one seeking to dominate the world by force].[7]

Chamberlain's speech represented a change in cabinet policy. Already Henderson had been called home to report. Before he left Berlin he was to inform the German government that the events of the past few days were "a complete repudiation of the Munich Agreement and a denial of the spirit in which the negotiators of that Agreement bound themselves to co-operate for a peaceful settlement." Weizsäcker begged Henderson not to present the note, but at last even Henderson had become unhappy with German actions. He insisted on presenting it. Weizsäcker accepted it as a matter of record.

When Coulondre presented a note from his government the same day, Weizsäcker turned the process into a farce. What did the note contain? It was a formal protest against German action, in violation of the letter and spirit of the Munich Agreement and the Hácha-Hitler accord. The French government refused to recognize the legality of the coup. Weizsäcker placed the protest back into the envelope unread and thrust it back at Coulondre. He would not receive it; the French government must revise it. Coulondre replied that his government would not revise the note and started to leave the note on the desk, but Weizsäcker shoved it at him again. Finally, Weizsäcker accepted the note as if it had come through the mails.[8]

In Paris there was indignation and some worry among the "men

7 Chamberlain, *In Search of Peace*, 269–75.

8 Halifax to Henderson, March 17, 1939, *DBFP*, Third series, IV, 291; Weizsäcker memorandum, March 18, 1939, *DG*, Series D, VI, 20–21; Coulondre to Bonnet, March 18, 1939, *Livre jaune*, 102–103.

of Munich." Hitler had violated the right of self-determination which he had so emphasized during the September crisis. He had ignored the Munich Agreement and even the Franco-German declaration of December 6. Although there were no indications of any new action, the Munich policy was re-examined.[9]

After the fall of Czechoslovakia, the Russian government could safely declare its indignation. Litvinov dispatched a note to the German embassy commenting on the coup but without formal protest. The Soviet Commissar declared that no head of state had the right to terminate the independent existence of a state without the agreement of the people. They should have the right of self-determination. The German action was "arbitrary, violent, and aggressive." The Soviet government could not recognize the incorporation of Czechia nor the action in Slovakia.

Litvinov, acting of course for Stalin, had merely gone through the motions of a complaint. This was for the record. Litvinov admitted to Schulenburg that the note had only been sent because the British and French had protested, and Roosevelt had issued a statement. When Schulenburg asked about the practical value of such a note, Litvinov only shrugged it off as the need for the government to make its point of view clear.[10]

In contrast to Litvinov, Halifax struck a new tone, hitherto unknown among the "men of Munich," when he addressed the House of Lords on March 20. He refused to accept the German contention that mistreatment of the Sudetens brought the intervention; these people had possessed exceptional rights since Munich. The bulk of the incidents were deliberately provoked; the Czechs had acted with the greatest restraint. Until now a good case could have been made that Hitler had only incorporated Germans within the Reich. Now that was ended because he had contradicted the principle of self-determination. This was a new method of "wars without declarations of war." Pressure had been exercised under the threat of force.[11]

The events of March 15 struck directly at Chamberlain's appeasement policy. A change would have to be made, but he did not intend to create an anti-German alignment. Instead he decided to seek a system which would prevent independent states' being compelled to

[9] Bräuer to the German Foreign Ministry, *DG*, Series D, VI, 77–80.
[10] Schulenburg to the German Foreign Ministry, March 20, 1939, *ibid.*, 52–55.
[11] *Parliamentary Debates, House of Lords,* Fifth series, Vol. 112, cols. 310–15.

surrender their independence under threat of force. From this decision followed a series of guarantees to Eastern nations. The most important guarantee was made to Poland on March 31.

Chamberlain promised his government's full support to the Polish government in any crisis which "clearly threatened Polish independence, and which the Polish government accordingly considered it vital to resist with their national forces." This promise contradicted everything he had said and denied to Czechoslovakia a year earlier. Now he accepted Poland as a vital British interest. Such a wide promise had been withheld from Czechoslovakia, because Britain might be drawn into a conflict in which her vital interests were not involved.

Apparently neither he nor his cabinet had fully considered the consequences: the Polish army was poorer than the Czech; Polish minorities were treated shabbily, and in Poland, unlike Czechoslovakia, Hitler possessed a valid claim that the Treaty of Versailles had robbed Germany of ancient territories.

The Prague coup influenced the British pledge to Poland. Chamberlain felt that German action in Czechoslovakia was in strong contrast to German pledges and indicated a desire to extend the process elsewhere. If Germany attacked one country at a time, where would it end? Chamberlain answered his hypothetical question: in the destruction of Poland and ultimately the British empire. This policy must be halted by making it clear that "if Germany pursued such a policy, she would be involved in a war on two fronts." The declaration of March 31 had been made, Chamberlain confessed, to prevent a "sudden coup or swoop."[12]

Such was the lesson he had learned from the Czech crisis. If Britain pledged to protect certain countries, Hitler would not attempt to swallow them. It did not matter that neither the British army nor navy was in a position to defend Poland. He did not consider the fact that France was in no position to aid Poland. In the Czech crisis he had not given such a pledge, and Czechoslovakia had fallen to Hitler. Now he would give a pledge supported by limited armament, Hitler would be brought to serious negotiations.

The decision of the British government to guarantee Poland was a direct result of the violation of the Munich Agreement. It did not

---

12 *Parliamentary Debates, House of Commons*, Fifth series, Vol. 345, col. 2415; conversation between Chamberlain and Beck, April 4, 1939, *DBFP*, Third series, V, 9–19.

represent a strong resolution to prepare for world war. Chamberlain still hoped to bring Hitler once more to the conference table for a final solution of the problems which harmed Anglo-German relations.

But what of Poland? How to resolve the questions of Danzig and the Corridor? Perhaps another Munich Conference over these questions might finally open the way to a stable peace if Hitler repented his past misdeeds.

# 25

## A Second Munich Conference?

DURING THE DEBATES in the succeeding weeks, Chamberlain tried to clarify the meaning of his pledge to Poland lest he seem to invite war. The pledge was effective only under specific conditions, and if these conditions never developed, he declared, the pledge would never be acted upon. His government would discuss a "general settlement" with Germany whenever the talks would be welcomed in Germany and Britain and have useful results. He wanted to be first convinced that Germany had no intention of aggression against other countries.[1]

Hitler had different ideas. At his conference with the military leaders of the Third Reich on May 23, 1939, he announced that Poland must be attacked at the first suitable opportunity. "We cannot expect a repetition of Czechia. There will be war." Because he expected Poland to fight, diplomatic isolation was imperative. Britain and France must be kept from the battle while Germany slaughtered Poland.[2]

Because of the Munich Agreement, there was serious doubt in the German Foreign Ministry of Anglo-French intentions to aid Poland. That the occupation of Czechoslovakia had produced a change seemed impossible. Surely the men of Munich would stand aside

[1] *Parliamentary Debates, House of Commons,* Fifth series, Vol. 345, cols, 2481–86; Vol. 346, col. 1113; Vol. 347, cols. 1827–31.

[2] Conference Minutes, May 23, 1939, *DG,* Series D, VI, 574–80.

rather than wage war. In the following weeks, German officials labored to bring off another Munich Conference over Poland.

Reichsmarshal Göring now joined the search for a new Munich Agreement, dispatching as his agent, Axel Wenner-Gren, a Swedish industrialist, who saw Chamberlain by appointment on June 6. He brought a memorandum containing Göring's demands and presented topics on which Britain should make proposals. Chamberlain rejected the proposition. "Since Hitler had already broken his word and brushed aside assurances which he had given on numerous occasions, of what value could fresh assurances be?" Wenner-Gren suggested a conference called by Hitler to settle the outstanding questions. The idea of another conference horrified the Prime Minister. "I should be swept out of office without a moment's delay!" For the present, he felt, "Hitler himself had made it out of the question for me to think of entering into any negotiations with this end in view." Confidence in Hitler had to be restored before conversations would begin.[3]

The German Foreign Ministry sent a former Rhodes scholar, Adam von Trott zu Solz, to England to pave the way for another Munich Conference. Trott zu Solz met Halifax at the home of Viscount Astor early in June. The Foreign Secretary admitted that after the Munich Agreement he had expected a "new consolidation of powers" in which Germany would be predominant in Central Europe. But the March 15 crisis had destroyed confidence in Germany; people were asking who would be next.

On June 8, Trott zu Solz met Chamberlain, who accused Germany of forcing him into the Polish guarantee because the public was so aroused that every concession was regarded as a capitulation to an aggressor. Chamberlain alleged that the British people were "passionately stirred" and would fight if another nation lost her independence. If Hitler could restore confidence in his intentions, Chamberlain would meet him halfway just as he always wanted to do after the Munich Agreement.[4]

Chamberlain hoped that spoken guarantees and limited military preparations would demonstrate to Hitler that forceful actions

[3] Conversation between Chamberlain and Wenner-Gren, June 6, 1939, *DBFP,* Third series, VI, 736–39.

[4] Memorandum by Trott zu Solz, June 12, 1939, *DG,* Series D, VI, 674–86.

could bring war. After the *Führer* had grasped this idea, perhaps he would be willing to seek his aims by peaceful means and give a guarantee of future good behavior. Once these conditions were met, they could all return to the spirit of Munich.

When Helmuth Wohltat, an official in the office of the commissioner for the Four Year Plan, came to London for a meeting of the International Whaling Commission, Robert Hudson, secretary of the department of Overseas Trade, offered plans for Anglo-German co-operation in world trade through new spheres of interest. On July 18 and 21, Wohltat conferred with Horace Wilson, who had requested the meetings. At Munich, according to Wilson, some thought Britain was unprepared for war, but now preparations were completed. He produced a memorandum, approved by Chamberlain but not found since in the files of the Foreign Office, calling for a joint Anglo-German declaration that forceful aggression would not be used by either side.

Wilson advocated secret Anglo-German negotiations on the highest level to lay down basic principles for joint policy, with France and Italy brought in later. Germany would also agree not to interfere in the British Commonwealth and Britain would agree not to interfere in the greater Reich. If Hitler accepted these discussions, "this would be regarded as a sign of returning confidence."

To confirm this proposal, Wilson invited Wohltat to meet with Chamberlain, but the German was unwilling. Ribbentrop was informed of the conversation with no result.[5]

The Anglo-German proposals were taken up on August 3 when Ambassador von Dirksen visited Wilson in his home. Wilson invited von Dirksen there to confirm the truth of his conversations with Wohltat. Wilson begged that Hitler take the initiative in a conciliatory measure because if Chamberlain expressed such statements, he and the cabinet might be overthrown.

Much of Wilson's line of argument was repeated by Halifax when he saw Amabssador von Dirksen on August 9. He had hoped for fifty years of peace after the Munich Agreement with "Germany the dominant power on the continent, with predominant rights in south eastern Europe," but the Prague coup had changed everything. Although the public was distrustful, Halifax believed that a return

[5] Memorandum by Wohltat, July 24, 1939, *ibid.*, 977–83.

to the Munich spirit could be achieved, but Germany must take the first step.[6]

The meetings of Wilson and Hudson with Wohltat and the von Dirksen conversations with Wilson and Halifax were indications of a desire to avoid war with Germany over the issue of Poland. Chamberlain hoped that by offering sufficient bait he could once more bring Hitler to negotiate over the conference table. Limited British rearmament would also make Hitler hesitate, see reason, and then seek a meeting with Chamberlain.

All Chamberlain's efforts toward conciliation were thwarted by the history of the Munich Agreement. Because of this failure, Chamberlain needed some public statement or action first from Hitler to restore confidence in his word. The first conciliatory move must come from Hitler lest such a gesture by Chamberlain appear as an invitation to another Munich Conference.

Because of the conduct of Britain and France in September, 1938, Hitler could not take seriously their threats to defend Poland in 1939. Chamberlain's attempts to resume negotiations only hardened Hitler's belief that another Munich Agreement could be reached over Poland. To some of his generals on August 14 he declared: "The men I got to know in Munich are not the kind that would start a new world war." He was convinced that while England "may talk big, even recall her ambassador, perhaps put a complete embargo on trade, she is sure not to resort to armed intervention in the conflict."[7]

The ghost of the Munich Agreement appeared again in the weird tale of Birger Dahlerus, a Swedish businessman, who had lived for some years in England and was a friend of Göring. After consulting with some English friends early in July, 1939, he decided to communicate to Göring his observations: the English were in earnest; the public was bitter over the fall of Czechoslovakia; the English government was not bluffing and did not want peace at any price.

---

[6] Record of Wilson-von Dirksen conversation, August 3, 1939, *DBFP*, Third series, VI, 579–82; Halifax to Henderson, August 10, 1939, *ibid.*, 647–48; von Dirksen to German Foreign Ministry, August 3, 1939, *Documents and Materials Relating to the Eve of the Second World War*, II, 116–25; minutes of conversation with Halifax, August 9, 1939, *ibid.*, 126–31.

[7] Notebook of Halder, August 14, 1939, *DG*, Series D, VII, 551–56.

Göring was not convinced by the story for he remembered the Czech crisis, but he consented to a meeting with some of Dahlerus' English friends. Even Halifax was agreeable to the meeting on August 7 at Sönke Nissen Koog in northern Schleswig.

There the Englishmen complained of Hitler's failure to solve international problems after Munich by negotiation instead of force. The occupation of Czechoslovakia indicated that Hitler's word was untrue because the Sudetenland was not his last demand. Göring blamed the British for the Czech failure to come to peaceful terms with Germany.

The conference ended with agreement on the need for a meeting of German and British representatives. Later the same night, the Englishmen convinced Dahlerus of the need for a four-power meeting of the Munich powers to achieve peace. Göring was naturally agreeable when he learned of the proposition.[8] Both sides waited for the other to request the meeting. Another telegram like that of September 28 would have been satisfactory to Berlin. Chamberlain, handicapped by the history of the Munich Agreement, feared that his cabinet would fall unless Hitler made the first move.

Using Henderson, the British government tried to convince Hitler that their pledge to Poland was sincere and that he ought to negotiate, but the Munich Conference had convinced him that there was little to fear. "Our enemies are small fry," he told his generals on August 22. "I saw them in Munich."

Chamberlain gave way first and dispatched a letter to Hitler on August 23, but it lacked the desired message. In the letter Chamberlain asked for direct German-Polish negotiations, with the results guaranteed by the other powers.

In his conversation with Henderson, Hitler accused the British of denying him a peaceful solution in Czechoslovakia and now in Poland. Henderson blamed the events of March 15 for altering British opinion, but Hitler retorted that conditions within Czechoslovakia had become intolerable for Germany. His solution of the Czech problem was the best. Even President Hácha was happy over the solution.[9]

Hitler hoped to convince the British government that war would

[8] *TMWC*, IX, 457–91; memorandum to Göring, August 7, 1939, *DG*, Series D, VI, 1088–93; record of conversation with Göring, *DBFP*, Third series, VI, 751–61.

[9] Speech of Hitler, August 22, 1939, *DG*, Series D, VII, 200–204; interview be-

be their fault. If they would withdraw from the East, as they had at Munich, peace would reign.

While Hitler spoke to Henderson, the world learned of the Nazi-Soviet Pact of August 23. Surely now the British would agree to Hitler's demand as they had in September. Perhaps Chamberlain's cabinet would fall, and those who wanted peace at any price would surrender to Hitler's demands over the Corridor and Danzig. But there was no surrender. There was no telegram from Chamberlain begging for another four-power meeting. Instead, the British government signed a full alliance with Poland on August 24.

On August 25, Hitler halted the invasion of Poland that had been scheduled to begin on August 26. Now he sought an agreement with the British because the Polish alliance implied that they were serious.

Dahlerus was called back to help achieve another Munich Agreement, as Göring confessed at his trial. On August 25 and 26, Dahlerus conferred with Halifax, giving him Göring's opinion that Germany wanted an understanding with the British. Perhaps this was the long-sought approach to peaceful negotiations. With Chamberlain's approval, Halifax sent a letter to Göring explaining the British position. Dahlerus delivered the letter to Göring on the night of August 26, and then Hitler received them.

After one of his ranting performances complete with shrieks, Hitler promised a guarantee of the Polish borders, agreement over colonies, and a German promise to defend the British Empire. In return for all of these considerations, Hitler asked that England "help Germany in the annexation of Danzig and the Corridor."[10]

Hitler wanted a repeat of the Munich conference and the Agreement over Czechoslovakia. With German armies poised on the Polish frontiers, just as they had been placed on the Czech frontiers a year earlier, the British would surely capitulate.

At the same time, on the ambassadorial level, Hitler labored to bring the British and French to concede that another Munich Agreement was possible in the case of Poland. To Henderson on August 25, Hitler announced his determination to end the Danzig and Corridor problems. If war came, it would be bloodier than World War I,

tween Hitler and Henderson, August 23, 1939, *ibid.*, 210–16; Henderson to Halifax, August 23, 1939, *DBFP*, VII, 161–63.

[10] L. B. Namier, *Diplomatic Prelude*, 417–33; Johan B. E. Dahlerus, *The Last Attempt*, 50–134.

but Germany would not fight on two fronts. There would be no profit for Britain in a war over these questions.

Coulondre, the French ambassador, also received a lecture from Hitler about the terrible Polish atrocities, including castration of Germans. "I will not attack France," he declared, "but if she enters into a conflict, I will go on to the end."[11]

To both ambassadors Hitler repeated tactics which had been successful in September, 1938. He rehearsed the story of terrible sufferings of the German minority, warnings of awful casualties—all unnecessary—and defensive tactics by Germany in the west forcing the French to leave the Maginot Line. If he were granted his last and final wish for Danzig and the Corridor, a catastrophe could be avoided just as one had been avoided over the Sudeten Germans.

In Paris rumor had it that Chamberlain and Halifax were preparing another Munich. Daladier swore to Bullitt that he would prevent the British from laying the basis for a new Munich.

When Coulondre delivered a message from the Premier to Hitler on August 26, Daladier's tough words were missing. Although France would stand by her pledge to Poland, there was nothing to prevent a peaceful solution of the crisis. Daladier guaranteed that Poland was prepared to submit the German grievances to the method of "free conciliation."

When Coulondre delivered Daladier's message, Hitler blamed the British promise to Poland for all of his troubles because he hoped that in Paris the inference would be plain. In September, 1938, he had wanted the Sudetenland, but there was no British promise to the Czechs. The Sudetenland was given to him, and there was no war. If the British and French would forget their promises and force the Poles to cede, as had been done to the Czechs, and if necessary have another conference, they could all have peace.[12]

On August 27, when Chamberlain, Halifax, Horace Wilson, and Cadogan conferred with Dahlerus, they had two offers from Hitler,

[11] Henderson to Halifax, August 25, 1939, *DBFP*, Third series, VII, 227–29, 236; statement of Hitler to Henderson, August 25, 1939, *DG*, Series D, VII, 279–81; Coulondre to Bonnet, August 25, 1939, *Livre jaune*, 312–14.

[12] Bullitt to Hull, August 26, 1939, *FRUS, 1939*, I, 376–77; Phipps to Halifax, August 26, 1939, *DBFP*, Third series, VII, 278; Bonnet to Coulondre, August 26, 1939, *Livre jaune*, 321–22; Coulondre to Bonnet, August 27, 1939, *ibid.*, 328–29.

Premier Édouard Daladier and Georges Bonnet stand at Le Bourget Field after the Premier's return from Munich, September 30. To Gamelin's assurances that he would be well received by the cheering crowd, Daladier replied, "Idiots! They do not know what they applaud."

*The National Archives*

HITLER was given triumphal acclaim in Berlin after the
Munich crisis, and General Alfred Jodl recorded in his
diary, "Czechoslovakia as a power is out. . . . The
genius of the *Führer* and his determination not
to shun even a world war have again won the
victory without the use of force."

*The National Archives*

one official, through Henderson, and one unofficial, through Dahlerus. Both added up to a repeat performance of a Munich Conference over the subject of Poland. The same basic reply was sent to Hitler: Britain would stand by the pledge to Poland; direct Polish-German negotiations ought to begin to settle the problems. But in the message for Dahlerus, an Anglo-German agreement of an unspecified nature was promised. Hitler had wanted more than this, but it was an opportunity for him to split the Poles away from the British and French, and isolate them just as had been done to the Czechs.[13]

Hitler reverted to the tactics of March 14–15, 1939, demanding that a Polish negotiator come on August 30 with full powers to negotiate whatever he wanted. He prefaced this with a promise to London that he accepted the British proposals. The British government hinted to Colonel Beck that they hoped for Polish negotiations with the German government as soon as the method and arrangement could be agreed on. There was no warning that Hitler's proposal was another repeat of the Hácha ploy.

Colonel Beck refused to follow the script written in Berlin and tried out on Schuschnigg and Hácha. No negotiator was sent. The Polish ambassador was instructed to make contact with the German government for a discussion but not to ask for German terms.

As if following the same old script, Mussolini proposed on August 31, that Britain and France first convince Poland to surrender Danzig. Then the four powers could have a conference on September 5 to revise the necesary clauses of the Versailles Treaty. If Britain and France were agreeable, he would present the proposition to Hitler.

Chamberlain would not reject the proposal outright, for he still hoped "to work out the whole European economic political problem" with Hitler if the Danzig problem could be solved. Because he feared lest a repeat performance of the Munich script have strong political repercussions in Britain,[14] his government requested prior German-Polish negotiations.

In Paris, Daladier again sounded belligerent. He would rather resign than accept an invitation to "a second Munich." Bonnet was

13 Ogilvie-Forbes to Halifax, August 28, 1939, *DBFP,* Third series, VII, 318–20; Halifax to Ogilvie-Forbes, August 28, 1939, *ibid.,* 330–32.
14 Kennedy to Hull, August 30, 1939, *FRUS, 1939,* I, 392.

eager for the conference if Poland were invited and other problems were discussed. This proposition he placed before the cabinet, adding that Chamberlain agreed with him. Daladier retorted: "It is a formal offer of a four power conference, it would be a copy of Munich." It was worse to accept because to carve up Poland would dishonor France and lose the few friends she had left. "The lesson of Munich is that the signature of Hitler is worth nothing." Chamberlain agreed with him, Daladier declared to the cabinet. The two ministers plunged into an argument over which one of them had Chamberlain's support. They were both right because the last messages each had received from London had been different. Although the French cabinet sided with Daladier, no rejection was sent.

During the night Bonnet sought support from London on the conference, hoping to swing Chamberlain and Halifax to his side and isolate Daladier. Halifax replied on September 1 that he doubted the workability of the conference idea.

German troops moved towards the Polish frontier during the night of August 31. War began on September 1. Hitler had tired of waiting for another Munich Conference. In his mind was the hope that Poland's cause would appear so hopeless that France and Britain would decide not to help her.

On September 1, Bonnet informed Berlin that the proposed conference was acceptable with the proviso that the problems of those powers present, including Poland, be discussed.

At Bonnet's insistence, Ciano contacted Berlin on September 2 and proposed a four-power conference to meet on September 5. Hitler was willing to consider the idea because, if his troops moved fast enough, they could conquer most of Poland while the meeting was in session.

The British cabinet, however, was unanimous in laying down a prior condition: the German troops must first withdraw from Poland. Ciano and Mussolini realized that the project was now useless and ceased to promote another Munich Conference.

The last appeal for a four-power conference came from Dahlerus at 10:15 A.M., September 3. From his contacts in the German Foreign Ministry, he was certain that such a conference could be arranged. He reported that the Germans were anxious to satisfy Britain and willing to give assurances on the independence of Poland, but he had been informed that "never before in world history had an army withdrawn before negotiations."[15]

Already Britain and France had demanded a cessation of hostilities, and Germany had refused. Before the day was over, Britain and France had gone to war. There would be neither a Munich Conference nor an agreement over Poland.

Because of the failure of the Munich Agreement, Chamberlain had insisted on some assurance that Germany would keep whatever agreements were made over Poland. Despite the Munich Agreement he was willing to negotiate with Germany, particularly in the economic sphere.

Because of the Munich Agreement, the Germans thought the British and French were only bluffing when they announced their determination to aid Poland. Why fight over a country whose strategic position was poor and whose army was weaker than that of Czechoslovakia? The events of September, 1938, led the Germans to think there could be another conference over Poland as there had been over Czechoslovakia.

Because of the Munich Agreement, all attempts at a conference over Poland were doomed. British public opinion seemed so aroused that Chamberlain dared not approach Hitler as he had in September, 1938. Chamberlain feared any meeting with Hitler until there was some conciliatory action. Because of his success in September, 1938, Hitler saw no need to conciliate. Because of the Munich Agreement, Hitler mistakenly believed that he could have Poland at nominal cost to Germany. His was a costly mistake.

[15] Memorandum by Weizsäcker, September 2, 1939, DG, Series D, VII, 509–10; François-Poncet to Bonnet, August 31, 1939, Livre jaune, 360–61; Bonnet to François-Poncet, September 1, 1939, ibid., 377–78; Zay, Carnets secrets, 78–82; minutes of Halifax, August 31, 1939, DBFP, Third series, VII, 442–43, 436–37, 465; minutes of Jebb, September 2, 1939, ibid., 518–19; minutes of Makin, September 2, 1939, ibid., 530–51; The Ciano Diaries, 136–37; memorandum of Ciano, September 2, 1939, I Documenti Diplomatici Italiani (Ministero degli Affari Esteri), Eighth series, XIII, 352.

# 26

## The Riddle

IN THE STORY of the Munich Agreement there is a riddle. Was it only surrender to Hitler's bluff? If Britain and France had stood fast, resolute in their determination to resist, would Czechoslovak independence and world peace have been saved? Or was the Agreement unavoidable under the circumstances? Was it a "tragic necessity?"[1]

To denounce the Munich Agreement as cowardly surrender is simple, but there is more to the tale. Other forces sent Chamberlain and Daladier to Munich. They did not go there out of sheer folly. They made the journey because it seemed the only alternative to a war no one wanted.

In 1938 the Munich Agreement seemed sensible to many who fancied themselves sane, sober, and Christian. It was far better than another world war. Because the Sudetens wanted to become a part of Germany, they seemed a poor excuse for bloodshed. The Treaty of Versailles was wicked; another world war was unthinkable. If appeasing Hitler with the Sudetenland avoided a world war, peace was preferred. There seemed to be no way to prevent German armies from overrunning Czechoslovakia.

There was an attempt to scientifically sample public opinion dur-

1 Cf. Lord Strang, *At Home and Abroad*, 153; Duff Cooper, "A Cynical Act of Cold-blooded Butchery," *The Listener*, Vol. XL (November 18, 1948), 757–58; Viscount Templewood, "The Lesson of Munich," *ibid.*, Vol. XL, (December 9, 1948), 879–80; Churchill, *The Gathering Storm*, 326–27; Viscount Simon, *Retro-*

ing the September crisis. This sampling revealed that 70 per cent of those contacted in one London borough reacted favorably to Chamberlain's flight to visit Hitler on September 15. At the time of the Godesberg meeting, the opposition to Chamberlain had risen to 40 per cent, according to a similar sampling; but the opposition dropped on September 30 to 10 per cent, with 54 per cent favoring him and 26 per cent expressing no opinion.[2] After September 30, however, the chorus of approval seemed proof of public assent, regardless of the wisdom of the Agreement. Every sign in France and Great Britain indicated the satisfaction of the man in the street with the Munich Agreement. The few dissenters were drowned out by those who wanted peace and had no wish to die for Czechoslovakia. To the politicians the Munich Agreement seemed justified by public opinion.

Of these politicians, none has been more condemned for the Munich Agreement than Chamberlain. He did not accept the Munich Agreement out of cowardice but because he was unwilling to drag the nation into a world war over an issue that did not seem worth the loss of countless lives. He doubted that the nation would have followed him into a war to coerce a minority who wanted to exercise the right of self-determination. He preferred to seek a formula satisfying Hitler's political demands and then to solve the Anglo-German economic problems because these were to him the most important.

To the end of his life, Chamberlain believed that his policy had been the only one possible in 1938, given the spirit of the time and the hostility of the Opposition. But the excuse of a strong Opposition meant little within the House of Commons where the Tories had a safe majority.

Chamberlain was strengthened in his resolution to appease Hitler by the pathetic condition of the French government and the Premier. Although Daladier accurately evaluated Hitler's aggression, he would not lead his nation into a war over Czechoslovakia. He blamed everyone else for the sins of France: British lack of armaments, Britain's refusal to support France, Polish hostility towards Czechoslovakia, Russian legalism over the alliance, and United States' isolationism.

spect: *The Memoirs of the Rt. Hon. Viscount Simon,* 238–39; Nevile Henderson, *Water Under the Bridge,* 210–13.

2 Charles Madge and Tom Harrison, *Britain by Mass-Observation,* 56–101.

It was sheer folly, he told the National Assembly in 1946, to fight Germany alone: France could be engaged to fight Germany only within a coalition.[3]

In 1938, France was alone except for the help provided by the British fleet. There was no mighty coalition. There had been hopes that, if war with Germany ever came, Poland, Russia and Czechoslovakia would attack Germany from the east while the French armies remained behind the Maginot Line; but in 1938, Poland was hostile and Russia preferred to watch rather than act. To save Czechoslovakia, France would be forced to mount an attack.

When the French government had concluded the 1935 alliance with Czechoslovakia, no one considered that France would ever be called upon to fulfill her obligations by attacking Germany. The alliance would provide a Czech attack on Germany, not a French one. Appalled at the bloody prospect of assaulting Germany in 1938, French politicians and generals deserted Czechoslovakia, using the Munich Agreement. The generals tried to excuse their desertion by launching a campaign to expose the inferiority of the Czech armed forces.

If France had ever seriously intended to aid Czechosolvakia, she would have made plans for an invasion of Germany. Such plans never existed, and without an invasion of Germany to draw off Hitler's armies, the Czech forces were doomed. No plans for an attack on Germany existed in 1938, because French strategy was defensive. The war of 1914–18 seemed to have proven the superiority of the defense over the offense. As a symbol of this philosophy, the Maginot Line had been constructed to withstand the expected German offensive.

Behind the Line the armies of France would be secure; casualties would be slight while French guns decimated the enemy. The Line made defensive strategy imperative; it nullified the Czech alliance; it confounded all hopes of a French offensive against Germany. If the French armies stayed on the defensive, however, the Czech armies would be left alone to face the German attack. The armies of France would become involved in the war only if Germany attacked the Maginot Line, but Hitler planned to attack only in the east.

There had not even been any planning with the Czech general staff. When General Ludvík Krejčí, the Czechoslovak chief of staff, pro-

[3] *Journal Officiel*, July 18, 1946, 2678–80.

posed to Gamelin, on June 18, 1938, that joint studies be made to insure unity of decision, Gamelin referred the question to his government. No action was ever taken because the French High Command had no intention of any offensive action to draw German troops away from the Czechoslovak frontiers. They followed the teachings of Marshal Henri Pétain, who believed that defensive strategy reinforced by the Line made alliances unnecessary.

There had not been any joint planning with the British general staff. Whatever plans the French may have had in September, 1938, were not passed on to the British, who only knew that French plans were based on defense rather than offense and that they would not leave the Maginot Line.

The failure of the staffs to confer was also a result of policy of the British chiefs of staff, who feared that talks with the French would anger the Germans when Chamberlain was seeking appeasement and would involve the British forces in commitments they could not fulfill. For similar reasons, cabinet instructions forbade any discussions of strategic plans with French generals. Until March, 1939, neither general staff had any definite idea of the strategic planning of the other.[4]

Any plan to aid Czechoslovakia required a massive striking force —heavy tank divisions, possessing powerful engines, and long-range artillery with armor-piercing shells—poised on the western frontiers of Germany prepared to thrust deep into the vitals of the Nazi empire and draw off the German forces fighting in Bohemia and Moravia. Such an offensive force did not exist in 1938, mainly because of the attitudes of certain French generals and Daladier. In September, 1938, the French army had two light, armored divisions capable only of limited reconnaissance and protection for the infantry from other infantry but not from tanks. With heavy armored divisions and a resolve to attack, French forces would have broken through Germany and saved Czechoslovakia. Without these forces, Czechoslovakia was doomed.[5]

Given the help of thirty to forty Czech divisions in 1938, France was stronger than Germany, but this strength was useless without

4 Sir John Slessor, *The Central Blue: Recollections and Reflections*, 146–47.
5 *Survey of International Affairs, 1938*, III, 545–55; Paul Reynaud, *In the Thick of the Fight, 1930–1945*, 165–66.

an offensive strategy and plans for an invasion of Germany. Had war come in 1938, the French armies would have remained along the Maginot Line, facing only eleven German divisions, while the bulk of Hitler's forces slaughtered the Czechs.

The French air force would have provided little help in a war. It was antiquated, weak, and crippled by defensive strategy.[6] In September, 1938, France had only seven hundred planes, and none was modern. The *Luftwaffe* had over twenty-eight hundred planes, and more than one thousand of these were bombers.

France lacked the industrial facilities necessary to sustain her air force in a modern world war. Between 1936 and 1938, the French government had ordered 761 planes, a month's production in Germany in 1938, and by September 1938, only 83 had been delivered.[7]

The faith of the French in their air force was not improved by the reports of so eminent an authority as Colonel Charles Lindbergh. Appearing in Paris and London amid the September crisis, he preached peace at any price because the *Luftwaffe* was the strongest air force in the world and would "flatten out cities like London, Paris, and Prague."[8]

The condition of the French air force was one more excuse that Daladier used to evade responsibilities which could have brought war. Another excuse was the condition of the British armed forces. Of these, only the Royal Navy approached a state of combat readiness when mobilized in 1938. However, there was no way for the fleet to aid Czechoslovakia because the sea coasts of Bohemia existed only in Shakespeare's mind.

The British army could offer no more than two divisions for service on the Continent, and Chamberlain was loath to promise even this. In 1938 only five, fully equipped, regular army divisions had been planned. They were to be trained for fighting a colonial war. Such a force would be unfit for offensive warfare against Germany. Noticeably lacking was any large force of mechanized armor, sufficient to

6 Slessor, *The Central Blue*, 148.

7 *Survey of International Affairs, 1938*, III, 511–19; Pierre Tissier, *The Riom Trial*, 53–92.

8 Slessor, *The Central Blue*, 218–22; Phipps to Halifax, September 13, 21, 22, 1938, *DBFP*, Third series, II, 310–11, 454, 473–74.

pierce the German defenses and race to the aid of the Czechoslovak armies.[9]

As late as November, 1938, the Chancellor of the Exchequer forbade the increase of the army to six divisions, using the argument of economy. One chief of staff observed that the Chancellor "was primarily concerned to insure that we had enough money left to pay the indemnity after losing the war."[10]

After the occupation of Prague, the British army undertook to prepare thirty-two divisions—a force comparable in size to the Czechoslovak army which had been surrendered to Hitler without a fight. If Hitler had been faced in 1938 with thirty-two British divisions, thirty-five Czech divisions, and over one hundred French divisions, prepared to drive through Germany with all their strength, protected by a mighty air armada, there would not have been a Munich Agreement.

Of the three British military services, the status of the Royal Air Force had the most decisive influence on British policy in the September crisis.[11] The R.A.F. did not measure up to the needs of the time either in defense or offense. In 1938 the R.A.F. could fight a German air force that had existed in 1936. The *Anschluss* forced the cabinet to approve a first line expansion to twelve thousand planes, to be ready within two years. This planned increase was known as *Schedule L;* only 10 per cent of the plan had been completed by the September crisis. This plan was consistent with the practice of expanding first line aircraft without creating the reserves, administration, and auxiliary services necessary to withstand a long conflict.

In September, 1938, less than 30 fighter squadrons were ready for duty. Only 5 of these were equipped with modern Hurricane fighters and none with Spitfires. In all there were 759 fighters, and the majority were outdated and so slow that German bombers could evade them easily. Although 93 Hurricanes were available, they were unable to fight above fifteen thousand feet even in summer because the guns could not be heated. Pilots for these squadrons were in short supply. The administration, reserve planes, and auxiliary services

9 M. M. Postan, *British War Production,* 29–30, 70–72, 81–82; James Leasor, *War at the Top,* 55–56.

10 Slessor, *The Central Blue,* 161; Postan, *British War Production,* 10–12.

11 Kemp, *Key to Victory,* 26.

were lacking for a long war. The situation was similar in the bombing squadrons—insufficiency in modern planes, personnel, airfields, and servicing facilities.[12] The R.A.F. was unfit for a world war.

Other means for air defense were lacking. Only 126 antiaircraft guns were available for the defense of London in September, 1938, and only 334 for the whole of the British Isles. The radar chain was incomplete, and the personnel were untrained in its use. Except for hastily dug trenches in parks, sufficient air raid shelters were lacking. Estimates of the probable number of killed and wounded that might result among the civilian population from air raids appalled the British government. Within sixty days of the first air assault, 600,000 dead were expected, creating an additional problem in the disposal of so many bodies. To build sufficient coffins would have required over twenty million square feet of timber. Hospitals would have been clogged with over 1,200,000 wounded. Psychiatrists anticipated three to four million mental casualties within six months of the outbreak of war. There were no plans whatsoever to feed the population during the air attacks.[13]

The inability of the British armed forces to wage modern war against Germany was known only too well within the government. When Chamberlain faced Hitler at Munich, the armaments and troops necessary to fight Germany did not exist, nor did the means to protect the civilian population. Thus it seemed wise to appease Hitler with the Sudetenland, for he could take all of Czechoslovakia if he desired while Britain could not stop him.

The riddle of the Munich Agreement is not solved by the testimony of the German generals, given after the war, that Germany was unprepared for a world war in September, 1938, and would not have fought had Britain and France resisted.[14] Although Germany was unprepared for a world war in September, 1938, her armed forces were ready for a war against Czechoslovakia.[15] Germany could not

12 Slessor, *The Central Blue*, 223–24; *Survey of International Affairs, 1938*, III, 497–99; Postan, *British War Production*, 14–19; Denis Richards, *Royal Air Force, 1939–1945*, Vol. I, *The Fight at Odds*, 30–31; Derek Wood and Derek Dempster, *The Narrow Margin*, 79.

13 Postan, *British War Production*, 54–55, 106–107; *Survey of International Affairs, 1938*, III, 504–505; Richard M. Titmus, *Problems of Social Policy*, 19–20.

14 *TMWC*, X, 509–10; XV, 361; XX, 606; memorandum of Moffat, December 22, 1938, *FRUS, 1938*, I, 735–36.

15 *NCA*, IV, 592–97.

have held out against the Anglo-French forces in the west if they had been prepared to invade Germany, but emphasis on defensive strategy, lack of modern arms, and the Maginot Line made these forces ready to sit out the war.

At the Nuremberg trials, the German generals argued that their armies would have been delayed by the Czechoslovak fortifications, but if they had been willing to suffer losses they would probably have gotten through. Czechoslovak forces planned a withdrawal to avoid being outflanked on the old Austrian frontier where the fortifications were slight. Such strategy would have succeeded if the Anglo-French forces had been ready to sweep into Germany.

Now we know that the German armed forces were not as well prepared in 1938 as they were in 1939 or 1940, but they were ready for a war against Czechoslovakia—a limited war on one front. There was no need to worry about war on two fronts, because the British had little with which to fight, and the French had no intention of attacking Germany.

Now we realize that the intelligence estimates of the size of the *Luftwaffe* were exaggerated; however, in combat readiness, it far exceeded that of the Anglo-French air forces. Intelligence estimates were colored by the effects of the Douhet theory that bombers could score a swift, knockout blow. The Spanish Civil War increased the fears of total destruction from the air.

Although the *Luftwaffe* lacked heavy, long-range bombers to pound London and Paris, there were enough planes to overwhelm the Czech air force. Only a skeleton force would have been needed on the western front where there was no intention of attacking Germany. Hitler's forces could have defeated Czechoslovakia at will, aided by the Poles and Hungarians, if they cared to share in the loot.

If war had come in 1938, would the story have ended differently? If the Czechoslovak army had not been forced to divert too many troops against Poland and Hungary, probably the German armies would have been delayed a little longer in their conquest. Their ultimate victory, however, would have been certain, given time to wear down the Czech resistance and willingness to sustain casualties. Czechoslovakia would have received no direct aid from Britain and France and even less indirect aid than Poland received in 1939. While the Germans conquered Czechoslovakia, Anglo-French troops would have remained on the defensive within the Maginot Line.

285

If Hitler had then taken only the Sudetenland, without direct aggression against Britain and France, these governments would have been sorely tempted to make peace. This policy would have seemed logical and moral because Hitler was only taking what many believed had been torn from Germany by the Versailles Treaty.

If a general European war had come in 1938, the fall of France could have come a year earlier. The R.A.F. would not have been ready for the Battle of Britain if it had come in 1939, for *Schedule M,* the plan under which the fighters for the Battle of Britain were produced, was not drawn up until October, 1938, as a result of the Munich Agreement. It is doubtful if the Hurricanes and Spitfires could have been built in sufficient numbers to be ready for an earlier battle. Time was needed to bring *Schedule M* to completion. Time was needed to complete the radar chain which provided the eyes and ears of the R.A.F. in 1940. Had the Battle of Britain been fought in 1939, there is serious doubt that the R.A.F. could have withstood the *Luftwaffe*.[16]

Arguments over the feasibility of war in 1938 prove little, however, because few in positions of responsibility in France and Britain wanted war over Czechoslovakia. Waging war would have meant that war had been accepted as the only alternative to a worse fate. In September, 1938, this did not seem to be the case either to the British and French peoples or to their governments.

If they would oppose Hitler, they must be resolved to go to the brink of war and beyond if necessary, but only Hitler was resolved to press on to war if such were necessary. Neither France nor Britain was resolved to stand fast against Hitler if war were the consequence. They were without the will and the means to resist. To those who prided themselves on their realism, there was no excuse for a world war and every excuse for appeasement.

When the four powers met at Munich, only Germany was prepared to pay the cost of victory—war. The governments of Britain and France wanted to avoid war over the Sudetens because such a cause was unworthy of the cost. Appeasement of Hitler through the Munich Agreement seemed worthwhile if it avoided a world war which

16 Basil Collier, *The Defence of the United Kingdom,* 69; Slessor, *The Central Blue,* 150, 178–80, 208. For a contrasting view, see William L. Shirer, *The Rise and Fall of the Third Reich: A History of Nazi Germany,* 426.

Britain and France never wanted and for which they were unprepared in armaments and in spirit.

Here is the answer to the riddle of the Munich Agreement: to wage war required sufficient cause, a will to war, and the men and armaments. Because these were lacking in 1938, Chamberlain and Daladier had no other choice than to sign the Munich Agreement.

# 27

## Liquidation and Legacy

No ONE from the Chamberlain government met Eduard Beneš when his plane landed at England's Croydon Airfield in 1938: official reception might arouse Hitler. He was ignored and almost forgotten.

There was little that Beneš could do then for Czechoslovakia, but in his heart there was one purpose, the repudiation of the Munich Agreement. When Hitler's troops invaded Bohemia in the early hours of March 15, 1939, Beneš no longer felt constrained to keep his silence, for Hitler had destroyed whatever validity remained in the Agreement; but the "men of Munich" chose to shun him because he represented their failure to appease Hitler.

When war came in September, 1939, Beneš was still without influence in either London or Paris. Now the Poles were heroes, their greed in 1938 forgotten. The Czechs, who had been urged a year earlier not to fight, were now damned for cowardice and subservience.

To the British and French governments, Beneš pledged the help of the Czechs and Slovaks. In his reply to the pledge, Chamberlain omitted all reference to the Munich Agreement and promised only to release the Czech people from the German occupation. Daladier ignored Beneš. His government deliberately supported a rival refugee Czech organization. However, Daladier did acknowledge the formation of an autonomous Czech army, much smaller and more poorly equipped than the thirty-five divisions which had been sacrificed to Hitler. By November, 1939, a Czechoslovak National Committee with

Beneš as a member was recognized by London and reluctantly by Paris.[1]

When the military collapse of France came in the spring of 1940, Czech troops retreated to the coast because of the danger of death in Nazi concentration camps. The French government refused to aid them in their escape and blocked efforts to rescue them. In London the Foreign Office did nothing. Bruce Lockhart, an old friend of Beneš, secured aid from the Admiralty, and the Czech troops were saved to fight again.

Despite the existence of the Czech army and the war being waged on its behalf, a provisional government was not recognized until after the creation of Churchill's wartime government. On July 21, 1940, after prolonged pleading by Beneš and others on his behalf, Halifax announced that he was happy to recognize the Czechoslovak National Committee as the provisional Czechoslovak government. There was no mention of repudiating the Munich Agreement or accepting the pre-Munich frontiers.[2]

Full recognition of the Beneš government in exile did not come until 1941, after the German invasion of Russia. With the Nazi-Soviet pact broken, Stalin could assume a new pose. On July 18, 1941, the Soviet Union renewed the prewar alliance with Czechoslovakia, promised assistance in the war, and agreed to organize a Czechoslovak army in the Soviet Union among those Czechs and Slovaks who had been interned.

Jan Masaryk, minister of foreign affairs in the provisional government, telephoned the news to Anthony Eden, now British foreign secretary. "So you achieved agreement with the Russians," Eden said, "and once again we shall be late." "As usual," Masaryk rejoined.[3]

Later the same day, the British government accorded full recognition to the Czechoslovak government in exile. On July 30, the United States followed the British in granting recognition.

1 Beneš to Chamberlain, September 3, 1939, Chamberlain to Beneš, September 29, 1939, Osusky to Daladier, November 13, 1939, Daladier to Osusky, November 17, 1939, Beneš to Halifax, December 20, 1939, Halifax to Beneš, December 20, 1939, *Czechoslovak Sources and Documents*, II, 41–46.

2 Halifax to Beneš, July 21, 1940, *Documents on International Affairs, 1939–1946*, II, 312.

3 Josef Korbel, *The Communist Subversion of Czechoslovakia, 1938–1948: The Failure of Coexistence*, 78–79.

On the second anniversary of the Munich Agreement, Beneš sought to have the Foreign Office announce that the Munich Agreement was non-existent. He argued that the Czechoslovak government had been forced by Britain and France to accept the Munich Agreement contrary to the constitution and that Hitler had violated the Agreement on March 15. The Foreign Office refused to admit that the Agreement had been forced on the Czech government. When Churchill spoke on the radio the night of September 30, 1940, he would only say that the Munich Agreement had been destroyed by the Germans.[4]

Beneš next insisted on full recognition of the legal continuity of the government of the Republic, arguing that Munich was null and void after March 15. He requested that the British government declare formally that it was in no way bound by the Munich Agreement or its consequences and regarded the pre-Munich status of the Czechoslovak government as restored.

Within the Foreign Office he met opposition. The British government could not make any statement concerning postwar frontiers because other countries would demand similar treatment: there was an agreement to this effect with the United States government. To declare that the Munich Agreement no longer existed would not annul the fact that it had been concluded. There had been a Munich Agreement, and it still was a legal document. It could only be superseded by a new agreement made by those nations who signed the old one. This argument led to the absurd conclusion that the Munich Agreement could only be annulled by another conference of four powers who were waging war against each other.[5]

The Foreign Office rejected Beneš' arguments because it was difficult for a sovereign government to confess that it had signed a diplomatic instrument which was either illegal or morally wrong. For a government to admit public error, required more courage and a stronger political position than Churchill's government had during 1940 and 1941. There were men still in the government who had held office under Chamberlain in 1938, cheered the news of the invitation to the conference at Munich, and supported the Agreement. A discussion of repudiation could open old wounds, causing grievous arguments within a coalition cabinet trying to wage war against a powerful foe. For Churchill there was a personal loyalty to his friends and

4 Beneš, *Memoirs*, 301.
5 *Ibid.*, 198–208.

CROWDS WERE SMALL, and the weather was wet and grim when Hitler led his troops into the Sudetenland on October 3, 1938.

*The National Archives*

FRANTIŠEK CHVALKOVSKY, Czechoslovak foreign minister,
October 1938–March, 1939.

colleagues. There seemed no pressing need to stir up the old quarrels amid a world war.

The Soviet government finally broke the impasse. On June 9, 1942, V. M. Molotov, Soviet foreign commisar, told Beneš that he could announce that the Russian government had nothing to do with the Munich Agreement and did not recognize anything related to Munich. In saying this, Molotov lied. The Soviet Union had played a prominent role in bringing the Munich Agreement to pass. The Soviet government had withdrawn recognition from Czechoslovakia on December 14, 1939, and had accredited a minister to the Slovak government in February, 1940.

Recognition from the Russian government provided Beneš with a lever to pry similar recognition from the British. Beneš pointed out to Eden that it was time to liquidate Munich, for the Russians had already beaten them to it. Eden had to agree. Serious discussions began which culminated with an agreement of August 5, accepted by Commons the same day without trouble. Eden acknowledged that the Munich Agreement had been completely destroyed by Germany, freeing the British government of responsibility. When the final frontier settlement came, the government would not be influenced by the terms of the Munich Agreement. Beneš' victory had not been complete, for the British government refused to admit the use of force to compel acceptance of the terms. The sinner was only willing to confess to a portion of his misdeeds.

General Charles de Gaulle, leader of the Free French forces, informed Beneš on September 29, 1942, that the French National Committee considered the Munich Agreement null and void. De Gaulle promised that his government would do everything to guarantee the pre-September 30 frontiers of Czechoslovakia. As the British had done before, De Gaulle admitted only part of his nation's sins.[6]

After four years, the Munich Agreement was legally ended, but its pernicious influence remained. The ghost of the Munich Agreement could not be stilled, for Beneš was still affected by the Russian attitude of September, 1938. Because the West had betrayed him, he wanted a guarantee of safety from the Russians against the German

6 Molotov statement, June 9, 1942, Eden to Masaryk, August 5, 1942, *Documents on International Affairs, 1939–1946*, II, 317–18; de Gaulle to Sramek, September 29, 1942, *Czechoslovak Sources and Documents*, II, 97; Lettrich, *History of Modern Slovakia*, 163–64.

menace without dependence on aid from France. He knew that Czechoslovakia was caught between the East and West; he must keep contact with both sides. He feared that Russia might try to exploit Munich, as they later did. To prevent such a policy Beneš wanted to stay on good terms with the Russian government. Believing that the West must become more involved in Eastern Europe if the peace were to be kept, Beneš did not hesitate to make Czechoslovakia a link between East and West. Thus he traveled to Moscow in 1943 to sign a treaty with Joseph Stalin.

Beneš received such special treatment as was usually accorded by Stalin only to distinguished statesmen. In a treaty signed on December 12, both pledged military aid against any future German attempt to conquer Eastern Europe. France was not mentioned; Beneš had deprived Stalin of his old excuse. Russia and Czechoslovakia were full allies because Beneš wanted a security against Russian acquiescence in another Munich Agreement. In a protocol to the treaty, other powers with common frontiers to either Czechoslovakia or Russia could join. By this means Beneš hoped to tie Poland down to preserving Czechoslovak frontiers.[7]

Within Czechoslovakia, Karl Hermann Frank, Henlein's deputy, fulfilled Hitler's orders to wipe out the Czech intellectuals, while dispersing the other Czechs to death camps and to forced labor in Germany. The assassination in Prague on May 24, 1942, of Reinhard Heydrich, the new Gestapo chief for Occupied Europe, loosed a wave of slaughter and terror among the Czechs. In 1943, Frank was rewarded for his labors with the title of Reich Minister and Minister of State in charge of the Ministry for Bohemia-Moravia; now the wishes of the Sudeten Germans would be satisfied.

On April 18, 1945, the United States Third Army, under General George S. Patton, crossed the Czechoslovak frontier. Beneš was delighted that a Western army would liberate his homeland, but he was sorely disappointed when Patton's advance stopped on orders of General Dwight D. Eisenhower, Supreme Commander of Allied Forces. To the Czechs the Allied halt meant that again, as at Munich in 1938, the West had forsaken them. General George C. Marshall had advised Eisenhower not "to hazard American lives for purely political

7 Beneš, *Memoirs*, 255–58; Taborsky, "Beneš and the Soviets," *Foreign Affairs*, Vol. XXVII (January, 1949), 306–307.

purposes."[8] Eisenhower agreed with this advice; he ordered his troops to advance across the 1937 Czech frontier, halting on the Karlsbad-Pilsen-Ceske Budejovice line, approximately sixty miles from Prague. The Russians accepted this plan because most of Czechoslovakia was left for occupation by their forces accompanied by Czech Communists who had sat out the war in Moscow.

Although the German armed forces had surrendered on May 7, fighting in Prague continued with the Nazis taking bloody reprisals on the Czechs. Soviet forces did not reach the city until May 10, securing it two days later. Arrests then began, but Konrad Henlein cheated Czech justice by committing suicide. Reich Minister Frank was arrested, tried, and eventually hanged.

Now the legacy of the Munich Agreement, the Sudetens, had to be settled. During the war, the problem of the future of the Sudetens in postwar Czechoslovakia was often in Beneš' thoughts. The presence of these peoples had created the Munich Agreement and aided the destruction of Czechoslovak independence. Many co-operated with the occupation troops and caused the death of Czechs and Slovaks. To avoid a repetition of these tragedies, Beneš concluded that the just solution would be to send the Sudetens back to Germany. They longed for their home in Germany, then home they would go. An exception would be made of those who had been loyal to the Czechoslovak Republic.

In 1943, Beneš obtained acceptance of his policy by the Russian, British, and American governments, including a personal agreement from President Franklin D. Roosevelt. The unwelcome citizens could be turned out of new, postwar Czechoslovakia. On April 5, 1945, the Czechoslovak provisional government announced that Sudeten Germans would be expelled and their property confiscated unless their loyalty to the Republic could be proven. Sudeten property was ordered confiscated on June 21, 1945. Sudetens were deprived of Czech citizenship on August 2, 1945, because they had become German citizens as a result of the occupation and subsequent Nazi decrees. The Sudetens could retain their Czechoslovak citizenship if they could prove their loyalty to the Czechoslovak Republic, if they had actively participated in the struggle against the occupation, or if they had suffered persecution at the hands of the Nazis.

8 Forrest C. Pogue, *The Supreme Command,* 468–69, 503–506.

Fighting and atrocities at the close of the war coupled with hatred building up since September 30, 1938, prevented an orderly expulsion in June and July 1945. Czech troops and police drove Sudetens from their homes without regard for politics or physical condition. Many were thrust into concentration camps. With only the clothes on their backs and perhaps hand luggage, thousands of Sudetens were pushed across the old Czech frontiers. Polish troops drove them back, but the Czechs would not have them; many succumbed to mistreatment and exposure.

At the Potsdam Conference, the three governments asked that the transfer of population take place in an "orderly and humane manner." The warning aided moderates among the non-Communist Czechs who had never wanted such outrages.

The expulsions proceeded but with less rigor. The exiles were allowed to take a week's food rations and fifty kilograms of baggage in addition to hand luggage. Gradually the restrictions were relaxed and proven anti-Nazis could depart with all their movables and even appoint administrators for their estates. Organized expulsions lasted from January, 1946, to the spring of 1947. Thousands more fled after the Communist coup of 1948. The ghost of Adolf Hitler should have been satisfied: almost three million Sudeten Germans had finally come home to Germany.[9]

The fate of the Sudetens is naught but cruel irony. Because of their condition in 1938, Hitler had brought them to a worse state after World War II. Although many Sudetens have aided the economic development of West Germany, others have dragged out a bitter existence far from their homes as a result of the Munich Agreement. Well can they join in the Czech anthem, "Where Is My Home?"

The Sudetenland did not easily recover from the exodus. For years it was a desolate waste land, filled with untended farms and ghost towns. Houses rotted, and the squares were empty of a people who could have lived peacefully in Czechoslovakia if Hitler had permitted. Instead, through the Munich Agreement, he gave them a legacy of hatred, unhappiness, and longing for their homeland.

9 *FRUS, Diplomatic Papers, The Berlin Conference,* II, 1495; Hubert Ripka, *Czechoslovakia Enslaved: The Story of the Communist Coup d'Etat,* 21; Elizabeth Wiskemann, *Germany's Eastern Neighbors: Problems Relating to the Oder-Neisse Line and the Czech Frontier Regions,* 100–12, 122–27; *The Expulsion of the German Population from Czechoslovakia* (ed. by Theodor Schieder), 63–128, 169–70.

# 28

## The Myth

THE MUNICH AGREEMENT soon became a myth, with truth distorted to serve new ends. Even before the Agreement had been liquidated in 1942, the West had begun creating the myth: had Russia been sincerely approached in 1938 by Britain and France, she would have eagerly rushed to the defense of Czech democracy, and Hitler's Reich would have been destroyed. Soviet Russia appeared to many as the only nation willing to fight Hitler and to defend Czechoslovakia, but Russia had never intended to do battle with Germany.

Diplomatic relations between the Western powers and the Russians during the war were colored by the myth that Russia had turned to the pact of August 23, 1939, because of pique over the Munich Agreement. No one profited so much from the Munich Agreement as the Soviet Union: she could pose as an opponent of Nazi Germany without being called upon to fight because of the French conduct in the Czech crisis.

By the same means, the Czech Communists and their leader, Klement Gottwald, who had led the party in a deliberate campaign to destroy the very existence of the Czechoslovak state, could appear as Czech patriots, eager to save the nation. The myth covered a tale of treachery when Communist informers betrayed the Czechs to the Gestapo during the occupation.[1]

For the Communists, "Munich Agreement" became a convenient peg on which to hang their anti-Western policy. The Western capi-

1 Korbel, *The Communist Subversion of Czechoslovakia*, 34–35.

talists had betrayed Czechoslovakia to induce Hitler to turn eastward against the Soviet Union. The loss of Czech lives in the fighting during 1944 and 1945 was blamed on the West as another trick to sacrifice Czechs to the Germans.

When Czech democracy fell before the Communist onslaught in 1948, it must have seemed to many Czechs that once more the West had betrayed them. Although the myth was not the sole cause for the coup, the Communists exploited it, saying that the capitalist West had deserted the Czech people in 1938 while the glorious Soviet Union had stood ready for action. Bourgeois capitalists had left the Czechs to the mercies of the Nazis because they feared the masses.[2]

On the twentieth anniversary of the Munich Agreement, the East German and Czech communist governments issued a statement to keep the myth alive. "The events following the signing of the Munich Agreement prove that Munich was an anti-Soviet plot . . . preparing aggression against the first Socialist state of the world."

Using the story of the Munich Agreement, it was easy for the Czech Communists to warn of West German rearmament and to point then to Russia as the only true friend. Reports in the Czech press of Sudeten agitation, propaganda, and meetings since 1945 have all contributed to bolster Communist rule in Czechoslovakia. Sudeten activity in West Germany has reminded the Czechs of Western connections with Munich. Among the leaders of the present Sudeten movement are Germans who were judges, generals, and officials in Czechoslovakia during the German occupation. Their names and activities are widely circulated in Czechoslovakia to remind the Czechs of the past and to make them willing to endure the present passively.

Each spring Sudeten refugees hold rallies at which ministers in the government of German Federal Republic extol the Sudetens' right to self-determination and demand the linking of Bohemia and Moravia to the future Germany. To some of the refugee leaders, the Munich pact still has international validity. Because these Sudeten groups have declared themselves as opposed to Communism, they have received fervent support from American congressmen.[3]

[2] Vladimir Reiskyde Dubnic, *Communist Propaganda Methods: A Case Study on Czechoslovakia*, 49; Korbel, *The Communist Subversion of Czechoslovakia*, 240. Rothstein's book, *The Munich Conspiracy*, is permeated by the Soviet version of the myth.

[3] *New York Times*, September 28, 1958, February 15, May 15, 16, 17, August 20, and December 12, 1959.

The myth of Munich became a potent force in American politics during the Korean war: it was present in the debate over the seating of Red China in the United Nations, the argument over bombing China, the firing of General Douglas MacArthur, and the collapse of French power in Indo-China.

When the North Koreans attacked South Korea in 1950, President Harry Truman and his advisers considered the attack similar to Nazi aggression in 1938. Memories of attempts to appease Hitler intensified their belief in the folly of standing by and letting South Korea succumb. Failure to meet this aggression could lead to World War III, just as the appeasing of previous aggressors had done.[4]

As the Korean War dragged on, charges of appeasement tended to smother all sane discussion of Far Eastern policy. Senator William F. Knowland declared that "appeasement was surrender on the installment plan." He equated lack of decisive and forceful action with appeasement: "Talk of seating the Reds in the UN is appeasement. Talk of establishing a neutral zone in Korea is appeasement. Waiting around for Mao Tse-tung to become Tito is appeasement."[5]

The question of the prosecution of the Korean War and the bombing of Manchuria produced the argument that the failure to wage total war was appeasement. General MacArthur informed Congress that such appeasement only bred more war. Speaking for those now branded as "appeasers," General Omar N. Bradley, army chief of staff, declared that appeasement was giving something to aggressor without making a struggle or paying a price. Because such was evidently not the case in Korea, Bradley did not think he was practicing appeasement.[6] Freed of any restraint after his firing by Truman in 1951, MacArthur proceeded to speak wherever opportunity afforded about appeasement policy in high places reminiscent of that practiced at Munich by Chamberlain and Daladier.

The Geneva Conference in 1954 over the division of Indo-China evoked cries of "another Munich." The United States observer, former General Walter Bedell Smith, defended the conference with another definition of appeasement. "Munich's a damned poor term,"

[4] Harry S. Truman, *Memoirs*, II, 463; John N. Spanier, *The Truman-MacArthur Controversy and the Korean War*, 29.

[5] Norman A. Graebner, *The New Isolationism: A Study in Politics and Foreign Policy Since 1950*, 68.

[6] Spanier, *The Truman-MacArthur Controversy*, 216–50.

he retorted. "At Munich things were given away when there was no fighting. This is a war!"[7]

When President Dwight Eisenhower returned from the Geneva Summit Conference in July, 1955, he had to make the usual airport speech immediately upon arrival. Although the weather was rainy, Vice-President Richard M. Nixon forbade umbrellas lest the nation be reminded of Neville Chamberlain and the Munich Agreement. To quiet those ghosts, Eisenhower spoke in the rain without any covering.

The Munich myth was given fresh life by Nikita Khrushchev when he opened the Berlin question in November, 1958. He announced that the West had failed to stop Hitler in 1938 when the Soviet Union had been so willing to oppose the *Führer*. The Western governments, he declared, had "tolerated and encouraged the policy of blackmail and threats pursued by Hitler."[8] In 1961, Khrushchev intensified the Berlin question by dividing the city and resorting to extensive testing of nuclear bombs. The charges of "another Munich" and "appeasement" again beclouded diplomacy. Some argued that Khrushchev was pursuing a policy modeled after that of Hitler's in 1938 regarding Czechoslovakia, with the East Germans playing the role formerly assigned to the Sudetens. Khrushchev was seeking to undermine the West by negotiation and threats, just as Hitler had done in September, 1938. Proposals to negotiate the crisis were damned as "appeasement" and "a new Munich."[9]

The meaning of appeasement has become a part of the Munich myth. Now appeasement means surrender to the foe without a fight. Such was never Chamberlain's intent for he meant to remove by negotiation the possible causes of conflict. He assumed good intentions on the part of Hitler and a mutual desire for peace and prosperity.

"No appeasement" has come to mean inflexible position offering no compromise whatsoever, thus making negotiation impossible. The danger of the "no appeasement" policy grows from the mistaken interpretation of the Munich story. According to the myth of Munich, Chamberlain and Daladier simply surrendered; if they had stood fast, refusing to compromise, Hitler would have backed down because he was really bluffing. There would not have been any war. Those who accept this myth demand a belligerent pose, thinking it will suffice to

7 *New York Times,* July 24, 1954.
8 *Ibid.,* November 28, 1958.
9 *Ibid.,* April 4, 1959, July 9, August 16, September 30, and October 2, 1961.

scare off the aggressor. If the aggressor will not be frightened, the supporters of "no appeasement" must then face war or back down entirely. "No appeasement" has come to signify courage to go to the brink of war. It does not mean courage to go beyond the brink and wage war if necessary.

To cry "No appeasement!" has become a symbol of courage and strength. The "non-appeasers" insist they are going to the brink of war, but they do not expect to back up their tough words with action. By misreading the Munich story, they have become convinced that the aggressor is always bluffing: to call his bluff will stop his aggression. The non-appeaser takes up an inflexible position, leaving no room for maneuver, and declaring, in effect, it will be his way or war. But is he fully prepared to fight a war? If need be, will he shoot first? Has he the necessary means to protect the population? Is he not himself bluffing and pursuing a course as potentially dangerous as that he condemns Chamberlain for taking?[10]

At Munich the Western powers believed they were unable to plunge into a war in order to find out if Hitler was bluffing. To avoid being caught in such a dilemma, Chamberlain took what seemed the more practical course.

To the non-appeaser it seems so easy to act the part of a gun fighter in a western cattle town encounter in the 1870's. He forgets that it was not only the fastest draw that won, but also the man who shot to kill. Each gun fighter had to accept the risk of being killed or else back down. The non-appeaser believes that merely by taking the gun fighter's pose he can ward off a fight. To actually go through with the fight is not his wish, because he is not prepared for it. Herein has the myth of the Munich Agreement become dangerous.

The Munich myth is a product of ignorance. The non-appeasers offer a glib, facile explanation for the Munich Agreement because they cannot see the entire story in all of its tragedy. It was more than surrender to bluff. It was the product of the revisionist historians and popular misconceptions about the Versailles Treaty. It was the result of minority problems inherited from the Austro-Hungarian Empire, with all the accompanying hatreds and bitterness. The Munich Agreement was aided by pacifists and frightened politicians who dared not face the threat of an unthinkable war now become thinkable. It was

10 Cf. Leo Perla, *Can We End the Cold War? A Study in American Foreign Policy*, 128–40.

created out of military weakness, fear of offensive warfare, and poor strategic planning. It was the failure of Europe and the United States to unite in a mighty alliance to stop the Nazi threat. It was the product of the decline of Britain and France as world powers. It was the tragedy of men who ignored the future danger to enjoy the ease of the moment. It was a story of free men who were unprepared to wage war against the tyrant: this was the truth of the Munich Agreement.

# Appendix

THE INTERVIEW of de Lacroix and Hodža, on the night of September 20, has confused those who have written on the Czech crisis of September, 1938. The problem has been confounded by the destruction of the files of the Quai d'Orsay and the reluctance of Czech Communists to publish all the documents.

Those who supported the Munich Agreement used the interview, as reported by Bonnet from telegrams sent by de Lacroix, to prove that the Czechoslovak government had no wish to fight Germany. They contended that the Anglo-French proposals were converted into an ultimatum by the Czechoslovak government to save face by thrusting the onus of capitulation on France.

The solution to the mystery begins with understanding the conditions when the pair conferred. Both de Lacroix and Hodža were under a great strain which affected their reporting and their memories. There are three accounts: de Lacroix's telegrams and accounts by Hodža and de Lacroix long after the events. To understand what occurred, all three accounts must be combined. De Lacroix's account and the telegrams are in *Les événements survenus en France de 1933 à 1945*, XI; I have relied on Hodža's account in Boris Celovsky's *Das Münchener Abkommen von 1939*.

De Lacroix claimed that the copy of his telegram found in the files of Georges Bonnet was mutilated. Originally the telegram began with Hodža's question: "In case of war, would France evade her pledge?" De Lacroix replied that he lacked instructions. Then Hodža said: "I admit, *a priori* that France will not fight and, if you can obtain from your government tonight, a telegram confirming this, the President of the Republic will give way. It is the only way to save the peace." Hodža had left unsaid a thought in the last sentence which de Lacroix never inferred. Hodža meant: "It is the only way to save the peace if France will not support Czechoslovakia. Without France it is suicide."

From the documents printed in *Les événements,* one telegram from de Lacroix, no. 2218, is missing. This undoubtedly contained Hodža's question: "In case of war, will France evade her pledge?" The surviving telegrams, nos. 2219 and 2220, were found in the private files of Georges Bonnet. Before a parliamentary investigating committee, de Lacroix attested to the truth of these documents. The telegrams from Bonnet's files read:

The President of the Council has just summoned me. In agreement, he told me, with the President of the Republic, he informed me that if I came that same night and declared to M. Beneš that in case of war between Germany and Czechoslovakia over the Germans in the Sudetenland, France would not fight because of her engagements with England, the President of the Republic would take note of this statement. Immediately the President of the Council would call the cabinet, all of whose members were at the time in agreement with the President and with himself in proposing to give way.

The rulers of Czechoslovakia have need of this pretext *(couverture)* in order to accept the Franco-English proposal. They are sure of the army, whose leaders declared that single combat with Germany would be suicide. M. Hodža stated that the step which he was suggesting was the only means of saving peace. He wished to have the matter settled before midnight, if possible, or in any case, during the course of the night. The President of the Council would make the same communication to the British minister.[1]

With the original question conveniently lost, these telegrams could be used by Bonnet to gain what he desired, but they must not be taken too literally because of the stress under which they were composed. De Lacroix did not disavow the telegram after the war; however, he

[1] *Les événements,* XI, 273.

confused what Hodža had said and what he had learned from other sources.

Much use was made by Bonnet of the sentence containing the word *"couverture."* In his excitement, de Lacroix may have interposed this sentence: it was not used by Hodža. The sentence related to information that de Lecroix already had learned from other sources before this interview. Thus, when Hodža asked a question which Beneš may have feared to ask, de Lacroix interpreted it as a *couverture*. From other sources, de Lacroix knew that members of the general staff viewed resistance to Germany as suicide.

Hodža sought accurate information about French intentions realizing that France would desert her ally. He knew that if France intended to violate her promise, swift decisions must be made by the Czechoslovak authorities. Few in the Czechoslovak government dared face reality by asking if France would keep her pledge. Hodža asked the question and learned the truth.

# Bibliography

## I. Primary Sources

### A. MANUSCRIPTS

Auswärtiges Amt, Records of the German Foreign Office, National Archives, Microfilm Rolls 126, 153, 154, 2402–11, 2443–44.

### B. NEWSPAPERS

London *Times.*
*New York Times.*

### C. PRINTED COLLECTED DOCUMENTS

*Czechoslovak Sources and Documents.* Vol. II, *Struggle for Freedom.* New York, 1943.

*Documents and Materials Relating to the Eve of the Second World War.* 2 vols. New York, 1948–49.

*Documents of American Foreign Relations, January 1938–June 1939.* Boston, 1939.

*Documents on British Foreign Policy, 1919–1939.* Third series. Vols. I–VII. Ed. by E. L. Woodward and Rohan Butler. London, 1949–54.

*Documents on German Foreign Policy, 1918–1945.* Series D. Vols. I–VII. Washington, D. C., 1949–56.

*Documents on International Affairs, 1938.* 2 vols. Ed. by Monica Curtis. London, 1942–43.

*Documents on International Affairs, 1939–1946.* Vol. II, *Hitler's Europe.* Ed. by Arnold Toynbee. London, 1954.

*Europäische Politik, 1933–1938, im Spiegel der Prager Akten.* Ed. by Friedrich Berber. 3d ed. Essen, 1942.

*Les événements survenus en France de 1933 à 1945. Témoignagnes et documents recueillis par la commission d'enquête parlementaire.* 11 vols. Paris, 1947–51.

*The Expulsion of the German Population from Czechoslovakia.* Ed. by Teodor Schieder. Bonn, 1960.

*Fifth Column at Work.* Ed. by B. Bilek. London, 1945.

*Foreign Relations of the United States.*
   *Diplomatic Papers, 1938.* Vol. I. Washington, D. C., 1955.
   *Diplomatic Papers, 1939.* Vol. I. Washington, D. C., 1956.
   *Diplomatic Papers. The Conference of Berlin (The Potsdam Conference), 1945.* 2 vols. Washington, D. C., 1960.
   *Diplomatic Papers. Soviet Union, 1933–1939.* Washington, D. C., 1952.
   *1919, Paris Peace Conference.* Vols. III, IV. Washington, D. C., 1943.

*Journal Officiel. Débats parlementaires.* Assemblée Nationale. Paris, 1946.

*Journal Officiel. Débats parlementaires.* Chambre des Deputies. Paris, 1938.

Ministère des Affaires Étrangères. *Le livre jaune française. Documents diplomatiques, 1938–1939, pièces relatives aux événements et aux négociations qui ont précédé l'ouverture des hostilités entre l'Allemagne d'une part, la Pologne, la Grande Bretagne et la France d'autre part.* Paris, 1939.

Ministero degli Affari Esteri. *I Documenti Diplomatici Italiani.* Eighth series. Vols. XII and XIII. Rome, 1954.

*Nazi Conspiracy and Aggression.* 8 vols. Supplements. Washington, D. C., 1946.

*New Documents on the History of Munich.* Prague, 1958.

*Parliamentary Debates. House of Commons.*

*Parliamentary Debates. House of Lords.*

*Soviet Documents on Foreign Policy.* Ed. by Jane Degras. Vol. III. London, 1953.

*The Trials of the Major War Criminals Before the International Military Tribunal, Proceedings and Documents.* 42 vols. Nuremberg, 1947–49.

D. PRINTED MEMOIRS, DIARIES, AND SPEECHES

Anfuso, Filippo. *Du Palais de Venise au Lac de Garde.* Paris, 1949.

Ashton-Gwatkin, Frank T. A. "The Personal Story of the Runciman Mission," *The Listener*, Vol. XL (October 21, 1948), 595–97.

Beck, Colonel Józef. *Final Report*. New York, 1957.

Beneš, Edvard. *Memoirs: From Munich to New War and New Victory*. Translated by Godfrey Lias. Boston, 1954.

Bonnet, Georges. *Défense de la paix*. 2 vols. Geneva, 1946–47.

Chamberlain, Neville. *In Search of Peace*. New York, 1939.

Churchill, Winston S. *The Gathering Storm*. Boston, 1948.

——. *Triumph and Tragedy*. Boston, 1953.

*The Ciano Diaries, 1939–1943*. Ed. by Hugh Gibson. New York, 1946.

*Ciano's Hidden Diary, 1937–1938*. Ed. and translated by Andreas Mayor. New York, 1953.

Cooper, Duff. *Old Men Forget*. London, 1954.

Coulondre, Robert. *De Staline à Hitler; souvenirs de deux ambassades, 1936–1939*. Paris, 1950.

Davies, Joseph E. *Mission to Moscow*. New York, 1941.

Davignon, Jacques. *Berlin 1936–1940. Souvenirs d'une mission*. Paris, 1951.

Dirksen, Herbert von. *Moscow, Tokyo, London: Twenty Years of German Foreign Policy*. Norman, 1952.

Fabre-Luce, Alfred. *Histoire secrète de la conciliation de Munich*. Paris, 1938.

François-Poncet, André. *The Fateful Years: Memoirs of a French Ambassador in Berlin, 1931–1938*. New York, 1949.

Gamelin, Maurice. *Servir*. 2 vols. Paris, 1946.

Halifax, Earl of. *Fulness of Days*. London, 1957.

Henderson, Arthur. *Eyewitness in Czechoslovakia*. London, 1939.

Henderson, Nevile. *Failure of a Mission: Berlin, 1937–1939*. New York, 1940.

——. *Water Under the Bridge*. London, 1945.

Hitler, Adolf. *The Speeches of Adolf Hitler, April 1922–August 1939*. 2 vols. Ed. by Norman H. Baynes. London, 1942.

*Hitler's Table Talk, 1941–1944*. London, 1953.

Hoettle, Wilhelm. *The Secret Front*. New York, 1954.

Horthy, Admiral Miklás. *Memoirs*. New York, 1957.

Hull, Cordell. *The Memoirs of Cordell Hull*. 2 vols. New York, 1948.

Kesselring, Albert. *Kesselring: A Soldier's Record*. New York, 1954.

Kirkpatrick, Ivone. *The Inner Circle*. London, 1959.

Kordt, Erich. *Nicht aus den Akten*. Stuttgart, 1950.

Lazareff, Pierre. *De Munich à Vichy*. New York, 1944.

Mantoux, Paul. *Les deliberations de conseil des quatre*. 2 vols. Paris, 1955.

Maugham, Viscount. *At the End of the Day*. London, 1945.
*The Moffat Papers: Selections from the Diplomatic Journals of Jay Pierrepont Moffat, 1919–1943*. Ed. by Nancy Harvison Hooker. Cambridge, 1956.
Monzie, Anatole de. *Ci-devant*. Paris, 1941.
Morell, Sydney. *I Saw the Crucifixion*. London, 1939.
Noël, Léon. *L'aggression Allemande contre la Pologne*. Paris, 1946.
Paul-Boncour, Joseph. *Entre deux guerres*. 3 vols. Paris, 1946.
Price, Ward. *Year of Reckoning*. London, 1939.
*The Public Papers and Addresses of Franklin D. Roosevelt, 1938*. New York, 1941.
Reynaud, Paul. *In the Thick of the Fight, 1930–1945*. London, 1945.
Ribbentrop, Joachim von. *The Ribbentrop Memoirs*. London, 1954.
Schmidt, Paul. *Hitler's Interpreter*. New York, 1951.
Shirer, William L. *Berlin Diary: The Journal of a Foreign Correspondent, 1934–1941*. New York, 1941.
Simon, Viscount. *Retrospect: The Memoirs of the Rt. Hon. Viscount Simon*. London, 1952.
Slessor, Sir John. *The Central Blue: Recollections and Reflections*. London, 1956.
Strang, Lord William. *At Home and Abroad*. London, 1956.
Szembek, Jean. *Journal, 1933–1939*. Paris, 1952.
Templewood, Viscount. *Nine Troubled Years*. London, 1954.
Truman, Harry S. *Memoirs*. Vol. II, *Years of Trial and Hope*. New York, 1956.
Weizsäcker, Ernst von. *Memoirs*. Translated by John Andrews. Chicago, 1951.
Whitaker, John. *We Cannot Escape History*. New York, 1943.
Zay, Jean. *Carnets secrets de Jean Zay (de Munich à la guerre)*. Paris, 1942.

## II. Secondary Sources

Beloff, Max. *The Foreign Policy of Soviet Russia 1929–1941*. Vol. II. London, 1949.
———. "Soviet Foreign Policy, 1929–41: Some Notes," *Soviet Studies*, II, (1950–51), 123–37.
Bloch, Camille. "La politique de l'U.S.S.R. pendant la crise de Munich (mars–septembre, 1938)," *Études d'histoire moderne et contemporaine*, Vol. I (1947), 172–208.
Bois, Elie J. *Truth of the Tragedy of France*. London, 1941.
Bowle, John. *Viscount Samuel: A Biography*. London, 1957.

Broszat, Martin. "Das Sudetendeutsche Freikorps," *Vierteljahrshefte für Zeitsgeschichte, Vol.* IX (January, 1961), 30–49.

Bruegel, J. W. "German Diplomacy and the Sudeten Question before 1938," *International Affairs,* Vol. XXXVII (July, 1961), 323–31.

Bullock, Alan. *Hitler: A Study in Tyranny.* New York, 1953.

Celovsky, Boris. *Das Münchener Abkommen von 1938.* Stuttgart, 1958.

Collier, Basil. *The Defence of the United Kingdom.* London, 1957.

————. *Leader of the Few: The Authorized Biography of Air Chief Marshal the Lord Dowding of Bentley Priory, G.C.B., G.C.V.O., C.M.G.* London, 1957.

*Czechoslovakia.* Ed. by Robert J. Kerner. Berkeley, 1949.

*Czechoslovakia in European History.* Ed. by S. Harrison Thomson. Princeton, 1953.

Dahlerus, Johan B. E. *The Last Attempt.* London, 1948.

Dinerstein, Herbert S., "The Impact of Air Power on the International Scene, 1933–1940," *Military Affairs,* Vol. XIX (Summer, 1955), 65–70.

*The Diplomats: 1919–1939.* Ed. by Gordon Craig and Felix Gilbert. Princeton, 1953.

Dubnic, Vladimir Reisky de. *Communist Propaganda Methods: A Case Study on Czechoslovakia.* New York, 1960.

Duff, S. Grant. *Europe and the Czechs.* London, 1938.

Dulles, Allen W. *Germany's Underground.* New York, 1947.

Emme, Eugene M. (ed.). *The Impact of Air Power: National Security and World Politics.* Princeton, 1959.

Eubank, Keith, "Conquest by Diplomacy," *The Southwestern Social Science Quarterly,* Vol. XXXIX (June, 1958), 18–27.

Falls, Cyril. "Should the Democracies have Fought in 1938?" *The Listener,* Vol. XL (November 11, 1948), 717–18.

Feiling, Keith. *The Life of Neville Chamberlain.* London, 1946.

Foertsch, Hermann. *Schuld und Verhängnis. Die Fritsch-Krise im Frühjahr 1938 als Wendepunkt in der Geschichte der Nationalsozialistischen Zeit.* Stuttgart, 1951.

Gauché, Henri. *Deuxième Bureau au travail (1935–1940).* Paris, 1953.

Gedye, G. E. R. *Betrayal in Central Europe: Austria and Czechoslovakia, the Fallen Bastions.* New York, 1939.

Graebner, Norman A. *The New Isolationism: A Study in Politics and Foreign Policy Since 1950.* New York, 1956.

Haight, John M., Jr. "France, the United States, and the Munich Crisis," *Journal of Modern History,* Vol. XXXXII (December, 1960), 340–58.

Hancock, W. K., and M. M. Gowing. *British War Economy: History of the Second World War*. United Kingdom Civil Series. London, 1949.

Henroit, Philippe. *Comment mourut la paix; le procés des responsables*. Paris, 1941.

*The History of the Times*. 4 vols. New York, 1952.

Johnson, Alan Campbell. *Viscount Halifax: A Biography*. New York, 1941.

Kemp, P. K. *Key to Victory: The Triumph of British Sea Power in World War II*. Boston, 1957.

Kennedy, John F. *Why England Slept*. New York, 1940.

Kerner, Robert J. *Bohemia in the Eighteenth Century*. New York, 1932.

Korbel, Josef. *The Communist Subversion of Czechoslovakia, 1938–1948: The Failure of Coexistence*. Princeton, 1959.

Leasor, James. *War at the Top*. London, 1959.

Lettrich, Jozef. *History of Modern Slovakia*. New York, 1955.

Lias, Godfrey. *Beneš of Czechoslovakia*. London, 1940.

Lockhart, Robert Bruce. *Comes the Reckoning*. London, 1947.

———. "September Crisis and After," *The Listener*, Vol. XL (October 28, 1948), 635–37.

Lukacs, John A. *The Great Powers and Eastern Europe*. New York, 1953.

Macartney, C. A. *A History of Hungary, 1929–1945*. 2 vols. New York, 1956.

Mackenzie, Compton. *Dr. Beneš*. London, 1946.

Madge, Charles, and Tom Harrison. *Britain by Mass-Observation*. London, 1939.

Micaud, Charles. *The French Right and Nazi Germany*. Durham, 1943.

Minney, R. J. *The Private Papers of Hore-Belisha*. London, 1960.

Namier, L. B. *Diplomatic Prelude*. London, 1948.

———. *Europe in Decay: A Study in Disintegration, 1936–1940*. London, 1950.

———. "Munich Survey," *The Listener*, Vol. XL (December 2, 1948), 835–36.

Nicolson, Harold. "The Commons and the 1938 Crisis," *The Listener*, Vol. XL (November 25, 1948), 795–96.

O'Donnell, James P. "The Case of the Crafty Frenchman," *Saturday Evening Post*, Vol. CCXXVI (August 8, 1954), 117–19.

Odložilík, Otoker. "Concerning Munich and the Ides of March,"

*Journal of Central European Affairs*, Vol. IX (January, 1950), 419–28.

Paux, Gabriel. "Les illusions de M. Beneš," *Revue de Paris*. Vol. LVII (June, 1950), 43–52.

Perla, Leo. *Can We End the Cold War? A Study in American Foreign Policy*. New York, 1960.

Pertinax (pseud. of André Géraud). *The Gravediggers of France*. New York, 1944.

Pogue, Forrest C. *The Supreme Command (United States Army in World War II: The European Theater of Operations)*, Washington, 1954.

Postan, M. M. *British War Production*. London, 1952.

Prochazka, Theodore. "The Delimitations of Czechoslovak-German Frontiers After Munich," *Journal of Central European Affairs*, Vol. XXI (July, 1961), 200–18.

Richards, Denis. *Royal Air Force, 1939–1945*. Vol. I, *The Fight at Odds*. London, 1953.

Ripka, Hubert. *Czechoslovakia Enslaved: The Story of the Communist Coup d'Etat*. London, 1950.

———. *Munich: Before and After*. London, 1939.

Ritter, Gerhard. *The German Resistance: Carl Goerdeler's Struggle Against Tyranny*. New York, 1958.

Rothstein, Andrew. *The Munich Conspiracy*. London, 1958.

Saundy, Robert. "The Uses of Air Power in 1939–1945," in *The Impact of Air Power*, ed. by Eugene M. Emme (*q.v.*), 216–24.

Schmidt, Dana Adams. *Anatomy of a Satellite*. Boston, 1952.

Seton-Watson, R. W. *Munich and the Dictators*. London, 1939.

Shirer, William L. *The Rise and Fall of the Third Reich: A History of Nazi Germany*. New York, 1960.

Simone, André. *J'Accuse! The Men Who Betrayed France*. New York, 1940.

Spanier, John N. *The Truman-MacArthur Controversy and the Korean War*. Cambridge, 1959.

Suarez, Georges, and Guy Laborde. *Agonie de la paix, 1935–1939*. Paris, 1942.

*Sudeten Bulletin.*

*Survey of International Affairs,*
   *1936.* By Arnold J. Toynbee. London, 1937.
   *1937.* By Arnold J. Toynbee. London, 1938.
   *1938.* Vols. I–III. By Arnold J. Toynbee, V. M. Boulter, R. G. D. Laffan, and P. E. Baker. London, 1951.

*1939–1946. Hitler's Europe*. Ed. by Arnold J. Toynbee and Veronica M. Toynbee. London, 1954.

*1939–1946. The Eve of War, 1939*. Ed. by Arnold J. Toynbee and Veronica M. Toynbee. London, 1958.

*1939–1946. The Realignment of Europe*. Ed. by Arnold J. Toynbee and Veronica M. Toynbee. London, 1955.

Táborsky, Edward. "Beneš and the Soviets," *Foreign Affairs*, Vol. XXVII (January, 1949), 302–14.

———. "The Triumph and Disaster of Edvard Beneš," *Foreign Affairs*, Vol. XXXVI (July, 1958), 669–84.

Taylor, A. J. P. *The Origins of the Second World War*. London, 1961.

———. *The Trouble Makers*. London, 1957.

Taylor, Telford. *Sword and Swastika*. New York, 1952.

Templewood, Viscount. "The Lesson of Munich," *The Listener*, Vol. XL (December 9, 1948) , 879–80.

Tetens, T. H. *The New Germany and the Old Nazis*. New York, 1961.

Tissier, Pierre. *The Riom Trial*. London, 1942.

Titmuss, Richard M. *Problems of Social Policy*. London, 1950.

Toma, Peter A. "Soviet Strategy in the Slovak Uprising of 1944," *Journal of Central European Affairs*, Vol. XIX (October, 1959), 290–98.

Vansittart, Lord. "A Morally Indefensible Agreement," *The Listener*, Vol. XL (November 4, 1948), 675–77.

Vnuk, F. "Munich and the Soviet Union," *Journal of Central European Affairs*, Vol. XXI (October, 1961), 284–304.

Wallace, William V. "The Foreign Policy of President Beneš in the Approach to Munich," *The Slavonic and East European Review*, Vol. XXXIX (December, 1960), 108–36.

———. "New Documents on the History of Munich: A Selection from the Soviet and Czechoslovak Archives," *International Affairs* (London) , Vol. XXXV (October, 1959), 447–54.

Watt, D. C. "Der Einfuss der Dominions auf die Britische Aussenpolitik von München, 1938," *Vierteljahrshefte für Zeitgeschichte*, Vol. VIII (January, 1960), 64–74.

Weinberg, Gerhard L. "Secret Hitler-Beneš Negotiations in 1936–37," *Journal of Central European Affairs*, Vol. XIX (January, 1960), 366–74.

Werth, Alexander. *The Twilight of France*. New York, 1942.

Wheeler-Bennett, John W. *King George VI: His Life and Reign*. New York, 1958.

———. *Munich: Prologue to Tragedy*. New York, 1948.

————. *The Nemesis of Power: The German Army in Politics, 1918–1945*. New York, 1954.

Wiskemann, Elizabeth. *Czechs and Germans*. London, 1938.

————. *Germany's Eastern Neighbors: Problems Relating to the Oder-Neisse Line and the Czech Frontier Regions*. London, 1956.

Wood, Derek, and Derek Dempster. *The Narrow Margin*. New York, 1961.

*The World at War*. Vol. I. Ed. by Geoffrey Dennis. London, 1951.

Zemskov, I. "New Documents on the History of Munich," *International Affairs* (Moscow), October, 1958, pp. 67–75.

# Index

Adam, General Wilhelm: 121, 123–24
Agreement of July 11, 1936: 11
Alexandrovsky, Sergei: 151, 223–24
Alphand, Hervé: 262
Anglo-French conferences: April 28–29, 1938, 47–51; Sept. 18–19, 1938, 137–41;
    Sept. 25–26, 1938, 170–74; Nov. 24, 1938, 244–45
Anglo-French ultimatum: 144ff., 251
Anglo-German declaration: 219–21, 236, 259
Anglo-German Naval Agreement of 1935: 21, 219, 221
Anglo-Italian Agreement of April 13, 1938: 43
*Anschluss*: 25ff., 283
Appeasement: 17, 24, 263, 298–99
Asch, Czechoslovakia: 8, 32, 99, 191, 230
Ashton-Gwatkin, Frank T. A.: 82, 85–86, 100, 209, 215, 234
Attlee, Clement: 203, 232
Attolico, Bernardo: 198, 200–201, 237, 244
Austria: 11, 118

Baldwin, Stanley: 16–17, 233–34
Beck, Józef: 106, 186, 275; and Czechoslovakia, 106–107, 152–53, 185; ultimatum
    from, 225
Beck, General Ludwig: 121, 123
Beneš, Eduard: 4, 5, 7, 13, 44, 153–54, 164, 183, 191, 233, 255, 289; biography of, 9;
    and proposed German Czechoslovak agreement, 11; and the *Anschluss*, 29, 33; on
    Czech policy, 23, 54–55; and nationalities law, 58; and May Crisis, 64, 67–68, 72;
    and Runciman mission, 79, 83, 102; proposes autonomous Sudeten districts, 86;
    Aug. 30 memorandum, 86–87, 90; and Karlsbad demands, 90–91; Sept. 4 meeting,
    92; and Fourth Plan, 92–93; radio speeches of, 96–97, 150; and U.S.S.R., 109–10,
    150–51, 223–24; and 1919 cession of Sudetenland, 140, 141–42; and Anglo-French
    ultimatum, 144–45, 148–50; and Poland, 185–225; and Munich Conference, 204;
    resignation of, 240; and repudiation of Munich Agreement, 288, 290–91; and
    treaty with Stalin, 291–92; and expulsion of Sudeten Germans, 293–94

MUNICH

Beran, Rudolf: 256
Berchtesgaden conference: 129, 132ff.
Berlin: 63, 197, 229–30, 298
Blomberg, Field Marshal Werner von: 13–14
Blum, Léon: 29–30, 39
Boehm, Nicholas: 61–62
Böhm-Tellelbach: 125
Bonnet, Georges: 106–107, 110, 129, 188, 203, 206, 228, 229, 250; biography and character of, 40; foreign policy of, 40–41; at Anglo-French conference, April 28–29, 1938, 47–51, 52; and sympathy for Germany, 52; pleads for peaceful settlement of Sudeten question, 52; and May crisis, 64–65, 70–71; and Runciman mission, 79; fears and moods, 88, 94, 119; complains to Welczeck, 88–89; speaks at Pointe de Grave, 89; and the British, 95–96, 136, 177; favors "peace at any price," 100–101; and Litvinov, 110, 113–14, 226; and Comnen, 113; and Russian aid, 112, 114; and Chamberlain's trip of Sept. 15, 1938, 131; and Anglo-French conference, Sept. 18–19, 1938, 137–41; and cabinet meeting, Sept. 19, 1938, 141–42; and Osusky, 143; and telegrams from de Lacroix, 146–47, 301–303; and Anglo-French conference, Sept. 25–26, 1938, 170–74; and cabinet meeting, Sept. 27, 1938, 179; plan for Sudetenland, 195–96; and Franco-German declaration, Dec. 6, 1938, 236–37; and Anglo-French conference, Nov. 24, 1938, 244–45; and occupation of Czechoslovakia, 260, 262; and proposal for second Munich Conference, 276
Boris III: 105
Bradley, General Omar N.: 297
Bratislava: 253–59
Brauchitsch, General Walther von: 121, 123, 253
Breslau: 66, 77
British Commonwealth: 182
Bulgaria: 105
Bullitt, William: 51, 95, 142, 195, 203, 236, 274

Cadogan, Alexander: 47n., 170
Carol II: 108
Celovsky, Boris: Das Münchener Abkommen von 1939, 301
Černy, Josef: 61–62, 68
Chamberlain, Joseph: 16
Chamberlain, Neville: 58, 222, 273; biography and character of, 16–17; appeasement policy formulated by, 17, 190, 263, 287–99; and Wilson, 18; and inner cabinet, 18; and Halifax' visit to Germany, 18, 20; and Central Europe, 20–21, 37; speaks in the House of Commons, Feb. 21, 1938, 23; and Ribbentrop, 23–24; reacts to the Anschluss, 26; speaks on the Anschluss in the House of Commons, March 14, 1938, 27–28; and March 24 policy statement, 35–36; Anglo-Italian Agreement of April 13, 1938, 43; Anglo-French conference of April 28–29, 1938, 47–51; May 10 interview, 55; May crisis, 71; and German relations, 76–77; and Runciman mission, 78, 80, 102; Sept. 15 trip, 101, 114, 115, 128–32; and Italy, 103–104; and U.S.S.R., 109–112; memorandum of Aug. 13, 1938, 116–17; and von Kleist, 125; and the generals' plot, 126–27; cabinet meeting of Sept. 14, 1938, 131; conference with Hitler, Sept. 15, 1938, 132ff.; reception after Berchtesgaden conference, Sept. 16, 1938, 135; cabinet meeting, Sept. 17, 1938, 135–36; Anglo-French conference, Sept. 18–19, 1938, 137–41; Godesberg talks, 155ff.; Czechoslovak mobilization, 166–67; and cabinet meeting, Sept. 24, 1938, 168–69; and international conference, 169; Anglo-French conference, Sept. 25–26, 170–74; letter to Hitler, Sept. 26, 1938, 175–76; press statement, Sept. 26, 1938, 178; charged with being an aggressor,

314